New International Poverty Reduction Strategies

The World Bank and the International Monetary Fund (IMF) launched a joint initiative at the end of 1999, stating that they intended to set the fight against poverty at the heart of their development policies. Under this initiative, low-income countries wishing to apply for financial aid from either of the organisations, or for debt relief, are required to draw up poverty reduction programmes. Given this new conditionality and the enormous importance that goes with reducing poverty, a first critical assessment of these new international poverty reduction strategies is required.

This book provides the expert, critical analysis of the poverty reduction strategies that are needed. Originally published in French and updated here for the first time in English, the book emphasises three main innovations brought about by these strategies:

* focus on poverty reduction;
* participatory process implemented for policy-making;
* better coordination of official development assistance.

The contributions also show that there remains a large gap between the principles of the World Bank and IMF's strategies and their application. That this valuable and insightful book will be of great interest to students and lecturers involved in development economics goes almost without saying. What also needs to be understood is that the lessons and policy implications drawn from the book need to be read and acted upon by those involved with the World Bank and the IMF.

Jean-Pierre Cling is director of DIAL (Développement et Insertion Internationale) where **Mireille Razafindrakoto** and **François Roubaud** are both working economists. The latter is a director of the research unit CIPRÉ (Croissance, Inégalités, Population et Rôle de l'État) of IRD (Institut de Recherche pour le Développement), to which they all belong.

The translation of this book received support from the French Ministry of Culture – Centre national du livre.

Routledge studies in development economics

New International Poverty Reduction Strategies

Edited by Jean-Pierre Cling,
Mireille Razafindrakoto and
François Roubaud

Routledge
Taylor & Francis Group

LONDON AND NEW YORK

First published 2002 as *Les nouvelles stratégies internationales de lutte contre la pauvreté* by Economica, Paris.

This English language edition published by Routledge, 2003
2 Park Square, Milton Park, Abingdon, Oxon, OX14 4RN

Simultaneously published in the USA and Canada
by Routledge
605 Third Avenue, New York, NY 10017

Routledge is an imprint of the Taylor & Francis Group, an informa business

Typeset in Baskerville by Wearset Ltd, Boldon, Tyne and Wear

British Library Cataloguing in Publication Data
A catalogue record for this book is available from the British Library

Library of Congress Cataloging in Publication Data
Cling, Jean-Pierre.
New international poverty reduction strategies / Jean-Pierre Cling, Mireille Razafindrakoto & François Roubaud.
p. cm. – (Routledge studies in development economics ; 35)
Includes bibliographical references and index.
1. Economic assistance–Case studies. 2. Poverty–Case studies.
3. World Bank.I. Razafindrakoto, Mireille.II. Roubaud, François. III. Title. IV. Series.
HC60.C526 2003
339.4'6–dc21
2002037165

ISBN13: 978–0–415–30700–0 (hbk)
ISBN13: 978–0–415–40694–9 (pbk)

DIAL, a centre of economic research on developing countries

DIAL (Développement et Insertion Internationale), established in 1990 by IRD (Institut de Recherche pour le Développement, ex-ORSTOM), the French government and the European Commission, is a scientific institute involved in economic research, studies and statistical surveys on developing economies. DIAL provides assistance to developing countries and to development institutions in France and Europe in the preparation and implementation of appropriate policies. DIAL's vocation is to be a centre of expertise at the service of the developing world and the international aid community. DIAL is the core unit of the research unit CIPRÉ (Croissance, Inégalités, Population et Rôle de l'État: Growth, Inequalities, Population and the Role of the State) from IRD.

In carrying out its research programme, DIAL benefits from the support of institutions such as IRD, the French Ministry of Foreign Affairs (DGCID), the French Ministry of Finances (INSEE, DREE) and the CESD-Paris. In addition, DIAL undertakes specific studies at the request of various bilateral and multilateral development institutions. DIAL's activities and research programme are supervised and monitored by a Management and Scientific Committee. A presentation of DIAL's work programme and activities is available on its website www.dial.prd.fr.

Contents

Figures

Tables

Boxes

Contributors

Anne-Sophie Bougouin, Executive Secretary of Association Conseil pour le Développement (ACDE), France, acdedevt@aol.com

Jean-Pierre Cling, Director of DIAL, Research Unit CIPRÉ/IRD, France, cling@dial.prd.fr

Denis Cogneau, Economist, DIAL, Research Unit CIPRÉ/IRD, France, cogneau@dial.prd.fr

Idrissa Dante, Economist, United Nations Development Programme (UNDP), Rwanda, passed away in July 2002

Michael Grimm, Associate Researcher, DIAL, Research Unit CIPRÉ/IRD, France, grimm@dial.prd.fr

Mohamed-Ali Marouani, Associate Researcher, DIAL, Research Unit CIPRÉ/IRD, Paris IX-Dauphine University, France, marouani@dial.prd.fr

Jean-David Naudet, Economist, Agence Française de Développement (AFD), France, naudetjd@afd.fr

Serge Paugam, Director of research at the Centre National de la Recherche Scientifique (CNRS), Director of Studies at Ecole des Hautes Etudes en Sciences Sociales (EHESS), France, serge.paugam@ensae.fr

Marc Raffinot, Associate Researcher, DIAL, Research Unit CIPRÉ/IRD, France, Paris IX-Dauphine University EURIsCO, marc.raffinot@wanadoo.fr

Mireille Razafindrakoto, Economist, DIAL, Research Unit CIPRÉ/IRD, France, razafindrakoto@dial.prd.fr

Anne-Sophie Robilliard, Economist, DIAL, Research Unit CIPRÉ/IRD, France, robilliard@dial.prd.fr

François Roubaud, Economist, DIAL, Director of Research Unit CIPRÉ/IRD, France, roubaud@dial.prd.fr

Daniel Verger, Head of the 'Statistical Methods' Unit at the Institut National de la Statistique et des Etudes Economiques (INSEE), France, daniel.verger@insee.fr

Foreword

As aid agencies learn from experience, their understanding of develop-ment changes the political climate within which they operate evolves and their policies go through distinct phases. By and large, it is the multilater-als – especially the World Bank – who set the fashion, with national aid ministries following with greater or lesser enthusiasm. For most of the 1980s and well into the 1990s the emphasis was on 'structural adjustment' – support for economic policies which combined strong macroeconomic management and 'structural' reforms intended to reorientate the state in more market-friendly, open and liberalised directions. The era of struc-tural adjustment is now over, symbolically put to rest by the current World Bank intention to re-label its policy-related loans as 'Development Policy Support Credits'.

As structural adjustment has declined two major new themes have come to the fore: *aid effectiveness* and *poverty reduction*, although, as always, not all donors have moved at the same speed. The aid effectiveness thrust brings forward from the structural adjustment era a (well-founded) con-viction that the quality of recipient-government policies is a crucial deter-minant of aid's ability to accelerate development. But the new thrust takes a different view of how policy improvements can be achieved. There is less belief now that aid can buy policy reforms, through conditionality, and greater acceptance of the reality that domestic politics decide policy choices. So great attention is now paid to what has come in the trade to be known as 'ownership' and to the desirability that donors be more selective than in the past in choosing the developing-country governments they assist. There is a searching for new, improved donor–recipient relation-ships, based more on trust, dialogue and recipient-led partnership, and a desire to support such relationships by providing aid monies as general budgetary support for governments' development programmes, instead of as investments in a multitude of discrete projects.

This greater concentration on ways of increasing the productivity of aid dovetails well with the second of the new donor themes – poverty reduc-tion. For the ways in which aid is being delivered for this objective also reflect concerns with policy, ownership and cost-effectiveness. It is with these new approaches to raising the welfare of the poor that this volume is principally concerned. The cornerstone of the new approach, at least in the poorer countries, is the production of Poverty Reduction Strategy Papers (PRSPs), around which future aid – including debt relief – is supposed to be coordinated. This is a new development, however, initiated in the late-1990s, and the importance of this book is that it offers, to my knowledge, the first systematic and substantial analysis of this new thrust of donor–creditor policies. They see the PRSP-based approach as offering an important opportunity for major changes from past practices, because this vehicle is not only intended to help forge new relationships between donor agencies and the governments of poor countries but also between those governments and their citizens, through the fostering of 'participatory' approaches to the design of anti-poverty measures.

The authors pose some critical questions, however. Will PRSPs really embody a break with policies which in the past have failed to bring many benefits to the poor? Will governments, for example, be willing to engage in policies of redistribution in countries where large inequalities are a fundamental cause of the persistence of poverty? Can consultation go beyond the formalism which it invites, to genuinely engage citizens – especially poor citizens – in policy debates and in holding their governments to account for the way they use state resources? Are the capacities there – within governments but also in civil society – for the idealism of the PRSP idea to be made good? Can a sufficient database be created and the techniques be developed for monitoring and evaluating the efforts that are undertaken? Is it sensible to link the PRSP idea to the provision of debt relief (the authors suggest not, rightly in my view)?

These are important issues to which this volume provides a major, well-informed and up-to-date attempt to suggest some answers, even if only a preliminary view is possible at this early stage. The authors are critical but constructive, never tendentious nor ideologically driven. For many English-language readers, the book has the added merit of introducing them to the results of a French-language literature with which they are unfamiliar. The authors' evidence and analysis lead them to conclude that there is a real risk that the promise offered by the poverty-reduction approach will not be realised. By the speed with which they have produced this well-integrated set of essays and the care with which they have gone about their task, however, the authors have provided an early warning which could help avoid the failure they fear.

Tony Killick
Overseas Development Institute
July 2002

Acknowledgements

We would like to thank all the people who have contributed to this book in one way or another. Our special thanks go to all the authors, for giving of their best, although they were often contacted at the last moment. We include Sandrine Mesplé-Somps; Tony Killick for his foreword and for sharing his wide experience with us; Jean Coussy, Gérard Winter and two anonymous referees for their fruitful comments; all those who took part in the numerous debates on the French version of the book in Europe (Belgium, France, Great Britain and Norway during the ABCDE-Europe conference in June 2002) and in several countries in Africa (Burkina Faso, Gabon, Mali). Inspired by our work on participatory processes, we had discussions with donors (World Bank, European Commission, French Development Cooperation Ministry, etc.), representatives from southern states and members of civil society, and hope to have enriched this version with their precious input.

We would also like to thank the translators, first and foremost Alison Bissery, Pauline Hammel, Duncan James, Michael Lavin and Elizabeth Turner-Guill, who by and large hopefully managed to contradict the saying 'traddutore = traditore'; also Loïc Le Pezennec for his lexicographical research.

Finally, we extend thanks to our elders – Maurice Cling, and Geneviève and Pierre Roubaud – and also to Alain Brilleau, Flore Gubert, Martine Lootvoet and Constance Torelli for their scrupulous proof-reading; to Maud Cling for her obscure but fruitful bibliographical research; to Sue for giving some of her precious time for the interest and the capital (on Vanves's terms); and to our young ones (Cam, Lu, Max, Paulo, Sam and Spart) for their cries of encouragement.

Abbreviations

ACBF	African Capacity Building Foundation
ACP	Africa Caribbean Pacific
AFD	Agence Française de Développement
AFRISTAT	Observatoire Economique et Statistique d'Afrique Sub-Saharienne
ATTAC	Association pour une Taxation des Transactions financières pour l'Aide aux Citoyens
BWIs	Bretton Wood Institutions
C2D	Contrat de Désendettement et de Développement (France)
CAS	Country Assistance Strategy
CDF	Comprehensive Development Framework
CFA	Communauté Financière Africaine
CGE	Computable General Equilibrium
CIPRÉ	Research Unit 'Croissance, inégalités, population et rôle de l'État'
CMDT	Compagnie Malienne de Développement des Textiles
CSLP	Cadre Stratégique de Lutte contre la Pauvreté (PRSP in French)
CSO	Civil Society Organisation
CWIQ	Core Welfare Indicators Questionnaire
DAC	Development Assistance Committee (OECD)
DFID	Department for International Development
DGCID	Direction Générale de la Coopération Internationale et du Développement (France)
DHS	Demographic and health surveys
DIAL	Groupement d'intérêt scientifique 'Développement et insertion internationale'
DNP	Direction Nationale du Plan (Mali)
DSA	Debt Sustainability Analysis
DSCN	Direction de la statistique et de la comptabilité nationale (Cameroun)
EC	European Commission
EDF	European Development Fund

EDM	Electricité du Mali
EMEP	Enquête Malienne sur l'Evaluation de la Pauvreté
ESAF	Enhanced Structural Adjustment Facility
EU	European Union
FGT	Foster Greer Thorbecke
FSD	Facilité Suisse de désendettement
FSP	Fonds de solidarité prioritaire (France)
GDP	Gross Domestic Product
GNI	Gross National Income
GNP	Gross National Product
HDI	Human Development Indicator
HDR	Human Development Report
HIPC	Heavily Indebted Poor Countries
HIV	Human Immuno-deficiency Virus
HPI	Human Poverty Index
IDA	International Development Association
IDG	International Development Goals
ILO	International Labour Organisation
IMF	International Monetary Fund
INSEE	Institut National de la Statistique et des Etudes Economiques (France)
INSTAT	Institut national de la statistique (Madagascar)
IREPAS	Initiative pour la Revue de l'Examen Participatif de l'Ajustement Structurel (Mali)
ISTED	Institut des Sciences et des Techniques de l'Equipement et de l'environnement pour le Développement
JSA	Joint Staff Assessment
LACI	Loan Administration Change Initiative
LDCs	Least-Developed Countries
LSMS	Living Standard Measurement Study Survey
MADIO	Madagascar–Dial–Instat–Orstom
MCA	Millennium Challenge Account
MDGs	Millennium Development Goals
MDS	Ministère du développement social (Mali)
MEF	Ministère de l'économie et des finances (Mali)
MTEF	Medium-term Expenditure Framework
NEPAD	New Partnership for Africa's Development
NGO	Non-governmental Organisation
NHDR	National Human Development Report
NPAS	National Poverty Alleviation Strategy (Mali)
NPV	Net Present Value
NSO	National Statistical Office
OAU	Organisation of African Unity
ODA	Official Development Assistance
ODHD	Observatoire du développement humain durable (Mali)

ODI	Overseas Development Institute
OECD	Organisation for Economic Cooperation and Development
PAIB	Projet d'Appui aux Initiatives de Base
PAMORI	Projet d'appui à la mobilisation des recettes intérieures
PARIS21	PARtnership In Statistics for development in the 21st century
PFP	Economic Policy Framework Paper
PPA	Participatory Poverty Assessment
PPP	Purchasing Power Parity
PRECAGED	Programme de Renforcement des Capacités nationales pour une Gestion stratégique du Développement (Mali)
PRGF	Poverty Reduction and Growth Facility
PRODEC	Programme décennal pour l'éducation (Mali)
PRODESS	Programme décennal de développement socio-sanitaire (Mali)
PRSC	Poverty Reduction Support Credit
PRSG	Poverty Reduction Support Grant
PRSP	Poverty Reduction Strategy Paper
PSIA	Poverty and Social Impact Analysis
RESAL	Réseau Européen de Sécurité Alimentaire
RMI	Revenu Minimum d'Insertion
RMSM	Revised Minimum Standard Model
RO	Rural Observatory
SAM	Social Accounting Matrix
SAP	Structural Adjustment Programme
SAPRIN	Structural Adjustment Participatory Review International Network
SDA	Social Dimensions of Adjustment
SMIC	Salaire Minimum Interprofessionnel de Croissance
SNLP	Stratégie Nationale de Lutte contre la Pauvreté (Mali)
SPA	Strategic Partnership with Africa
UE	Union Européenne
UNAIDS	Joint United Nations Programme on HIV/Aids
UNCTAD	United Nations Conference for Trade and Development
UNDP	United Nations Development Programme
UNECA	United Nations Economic Commission for Africa
UNICEF	United Nations International Children's Emergency Fund
USAID	United States Agency for International Development
WAEMU	West African Economic and Monetary Union
WDR	World Development Report
WTO	World Trade Organisation

Introduction

Have the changes actually changed anything?

Jean-Pierre Cling, Mireille Razafindrakoto and François Roubaud

The World Bank and the International Monetary Fund (IMF), known as the Bretton Woods Institutions, launched a joint Initiative at the end of 1999 setting the fight against poverty at the heart of development policies. Under this Initiative, low-income countries wishing to apply for financial aid from either of the organisations, or for debt relief under the HIPC (Heavily Indebted Poor Countries) Initiative, are required to draw up poverty reduction programmes known as Poverty Reduction Strategy Papers (PRSP).

Since then, the Bretton Woods Institutions (BWIs) have mobilised considerable human and financial resources to implement the Initiative and to ensure its success. They began by reorganising and renaming their aid programmes so as to explicitly include the fight against poverty in their key goals. The World Bank's financial support for low-income countries, handled by the International Development Association (IDA), now comes within the framework of Poverty Reduction Strategy Credits (PRSC) and the IMF's within the Poverty Reduction and Growth Facility (PRGF). The BWIs also gave much thought to defining precise guidelines to help low-income countries prepare the PRSPs. The World Bank's *World Development Report 2000/2001* (World Bank 2000a), entitled *Attacking Poverty*, was duly followed in 2001 by a reference document, or sourcebook, designed as a practical guide for the approximately sixty countries concerned (World Bank 2001a). Finally, unparalleled efforts were made to consult the developing countries' governments and civil societies, with the organisation of a wide series of international, national and regional seminars.

All the other donors rapidly decided to follow suit and link their aid policies to the PRSP system. Some, such as the European Commission and Scandinavian countries, did so readily as they were already very much aware of the whole issue of poverty; others, such as France, followed with more caution.[1] Whatever the case may be, it is quite remarkable that just a few years after the initiative was launched, the new poverty reduction programmes now channel all official development assistance to low-income countries; that is, all these countries' external resources. This is a major change, given that interventions from the donor countries and organisations were traditionally criticised for their incoherency.

Given the enormous scope of the efforts made to introduce these programmes, their increasing importance for the countries concerned and the strong mobilisation of the international community, we believe that it is now very important to make a first critical assessment of the new international poverty reduction strategies applied in developing countries. This is the aim of this book. To our knowledge, it is the first attempt to summarise the current state of affairs on this issue.

The book demonstrates that the underlying principles of the PRSPs provide three major innovations, which should be recognised as such: first, it is to be welcomed that the BWIs have adopted poverty reduction, and not structural adjustment, as their main goal;[2] second, adopting a participatory process for defining and monitoring the PRSPs certainly has great potential for strengthening democracy in countries where the people generally have very few means of making themselves heard; third, the new approach increases the overall coherence of aid, as debt relief granted within the HIPC Initiative (which is a main source of funding for poverty reduction policies) is managed collectively, and the major donors are aligned on the PRSP framework.

At the same time, a number of points still remain unclear concerning the real scope of these innovations: has the content of the policies really changed and are they capable of meeting the goals that have been set? Will the participatory process really bring the developing countries ownership of their policies and will it enhance accountability of their governments and increase empowerment of the populations? Also, what means are available for monitoring and assessing the new policies? These are some of the main issues covered in this book.

After a reminder of the reasons why the new poverty reduction strategies were launched, this introduction presents a summary of the book and its main conclusions, finishing with a brief outline of certain issues to be explored.

The increase in importance of poverty-related issues

Today's acute awareness of the problem of poverty in developing countries is the result of a long process that began at the end of the 1980s. The United Nations, particularly the UNICEF (United Nations International Children's Emergency Fund) and the UNDP (United Nations Development Programme), were the precursors in this field, whereas the Bretton Woods Institutions took more time to include the issue in their policies.

In 1987, the UNICEF published a report that was to have a tremendous impact. Entitled *Adjustment with a Human Face*, it alerted people of the disastrous effects of structural adjustment policies, and put forward various possible solutions (Cornia *et al.* 1987). Throughout the 1990s, the United Nations organised several international conferences that helped create a new awareness of poverty-related issues. One of the most important ones was doubtless the World Summit for Human Development, held in Copenhagen (Denmark) in 1995. The Final Declaration and Action Programme ratified at this summit made poverty reduction a priority of development. The United Nations General Assembly followed this by declaring 1996 'International Year for the Eradication of Poverty' and the decade 1997–2006 as the 'First United Nations Decade for the Eradication of Poverty'. Also in 1996, the OECD's Development Assistance Committee (DAC) decided to focus its attention on poverty and drafted the International Development Goals, which were enlarged and renamed as the Millennium Development Goals (MDGs) by the United Nations in 2000. The first of the MDGs aims to reduce the proportion of the world's population living in extreme poverty by half between 1990 and 2015.

The World Bank also accompanied this gradual move towards recentring development policies on the question of poverty. First indirectly, by introducing the Social Dimensions of Adjustment Programme, in partnership with the UNDP and the African Development Bank, designed to lessen the short-term negative effects of reforms on vulnerable populations. Then more directly, by devoting the *World Development Report 1990* to the subject of poverty. By publishing this report (followed by a second one on the same theme ten years later), the Bank stressed how much importance it attached to the fight against poverty.[3] It then provided itself with the analytical means of carrying out its mission, by undertaking a series of studies based on data obtained from surveys on this theme, whilst also systematically preparing documents to help define the nature and determining factors of poverty in each country, i.e. the poverty profile, poverty assessment, etc. In fact, only the IMF stayed on the fringe of this movement.

At the end of the last decade, the Bretton Woods Institutions had three main reasons for enhancing their positions in this field by launching new poverty reduction strategies that put this theme at the very centre of their actions, particularly in the case of the World Bank.

The first is related to an increase in poverty in many parts of the world. However uncertain the figures may be, there can be no question that poverty has risen in the past few years, particularly if the figures for China are excluded, as the poor population seems to have been significantly reduced there since economic expansion started in the 1980s.[4] The increase in poverty has been particularly significant in sub-Saharan Africa and transition countries in Europe and Central Asia. According to the World Bank's statistics, nearly half the world population lives with less than two dollars per day and a fifth with less than one dollar per day, the amount generally considered as the threshold of absolute poverty.

Perhaps the most worrying phenomenon in this respect is that certain countries appear to have fallen into a 'poverty trap', illustrated by the fact that the number of least-developed countries (LDCs) has doubled in the last thirty years, rising from 25 in 1971 when this category of country was

first created, to 49 in 2001. Given the demographic trends in these countries, their population will be tripled by 2050 according to United Nations
forecasts, rising from 660 million to 1.8 billion, representing nearly 20 per
cent of the world population (compared with 11 per cent at present). In
this context, urgent action must be taken to prevent entire populations
from literally dying of hunger.

The second reason that forced the BWIs to change their policies is
related to the failure of structural adjustment policies, and the questioning of the 'Washington Consensus' on which they were based, with the
three-pronged solution of macroeconomic stabilisation, external and
internal liberalisation. The above figures suffice to prove the failure of
structural adjustment. After twenty years of recommending these policies,
the BWIs cannot produce a single case where they have been successful.
Even the 'Asian miracle', for many years given as an example to the other
developing countries, has been questioned since the 1997 crisis. The same
applies to the programmes applied with the BWIs' support in other large
emerging economies (Argentina, Brazil, Mexico, Turkey, etc.) and transition economies (Russia), which have also experienced serious crises that
are still far from being resolved. As for the 'front-runners' in Africa, successively praised for their success stories, none has managed to live up to
expectations in the long term (it is doubtless rather cruel to point out that
the Democratic Republic of Congo, formerly Zaïre, was once ranked in
this category).

By and large, the 'Washington Consensus' failed in most countries, as
even the World Bank now admits. It is interesting to hear what Joseph
Stiglitz, former chief economist of this institution and Nobel prizewinner
for Economics in 2001, has to say on this subject:[5]

> The IMF is supposed to guarantee international financial stability. As
> for the WTO, it is designed to facilitate international trade. Unfortu-
> nately, the way these two institutions try to carry out their mandate has
> probably contributed to increasing poverty ... The cocktail obtained
> from the combination of liberalisation policies and restrictive eco-
> nomic policies imposed by the IMF has had the most dramatic effects
> for developing countries.

His criticism may spare the World Bank, but our analysis shows that there
is no reason why it should be given preferential treatment, at least not
until recently.

Apart from calling past strategies into question, the failure of structural
adjustment policies has led to the multilateral debt crisis, which has an
adverse impact both on developing countries and on the BWIs. The crisis
is the direct result of twenty years of debt rescheduling without economic
growth. The international financial institutions, particularly the World
Bank, are on the front line in a situation in which poor countries are

heavily indebted and the multilateral element has gradually become preponderant. Faced with the states' insolvency, it is the principle of the intangibility of the BWIs' debts that was at stake.

The third factor involved in their change of attitude is the crisis in the legitimacy of the Bretton Woods Institutions. To a great extent, this stems from the other two factors: given the increase in world poverty and the overall failure of their policies, it is quite natural that more and more people should criticise them and call for changes to their policies (some even suggesting to close them down). These changes were especially a way of responding to aid fatigue in developed countries, where public opinion was beginning to wonder whether it was really worth while continuing to spend so much on development aid. The theme of poverty was used to combat their disenchantment, the perspective of humanitarian solidarity helping to rehabilitate development aid (Severino 2001a, 2001b). They were also a means of answering criticisms from civil society and the various protest movements. It is important to remember that the decision to launch the PRSPs took place against a background of increasingly strong protests against international organisations, which forced the G7 countries to launch the enhanced HIPC Initiative at the Cologne Summit in 1999, culminating at the Seattle Conference in November 1999 and the G7 Summit in Genoa in June 2001.

Aim and summary

This book presents a critical analysis of the new strategies for poverty reduction in developing countries recommended by the BWIs. We believe that the term 'strategies' is more appropriate than 'policies' as, contrary to the previous generation of reforms relating to structural adjustment, the current approach aims at establishing close links between economic policies and the political economy of the reforms. Consequently, the analytical content of the actual policies is only one aspect of the new architecture, as the way in which the policies are drafted and implemented is considered to be just as important as far as the expected results are concerned. For this reason, we believe that it is vital to look jointly at the three main components of the new strategies, devoting a section of the book to each: general assessment on poverty and on the content of recommended policies; guiding principles of the new approach based on a participatory process and implementation in practice; monitoring and evaluation systems.

One disadvantage of undertaking our analysis at such an early stage is that it can only be partial. Not enough time has passed to enable us to look at one of the fundamental dimensions of the question; that is, the real impact of the policies. It is still obviously too early to judge the success or failure of the proposed strategies as they have not yet been fully implemented.

On each of the three themes mentioned above, our book presents work with a general scope (critical analysis of the World Bank's positions on poverty reduction, description of the HIPC Initiative, comparison with European approaches to poverty, etc.) plus work on specific countries in sub-Saharan Africa (Madagascar, Mali, etc.).

Our analysis puts special emphasis on the African continent. This is justified first by the fact that most of the countries concerned by the PRSP and HIPC Initiative are in Africa.[6] Also, almost half of the population lives in a situation of extreme poverty, which is a higher proportion than in any other part of the world. Finally, only in Africa will the number of poor keep increasing during the next few years according to the World Bank's forecasts (World Bank 2001b). To complete the approach adopted in this book and particularly highlight the specificity and diversity of national contexts, a second book on the case of Madagascar is currently in the pipeline.[7]

Although this book is a collective work by authors from different backgrounds, we have tried to avoid the frequent failings of this sort of publication, where, behind the façade of a federating title, there is often just a juxtaposition of heterogeneous, if not contradictory, studies and points of view. Nonetheless, the questions handled and the angles from which the studies are approached are highly diverse, and are backed by a wide spectrum of information sources and analytical techniques (production of first-hand data, processing of surveys, reviews of literature, content analysis, etc.).

We have also been able to bring together a whole series of original studies carried out by DIAL researchers in recent years. The overall harmony in the different analyses enables us to develop a coherent set of arguments and to come to common conclusions concerning the contributions made by the new policies and their limits.

Finally, we have tried to focus our thinking in an international perspective that goes beyond the mere context of developing countries. Although the issue of poverty is also at the heart of debate in industrialised countries, the approaches adopted in the two geographical camps are usually unconnected. In the two chapters dealing with poverty in Western Europe, we are able to put the specific nature of the new initiatives in the southern economies into perspective and initiate comparative analysis on this theme, thanks to the two-way study.

The first part of the book presents a general diagnosis on poverty and some reflections on poverty reduction policies. The first two chapters directly concern the economic policies. Chapter 1 analyses the World Bank's stance on poverty reduction, based on the World Development Report *Attacking Poverty*, which can be seen as the founding document for the new approach, published ten years after the Report on the same theme. The chapter highlights how innovative the ideas are, but also underlines their limits. Chapter 2 is aimed at explaining the goals of the new policies, in the light of contemporary theories on distributive justice. The author argues that the policies should be more careful to consider, on the one hand, factors of individual mobility to escape poverty and, on the other, to accept the redistribution of income implied by the increase in this mobility. The chapter particularly looks at education and health policies from this angle.

Chapter 3, which analyses the methods used to regulate poverty in Europe, gives an interesting perspective to the way the problem is handled in Western societies. Two of its conclusions are particularly worth underlining: first, the vital importance of state intervention in handling poverty, even though these countries are supposed to be archetype models of consolidated free market economies; and second, the great variety of solutions to be found from one country to another, despite their relatively homogeneous culture. It can therefore be assumed that there will be even greater diversity in developing countries.

Each of the following two chapters look at a specific question relating to poverty reduction policies. In Chapter 4, the authors analyse the rise in urban poverty in Africa in the past decades, attempting to quantify the phenomenon and describe its main characteristics. The analysis points to a blind spot in the recommended policies, stemming from the World Bank's 'ruralist' stance. Chapter 5 looks at empowerment and the participation of the poor. This chapter proposes an original method for revealing the demands and aspirations of the poor (the so-called 'voices of the poor'), with examples taken from the case of Madagascar. By highlighting that the poor express a strong need for a welfare state, the authors ask how this demand can be satisfied when it appears to be in contradiction with the planned strategies.

The second part of the book highlights the scope and limits of the new international initiatives. The five chapters in this part are aimed at assessing the extent to which the new initiatives recommended by the Bretton Woods Institutions are implemented in the field. These chapters are particularly interesting because they look at the same subject from three different angles – the first seen from the world of research, the second from aid and cooperation specialists working in the field, and the third from that of development NGOs – but with views that nonetheless converge.

Chapters 6 and 7, the linchpin of our work, set down the guiding principles for drawing-up PRSPs and the problems that arise in practice. Chapter 6 analyses current and future contradictions of the participatory process, together with the stakes involved, with a two-way table taking into account the stakeholders – donors, civil society and the state – and the relationships between each of them. Chapter 7 focuses on the contents of policies and arrives at two main conclusions: first, the global content of policies has not changed significantly in spite of the participatory process;

second, the PRSPs' shortcomings reflect mainly weaknesses in the strategies recommended by the BWIs, analysed in Chapter 1. Chapter 8 asks whether the countries concerned are capable of defining their own strategies to combat poverty given the weakness of their institutions. It backs its arguments with the example of Mali. This field study serves as a concrete example to support the general arguments developed in the previous chapters.

The next two chapters look at the link between the fight against poverty and debt relief. They highlight the incompatibility of the underlying principles of the two initiatives launched simultaneously, the HIPC and the PRSP. This mainly stems from their different objectives: the HIPC Initiative is finance-oriented as it aims to make debt bearable; the PRSP Initiative is aimed at poverty reduction. These are different preoccupations, even though the funds resulting from debt relief are used to finance the fight against poverty. Each of the two chapters illustrates this contradiction in its own way, demonstrating the practical consequences in terms of the allocation of development aid and the way policies are drawn up. Chapter 9 supports the view that the interlinking of debt relief and PRSPs heralds the end of the principle of aid selectivity previously favoured by the World Bank, as all heavily indebted poor countries will be eligible for debt relief in the long term. In addition, in practical terms the interlinking also leads to incoherency in terms of timescale. The urgency of releasing funds for debt relief is contrary to the aim of drawing up well-thought-out economic strategy within the framework of a participatory process that inevitably takes time to implement. Based on an assessment of financial impact of the debt relief initiative, Chapter 10 demonstrates its highly inequalitarian nature and the uncertainty with respect to its potential impact, as it is decided on the basis of criteria of sustainability and not of the poor countries' needs in terms of development.

The third part of the book deals with the mechanisms for monitoring and evaluating the new poverty reduction policies. These have become more important than in the past, partly because they are supposed to guide action in real time, using their findings as a basis for redirecting policies, but also because the emphasis on citizens' participation in leading reforms implies a wider access to information. But at the present time, input to thinking on these mechanisms is one of the main weaknesses in the current process.

Chapter 11 proposes a critical analysis of the statistical surveys generally used to monitor poverty in developing countries, particularly in Africa. The authors come to the paradoxical conclusion that the multiplication of household surveys during the last decade may not have led to a better understanding of the phenomenon, because of problems of methodology and data quality. In the light of the conclusions of European thinking concerning the measurement of poverty, Chapter 12 tries to identify the main lessons that could be learned from this for the poor countries. It shows that, even in a context where human and financial resources are far more favourable, a large number of difficulties still subsist, and the scientific debate is still very open. This especially concerns the concepts to adopt, the dimensions of poverty to measure, the choice of indicators and the surveying techniques to be used. Chapter 13 presents two original survey systems for analysing poverty that have been developed by DIAL and successfully used in several developing countries: 1-2-3 surveys for urban areas and Rural Observatories for country areas. They are compared to the main surveys traditionally used on an international level, highlighting the potential complementarities.

Finally, Chapter 14 assesses the different tools available for evaluating the impact of poverty reduction policies, both in terms of growth as well as of income distribution and poverty. The authors remark that none of these tools are currently being used for the definition of PRSPs, due to various human and data constraints (analysed below), as well as to technical difficulties. This chapter focuses on a presentation of micro-simulation techniques, which are particularly useful for this kind of evaluation, but which are still at an experimental stage. It presents the guiding principles of these techniques and some applications to three case studies on Côte d'Ivoire, Indonesia and Madagascar.

In the end, have the changes actually changed anything?

As you will have gathered from reading this presentation of our book, our conclusions regarding the new international initiatives are uncompromising and, in many respects, extremely severe. Whether it be in terms of the content or the way in which the strategies are implemented, the analyses clearly highlight operational shortcomings, weaknesses and defects in the current processes. However, it is important to ask whether ultimately, all things considered, the new strategies are capable of changing the order of things and whether they are a step in the right direction in the fight against poverty. Of course, this sort of judgement can only be subjective, given that no objective procedures are available to weigh up the positive and negative aspects of our diagnosis.

However imperial the BWIs may be (with the donors and other international organisations, but also, and above all, in their dealings with the southern countries), it is perfectly natural to try to take a stand on this question since they are being heavily criticised for their new initiatives. Paradoxically, the crossfire of criticisms comes from both sides of the political scene: rejection on the right, in the name of scientific objectivity and a technocratic approach, of the inevitable interference with politics inferred by the participatory processes; or on the left, suspicions regarding the BWIs' duplicity, on the lines that they only adopted the slogan of poverty reduction as a way of sweetening the pill of liberalisation. But, on closer scrutiny, it appears that neither side has put forward very convincing arguments. In turn, both sides typically use the three rhetorical effects, so subtly used by Hirschman (1991) to describe those who have fought against political and social reforms in the last two centuries (civil and political, as well as economic and social rights) – namely, the argument of *perversity*, whereby any attempt to change the order of things produces exactly the opposite of the intended effect; of *futility*, whereby all attempts at political and social engineering are powerless to alter the natural order of things; and *jeopardy*, whereby reforms are to be avoided as they threaten previous hard-won reforms.

In the end, we do not think that the theory of a plot holds out under closer scrutiny. It cannot be denied that the BWIs were forced under pressure to adopt the theme of poverty reduction, that the ideological bias that existed with the adjustment policies has not suddenly disappeared, that they are using the new strategies to restore their international credibility, that the current process has weaknesses and seriously risks going astray, or that there is little hope that miraculous solutions to the recurrent problems of development will suddenly be found in this way – and all this must be underlined.

But, although these warnings are necessary and prevent us from having blind faith in what is still a very imperfect strategy, this does not mean that the current process should be irrevocably condemned. The main progress at this stage is probably not to be expected on these levels at all. The underlying principles of the PRSP/HIPC Initiatives are a radical breakaway from past practices and bring much hope. They offer a real opportunity of seeing changes in the nature of public policies and international aid, in a manner that favours development and calls on greater participation from citizens. Of course, nothing guarantees that this opportunity will actually be grasped. This will depend on the ability of social forces, in local contexts, to work to this end (as well as on the actual commitment of the donors to this approach in the long term); but the formal conditions allowing these new voices to emerge have never been so favourable. One thing is for certain, it cannot be said that the outcome is settled in advance.

To reinforce our relatively optimistic view of the new guidelines for development policies adopted at the instigation of the BWIs, a significant parallel can be drawn with trends in international negotiations on trade liberalisation under the auspices of the World Trade Organisation (WTO). The promotion and close coordination of the three parties involved – developing country governments, civil society, international institutions – are not specific to poverty reduction policies. There is astonishing symmetry between the new poverty reduction strategies promoted by the BWIs and the new tendencies of the trade liberalisation policies supported by the WTO (the two are obviously closely linked by a broad common denominator): same mediocre results of policies implemented to date, from the developing countries' standpoint (structural adjustment in one case, trade liberalisation in the other); same marginalisation of these countries in the decision-making processes that determine the policies imposed on them; same pressure of criticism/recrimination/dispute, particularly from international civil society; same promises of reform in response, with the same key words: transparency, confidence, consultation, participation from civil society, communication, capacity building.[8]

Nonetheless, in the case of the WTO the changes seem to be cosmetic as far as poor countries are concerned. It has not questioned the dogma whereby trade liberalisation is always the right thing, everywhere and in all circumstances; it confuses ends and means (poverty reduction is an end on which a consensus can be reached, but this is not the case for trade liberalisation);[9] lacks democracy (between northern and southern countries); marginalises civil society: the 'sanctuarisation' of the WTO conference in Doha (Qatar) in November 2001 was symptomatic in this respect; and fails to take into account the interests of the poorest countries (although the question of relaxing the conditions of agreements with developing countries was put on the agenda for the forthcoming negotiations).[10]

On the contrary, the BWIs' reform guidelines are being put into practice, particularly those launched by the World Bank. In each country, the different players are systematically able to confront their views in the numerous workshops programmed at the drafting stage of the PRSPs, albeit in a far from perfect manner.

A turning point has been reached as far as the principles and goals are concerned. The current weaknesses result from a still fragmentary understanding of the practical implications of the new tendencies. The way they should be conveyed in terms of prioritisation, defining target populations, sharing responsibility amongst the different players and means of implementation, remains vague. Also, the implied arbitration processes, the preconditions to be satisfied and risks to be run have not yet been fully measured. In more concrete terms, apart from the questioning about the relevance of the recommended policies, the new strategies always come up against a certain number of recurrent problems neglected in the past. How can capabilities (of the authorities and civil society) be strengthened in poor countries? How can the institutions be made accountable and legitimate?

Despite all the above difficulties, it would not be fair to say that the new poverty reduction strategies are simply a facelift or a passing fashion, because the institutional mechanism is already deeply imbedded in the development aid procedures, whether it be for PRSPs, the HIPC Initiative, PRSCs, PRGFs, MDGs, etc.

More generally speaking, even though the BWIs' approach and their instruments may have weaknesses, we must stress something that people tend to forget: given the choice between the World Bank or a classic example of a despot in a developing country systematically bleeding its economy, surely it is obvious that the first is more inclined to make an effort to reduce poverty.

In the end, given that one of the main aims of the new strategies, as we pointed out above, is to ensure that international financial relations continue to operate as they do at present, it is tempting to attribute to the BWIs the declaration made by a threatened aristocrat in *The Leopard* (Lampedusa 1958): 'If we want things to stay as they are, things will have to change.'

Challenges and future policies

As we have already said, we can only make a partial assessment of the new poverty reduction initiatives. At this stage the only elements that can be assessed are the processes used to draw up the strategies and their content. The history of development has shown that this is probably not the most important part of the issue. For example, a similar exercise carried out in the 1960s or 1970s would have analysed the options adopted in the long-term plans drawn up in most developing countries. A large number of economists did just that at the time, but none foresaw their real results. We have to admit that it is unlikely that we are much more clear-sighted today. In retrospect, although the failure of these plans was partly due to mistaken assessments of their future impact, it was at least as much due to the countries', and particularly their public authorities', failure to implement their principles.

Hence, in the coming years, the challenges will concern both the validity of the policies and the ability to implement them, while monitoring and evaluation tools will be required to both assess the situation and evaluate the results of the policies implemented. On all three levels, which correspond to the three parts of this book, participation is supposed to play a key role. It is also the main unknown factor.

On the content of the policies, the fact that the majority of PRSPs simply renewed the previous policies shows that there is strong resistance to any questioning of them, however necessary this may be. Of course, the adoption of new poverty reduction strategies implicitly recognises the failure of the previous policies, even if BWIs have pleaded their own case many times by continuing to put most of the blame for the failure of structural adjustment down to the developing countries' failure to implement them rather than to their content (World Bank 1994, 2002a). Nonetheless, as our book suggests, there is reluctant recognition of the need for an innovative approach to the content of the policies in areas such as the need for better balance between the state and markets; taking into account the specific national and local contexts; the relativisation of the benefits of liberalisation, etc. If countries are to do more than simply making a few marginal changes to the content of policies, it is vital that they try to identify viable, coherent alternatives to the previous policies. If this challenge is taken up seriously, the participatory process should be of great help in taking into account specific national cases, in identifying the population's real needs and gaining a better understanding of the positions adopted by each of the parties.

As for the implementation of the strategies, the principle of participation from different members of society opens up new prospects that will have an impact on the way national affairs are led. By favouring respect for the right to information and expression, participation fulfils one objective in that it deals with one of the key factors of poverty, namely exclusion and marginalisation. But the potential impact of this precept goes way beyond this aspect. Participation will only take on its full meaning if it really helps solve the problem of the lack of democracy in poor countries. It should give extra capabilities and power to intermediate bodies (the media, trade unions, associations, etc.) in drawing up, monitoring, controlling, assessing and redirecting the policies. Information is of course of utmost importance in this respect, and its formative nature must be underlined. It makes public choices explicit and increases transparency in the management of state affairs, whilst offering the different players in society the possibility of exerting pressure, or even taking sanctions in the case of failure. In short, making the state accountable for its actions before its citizens is at stake.

The majority of the players do not seem to be fully aware of these new prospects, as they lack guidelines and are used to being excluded from decision-making circles. Also, the real influence of the participatory process on economic policy decisions has yet to be defined. No help on this matter can be found either in the World Bank's sourcebook on PRSPs or in practice in the field, although the BWIs' and the governments' natural inclination probably works in favour of making it a purely consultative process. Once the PRSPs have been drawn up by the countries and validated by the BWIs, can we hope to see an attempt to institutionalise these processes of popular expression? If this intention does exist, the real problems will arise at that stage, because the participatory process approach challenges the way in which the so-called representative institutions usually work in developing countries. If things are to change, they will need to have a great deal of courage, or, more probably, there will need to be an enormous amount of pressure from the public.

The players' ability to define adequate policies depends on whether they have access to information on the problems as they stand and on the real or expected impact of the options which have been implemented or are planned. Unfortunately, we only have very fragmented information on poor country economies, and lack relevant, reliable data. In this context, it is very difficult, if not impossible, to assess the impact of the policies.

It follows that it is now urgent to mobilise all the means required to deepen our knowledge of the situation and the mechanisms in force in poor countries, both in economic and socio-political terms, given that these two factors are very closely related. Defining an effective strategy to fight against poverty particularly requires a careful assessment of the distributive impact of the economic policies that are planned or implemented.

The World Bank's and IMF's Poverty and Social Impact Analysis (PSIA) programmes respond to this need. These recent programmes represent an immense project in terms of operational research and applications. They will be faced with three types of difficulties, described hereafter.

First of all, the natural order of things would have been to use these techniques from the beginning when drawing up the PRSPs and defining policy priorities. However, the PRSP system was set up in such haste that this was not possible.

More fundamentally, there are no instruments available at the present time to enable precise assessment (*ex ante* and *ex post*) of the impact of the policies on poverty. Certain innovative paths of research, such as microsimulations techniques presented in this book, represent promising methodological progress in this direction. But two fundamental problems remain unsolved. How can the multidimensional nature of poverty be taken into account when analysing the policies' distributive effects? How can the impact of alternative measures be measured in terms of poverty (with a given budget, is it better to construct rural tracks or improve the quality of primary schooling)? A programme of this sort must be based on an analysis of what are still widely unknown interactions between the different forms of poverty and the wide range of alternative policies.

Finally, assuming that researchers solve these analytical difficulties and that the data required to implement the new methods is produced, the constraints of local technical and institutional capabilities will need to be lifted, and the means of dialogue between those 'in the know' and society will need to be rethought, in order to bring the key principles of ownership and participation, empowerment and accountability into being. Although this very ambitious project is clearly inaccessible in the short term, it is nonetheless vital to make a firm commitment in this direction. Creating and transferring appropriate instruments to be mobilised for this project will be a final challenge, and by no means the easiest.

In the end, the BWIs have opted for a path over which they have no control. In a way, they have opened a 'Pandora's box' by creating expectations that they may be unable to satisfy, running the risk of disappointment and retreat. They may be taken at their word by the southern countries and have to adapt to radical changes that they have not fully anticipated. In any event, new paths have been opened by the PRSP Initiative. It remains to be seen whether the numerous obstacles and constraints that still exist can be overcome, and whether the different players at national and international levels are aware of the real stakes involved and are ready to mobilise the resources needed to make the process a success.

Notes

1 Whilst insisting that it attached great importance to the question of the fight against poverty, France wished to widen the issue to cover inequalities and exclusion (see DGCID 2001).

2 We will not take part here in the debate on the oversimplified aim of reducing poverty compared with the more global aim of development. The PRSPs are also development policies, at least as far as their principles are concerned.

3 In fact, the *World Development Report 1980* was already devoted to poverty and the World Bank's interest for poverty goes back to the beginning of the 1970s, during McNamara's presidency. But the focus put on structural adjustment policies from the 1980s moved poverty issues to the background.

4 Although it should be noted that there is much uncertainty as to the reliability of the Chinese statistics.

5 Interview in *Le Monde*, 6 November 2001.

6 Among approximately sixty countries concerned by the PRSPs, the 35 in Africa account for the great majority of the population living in a situation of extreme poverty. Of the 37 countries eligible for the HIPC Initiative, 32 are in Africa.

7 This second book, together with some of the chapters in this one, is based on papers presented at the international conference on poverty organised by DIAL/CIPRÉ, INSTAT/MADIO and RESAL/EU, held in February 2001 in Antananarivo for the drafting of the PSRP for Madagascar. All the papers can be consulted on the DIAL website [www.dial.prd.fr].

8 The WTO's priorities, drawn up in answer to protests and in a view to gaining a better image in public opinion, include better integration of developing countries and other poor countries; more active participation of all parties (technical assistance and training sessions); improved consultation processes and the promise to take into account concerns relating to the implementation of agreements made during the Uruguay Round.

9 On this subject, Rodrik points out that the current tendency to consider development almost exclusively from the angle of integration into the world economy closes other possible paths, and even goes as far as distracting attention from the key goals of development (Rodrik 2001).

10 Most of the advantages granted to LDCs (concerning market access in particular) are done so unilaterally, not within the scope of the WTO (see, for example, the EU Initiative *Everything but Arms* or the American *Africa Growth and Opportunity Act*).

Part I

Diagnosis and reflections on poverty reduction policies

The launching of the new international poverty reduction strategies is an enormous challenge for the international community. The initiative is based, amongst other things, on two key observations: the scale of poverty in some regions such as sub-Saharan Africa where nearly half of the inhabitants live in extreme poverty; the progression of the affliction, with the deterioration of living conditions in many countries. According to the World Bank, the number of poor people (based on the threshold of two dollars per day) increased throughout the world in the 1990s, except in the Latin American region where it stagnated and in eastern Asia and the Pacific where it fell.

Apart from being able to stir people into action, global statements of this sort are of little interest, particularly as some of the results are marred by uncertainties. Up until now, not enough attention has been paid to the fact that, if appropriate strategies are to be drawn up, they must be based on a precise description of the current state of affairs, drawing lessons from thinking on the nature and evolution of poverty and from past poverty reduction policies. Cases of policies crowned with success are the exception, particularly in the poorest regions. Nonetheless, the decision-makers act as if they had a wide range of effective, appropriate measures at their disposal and that there is no question of their ability to fight against poverty. We must face the facts: at the present time there are still very serious gaps in our knowledge of the characteristics, evolution and determining factors of poverty, and also of the means of curbing it.

Taking this observation as its starting point, the first part of the book takes a close look at current diagnoses of poverty, and also the way in which it is generally tackled. Based on specific case analyses, various paths are suggested to enable us to understand the different dimensions of poverty, to improve our knowledge of changes over time, but also to find a way of making policies more effective. The aim is not so much to give a comprehensive overview of the situation of poor people and of ways of improving their conditions, as to cast a new light on a certain number of essential points that are very often neglected.

Chapter 1 analyses the WDR 2000/2001 entitled *Attacking Poverty*, the core document that defines a new conceptual framework on this issue, and highlights the scope and limits of the World Bank's position. This analysis is of great interest for two main reasons: the first concerns the role assigned to the World Bank, or that it assigns to itself, on the international scene in terms of poverty reduction; the second results from the fact that the Report lays the foundations of the institution's new position by presenting new approaches on the basis of a diagnosis of world poverty which is linked with the results of past strategies. This chapter, which presents a historical and conceptual framework from a critical standpoint, helps measure immediately the challenges involved in the new poverty reduction initiatives.

The other chapters in this part examine little-studied paths of analysis, in a view to making up for the shortcomings in past approaches but also those in the new guidelines recommended by the Bretton Woods Institutions. Chapter 2 makes a precious input to thinking on the principles of justice underlying the objective to fight against poverty, and on their impact in terms of the policies to be implemented. The author argues that such policies must aim at equal opportunities from one generation to another and also at redistribution amongst adults of the same generation. However, analyses and policies recommended under the new poverty reduction initiatives seldom consider the issues of intergeneration social mobility or redistribution. Starting from a global theoretical analysis, the chapter particularly addresses social policies for education and health, a major element in PRSPs. Chapter 3 is also concerned to further thinking on the aims to be set and the means to be mobilised for a political and socio-economic approach to poverty and the poor. Comparative analysis of experiences for regulating poverty in West European societies opens up paths of research for developing countries. The author of this chapter seeks to explain, for each country, how institutional responsibilities are shared, the target populations, the principles underlying the assistance given to the poor, and the means used. Two conclusions are particularly noteworthy: first, the key role of the state; second, the diversity of responses particularly depending on historical and cultural contexts, although they are relatively similar throughout Europe. Questions are raised by the fact that these principles seem far removed from current poverty regulation practices in southern countries.

The following two chapters propose, from specific angles, a diagnosis of the different dimensions of poverty and its determining factors in badly hit regions. On the basis of an empirical study using temporal data on several African countries, Chapter 4 takes stock of the characteristics of urban poverty and assesses its evolution in Africa during the 1990s. This analysis is original, first because it puts the accent on the deterioration of the living conditions of urban populations who tend to be ignored, as the focus is usually on poverty in rural areas; and second, because it tries to clarify the economic mechanisms that led to this situation, an approach that it seldom adopted when studying poverty. It looks at the impact of demographical phenomena, the deterioration of the labour market and also the limits of the possibilities open to households to counter the impact of the macroeconomic shocks they suffer. Chapter 5 also aims to explore the characteristics of poor populations. Using 'voicing', an original method for revealing people's aspirations and demands, applied to the case of Madagascar, poor people are no longer seen as a homogeneous, distinct social group. Whilst pursuing initial paths of analysis, this chapter highlights the need for more in-depth thinking on the appropriate stratification criteria required to explain the rationale behind the demands and to target specific populations. In the case of Madagascar, the only trait that distinguishes poor people is that they express a strong need for the welfare state. But how can such a demand be satisfied when, in principle, it goes against the policies usually considered?

1 A critical review of the World Bank's stance on poverty reduction

Jean-Pierre Cling

Since it defined the concept of Poverty Reduction Strategy Papers (PRSP), the World Bank has officially made the fight against poverty one of its major priorities. Poverty reduction is now being recognised as the basis for development strategies in poor countries. Rising concern for the issue stems from the fact that, although in income terms the number of poor people has been stable overall for the last ten years or so, poverty has nonetheless increased in all regions of the world except East Asia, where it has fallen significantly.

The World Bank's *World Development Report 2000/2001: Attacking Poverty*, helps understand the conceptual framework used as a basis for the new policies promoted by the Bretton Woods Institutions. It is also an opportunity, ten years after the *World Development Report 1990*, devoted to the same subject, to see what progress has been made since then in understanding this issue and finding new ways to deal with it. The first part of this chapter presents the state of world poverty as described in the WDR, and the macroeconomic elements it contains on the relationship between growth and income poverty on a world level, which lead to relatively pessimistic estimates of the evolution of poverty in the coming years. The second part underlines how innovative the Bank's positions are, as it has widened the concept of poverty and put more emphasis on the role of institutions whilst also criticising certain aspects of its own policies. The third part points out the serious limits of these proposals from an operational standpoint.[1]

At the beginning of the twenty-first century, poverty is still a global calamity

Half of the world's population is poor, on the basis of the accepted international monetary indicators. In the long term, there is a close relationship between countries' macroeconomic performances in terms of GDP growth and the evolution of income poverty. But even with very favourable world growth forecasts, it is impossible to foresee any significant reduction in poverty in low-income countries in the coming years, with the notable exception of China.

Poverty and inequalities are rising in many countries

The WDR begins with a summary of the current state of world poverty and recent trends. It starts by underlining the fact that poverty is very common throughout the world: of the world's 6 billion people, 2.8 billion (i.e. almost half) live on less than $2 a day; 1.2 billion, or a fifth of the world's population, live on less than $1 a day, the figure generally accepted as the international threshold of absolute poverty.[2] According to the same sources, 44 per cent of the world's poor living in extreme poverty are to be found in South Asia. The Report remarks that less than one out of every hundred children born in rich countries does not reach its fifth birthday, whereas it is the case for a fifth of the children born in the poorest countries. Similarly, whereas less than 5 per cent of children under five suffer from malnutrition in rich countries, this proportion is approximately 50 per cent in poor countries.

In the last decade (1990–9), the number of people living on less than $1 a day in East Asia fell from approximately 450 million to 260 million, despite the impact of the financial crisis. This reduction was particularly rapid in China, where the number of poor people is said to have fallen from 360 to 215 million (apparently, the reduction took place mainly in urban areas). On the contrary, the number of people living in extreme poverty increased in sub-Saharan Africa and in South Asia. In Europe and Central Asia, the numbers of poor more than doubled during transition to market economies. At the same time, major progress has been made in non-income aspects of poverty. Social indicators have improved substantially on average in developing countries over the past three decades. For example, the infant mortality rate fell from 107 to 59 per 1,000 between 1970 and 1998.

These overall figures conceal large differences from one region to another. For instance, life expectancy was only 52 years in sub-Saharan Africa in 1997, that is 13 years less than the average in developing countries and 25 years less than the OECD average. This can be related in particular to Africa's extraordinarily high infant mortality rate, which amounts to 90 for every 1,000 births, compared with six for 1,000 in the OECD. The situation has of course worsened due to the Aids epidemic, which led to a rise in infant mortality in several African countries: from 62 to 74 in Kenya, and from 52 to 69 in Zimbabwe. Maternal mortality rates are also high in Africa.

In India's most advanced state, Kerala, life expectancy is higher than in Washington, despite incomparably lower average income levels. In the countries that are most affected by the Aids epidemic, all in Africa, the gains in life expectancy obtained in the last 50 years will soon be wiped out. According to United Nations estimates, life expectancy at birth, which rose from 44 years at the beginning of the 1950s to 59 years at the beginning of the 1990s, will fall to 45 years between 2005 and 2010 (UNAIDS, 2000). In Botswana, life expectancy will even fall to less than 40 years.

Regional differences are also very marked in education indicators. East Asia increased its gross primary school enrolment rate from 77 per cent to over 100 per cent between 1982 and 1996,[3] but the rate remained unchanged at 74 per cent in sub-Saharan Africa. Consequently, whereas nearly the entire decline in the illiteracy rate in developing countries can be attributed to East Asia, the number of illiterate people increased by 17 million in South Asia and 3 million in sub-Saharan Africa.

According to the World Bank, there has been a significant divergence between the richest and the poorest countries over the last decades: in the last 40 years the gap between incomes in the richest 20 countries and the poorest 20 has doubled, giving extraordinary differences between countries,[4] certain countries have fallen into a 'poverty trap', as proved by the fact that the number of least-developed countries (LDCs) has doubled in thirty years, rising from 25 in 1971, when this category of country was first created, to 49 in 2001. Only one country, Botswana, has managed to 'graduate' from this group. According to the Report, there is greater diversity in inequality trends within countries. They increased considerably in certain countries (Bangladesh, China, Mexico, etc.), but fell in others (Brazil, Uganda, etc.). Basing its conclusions on a study by Bourguignon and Morrisson (1999), the World Bank considers that worldwide inequality between individuals (combining inequalities between countries and within countries) has increased in past decades, although evidence suggests that the increases observed in recent years are small.

While the above-mentioned divergence is unanimously recognised, the latter conclusion is contradicted by other studies. Overall, there are serious debates among economists concerning the recent evolution of world inequalities between individuals, as well as those between and within countries.[5] In fact, what matters is not only the recent evolution of these inequalities but also their actual level, which is properly astonishing as 20 per cent of world population (in short, the OECD countries) concentrates approximately 80 per cent of world income. No country world wide has such an unequal income distribution; in other words, inequalities between countries are far higher than inequalities within countries (Bourguignon and Morrisson 1999; Schulz 1998). This is why UNDP's expression 'Global inequality – grotesque levels, ambiguous trends' seems very adequate to us (UNDP 2002).

As the World Bank remarks, empirical observations show that countries that recorded high growth rates were able to reduce poverty, whereas poverty usually remained stable or increased in other cases. In the past two centuries, per capita income in West European countries increased tenfold in real terms, in China more than fourfold and in South Asia, threefold. Consequently, the number of poor people (at the $1 threshold) is practically nil in Western Europe. It is higher in China (approximately 20 per cent of the population), where growth was slower. In South Asia, where growth was slower still, it amounts to 40 per cent.

The lack of growth in a certain number of countries helps explain their high poverty levels. This is particularly the case in Africa, where in most countries the GDP per capita has not increased since the 1960s, and where the percentage of the population living in extreme poverty is the highest of all the major geographical zones.

The Report considers that differences in countries' growth rates explain the greater part of the variations in income poverty evolution patterns – as this is the case in the long term, growth in GDP per capita is an important factor in explaining poverty reduction. On average, one additional percentage point of growth in average household consumption is supposed to reduce the share of people living on less than $1 a day by about 2 per cent.

In general, the richest countries in terms of GDP per capita are those with the lowest percentage of poor people measured in income terms (at a given threshold) – the higher the GDP per capita, the higher the average level of consumption of the first quintile of population (the 20 per cent with the lowest consumption), and the lower the share of the population living on less than $1 per day. Nonetheless, this relationship varies from one country to another. Two countries with the same GDP per capita can have very different percentages of poor people (defined at a given threshold) if they do not have the same scale of income inequalities.

It will be difficult to meet the Millennium Development Goals

If, to quote the Report, 'economic growth is a powerful force for poverty reduction', it is clearly important to take a close look at the growth prospects in the world's major economic areas for the coming years, in order to study the possible evolution of income poverty in these areas. As the world population is expected to increase by one billion people by 2015 (97 per cent of which in developing countries), halving the percentage of people living in extreme poverty by then would amount to reducing world poverty at an annual rate of 2.7 per cent, compared with an average rate of 1.7 per cent per year between 1990 and 1999.

Table 1.1 presents the World Bank's main forecasts for the evolution of poverty in developing countries by 2015, taken from its *Global Economic Prospects 2002* (World Bank 2001b). In the basic scenario – based on very rapid growth (an average of 3.7 per cent per year of GDP per capita for developing countries, i.e. twice the rate recorded for the 1990s)[6] – the target of halving the share of the world population living on less than $1 dollar a day (compared with 1990) would be reached. The figure, that stood at 29 per cent in 1990, would be reduced from 22.7 to 12.3 per cent between 1999 and 2015.

Table 1.1 Evolution of poverty in developing countries, by geographical zone

Region	People living on less than $1 per day (millions)			People living on less than $2 per day (millions)		
	1990	1999	2015*	1990	1999	2015*
East Asia and Pacific	452	260	59	1,084	849	284
Excluding China	92	46	6	285	236	93
Europe and Central Asia	7	17	4	44	91	42
Latin America and the Caribbean	74	77	60	167	168	146
Middle East and North Africa	6	7	6	59	87	65
South Asia	495	490	279	976	1,098	1,098
Sub-Saharan Africa	242	300	345	388	484	597
Total	1,276	1,151	753	2,718	2,777	2,230
Excluding China	916	936	700	1,919	2,164	2,040

Region	1990 (%)	1999 (%)	2015 (%)*	1990 (%)	1999 (%)	2015 (%)*
East Asia and Pacific	27.6	14.2	2.8	66.1	46.2	13.5
Excluding China	18.5	7.9	0.9	57.3	40.4	13.3
Europe and Central Asia	1.6	3.6	0.8	9.6	19.3	8.7
Latin America and the Caribbean	16.8	15.1	9.7	38.1	33.1	23.4
Middle East and North Africa	2.4	2.3	1.5	24.8	29.9	16.7
South Asia	44.0	36.9	16.7	86.8	82.6	65.5
Sub-Saharan Africa	47.7	46.7	39.3	76.4	75.3	68.0
Total	29.0	22.7	12.3	61.7	54.7	36.3
Excluding China	28.1	24.5	14.8	58.8	56.5	43.0

Source: World Bank (2001b).

Notes
*Estimates.

The reduction is split very unequally between the different countries. Extreme poverty would practically disappear in China and East Asia. It would be very rapidly reduced in South Asia (in particular in India). On the other hand, despite the optimistic or perhaps unrealistic hypothesis of an average growth in GDP per capita of 1.5 per cent per year (compared with −1.2 per cent in the 1980s and −0.5 per cent in the 1990s), the numbers of poor would apparently still continue to rise in sub-Saharan Africa – from 300 million to 345 million at the $1 per capita threshold, between 1999 and 2015, which corresponds to a slight reduction in the share of the population living in extreme poverty (from 46.7 to 39.3 per cent). The evolution would be very similar for those living on less than the $2 threshold.

Overall, even if the international goal of halving the number of the world's citizens living in extreme poverty between 1990 and 2015 is met (i.e. that the World Bank's extremely optimistic forecast for overall growth proves to be correct), this will mainly be due to the drastic reduction in poverty in China and India, given these two countries' demographic weight. By contrast, the least-developed countries (most of which are in sub-Saharan Africa) will probably not be able to reduce poverty during this period, and these countries' share of world population will continue to increase: according to United Nations forecasts (based on the hypothesis that their number will remain constant), the share will rise from 11 to 20 per cent between now and 2050 (United Nations 2001).

In the overview at the beginning of the WDR, the World Bank also expresses its concerns regarding the other international development goals set at different United Nations conferences in the 1990s, and these concerns are shared by other studies (see in particular Hanmer and Naschold 1999; UNDP 2002). Table 1.2 lists these goals, which have been extended to include the aid and trade agenda and renamed Millennium Development Goals (see Chapter 11).[7]

For instance, at the current rates, there is little hope of attaining universal primary education by 2015, particularly in sub-Saharan Africa. For infant mortality rates to be reduced by two-thirds between 1990 and 2015, a 30 per cent drop would have been needed between 1990 and 1998, but the figures actually only fell by 10 per cent during that period. The World Bank *Global Economic Prospects 2002* (World Bank 2001b), based on estimates of long-term growth and trends in urbanisation, considers that only South Asia is likely to reach the goal in 2015. Three other regions should come quite close to reaching it (East Asia, North Africa and the Middle East, Latin America), whereas Eastern Europe and Central Asia would be far off; and infant mortality would remain more or less stable in sub-Saharan Africa.

In this context, the challenges behind the fight against poverty and human deprivation of all kinds are not only macroeconomic (i.e. to

Table 1.2 The main International Development Goals

Goal	Conference
1 Reduce the proportion of people living in extreme poverty by half between 1990 and 2015.	Copenhagen (1995)
2 Enrol all children in primary school by 2015	Jomtien (1990), Beijing (1995), Copenhagen (1995)
3 Make progress towards gender equality and empowering women by eliminating gender disparities in primary and secondary education by 2005	Cairo (1994), Beijing (1995), Copenhagen (1995)
4 Reduce infant and child mortality rates by two-thirds between 1990 and 2015	Cairo (1994)
5 Reduce maternal mortality ratios by three-quarters between 1990 and 2015	Cairo (1994), Beijing (1995)
6 Provide access for all who need reproductive health services by 2015	Cairo (1994)
7 Implement national strategies for sustainable development by 2005 so as to reverse the loss of environmental resources by 2015	Rio (1992)

Sources: World Bank (2000a), Hanmer and Naschold (1999).

obtain a higher economic growth rate), but also microeconomic (i.e. to ensure that growth helps the segments of the population that suffer the most hardship and to define policies targeted on reducing extreme poverty). The overview to the World Development Report, whose main proposals are analysed in the next part of this chapter, summarises the issues at stake as follows:

Attaining the international development goals will require actions to spur economic growth and reduce income inequality, but even equitable growth will not be enough to achieve the goals for health and education. Reducing infant and child mortality rates by two-thirds depends on halting the spread of HIV/AIDS, increasing the capacity of developing countries' health systems to deliver more health services, and ensuring that technological progress in the medical field spills over to benefit the developing world. And meeting the gender equality goals in education will require specific policy measures to address the cultural, social, and economic barriers that prevent girls from attending school ... Hence the need for a broader, more comprehensive strategy to fight poverty.

(World Bank 2000a)

The World Bank has adopted an innovative stance

As we shall see in this section, the stance adopted by the World Bank in its Report is innovative in that it is not limited to the macroeconomic approach, focused on the relationship between growth and income poverty, but widens the concept of poverty to non-income factors, and proposes a series of widely varied policies for attacking poverty.

Considerable progress in analysing poverty

The 1990 Development Report extended the definition of poverty to include the deprivation of fundamental rights (education, health, nutrition), but in fact carried out most of its analyses from a monetary standpoint.[8] The WDR 2000/2001 describes the many different dimensions of poverty, each requiring equal attention. There is a move from the notion of lack of goods (monetary or essentials) to the notion of lack of ability to choose. It takes into account new dimensions such as exclusion and vulnerability (see Figure 1.1). Ten years after the UNDP, which adopted this approach for its Human Development Reports, the World Bank uses a conceptual framework inspired by the works of Amartya Sen, Nobel Prizewinner for Economics, quoted on the first page of the first chapter: '[all these forms of deprivation severely restrict] the capabilities that a person has, that is, the substantive freedoms he or she enjoys to lead the kind of life he or she values'.

Three key issues: opportunities, empowerment and security

In 1990, the World Bank's analysis of the situation encouraged it to focus its fight against poverty on three main areas: first, economic policies based on liberalisation and market incentives, designed to create rapid, labour-intensive growth;[9] the second element consisted in ensuring minimum levels of social services for poor people, including basic healthcare, family planning, nutrition and primary education; third, a comprehensive approach to poverty reduction also called for well-targeted actions offering safety nets for people exposed individually (illness, old age) or collectively (natural disasters) to shocks.

As in the previous report on this theme, the *World Development Report 2000/2001* focuses its strategy on three different issues – opportunities, empowerment, security – which we describe below. As Mosley (2001) points out, security and opportunities stem directly from safety nets and investment in the human capital of the poor, whereas empowerment is a new idea that was not mentioned in the previous report (Table 1.3).

With the approach in terms of *opportunities*, microeconomic free-market reforms should follow the macroeconomic reforms. Markets must be pro-poor to enable the poor to acquire assets and gain the best opportunities

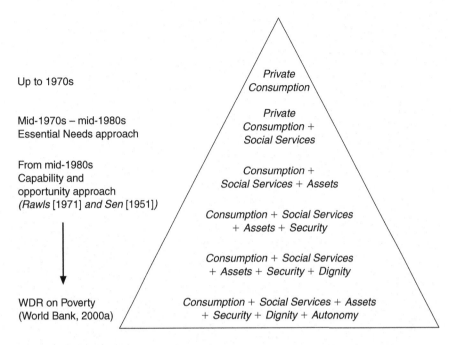

Up to 1970s

Mid-1970s – mid-1980s
Essential Needs approach

From mid-1980s
Capability and
opportunity approach
(Rawls [1971] *and Sen* [1951])

WDR on Poverty
(World Bank, 2000a)

*Private
Consumption*

*Private
Consumption +
Social Services*

*Consumption +
Social Services + Assets*

*Consumption + Social Services
+ Assets + Security*

*Consumption + Social Services
+ Assets + Security + Dignity*

*Consumption + Social Services + Assets
+ Security + Dignity + Autonomy*

Figure 1.1 Gradual widening of the concept of poverty since the 1970s.
Source: from SPA (1999).

from them. But markets are subject to a large number of obstacles of
micro origin, resulting from bureaucracy or corruption, which call for
deregulation at the microeconomic level. Also, at micro and local levels,
economic efficiency cannot be considered separately from institutional
efficiency, and it is the complementarity of the different players – state,
private sector, civil society and population – that frees economic forces
and increases opportunities for the poor. The policies proposed in this
area are extremely varied, calling on one or several of the players at the
same time, depending on the case. They include microfinance, land
reform, tax policies, human capital development policies for the poor
(health, education) etc.

A new concept of *empowerment* is put forward by the World Bank. The
political, institutional and social causes of poverty are strongly emphasised, and deemed inseparable from the economic causes. For individuals
and households, but also for all human societies, possessing social assets is
essential to escape poverty. Social cohesion and the absence of discrimination or of striking inequalities also determine the quality and level of economic growth. Social capital is considered just as important a factor of
poverty as human capital or physical capital. The way in which institutions

Table 1.3 Comparison of the 1990 and 2000/2001 Development Reports. Themes and related policy recommendations

World Development Report 1990		*World Development Report 2000/1*	
'Pillars'	*Associated policies*	*'Pillars'*	*Associated policies*
Labour-intensity	Small-scale industry; special employment measures; promotion of green revolution in small-farm agriculture		
Investment in the human capital of the poor	Promotion of primary health and education, especially amongst females; microfinance	Opportunity	Microfinance; land reform and other asset redistribution policies; fiscal and other measures to reduce inequality; pro-poor public expenditures patterns
Social safety nets	Food subsidies; social funds; support for community-based redistribution	Security	'Tailor-made' social protection measures; measures to support asset diversification; insurance; 'international public good' defences against economic crisis, e.g. financial regulation; conflict prevention
		Empowerment	Democratisation, decentralisaton, measures to build 'social capital'

Source: Mosley (2001).

listen to and address the aspirations of poor citizens is a vital element in the fight against poverty, now commonly referred to as empowerment. Ensuring a pro-poor approach from public institutions (particularly, the struggle against corruption), promoting the diversification of social assets and strengthening national cohesion are thus essential political, institutional and social aspects of any effective poverty reduction strategy.

Finally, official policies must not only promote efficiency but also *security*. Vulnerability to shocks is one of the main reasons for falling into poverty. Adverse shocks are not only detrimental to the living standards of poor people but also lead to situations that are extremely difficult to reverse and affect 'their ability to escape from poverty'. The Report looks at protection from and prevention of a certain number of shocks, including idiosyncratic shocks (e.g. illness), market instability, financial crises and natural disasters. The concept of security is by nature the most antithetical in a pure market economy approach and is therefore potentially the most subversive and conflictual. Depending on the way it is interpreted, it can be used to defend, to reform or to condemn economic liberalisation policies (Mosley 2001). On this subject, the Report more or less recognises that the reform policies carried out in the last two decades can produce losers: 'liberalizing markets (say, by privatising state commodity boards) can have mixed effects and will not always benefit poor people' (World Bank 2000a: 147). One of the aims of security policies must be to protect these losers. Safety net mechanisms, touched on briefly in 1990, are given more attention in the 2000 Report that advocates a modular approach based on different combinations of instruments such as insurance, targeted aid, redistributive transfers, social funds, etc.

Challenging the Washington Consensus?

One point that was particularly long awaited was the way the World Bank would analyse the impact of past economic reforms that it had fervently supported and often promoted in the past. It is no secret that there was some quite heated internal debate during the drafting of the Report, leading to the resignation of its team director, Ravi Kanbur, shortly after that of the Bank's chief economist, Joseph Stiglitz, who won the Nobel Prize in Economics in 2001. Despite the relative independence of the editorial team in principle, the Report does nonetheless commit the Bank – particularly on such a sensitive subject. The terms of the Report therefore reflect a certain compromise between the initial version, far more daring in its criticisms of trade and financial liberalisation, and political pressures, particularly from the American Treasury (Wade 2001).

The validity of free-market reforms is not questioned as such, but through the reservations it makes concerning the optimal rate or extent of reform processes and the institutional conditions required, it is in fact a criticism of the mixed results obtained by two decades of liberalisation. In particular, it challenges the model of economic openness that was the basis of the strategies recommended in the 1990 Report, although its position was very much watered down between the draft version and the final version of the Report.

The authors recognise that 'the initial push for trade liberalisation as an instrument for poverty reduction was influenced by a narrow reading of predictions from trade theory' (World Bank 2000a: 70). In some countries, trade barriers benefited poor people by increasing the prices of the goods they produced. This was particularly true in the labour-intensive textile and clothing sector. A study quoted in the Report found that in Mexico about a quarter of the decline in unskilled wages since the mid-1980s (−20 per cent), shown in the Figure 1.2, was due to the reduction in tariffs and the elimination of import licence requirements. Also, in countries where the abundant factor of production is land rather than labour (Latin America, Africa), liberalisation does not necessarily benefit the latter.

Written in the aftermath of the Asian crisis, the Report also mentions the criticisms voiced regarding the financial liberalisation policies recommended by the Bretton Woods Institutions, provoked by the crisis. A draft version of the Report actually questioned the financial liberalisation implemented since the 1980s on these institutions' initiative, stating that this policy was responsible for the recent crises. The final version is far more timid in its criticism, although it does recognise the need for control on capital flows in certain circumstances to help prevent financial crises.

Finally, a chapter was added (Chapter 3) that did not exist in the original version, on the relationship between growth, poverty and inequalities. Above all, the chapter aims to strengthen the World Bank's central message that growth is good for the poor, but on the condition that the economic policies implemented by the countries in question, which are of course needed to favour growth, follow its recommendations. Referring to the results of what are extremely fragile econometric estimates (Dollar and Kraay 2001), the Report notes that 'good' policies have a pro-poor impact on growth:

A recent study of growth and poverty reduction in a sample of 80 industrial and developing countries found that macroeconomic policies such as a stable monetary policy, openness to international trade, and a moderate-size government raise the incomes of poor people as much as average incomes. In other words, these policies did not systematically affect income distribution. Other policies, such as stabilization from high inflation, may even disproportionately favour poor people . . .

(World Bank 2000a: 52–3)

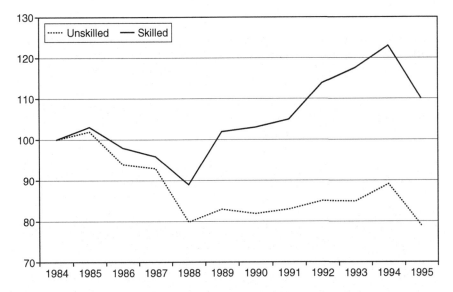

Figure 1.2 The gap between skilled and unskilled wages widened in Mexico *(base 100 = 1984)*.

Source: World Bank (2000a).

Whilst being forced to moderate its position on the advantages of liberalisation, under pressures from within and without and in the light of the facts, the World Bank ended up by not taking a clear stand on the issue, thus making its message somewhat incoherent.

Despite considerable progress, the World Bank still lacks a coherent political framework for attacking poverty

The 2000/2001 Report is far less operational than previous World Development Reports, particularly the one published in 1990. The growing complexity of poverty issues and certain reservations regarding the results of past reforms tend to make the recommended strategies federating rather than mobilising.

Although the Report partially calls into question the Washington Consensus it does not suggest any alternative model, thus giving the impression of a somewhat agnostic stance on the part of the World Bank. Contrary to the 1990 Report that proposed a clear, universal strategy, *Attacking Poverty* limits itself to defining general guidelines. The social and institutional analysis of the causes of poverty is convincing, but is not backed up by precise political recommendations, and a large number of questions remain in the air.

The poor are elusive

The fact that the Report recognises the multidimensional nature of poverty unquestionably adds to the wealth of its analysis. It describes phenomena such as material deprivation, malnutrition, illiteracy, sickness, exclusion, vulnerability, insecurity and marginalisation as different facets of a single concept. The disadvantage of this approach is that the poor and poverty become relatively elusive, changing their form and nature depending on the angle being considered.

Razafindrakoto and Roubaud (2000a) tested the links between the different forms of poverty in the case of Madagascar. They came to the conclusion that the different categories of poor people hardly overlap at all. This obviously has an impact on poverty reduction strategies. Their findings invalidate those of Kanbur and Squire (1999) who concluded in a recent article that 'broadening the definition of poverty does not change significantly who is counted as poor ... it reflects the fact that the many aspects of poverty – income, health, education, political rights, and so on – are often closely correlated'. The observation that there is very little overlapping between the different dimensions of poverty challenges the nature and causes of poverty highlighted by studies based on a purely monetary approach, and consequently questions the appropriateness of any policies drawn up on the basis of such studies (see also the case of France in Chapter 12).

Should we count as poor only people who suffer all the different dimensions of deprivation identified? Should one particular dimension of poverty be considered more important than the others – because it causes the greatest suffering, or because it conditions the others – and hence be the main focus for identifying poor people and measuring poverty?

There is obviously no single, clear-cut answer to this type of question and it would be unfair to criticise the Report for not giving us definitive solutions. But we would have liked at least to find a few answers, an outline of priorities, or perhaps ideas for future research. Failing which, poor people come over as a large, undifferentiated mass, covering a very wide section of the population, or even the majority in low-income countries. Also failing which, it seems difficult to establish priorities and define policies that will enable us, in the words of the Report's title, to 'attack poverty'.

The only approach proposed for aggregating the different forms of deprivation (i.e. calculating the 'well-being' function) may be intellectually attractive, but does not work very well in practice when trying to take into account non-income criteria such as social exclusion. The best-known attempt at aggregation of this sort is that of the UNDP, which calculates Human Development Indexes that combine, in a totally arbitrary manner, three quantitative indicators (life expectancy, level of education and GDP per capita).

Amongst other examples, the passage in the Report that states that 'poverty is also fear for the future', gives the impression that, through poverty, it is in fact 'ill-being' that is being addressed. Experience shows that such concepts are rarely workable, particularly because the poor defined in this way are statistical aggregates of population and not groups in the sociological sense of the word. Old people, marginalised families and lower-income deciles are ways of grouping the poor; but they are not living social structures with their rules and norms. Social and political relations between the poor and the rest of the population can only be analysed by looking at pertinent social groups with common interests (Winter 2001). In practice, the fight against poverty cannot be based on segments of the population but must be made on the level of village groups, associations of producers, rural communities, urban cooperatives, all of which groups, incidentally, do not only include poor people but also have their own elites.

The frequent references to civil society are not differentiated either. The Report often makes a distinction between the 'elites' and 'people in power' and the others, the civil society, lumped together with the vast majority of poor. But we must go beyond these all-purpose categories and get down to the grass-roots level of the groups of people actually involved if we are really to analyse the social and political relations between 'the poor' and the rest of the society, and then go on to define the poverty reduction strategies called for in the Report.

The link between growth and poverty reduction is only treated superficially

Adopting the distinction made by Klasen (2001), the link between growth and poverty reduction can be analysed in two different ways: first, on the global level, by studying the interrelationship between growth on a macro-economic level and the different types of poverty; and second, by focusing on the sectoral, regional and functional make-up of growth, in relation to its impact on poverty. In the WDR, the World Bank's analyses of these two aspects seem relatively superficial. A closer study and a synthesis would have been welcome.

Although one of the main contributions of the Bank's new approach is, precisely, to take into account the multidimensional nature of poverty, the Report only briefly analyses the interrelations between growth and income-poverty alone. The cross-section studies on which the analysis is based (see p. 32) establish a link between evolutions in these two variables over the long term for samples of developing countries. Growth is considered pro-poor when it offers a high level of elasticity between growth and a reduction in this type of poverty. It is most regrettable that the correlation between growth and non-income poverty, such as the synergies between human development and economic development, is only mentioned in passing: 'across countries, and across individuals within countries, there are strong correlations between health and education outcomes and incomes' (World Bank 2000a: 57). Chapter 2 of this book aims to give a new impetus to thinking on this issue.

The relationship between an additional percentage point of growth in per capita consumption and the reduction in the share of the population living in extreme poverty (by 2 per cent on average) varies depending on the initial level of inequalities in income and in assets and the way it evolves. According to the Bank's estimates, 1 per cent growth in consumption per capita should lead to a 1.5 per cent reduction in poverty (share of population living on less than $1 per day) with the Gini index (index measuring inequalities) at 0.6; the poverty reduction would be doubled (3 per cent) with the Gini index at only 0.2. The mediocre quality of statistical data on income distribution in developing countries makes such estimates extremely fragile. The elasticity in question is very sensitive to the poverty threshold chosen, although we know perfectly well that the choice of these thresholds is highly arbitrary.[10]

More fundamentally, there is no in-depth study of the link between growth, poverty and inequality: referring to the estimates made by Dollar and Kraay (2001), it is stated that, on average, growth favours the different population quintiles in the same proportions; in other words it does not distort income distribution, hence the title of the above mentioned paper *Growth is Good for the Poor*. This relationship is subject to the right combination of policies. These conclusions are rejected by an IMF study, according to which growth disfavours the poorest quintile on average and some of these macroeconomic policies affect the income distribution (Ghura, Leite and Tsangarides 2002). Going beyond these technical debates, it should be stressed that this purely instrumental approach to inequalities should be widened: their reduction should not be considered as a simple means to increase the share of growth that accrues to poor people (and possibly to speed up economic growth) but also as an end, which is intimately interconnected to any poverty reduction strategy (see Chapter 2).

The second area in which the Report analyses the link between growth and poverty concerns the distribution of growth, an issue that is all the more important because, as we mentioned above, the spread in numbers of poor people can vary considerably within a country, depending on the economic sector or the region.

It may seem obvious, but there is one point that must be repeated in this respect: pro-poor growth aimed at directly reducing poverty must be concentrated in the sectors where the poor are to be found and must use the factors of production that they possess. The majority of poor people live in rural areas and make their living out of farming; their most abundant factor of production is their labour force, and sometimes their land. Hence, according to Klasen (2001): 'The experience of virtually all successful developers suggests that rapid growth and poverty reduction always involves an emphasis on improving productivity and incomes in agricultural and non-farm rural occupations.' There is also the need to invest in 'spatial poverty traps' where concentrations of extreme poverty make public intervention an absolute necessity (e.g. the case of the former homelands in South Africa).

The Report mentions a few successful examples of growth in farm productivity in India (the famous 'green revolution' of the 1960s) and growth in non-farming income in China, accompanied by migrations that have tended to equalise income from one province to another. But on the whole, the World Bank remains prudent on this question and does not come to any final conclusions. This is no doubt related to its lack of commitment to targeted, prioritised recommendations that we will analyse later on in this chapter, but also to the fact that although there is a relative consensus on all these subjects as far as diagnoses are concerned, there are still heated discussions concerning the alternative solutions to be adopted in terms of policies (see pp. 44–7).

Conflicts and the need for state arbitration are underestimated

On a number of points, the Report minimises or even completely ignores the existence of potential conflicts that could give rise to either political compromises or violent confrontations. The result is a somewhat idealistic picture of the situation, with the great disadvantage of not offering practical assistance to politicians striving to find poverty reduction policies and to implement them on a day-to-day basis.

This tendency to minimise or ignore possible contradictions is to be found in both the theoretical analyses and the practical recommendations given in the Report. For instance, from a theoretical standpoint, the Report observes the change in scientific opinions regarding the possibility of a trade-off between growth and equality. After indicating that this was accepted as a fact in the past, the Report notes that recent empirical studies weaken the case for such a trade-off and concludes that: 'lower inequality can increase efficiency and economic growth through a variety of channels' (World Bank 2000a: 56).

This conclusion is, in fact, exactly what we all want to hear: choices would be so much simpler if equality and efficiency were always synonymous! But although the conclusion appears satisfactory, it may perhaps be premature. Other studies, including recent work by Cogneau and Guénard (2002), show on the basis of in-depth econometric studies that the relationship between equality and growth is, to say the least, elusive and that there may be a trade-off between greater equality and more rapid economic growth.

However, even if there is a positive relationship between equality and growth, this does not mean that choices between different economic policies would simply disappear. A policy can make the situation worse for certain poor people in the short term, whilst being favourable to growth and therefore poverty reduction in the long term. For instance, this is often the case of policies that liberalise prices of farm inputs. Other policies can improve the well-being of underprivileged groups whilst having an adverse impact on others. For example, studies by DIAL came to the conclusion that the devaluation of the CFA franc resulted in improvements for disadvantaged rural populations but worsened the situation for the urban poor (DIAL 2001). There is hardly any mention in the Report of the need to make choices, or of the issue of conflicts of interests between groups or social categories.

As the Report fails to differentiate sufficiently between the different groups of poor people, it often gives the impression that the large mass of poor are to be found side by side with a minority of privileged people, albeit without necessarily being opposed to them. It uses the terms of privileged or elite indiscriminately, but the category is no more workable in practical terms than the vast group of the poor.

According to the Report, the impact on poverty of inequality in the distribution of assets and income mainly stems from the fact that it puts a brake on growth, and not from any conflict of interests between the different parties. This position would perhaps be more convincing if it was less systematic. There is no need to extol class war to observe that there are many cases where there are obvious conflicts of interest between rich and poor and where political arbitration is necessary. As it ignores these possibilities, the Report is, once again, of little practical assistance to politicians who are confronted with these problems every day.

Let us take a few examples. Chapter 6 of the Report ('Making State Institutions more Responsive to Poor People') makes no mention of such conflicts of interests and devotes a whole section ('Pro-poor Coalitions') to showing why elites have several reasons for working with the poor to fight against poverty. The reasons are based on very legitimate ethical grounds, but seem very abstract in terms of the short-term interests of more favoured groups. For instance, an African civil servant – who belongs to the category of privileged people – can no doubt understand that mass education is good for his country's long-term growth. But he also knows that 'in the long term, we'll all be dead' and that, in the shorter term, mass education will be financed by an increase in his taxes or cut-backs in the subsidies granted to the universities his children attend. It is obviously a good thing to try to convince privileged groups of the need to attack poverty, but we should not delude ourselves: for the time being there will continue to be conflicts of interest between the rich and the poor, and even between different groups of poor people.

In this respect, it is highly significant that the Report totally ignores fiscal policy. This is, of course, a complicated issue, as it is difficult to measure the global impact of tax on the distribution of income and assets. But it is an instrument that governments have frequently used in their fight against inequalities and poverty, at least in developed countries (Piketty 2001). It is also a tool for which there is an obvious conflict of interests between groups of rich and poor. Whatever the case may be, the potential importance of this instrument for attacking inequalities and poverty is such that it is surprising that the Report has nothing to say about it.

Similarly, the Report has very little to say about the issue of restructuring public expenditure. It notes that, although the issue has been in the forefront for over ten years, little has been done to redirect this spending towards underprivileged people, particularly in areas such as health and education. The Report does not study the reasons why this has not been done, although this would be most useful in ensuring the implementation of such restructuring policies. However, it seems likely that one of the main reasons for the failure of attempts made so far is that the current beneficiaries of the spending have simply defended their own interests.

Paradoxically, despite recognising the acute need to reduce inequalities in a certain number of countries, the only strategy proposed is a win–win strategy, consisting in redistributing the capital in such a manner as to have no impact on incentives and to avoid conflict (Maxwell 2001). It gives examples of land market reforms in Bangladesh and Brazil, grants for families to send their children to school in Mexico (the *Progresa* programme) and the South African retirement scheme.

More authoritarian measures are rejected, with fairly weak arguments: 'Coercive land reform under highly unequal land ownership, while potentially good for poor people and good for efficiency, rarely has enough political support to be effectively implemented' (World Bank 2000a: 80). However, the example of structural adjustment demonstrates that the World Bank has not always hesitated in proposing politically sensitive reforms when it considered them necessary.

The Report points out that: 'access to land plays an important part in poverty reduction. Better access to land, accompanied by access to such assets as credit and infrastructure, can improve the productivity of land and labour for poor people. Thus liberalizing land markets has large potential benefits' (World Bank 2000a: 67). Improving security for property rights is also considered a priority. Improving poor people's access to land is only seen from a market-based standpoint. The Report advocates negotiated land reform, whereby large landowners would be given incentives to sell their land to poor peasants on a voluntary basis.

However, we must bear in mind that in all the cases where countries have carried out successful land reforms in the past, they were preceded by violent upheavals (South Korea, People's Republic of China, Taiwan). Gunnar Myrdal noted this at the end of the 1960s (Myrdal 1968), when he was already pessimistic about the chances of success for land reforms that respect the rules of democracy and the free-market economy. His judgement is confirmed by the fact that no successful examples of this approach have been recorded over the last three decades. This is perhaps another example of the limits of the free-market economy that the Report should have recognised.

As it minimises the possibilities of conflict, the Report does not put enough emphasis on the need for arbitration procedures and particularly for respected, competent public administration. And yet, one of the main reasons for the failure of adjustment policies in the poor countries in Africa is the limited competence of their national administrations. This is true in technical terms, but also in their ability to arbitrate in favour of the poorest people in the event of conflicts. In fact, the problem of the states' lack of ability to define and implement suitable economic policies becomes even more acute in the case of poverty reduction policies.

The international environment is not studied in enough detail

The final part of the Report, on the links between international relations and evolutions in poverty, is very incomplete. Paradoxically, the burning question of the hour, world governance, is not mentioned. Despite being the focus of much attention since the World Trade Organisation's Conference in Seattle (1999), international trade relations are hardly touched on, and then only from the angle of developing countries' access to markets in industrialised countries, although it is true that the reports on global economic prospects (World Bank 2000b, 2001b) cover the developing countries' multilateral trade interests in great detail but without looking closely at the impact of trade on poverty. Financial relations are only brought up in its analysis of the Asian crisis and development aid.

As we have already indicated, the Report highlights the causality between inequalities and poverty, and quite rightly puts the accent on geographical inequality as a fundamental aspect of world poverty. It also underlines the decisive importance of inequalities between countries. It is macroeconomic forces that determine inequalities on the world level, determining the modes of growth and convergence between countries. Inequality within countries and its relation to a country's growth performance plays only a small role in global inequality dynamics.

One of the causes of divergence on a world level is presented as the difference in 'quality' of the policies adopted by the different countries. But is it not true to say that the nature of international relations also has an impact on this trend towards growing inequalities? Although it is recognised that national policies of openness have often helped aggravate inequalities on a national level, the Report does not analyse the hypothesis that wide-scale liberalisation may have contributed to differences between nations.

Some of the arguments put forward in the Report, admittedly in a different context, would have been sufficient to justify making this issue of growing inequalities between nations a central focus of its analyses and recommendations. If, as the Report states, inequalities within a country put a brake on its economic growth and its ability to produce collective goods, in principle it should also follow that inequalities between nations or individuals at the world level slow down world growth and hamper the production of international public goods. And the same reasoning that leads to encouraging elites within each developing country to recognise that it is in their obvious interests to improve the living standards of the poorest people, should induce the Report to argue, *mutatis mutandis*, that the rich countries' economic interests will be served by encouraging development in poor countries.

For all of these reasons, we would have expected the Report to include an in-depth analysis of international economic relations and their impact on poverty in developing countries. Instead, the analysis is limited to global public goods (a fashionable subject, but its relationship to poverty is not always very clear) and to development aid. On this last point, the presentation offers very little new material as most of the World Bank's ideas on the subject are already well known (in particular, see World Bank 1998a).

In addition, the fact that there has been near stagnation over the long term in poor regions such as the Indian sub-continent and sub-Saharan Africa whilst there has been economic growth in other regions in the world, raises the question of whether this situation is not partly caused by structural problems. For example, we know that in the case of sub-Saharan Africa several studies have concluded that physical factors such as land-locked situation, soil infertility, climate or endemic diseases, are major causes of this situation (Sachs and Warner 1996; Collier and Gunning 1997; Bloom and Sachs 1998). If this is the case, the solution to the problem of poverty cannot be found solely in internal policies implemented by the countries concerned. Is the answer to structural poverty to be found simply by producing global public goods? This is far from obvious.

The final chapter on development aid does not analyse the impact on poverty or the long-term effects of the HIPC Initiative, designed to relieve the debt burden of heavily indebted poor countries. Only three pages are devoted to this Initiative, despite the fact that the question of debt relief for the poorest countries is, as it states: 'the most prominent issue in development cooperation at the end of the twentieth century and the beginning of the twenty-first'! The chapter deplores the decline in development aid in the 1990s, due to political and strategic reasons, but also to aid 'fatigue'. However, beyond the now traditional message from the Bank whereby aid should be given in priority to countries that practice good policies (under the principle of selectivity), wider issues are not touched on, such as:

> whether and how increased aid might reduce poverty more rapidly (particularly where governance is weak), how to reverse the decline in

> aid resources (getting to the 0.7 per cent of GDP, alternative sources
> of aid revenue) and how to achieve a better balance of grants to loans.
>
> (Hubbard 2001: 297)

In its introduction, the Report begins by underlining the seriousness of
the Aids epidemic, which is bound to have a considerable impact in the
coming years, both in terms of life expectancy and income levels and distribution (see pp. 22–3). Nonetheless, the impact of the epidemic is not
really analysed in detail (one box is devoted to it in chapter 8). Out of 36
million people affected by the virus at the end of 2000, 70 per cent live in
sub-Saharan Africa (which has 80 per cent of the infected children),
where the average prevalence rate is estimated at nearly 10 per cent of the
adult population (UNAIDS 2000). In the most badly affected southern
African countries (South Africa, Botswana, Zimbabwe, etc.) the prevalence rate is over 20 per cent, and cautious estimates consider that a third
of today's 15-year-olds will die from Aids.

Although it is obviously very difficult to measure the macroeconomic
impact of Aids, ample, clear information can be found in a number of
prospective studies on the subject that confirm its extreme gravity. For
instance, although Botswana currently has one of the highest GDP per
capita in sub-Saharan Africa, a survey suggests that the number of poor
households (living on less than $5 per person, per month, the threshold
used by UNAIDS) will increase again in the next decade. During this
period, the poorest families will suffer from a 13 per cent drop in income
at the same time as an increase in their size, as the Aids epidemic means
that workers have to support more and more people (UNAIDS 2000). By
2025, GDP will be more than 30 per cent lower than it would have been
without the epidemic.

Such a terrible drama obviously calls on society as a whole and the
international community to join forces to fight against the spread of the
epidemic and to care for the sick, but also to help the populations and
their governments to face up to the consequences. Although households
and communities obviously bear the brunt of Aids, there is bound to be
an adverse impact on states (such as the risk that health and education
systems may collapse due to high death rates amongst civil servants,
increased expenditure, etc.), as well as on businesses and the economy as
a whole. It is disappointing that the Report is not more precise in its recommendations to fight against Aids, although in this respect the Bank's
precise role in relation to the other international organisations (especially
the World Health Organisation) is yet to be defined.

The economic policy recommendations are not sufficiently clear or prioritised

The World Bank's World Development Reports have always fulfilled two complementary functions. First, they present a comprehensive analysis of a specific subject, backed up by a full summary of the research in that area to date. Second, they propose a series of recommendations designed to guide the development community in its actions in the given area. The 2000/2001 Report is excellent with respect to the first part, but more disappointing regarding the second. Based on the Report, Table 1.4, taken from Klasen (2001), summarises the main findings of research on these issues, the consensus on economic policy implications and the areas remaining open to debate.

Although it was based on a more limited concept of poverty and was backed by less detailed analyses, the previous Report on poverty (1990) had the advantage of presenting a clear message. This was the now well-known idea of a labour-intensive growth strategy, backed by the recommendation to focus public expenditure on basic social services. These relatively simple precepts served to guide – either well, or not, this is not the point here – the Bank's, the other donors' and the developing countries' actions over the last decade. It is not so easy to see in concrete terms what the three key issues proposed in the latest Report – opportunities, empowerment and security – will mean as far as the actions of governments and donors are concerned; particularly the first two points.

Due to a combination of several factors, the proposed guidelines lack clarity. First, as we mentioned above, the group of poor people is too vast and too heterogeneous to be clearly identifiable. It is also too abstract to lend itself to concrete actions on the part of public authorities or donors. Who are these people who lack social capital or are living in precarious situations, and where are they? Second, although the new dimensions included in the concept of poverty help to improve our understanding of the phenomenon, they are not easy to interpret in operational terms. How can we increase the social capital of the poorest people? How can we measure, and above all, how can we correct vulnerability? It seems impossible for governments in poor countries to set up safety nets to cover all vulnerable populations, due to the sheer numbers of people concerned. In this respect, we must recognise that by widening the concept of poverty in this extremely useful way, the authors of the Report made the task of deducing the operational implications far more difficult.

The third and most important reason why the Report remains vague is the lack of clearly stated priorities, both in terms of the targeted groups and the recommended actions. By multiplying different concepts of poverty, we risk forgetting simple things, such as the fact that the highest concentration of poverty is in sub-Saharan Africa and the Indian sub-continent. Also, should public authorities not focus their attention on certain dimensions of poverty, either because they condition to a great extent the other dimensions, or because they lend themselves more easily to corrective action? It is essential to draw up priorities of this sort because the poor countries have limited capacities. Failing this, poverty reduction policies risk getting lost in a myriad of different forms of actions that have very little effect.

In its recommendations, the Report sometimes seems to ignore the majority of poor people and the priority measures required to help them. We would like to give three examples:

1 The Report recognises the crucial importance of growth in agriculture in order to reduce rural poverty in India and China, and more generally to reduce inequalities. It would therefore be logical that this should serve as a guide in defining poverty reduction policies. However, as we have seen, the Report focuses very little attention on the role and content of agricultural policies.

2 On the issue of health, the Report devotes several paragraphs to public insurance mechanisms to guard against catastrophic health shocks. Although this is obviously a good idea for middle-income countries, it hardly seems appropriate for the hard core of poverty, the rural poor in sub-Saharan Africa and South Asia. The sort of public health services that would really help this category of poor people (i.e. primary healthcare services) are not mentioned in the Report.

3 Finally, the chapter dealing with the protection of poor people during crises (Chapter 9) is very much marked by the recent Asian crisis and, to a lesser extent, by the Latin American crisis, but practically ignores sub-Saharan Africa. And yet this region has been in a state of crisis for 20 years and has more poor people than East Asia (excluding China) and Latin America put together. The Report chose to overlook the World Bank's own experience in the protection of poor people in Africa at the end of the 1990s. Its analysis of the impact of crises on deprived populations almost completely ignores the situation of the many poor people in Africa.

The above examples are just a few amongst many that can be found in the Report. However useful the proposed policies may be, they seem difficult to apply in the case of the poorest countries. More than any other document, the *World Development Report 2000/2001* helps widen our understanding of the many different dimensions of poverty. The negative side of this broadening of the concept is doubtless that we have more difficulty in finding clear policy guidelines in it to attack this problem.

Conclusion

Is the World Bank in the process of completely changing its assessment of poverty and its policies to fight against it? In the light of the Report studied here there can be no doubt that changes are underway, as it reveals what may be a change of culture on the part of the World Bank. Its criticism of the 'Washington Consensus', or at least the excesses of past liberalisation policies, shows that there is internal debate on this subject at the Bank. To a certain extent, the Bank now seems to be focusing its policies on the motto to be found in the entrance hall at its headquarters, and which is also printed on the back cover of the Report: 'Our dream is a world free of poverty'.

At the same time, the approach is incomplete as we have seen above: although the Report criticises the trade and financial liberalisation policies, it does not fundamentally challenge them; social redistribution policies are only analysed from an instrumental standpoint without taking into account the ethical and intrinsic goals of creating a society with fewer inequalities. On this point, we willingly agree with the proposal put forward by Maxwell (2001) to introduce a new International Development Goal that would add social redistribution to the list of the economic and social development goals adopted by the various United Nations summits over the last ten years.

In truth, the Report's failings stem from its qualities. Although it may be considered insufficiently operational, this is mainly because it avoids laying down a ready-made doctrine, a criticism that has often been made of past work coming from this institution. At the very beginning of the Report, the World Bank shows new-found humility by refusing to propose a single model to fight against poverty: There is no simple, universal blueprint for implementing this strategy. Developing countries need to prepare their own mix of policies to reduce poverty, reflecting national priorities and local realities' (World Bank 2000a: 7).

The new position sought by the World Bank as advocate of the world's poor is far removed from its international image. But how far will the institution really be able to stand up for poor people's rights if they go against the Bank's traditional positions on globalisation, openness and liberalisation for example? It is also true that the institution positions itself above all as the defender of the poor against their own governments. It is less at ease when it comes to defending these same poor people on the international scene, with respect to policies laid down by the international institutions and the rich countries. The problem is perhaps that in this area the Bank is both judge and judged.

Notes

1 This analysis is partly based on a critical study by DIAL (2000b). The author has updated the study, which analysed a draft version of the World Bank Report, and has made additions as and when appropriate.

2 Comparisons are generally based on a threshold of income or consumption per capita, expressed in dollars at 1993 prices. Local currencies are converted to dollars using purchasing power parity (PPP) factors.

3 The gross primary school enrolment ratio is defined as the number of children enrolled in primary education as a percentage of the official school age population for that level.

4 According to the World Bank, the GDP per capita in the 20 richest countries was 18 times higher than that in the 20 poorest countries in 1960. This ratio rose to 37 in 1995.

5 The conclusions of the studies vary according to the methodological choices (choice of indicators, aggregation methods, etc.) and the period of reference. The size of the time variations is most probably inferior to the measurement error. It is especially important to note in this respect that in most developing countries there is actually often very little, if any, statistical data available for calculating inequalities.

6 According to the Report, two-thirds of the acceleration in growth will in fact be due to a structural effect, as the weight of rapid-growth countries (in particular China) will increase significantly between the two periods.

7 The *World Development Report 2000/2001* refers to International Development Goals (IDGs), but since the year 2000 effort has been undertaken to harmonise the IDGs with the development objectives contained in the United Nations Millennium Declaration (September 2000) to arrive at a common set of objectives and indicators: the Millennium Development Goals (MDGs); see Chapter 11.

8 The *World Development Report 1980* was devoted to 'Poverty and Human Development'. It affirmed that 'the solution to poverty is economic growth' and stressed 'the role of human development as investment, contributing to growth', taking into account other dimensions of poverty (ill health, illiteracy). But the diagnosis and recommendations on these other dimensions were still rather superficial.

9 Liberalisation and competition were seen as a means of increasing the returns on the poor countries' most abundant asset, namely unskilled labour.

10 These reservations do nothing to stop the World Bank from stating in another publication (2001b), referring to these elasticities (but in this case on the basis of the $2 poverty threshold) that are based, in its words, on historical experience, that multilateral trade liberalisation on a world scale would reduce the numbers of poor by 300 million by 2015.

Table 1.4 Policies to promote pro-poor growth: consensus and remaining debates

Policy issue	Research finding	Agreed policy implication	Areas of debate
Macroeconomic stability (see also individual areas of macro policy)	Macroeconomic stability critical; necessary (though not sufficient) condition for pro-poor growth; poor hurt particularly by high inflation and high macro volatility	Monetary and exchange rate policy should aim for low inflation and competitive exchange rates; fiscal policy should aim for low budget deficits; financial policies should promote savings and investment	Role of exchange rate policy to fight inflation; role of financial sector deregulation; how to promote domestic savings
Monetary and exchange rate policy	Overvalued exchange rates and high black market premia hurt economic growth and tend to be anti-poor	A competitive and possibly undervalued exchange rate a critical ingredient to ensure macro stability; government intervention necessary to manage capital flows	Fixed or floating rates; role of capital controls?
Fiscal stance	Large budget deficits hurt growth and are unsustainable	Governments should aim for moderate budget deficits through broadening of the tax base and, if necessary, a focusing of expenditures (esp. cuts in subsidies to state-owned enterprises and unproductive sectors); during crises not feasible or desirable to cut expenditures fast	Mix of tax increases, tax broadening, and expenditure cuts
Financial sector	Poorly sequenced financial sector reforms can be counter-productive and destabilising	Capital account and financial sector reform should be phased slowly, be implemented only if macro stability has been achieved, and be accompanied by tight regulation, competition policies, and policies to improve access of the poor	State allocation of credit to priority sectors? Other policies to mobilise savings?

Table 1.4 continued

Policy issue	Research finding	Agreed policy implication	Areas of debate
Trade policy	Anti-export bias hurts growth and the poor; import liberalisation can be anti-poor and not sufficient to generate supply response. Diversification essential for long-term growth	Focus on removal of anti-export bias (competitive exchange rate, duty draw-back schemes, etc.); provision of infrastructure to assist exports, esp. for export diversification	More activist state intervention to boost non-traditional exports (e.g. export subsidies)?
Industrial policy	Removal of distortions necessary but not sufficient for vibrant industrial sector	Focus on providing infrastructure and services to industrial sector	Activist industrial policy?
Human capital	Human capital is essential for overall growth, and low disparity in human capital increases growth and increases the poverty impact of growth	Increased investment in education and health, particularly basic education and primary healthcare; greater focus on quality; reallocation of spending to the poor and use of subsidies and other measures (lifting of user fees) to promote education and health of the poor	How much new funding (from where?), how much reallocation from higher education without destroying quality in secondary and tertiary education systems?
Land inequality	Large land inequality reduces economic growth	Removal of subsidies to large landowners, land taxes to increase land for sale; land redistribution necessary	Market- and subsidy-based land reform versus quick one-off (partly) confiscatory land reform
Agriculture	Raising agricultural productivity critical for pro-poor growth; removal of distortions necessary but not sufficient in the presence of other market failures; protection and subsidies in North hurt poor in South	Renewed emphasis on agricultural research and extension, rural infrastructure, and competitive marketing and input supplies; open access to OECD markets and removal of OECD subsidies critical	How to stimulate non-traditional agricultural exports? Role of subsistence production for poverty?

Table 1.4 continued

Policy issue	Research finding	Agreed policy implication	Areas of debate
Gender inequality	Gender inequality reduces growth and makes growth less pro-poor	More supply of education for girls plus targeted subsidies to boost enrolments; removal of restrictions on female control of other assets; affirmative action policies; political empowerment of women	How to fund expansion of female education?
Regional inequality	Regional inequality can sharply reduce impact of growth on poverty; possibility of regional poverty traps	Targeting of state transfer programmes and safety nets on regions with high poverty concentration; regional inequality to be considered in programmes of decentralisation and fiscal equalisation	How to promote economic growth in backward regions? The role of regionally targeted industrial policy?
Security	Physical and social security essential for pro-poor growth	Safety nets and greater physical security essential measures to promote pro-poor growth	Public and private roles in safety net? How extensive? How funded?
Donor policies	Donors can assist with pro-poor growth when aid and advice is focused on poorest countries and those with highest poverty impact of policies	Aid should be focused on poorest countries that promote pro-poor growth, should flow through budget and be accounted for using national processes, observe country leadership	What to do in poor countries with poor policies? Interactions between donors and civil society?
Public sector	Able and functioning state essential for delivering policy package for pro-poor growth	Public sector reform focused on improving management and capacity of public service; strengthen public accountability	Role of the state where state capacity is weak? How to strengthen capacity effectively?

Table 1.4 continued

Policy issue	Research finding	Agreed policy implication	Areas of debate
Private sector	Indigenous private sector critical for employment growth and dynamic economy	State assistance with capacity-building, finance (esp. microfinance), dialogue between state and domestic private sector	Role of national vs. multinational companies?
Political economy of reform	Domestic political economy crucial for success; pro-poor coalitions necessary to implement package	Dialogue to replace donor conditionality; empowerment of poor and local analytical and research capacity critical for implementation	Role of financial aid and conditionality under some circumstances? Empowerment from outside possible/desirable?

Source: Klasen (2001).

2 Poverty, inequality of conditions and inequality of opportunities

Chances and risks of new strategies

Denis Cogneau

Justice without might is helpless; might without justice is tyrannical.
(Blaise Pascal, *c.* 1650, *Pensées*, fragment 94, trans. W.F. Trotter)

It is not very long ago that States became units of integration to which are attached, though in an ambivalent form, feelings of belonging to an 'us', relatively deep commitment and solidarity between all their nationals. The image of 'us' has changed; so it can change yet again.
(Norbert Elias, 1987, *Die Gesellschaft der Individuen*)

Anyone working in the field of development economics or sociology is often compelled to ask about the meaning of the word 'development' and to examine notions of international or global justice and their implications for the rights of people or peoples. This kind of interrogation arises perhaps from a concern with the humanities, but it may also be from the fact that development policies are constantly changing. Hence, the initiative targeted at heavily indebted poor countries has led to the World Bank's elaboration of a new document – the 'Poverty Reduction Strategy Paper' (PRSP), a synthesis of national strategies for growth and poverty reduction in the world's poorest countries. PRSPs have to fulfil two main requisites: in terms of substance, they should outline a strategy that promotes a pro-poor market economy; in terms of form, they should set up participatory processes for developing the strategy. In practical terms, they pose the problem of the universality of the notions of justice and democracy at the heart of the political economy of development, which can be observed in action between so-called developed and developing countries.

PRSPs in fact represent an attempt to confer a democratic, rather than a purely bureaucratic, legitimacy on reforms. Somewhat paradoxically, the liberal policies of structural adjustment recommended in the past invoked the legitimacy of bureaucratic rationality, expressed in the pursuit of the greatest economic efficiency. Externally imposed economic deregulation was authoritarian and centralising, a fact reflected in the rigorous conditionality attached to the financing provided by donor organisations, as well as in the uniformity of policy packages. These packages, criticised by several economists as contractionary, consisted basically of short-term macroeconomic stabilisation policies combined with structural policies aimed at liberalising product and factor markets. This situation produced a great many adverse effects, ranging from an increase in corruption to blatant socio-political deadlock. The negative social, environmental, and institutional effects of structural adjustment have by turns been stigmatised, and there is a demand for democratic monitoring in order to offset these effects. For the moment, the reality of participatory processes leaves much to be desired in this area (see Chapters 6 and 8). Similarly, when existing PRSPs amount to broad statements of generous general principles without any practical consequences, their content tends to duplicate the uniformity of previous documents,[2] minus their rational coherence. This rational(-bureaucratic)/(social-)democratic 'double bind' may well result in paralysis, rather than the hoped-for social contract.

After having observed the nefarious effects of enforced liberalisation, will we ten years hence be sifting through the rubble created by uncontrolled 'democratisation'? We should in any case be just as wary of a certain populism based on some vague notion of the intrinsic lucidity of social subjects, as of the previous miserabilism based on the existence of a benevolent and omniscient planner or his 'invisible hand'. Participatory processes could be manipulated by status or interest groups, or (not exclusively) drift into demagogy, or favour the outbreak of violent distributive conflicts.[3] Now because institutions connected to the functioning of the state apparatus and the market economy are not well developed, the capacity for mediation and arbitration of distributive conflicts is weak, a causal relation which is no doubt circular. We still know very little about the various dimensions of these conflicts, and we know little more about how the accompanying inequalities define the affiliations of social subjects and affect their evolution. The problem of the uniformity of policies, however 'well-intentioned' and 'universalising' their vocation, is related both to geopolitics, which is not dealt with here, and to the economic anthropology of the diversity of societies and their demand for justice.

If these new policies are to be more successful than the old ones, their goals need to be fully measured. There is, moreover, a consensus that the new policies should be assessed more scrupulously than they used to be, which makes it all the more necessary to clarify their goals.

We will try therefore, in the first part of this chapter, to analyse the offer of justice implicit in the PRSPs. We will reinterpret the goal of multidimensional poverty reduction as the combination of two requirements: a certain equalising of intergenerational social opportunities and a certain redistribution of resources within adult generations. We will argue that, in order to be consistent with their initial philosophy, the new policies being developed in the world's poorest countries must scrupulously examine the factors of mobility across the poverty line, and accept the concomitant income redistribution that increased mobility implies. And we will point out that if they are also to conform to their other requisite, democratisation, then they must take into account a pluralistic principle of equality of opportunity. Only in this manner will they be able to reconcile a reflective, universalistic goal of reducing tyranny with the diversity of societies' demands for justice.

In the second part of the chapter we will review the consequences in terms of economic policy of the welcome reinjection of dynamicism into the issue of poverty reduction. We will revisit the hotly debated relationship between economic growth, inequality and poverty, before underscoring, as others have, the absence of general laws, the accumulation of possible relations, and the importance of the perspective under consideration. We will then discuss education policies, which the PRSPs particularly emphasise. Equal education and healthcare for children does play a central and exemplary part and is the necessary condition for equality of opportunities amongst future generations. It also entails a redistribution of resources in the current generation of parents. We will finally analyse questions of dualism – intersectoral mobility and distribution of earned income.

Poverty reduction: what poverty, for what society?

The view of inequality first presented by John Rawls, and later developed and amended by Amartya Sen, seems to have been incorporated, at least as a line of thought, by the major international institutions. A synthesis of this view and prior concepts related to welfarism[4] is being elaborated, albeit progressively.

> John Rawls, it can be recalled, considers distributive justice the basic and enduring problem of life in society.[5] Amartya Sen claims, moreover, that any theory of justice is a theory of equality, the question of justice being not 'equality or not', but 'equality of what'.[6] These premises are not called into question. In the second half of the twentieth century economics gave rise to two broad views of inequality: first welfarism, and, second, the opportunities approach, which Sen's theory of capabilities belongs to. To sum up the divergent points rapidly, the welfarist current of thought emphasises the inequalities associated with a certain number of outcomes affected by the preferences of individuals and society as a whole (the social welfare function). This current follows upon the utilitarian approach which recognised only the Pareto optimality criterion and arrives at arbitrations between efficiency and equity, resulting from the comparison between 'second-best' optima.[7] The opportunities approach is critical of utilitarianism and welfarism for not respecting the diversity of individuals' preferences or ideas of good. It stresses opportunities at the start rather than outcomes.
>
> Rawls's theory of justice as fairness is initially presented as a synthesis of welfarism and the equality of rights and opportunity. It goes beyond the

well-known difference principle, a principle of fair inequalities. The other two principles, the first of which has priority in terms of lexical order, are on the contrary unconditional principles of equality of rights and opportunity:

> First: each person is to have an equal right to the most extensive scheme of equal basic liberties compatible with a similar scheme of liberties for others ... Secondly: social and economic inequalities are to be arranged so that they are both a) to the greatest expected benefit of all the least advantaged and b) attached to offices and positions open to all under conditions of fair equality of opportunity.
>
> (Rawls 1971: 53, 72)

It is not easy to interpret this last principle. John Roemer (1998) recently proposed a meritocratic principle of equality of opportunity that consists in placing individuals on a 'starting line' of social competition, without worrying about *ex post* achievements attributable to effort, merit, and individual responsibility, which are the source of justifiable inequalities. Unlike Roemer, John Rawls (1971: 87) refuses to consider merit a justification of fair inequalities, which can also mean that he gives the expression 'positions open to all' a strictly legal and formal meaning. We also see that the difference principle introduces the category of 'the more disadvantaged', who could just as well be called 'poor', and a notion of 'perspectives' rather than a *de facto* situation.

Amartya Sen arrives at a concept of absolute poverty as deprivation of the minimal resources ('capabilities') necessary for the free exercise of inalienable human rights: obtaining food and healthcare for oneself and one's children, choosing a profession in accordance with one's abilities, taking part in society, enjoying self-esteem, and so on. Insofar as the list of human rights is extensive, poverty is 'multidimensional'. The goal of multidimensional poverty reduction is therefore the application of the principle of the universality of human rights to development policies. In principle as well as in practice, this goal is no doubt preferable to welfarist-inspired uniform planning which reasons solely in terms of goals of growth and income distribution. Putting it into practice, however, raises several questions which should be answered only by an ethical and political and, if possible, 'participatory' debate.[8]

Poverty reduction, equality of opportunity and equality of condition

For both Rawls and Sen, extending the problem of justice beyond simple formal rights to a certain number of economic rights ('primary goods') is based on a realistic principle of equality of opportunity. In this spirit the problem of poverty is the link between present inequalities of conditions and future inequalities of opportunity.

Mobility out of poverty and individual responsibility

The notion of absolute poverty, first of all, can be considered as a border-line version of equality of opportunity, just as Rawls's principle of difference is a borderline version of welfarism. One could argue, along with Sen, that bringing the poorest to the poverty line consists in getting them to regain a certain number of universally required capabilities to put their opportunities to good use. There is therefore a strong relation of causality between an individual's present condition of poverty in the sense of his inability to seize opportunities, and his future opportunities, absolute poverty being conceived as a trap or absorbing state that reduces the likelihood of escape to zero. The mortality associated with situations of extreme poverty constitutes the most dramatic kind of poverty trap. Aside from this borderline case, instantaneous indices of poverty are not the only suitable indicators; matrices of mobility can also be used to measure poverty. If, for example, we distinguish between different degrees of poverty, as is usually done,[9] mobility within poverty is just as important as flux between poverty and non-poverty. We know moreover that a high level of monetary poverty and/or inequality is perfectly consistent with a high level of social or economic mobility, and vice versa. Therefore a decrease in poverty can go hand in hand with an increase in the risk of falling into poverty. A dilemma can arise between the equalising of opportunities and greater inequality of outcomes.

Insofar as policies are concerned, everything depends on the degree of individual responsibility attributed to descent into and escape from poverty, and its relation to hazards and constraints beyond the individual's reach. This assessment of the degree of individual responsibility can be considered ethical and political, and can in fact be the subject of public debates connected to participatory processes.[10] The issue is recognised as being a very complicated one, especially in terms of the phenomena of statistic discrimination and adaptive preferences that can lead to the emergence of a 'culture of poverty'. Moreover, the notion of individual responsibility loses its meaning when poverty is extreme; that is, when survival is at stake. Only a tyrannical society can hold the individual responsible for endangering his own life. We will return to this point in the next section.

Like responsibility, the question of 'individualising' poverty can also be debated. Competition between socially constituted individuals does not, in fact, have the same meaning everywhere. Let us imagine, for example, that an individual's well-being depends on the reference community he compares himself to, but let us assume too that the size of this community is variable in different societies. Let us put forward the realistic conjecture that in Western societies, which are open and competitive, and in which, at the same time, the state plays an important role, the reference community is the group of individuals of the same generation. Let us then suppose that in a relatively closed, uncompetitive society – such as an African one – this reference model is restricted to the extended family. In the first model, which Norbert Elias[11] calls the 'society of individuals', in which the competitive space is both wide and peaceful, equality of individual social opportunity carries great weight. It is the criterion of justice suited to individualistic competition. In the second model, a lineage-based society in which competition is segmented among 'brothers' for recognition by fathers and ancestors on the one hand, and among 'big men' of the lineages for possession of land and territory on the other, there is a different meaning to equality of opportunity between two members of two different lineages, since they are not in direct competition with each other.

The 'big men' of lineage-based societies agree to perform a certain number of services for their community, notably in the area of health and schooling for children, and marriage and funerals for adults. The logic of gift and counter-gift stems, in fact, from a deferred exchange of material resources and symbolic capital.[12] Nevertheless, these transfers are very far from attaining the level of socialised redistribution made possible by the systems of social protection in effect in Europe and even in the United States. They have also probably decreased as the societies have modernised.

The issue here for policies is whether they are being addressed to individuals, families, lineages or communities. It could be dangerous to allow free rein to group redistribution mechanisms, since they could lead to situations of serious exploitation and deprivation.

Mobility across the poverty line and distribution of resources

We have just seen that the reduction of poverty raises various problems connected with equality of individual social opportunity and presupposes a firm grasp of phenomena linked to social mobility. But its logic implies a certain equalisation of present living conditions (i.e. redistribution).

First of all, beyond the fragile universal notion of the individual, the nature of society and community makes the notion of relative poverty inevitable. Being 'relatively poor', for example, implies not being able to find a spouse and, more generally, running the risk of being excluded. Similarly, 'appearing in public without shame' implies incurring variable expenses, depending on the social context. More simply, the process of development increases the number of possibilities such as travel, but can leave some people on the sidelines because they cannot afford the new services. People are always poor 'relatively speaking', as Sen (1983) puts it. So it is difficult to evaluate relative poverty even in terms of basic rights. The reduction of poverty in its multidimensional version justifies a certain reduction in present inequalities, whatever the degree of each individual's responsibility for his or her position in the distribution of income, especially

Box 2.1 Extreme poverty, absolute poverty, and duration of poverty

There have been many scientific debates about defining and measuring poverty. We can nonetheless consider that the issue is as yet unresolved. There is a consensus that poverty should represent basic deprivation. On this basis an 'absolute' line of poverty seems essential, whether it is a monetary standard like the famous $1 a day, a physiological standard like 1,250 kilocalories a day, or any other type of threshold. The line of absolute poverty is supposed to represent a threshold of minimum subsistence beyond which the risk of mortality increases sharply. It might seem strange, then, to differentiate amongst the poor included in this definition. Would not a discontinuous measurement be more consistent with an absolute threshold? If the answer is yes, the incidence of poverty (FGT0 indicator), which is simply the proportion of poor people in a population, suffices for measuring the phenomenon. If the dynamics are taken into account – that is, the number of individual entries and exits across a poverty line fixed in time – a 'stationary' rate of poverty could be defined. This suggests that the number of poor measured at a given moment in time is a mix of long-term poverty and short-term poverty. The spread of poverty over different durations is likely to result in two types of policy: insurance policies for the short term and structural ones for the long term. The longest-lasting cases of poverty are also more likely to be furthest from the line, so that a static gauge that gives more weight to individuals furthest from the line, such as the FGT2 indicator, allows this phenomenon to be taken into account, albeit indirectly. Furthermore, the FGT2 indicator avoids certain bothersome axiomatic features of the FGT0 such as the fact that a transfer from a poorer person to one who is less poor can lower poverty. It is, however, more sensitive to measurement errors at the bottom of the income distribution. Furthermore, it emphasises policies aimed at the poorest of the poor.[25] But the fact remains, in the end, that a static gauge is fairly unsuitable for analysis, whether normative or positive.[26] It would be wise to distinguish between extreme poverty and extended poverty. Individual responsibility would hardly be an issue in the case of extreme poverty, and the policies for dealing with it would be mechanisms of direct transfer, insurance, or aid depending on the duration; whereas the policies suitable for extended poverty would be the policies of equality of opportunity which are our focus here. Neither type would be exempt from problems of information connected to targeting, and the former would perhaps be even less so. It seems impossible in fact to decide on this distinction or statistically identify a single category of 'extreme poor' (Razafindrakoto and Roubaud 2000a). It is preferable to deal with the different dimensions separately according to a principle of equality of opportunity which does not of course rule out certain types of redistribution, as we will argue.

in that, to obtain the same reduction in 'multidimensional poverty', certain societies will have more need for redistribution than for growth.

Lastly, as always happens with the issue of equalising opportunities, we encounter the problem of the 'starting line'. Thus education and child nutrition policies are supposed to address the root causes of the inequality observed within a generation. Whatever the terms of the social contract of individual responsibility, we cannot hold children 'responsible' for their parents' living conditions. So long as the parents' living conditions determine the future poverty of their children once they reach adulthood, there is always necessarily 'something to redistribute' amongst the children and, consequently, amongst the parents. Clearly, as research on collective household models has shown, redistribution between households may not necessarily benefit children. Even assuming that children who have reached adulthood have all had the same opportunity to escape from poverty, there is no reason to believe that they should not get at least a second chance. This is not ruled out by either Rawls or Sen[13] – who recommend, for example, compensation for accidental handicaps – but is often disregarded in practice. In this case, a 'once and for all' approach to redistribution not only fails to settle the question but also raises the issue of insurance.

The problem of the 'finishing line' also needs to be addressed. Any policy of equal opportunities is a bet on the future. Emphasising schooling for children, for example, implies betting on the fact that the return on education will be sufficient to ensure that the likelihood of educated children from poor backgrounds escaping from poverty is relatively similar to that of educated children from more advantaged backgrounds. In particular, bets are being placed on sufficiently strong growth in more highly skilled jobs and on these jobs being fairly distributed. In order to deal with problems of segmentation and discrimination, which could potentially render null and void all previous efforts, a close eye must be kept on job distribution. Moreover, it is known that the virtuous trickle-down effects of growth on poverty increase when income distribution is more equal.

In summary, we cannot establish a clean break between policies for equalising resources or initial allocations, and redistribution policies for current revenues or living conditions, as is so often done. This is already true with regard to equality of opportunity, for in practice it is difficult to redistribute productive resources (capital, land, education) without redistributing the income that serves to produce them in the first place. When insufficient attention is paid to some of the positive dynamic effects of redistribution, its static risks (distortions in the price system, disincentives to work) are overemphasised. And this is even truer for poverty reduction because of relative poverty, problems of insurance, and trickle-down effects. We will discuss these points further in the second part of this chapter.

It follows from this initial analysis that poverty reduction should be conceived of as a dynamic process centred on the 'acceleration of individual exits from poverty', and as an issue inextricably linked to divergences in living conditions and therefore to the reduction of certain inequalities. There are many factors at play in the relationship between the current distribution of resources and the mobility of individuals. But having raised the important issue of universalism, we will now make a digression. Due to a certain ethnocentrism concerning Western values, there is a danger that the obsessions of contemporary developed capitalist societies might be projected onto developing societies somewhat over-enthusiastically. We have briefly touched on the fact that equality of individual social opportunity does indeed seem to be the central issue of so-called Third Way policies, a kind of prolongation of the liberal policies that led to increased competition between individuals.[14] But the fact that all the developing countries have applied this type of policy for the past 20 years does not imply, except by pure sophistry, that equality of individual social opportunity is the be-all and end-all of social justice.

Poverty reduction and pluralism

The 'reluctance' of societies to planned development

In the 1960s and 1970s development planning policies involved the accrual of debt and a recourse to state intervention to promote industrial and urban modernisation. The Brazilian experience had already shown that this type of modernisation did not necessarily lead to progress in social justice. In the 1980s and 1990s, with debt at unsustainable levels and growth stagnant, liberal development policies attempted to introduce a factor that seemed to be absent from this approach to modernisation – competition. Now the emphasis is being placed on democratisation, as if it were a means whereby any remaining blanks in the ideal image of Western society could somehow be filled. But it seems that the societies of the South have, to varying degrees, 'resisted' this preconceived pattern.

The societies historically most integrated into this model – those of East Asia, as well as some in South-East Asia (Singapore and Malaysia) – accepted only what suits them in these policies, and, what is most important, did so at their own pace. Moreover, they never had to solicit any significant backing from the Bretton Woods Institutions. In fact, what they absorbed was, primarily, industrial modernisation; the idea of competition was taken on board, but the impact of democratisation was limited. Furthermore, in response to Western recriminations, the theme of 'Asian values' was radicalised. In terms of economic success, the picture was very different in Indonesia, Thailand and the Philippines during the 1970s and 1980s, and has been particularly gloomy since the crisis of 1997.

Most of the Latin American countries, under the more direct influence of the United States, applied the successive recommendations to the letter. The resistance of these societies manifested itself in forms more familiar to Westerners – revolutionary civil wars, nationalistic populist movements, and elections pitting Right against Left. In the case of these Latin American societies, the genuine demand for justice seems, ultimately, to conform more or less to the criteria of Rawls and Sen. The least that can be said is that judged by these criteria, the policies which have been applied are very much open to question.[15]

In sub-Saharan Africa (with the exception of South Africa), the weakness of states and economies has meant that policy packages have been formally accepted without conditions (though with conditionality),[16] but it has also led to strong resistance on the part of these societies to the pace of modernisation promulgated by their elites and their Western donors. There has been wave after wave of planning, liberalisation, and democratisation, but here more than anywhere else, countries are still not industrialised, free open competition is still only in its embryonic stages, and electoral democracy lacks a credible political offer. In reaction to the situations of rupture endured by various generations, there is a re-emergence of the theme of 'African values'. This marked resistance should come as no surprise, for Africa has always been and still is the continent farthest removed from the West, not only in terms of per capita income or poverty but also in terms of family structures, technical agricultural development,[17] and the non-state organisation of society.

This overview of part of the developing world should not, of course, obscure the fact that each of the countries concerned has its own history, during the course of which a whole series of original combinations of modernity and tradition, westernisation and native cultures have succeeded each other. Moreover, the use of the word 'resistance' does not mean that there is an opposition between so-called African or Asian values – which are fairly frequently manipulated or reinterpreted for tyrannical purposes – and processes of industrialisation, liberalisation and democratisation, as if the subjects of these societies did not *also* want more industrial jobs, more competition and more democracy. It is merely a question of insisting on the fact that the form and pace of these processes cannot be determined independently of the social structures actually existing at a given moment in history, and of the corresponding demand for justice. In the long run, form and pace are eminently *political* questions, and the ambition that should be conferred upon the participatory processes of the PRSPs is probably to contribute to respecting this political determination of the demand for justice.

Reduction of poverty and reduction of tyranny

Neither is it our intention to contest the relevance of a specific criterion of poverty reduction. Furthermore, the kind of intra-community redistribution mentioned in the preceding section provides evidence of the existence of a universal requirement – the aid and assistance the powerful owe to those they govern. This no doubt corresponds to a sphere of every human society's demand for justice rooted in every living creature's basic need for safety and protection. There is hardly any need, then, for a sophisticated participatory process in order to highlight the need for an egalitarian distribution of means of survival. Or if you will, Rawls's anonymous individuals belonging to the human species, in their original position and behind a veil of ignorance, would be unanimously in favour of a social contract minimising every person's risk of dying young of hunger or disease, being subjected to intolerable physical and mental violence, living with no roof over their head, or subsisting in moral distress.

Two ultimately interlinking questions follow from this. First, does poverty reduction imply a modification of the 'rules of the game' in society as a whole, and, if so, to what degree? And second, can societies' demand for justice stop at the reduction of poverty?

The work of Amartya Sen deals just as much with the issue of poverty as with that of democracy. According to his well-known theory, famine does not stem from a lack of food supply but from poor distribution of access to goods. Rationing of part of the supply can, moreover, result in runaway prices and consequently reduce the purchasing power of the poorest. Representative democracy provides the most impoverished with influential spokesmen, while a free and wide-ranging press serves as an early alarm system and a means of pressure on states (Sen 1981; Besley and Burgess 2001). Major famines, such as the one recently discovered to have ravaged the capital of Madagascar in 1985, most often occur in silence (Garenne *et al.* 1999).

Michael Walzer (1983) puts forward a universalistic theory of justice as pluralism, as an explicit alternative to that of John Rawls on justice as fairness. His argument is based on historical and anthropological examples rather than on a procedural demonstration. It is inspired by Pascal's definition of tyranny. His criticism of Rawls starts from the observation of the anthropological multiplicity and diversity of what Rawls calls primary goods, a problem also addressed by Amartya Sen in his theory of basic 'capabilities'. In Walzer's view, in fact, these multiple primary goods cannot be aggregated for the basic reason that they generally relate to distinct social distribution principles. Walzer calls the association of a primary good and its specific principle of distribution a 'sphere of justice'. And justice as pluralism consists in ensuring that one sphere does not predominate over others, with legitimate possession of one primary good ensuring access to all the others. American society, for example, is said to be characterised by the tyranny of money and its principle of distribution – competition. Indian society, on the other hand, is characterised by the possibility of a tyranny of caste, and by its principle of distribution – purity. The latter example reveals the reflective advantage of a theory which allows for the incorporation of a certain form of relativism, without necessarily forgoing universalism. Walzer's two proposals can be expressed as follows:

1   There exist several spheres of justice; that is, several types of primary social goods which have different legitimate principles of distribution: money, education, security and welfare, access to public office, honour, and so on.
2   The primary form of injustice consists of one sphere of justice encroaching on another, which borders on tyranny.

Amongst the essential goods, Walzer singles out security and welfare, money, education, and access to public office, which are regulated respectively by distribution principles of pure equality, productive competition, merit, and devotion to the public good.

Tyranny does not recognise the multiplicity of spheres of justice; all primary goods are subsumed under a primary imperative (be it noble birth, wealth, education, party membership, or geographical origin) while, if necessary, tyranny is justified as the defence of a 'common good' (the welfare and security of its citizens, the purity of its race, the power of the nation, the glory of science, the carrying out of God's work, and so on). In a society that functions tyrannically there is a particular possibility that certain categories of people might be denied access to even the lowest levels of welfare and security because they lack a predominant primary good – in the United States, for example, the poor; in India, members of the untouchable caste; and in France, the uneducated.[18]

To a certain degree extreme poverty cannot be combated without changing the rules of the social game, which exclude the most disadvantaged from access to the means of survival. But it is clear that this approach can be applied to other primary goods and to a broader notion of poverty as a deficit in rights and capabilities. Thus, the development of education is also the focus of a whole area of political economics. For example, as soon as education begins to exert an important influence on participation in the public arena, an oligarchic government might decide that it was in its interest to keep people ignorant in order to stay in power (Bourguignon and Verdier 2000). Therefore, since the demand for the reduction of tyranny goes hand in hand with the reduction of multidimensional poverty, it will be necessary to develop an expanded equal opportunities programme offering access to various spheres of distribution in society, which, to use Rawls's term (though not exclusively formally or legally), should be 'open to all'. The importance attributed to individual responsibility could vary according to the various spheres of distribution – none in the case of means of survival and basic education; more in other cases. This means once again that policies must focus on the multidimensional nature of inequality of opportunity.

Mobility, growth, and inequalities of condition and education

Let us return now to the central aim of the PRSPs as we presented it in the Introduction – namely, the establishment of pro-poor economic growth. We will not attempt to list the achievements and omissions of the debate on this issue, as this has already been done more competently (Klasen 2001; Lipton 1997). We are of the opinion that the approaches to poverty reduction proposed in the PRSPs still suffer from an excessively static and aggregated bias.

> The fourth volume of *Principles of Political Economy* by James E. Meade, winner of the 1977 Nobel Prize for Economics with Bertil Ohlin, is entitled *The Just Economy* (1976). The three preceding volumes were devoted, respectively, to issues of equilibrium and efficiency (*The Stationary Economy*), macro-dynamics and growth (*The Growing Economy*) and regulation (*The Controlled Economy*). It is striking that dynamic, demographic and intergenerational problems represent almost two-thirds of the 250 or so pages of the book (economic and social mobility, accumulation and inheritance, marriage, and differential fertility). Yet these themes are, for the moment, virtually absent from the World Bank sourcebook.
>
> The catalogue of redistribution policies developed by Meade in his conclusion includes promoting the preconditions necessary for free competition, regulating certain prices and quantities, organising the public provision of certain goods, redistributing private property, socialisation of ownership for certain resources, controlling distribution of individual savings, introducing demographic policies, and directly redistributing income. Here again it is striking that the policies envisaged in the sourcebook are limited to the first three entries of Meade's catalogue.

In effect the 'new policies' are still characterised by the kind of global and sectoral efficiency issues typical of the structural adjustment policies which preceded them. This slant raises a series of macroeconomic problems which will not be our subject here (Herr and Priewe 2001). We shall instead attempt above all to defend the idea that an approach focused on the mobility of individuals and groups constitutes a useful way out of a number of aporias concerning the links between growth, inequality, and poverty. In the preceding section it has been our aim to demonstrate, in light of contemporary theories of distributive justice, that the goal of poverty reduction consists in a combination of issues concerning both the equalisation of opportunities and the reduction of inequality of conditions. We will now deepen our analysis of this combination of issues in the dynamic framework of the structural change specific to economic development.

The elusive macroeconomic relation between growth and inequality

Economists have been asking questions about the relation between distribution and production for a long time now; the great historical theories of production and allocation of resources were also theories of the distribution and price formation of resources. A considerable literature re-examined this question in the 1990s in the wake of 'new' theories of growth.

The years between the 1960s and the early 1990s saw the publication of numerous articles[19] on the causal link running from growth to inequality, in the tradition of the work of Kaldor and Kuznets. The models of Stiglitz and, later, of Bourguignon, for example, took Solow's framework as a starting point and discussed the necessary preconditions of a Kuznets curve, and more generally the assumptions under which growth could generate, or on the contrary reduce, inequalities of income. In the 1970s and 1980s, transversal data on developing countries seemed to corroborate the Kuznets curve. Nevertheless, it became apparent little by little that estimates were sensitive to the functional forms tested and to the make-up of the samples. On the basis of transversal data, the curve showed a certain resistance, once the effect of other variables, such as human capital and dualism, had been controlled for. However, it passed the longitudinal data test with more difficulty.

From the 1990s on, economists turned their attention to the inverse causal links running from inequality to growth. In the mid-1990s a new stylised fact emerged from the field of growth econometrics – a negative correlation between 'initial' inequalities and long-term growth. Many theoretical models were developed to account for this striking regularity, which for a short time was considered tried and true. A great many initial series of theoretical models were based on a central hypothesis of the imperfection of credit markets, whether for financing individual material investment or education projects. A second series of models focused on political economy. This seemed all the more justified in that the negative effect of inequalities on growth seemed to persist despite the inclusion of physical and human investment in the tested econometric equations. The results of this series of models are more complex and, to date, have not been empirically corroborated. Lastly, other arguments have been put forward to account for the negative link between equalities and growth: mechanisms of local externality and population distribution, the effects of market size in the presence of growing returns of scale, and the effects of inequalities on fertility.

The availability of the wide-span international database on income inequalities, set up by Deininger and Squire at the World Bank, helped stimulate a series of econometric studies. Nevertheless, the new curve, like the Kuznets curve, soon proved to be fragile, even on transversal data. An inverse relationship – that is, inequalities favourable to growth – seems to be revealed in the longitudinal analysis of Forbes (2000).

Our point of view concerning an assessment of the econometric work of the past decade is that, *on the macroeconomic scale of countries,* no link can be found between growth, or GDP, and income inequality. Indeed, the use of econometric techniques suitable for the analysis of causality, and the control of the selection of samples, leads us to question the reliability of previous results (Cogneau and Guénard 2002). This assertion is valid for both possible causal relations – from growth to inequality and vice versa.

On the macroeconomic scale, the absence of a significant correlation between growth and inequality was the inspiration for the idea of unit elasticity between growth and monetary poverty in a paper by Dollar and Kraay (2001). This simplistic idea stems, however, from a confusion between a macroeconomically non-significant relation and a non-correlation valid at any time and any place. As Ravallion (2001) puts it, we should already be looking 'beyond averages'. In doing so we notice that individual societies' national development strategies and historical and structural configurations leave considerable room in which to determine the interlinking evolution of income and income distribution. Even if it is not too hard to accept that 'growth is (more often than not) good for the poor' – to employ a toned-down version of Dollar and Kraay's title slogan – neither the theory that growth *per se* can suffice to reduce poverty, nor the notion that growth is a phenomenon independent of poverty reduction, can be considered exact.

So one cannot expect to learn too much from a fundamentally negative econometric result.[20] In fact, it would have been surprising to find anything at all. First of all, the theoretical literature emphasises the quantity and diversity of mechanisms that potentially link income growth to income distribution. Second, for any mechanism considered in isolation, everything points to the fact that, theoretically, the parameters of interest depend on the country under consideration. Third, there is no law stating that relations between growth and inequality have to be linear (Cogneau and Guénard 2002).

> We return now to two types of model amongst those which seem most convincing to us – the one belonging to Simon Kuznets and the credit market imperfection models developed by Glenn Loury.
>
> Kuznets (1955) bases his argument on the shift of labour from low-productivity sectors to high-productivity ones that occurs during the structural changes characteristic of development. As the population shifts, inequality should first increase and then decrease once labour becomes predominantly 'formal'. This unequivocal argument includes several barely credible hypotheses, notably the stability of the exchange terms between the two sectors (Bourguignon 1990), the constancy of intrasectoral inequalities (absence of selection in mobility), and the absence of a differential demographic process. The advantage of Kuznets's simple model, however, lies in its emphasis on the role of job mobility (intragenerational or intergenerational) in the development of inequality and poverty, and on the importance of dualism.
>
> The models of Loury (1981) and his successors also stress social mobility, while focusing on the behaviour of accumulation and inheritance against the

backdrop of imperfect credit markets (Loury 1981; Becker and Tomes 1986; Banerjee and Newman 1993; Galor and Zeira 1993; Aghion and Bolton 1997; Piketty 1997). These models suggest formalising the persistence of inequality over time and provide arguments for the theory that too high a level of inequality is dynamically inefficient – that is, harmful to overall growth because it reduces the possibilities for investment. The model of Maoz and Moav (1999) fits intergenerational mobility into the framework of an equilibrium of the labour market. The originality of their contribution resides mainly in the endogenous interactions existing between the level of educational mobility and returns on education. Individuals in one generation receive a monetary inheritance from their parents and have varying capacities for learning at school which influence the cost of their education. There is no credit market for education. In the system central to this model, in each generation some children of educated parents will once again become unskilled workers (downward mobility) while some children of non-educated parents will become skilled workers (upward mobility). Social mobility promotes growth through accumulation of human capital (skilled work) and by allocating it efficiently – that is, creating the best correlation between schooling and learning capacities (which lowers its cost). Conversely, growth in income increases social mobility by lifting the cash constraints that the very poorest face in their choice of education; but it also means a reduction of the returns on education (in the absence of a technical progress bias). Redistribution of income from skilled to unskilled workers has two contradictory effects on growth: on the one hand, it decreases the returns on education and discourages investment in human capital; but on the other, it enables some of the most poverty-stricken to educate their children. The latter effect predominates in the first stage of development. The growth rate follows an inversed-U curve similar to the Kuznets curve, reflecting the size of the salary gap between the skilled and the unskilled.

There is no universal macroeconomic relation between growth and inequality. Nevertheless, the association of three elements – the productive role of education, the imperfection of credit markets, and the importance of earned income for the most impoverished – suggests that there is a virtuous relation between the four variables: growth, education, income redistribution, and poverty reduction. On the microeconomic scale, the link between the latter three variables seems fairly certain to us; this will be the subject of the next section.

The role of education in growth is a more sensitive empirical issue. Here again, the macroeconomic results are unreliable and contradictory. And this should not come as a surprise, for the simple reason that there are not necessarily any skilled jobs in the labour demand, at least in the short and medium term. It all depends on the quality of a country's international specialisation and the persistence of imperfections in the job market, two elements largely absent from the above-mentioned models. The last section of this chapter focuses on these points.

Educational mobility and redistribution

Progress in education can constitute an important factor in intergenerational income poverty reduction, which it influences through different channels.

In several cases, econometric estimates suggest that education has only a fairly moderate direct impact on current agricultural revenues. It may have greater impact on the time variance of this income, allowing for better risk management. Moreover, it encourages diversification into informal non-agricultural gainful activities where the return on education is higher (Jolliffe 1998). Education also facilitates geographical mobility towards higher-density areas where product markets are more highly developed. Finally, it is the key to formal or industrial jobs: primary education for unskilled jobs, secondary or higher education for skilled jobs. The strength of this last incentive, however, depends on the extent to which such jobs are rationed – that is, how persistent dualism is on the job market (see next section). In the longer term, educating mothers results in better control of fertility and children's health and a cumulative reduction of poverty.

On the basis of the sparse reliable data available, it appears that intergenerational educational mobility is much lower in developing countries than in developed ones. For many poor households, in fact, children's schooling involves considerable expenses, and the benefits gained in compensation are doubtful. This is partly due to the content, proximity and quality of instruction dispensed in state-run schools. But it is mainly due to the fact that parents often prefer to pass on their practical skills directly to their children and keep them at home or have them help out with productive household chores.

> The question of the impact of income on decisions about school enrolment in developing countries has already prompted a great deal of research, but remains largely unresolved.[21]
>
> Generally speaking, the existing literature has focused mainly on reducing hereditary biases – that is, biases caused by resources unobserved and transmitted from generation to generation. One of the most widely used econometric strategies consists in analysing the differences in enrolment and academic performance amongst descendants of a given lineage. Using data gathered in Nicaragua, Behrman and Wolfe (1987) analysed the gap in years of education between pairs of cousins compared to gaps in income and educational level between their parents. They found no significant relation between the differences in schooling and observed differences in resources. They concluded that the correlation generally observed between parental

resources and children's schooling derives from unobserved aptitudes and resources transmitted from one generation to the next. Another method consists in simultaneously analysing the schooling of parents and that of their children from data over several generations. Using Malaysian data over four generations, Lillard and Willis (1992) simultaneously assessed a model of educational transition for parents and children, without ruling out the possibility of a correlation between the unobserved determining factors of parents' and children's transition. Assuming the exogenous nature of parental income, they concluded that parents' education affects children's, but did not identify a significant effect on income. As the authors themselves admit, the effect of parents' income is nevertheless difficult to interpret, because their analysis also takes into account a certain number of variables potentially linked to income (such as quality of housing).

But hereditary biases are not the only ones involved. Also at play is the simultaneity of decisions about enrolment in school on the one hand, and organisation of labour and production within the family on the other. A prime example of this is the profit gained from children's labour. Suppose in addition that the professional skills acquired by parents throughout their lives are at least partially transmitted to their children. In cases in which these skills are in some degree a substitute for academic skills, the parents who are the most highly skilled in their professions are then those who earn the highest income and, at the same time, have the least to gain from sending their children to school.

Cogneau and Maurin (2001) propose a semi-parametric assessment method that allows hereditary biases and simultaneity to be dealt with jointly. This leads them to a sharp upward reassessment of the effect of income on primary school enrolment in Madagascar.

When econometric assessments are correctly controlled, they suggest that the demand for education is highly sensitive to income, whatever the offer of services available (Cogneau and Maurin 2001). Cash constraints also appear as an important explanation for school drop-outs (Jacoby 1994).

We can therefore consider that the decline in school attendance observed in many developing countries during the crisis of the 1980s can be explained at least as much by the drop in real household income as by the deterioration of infrastructures and the quality of teaching, or the drop in anticipated returns on education attributable to the rationing of formal jobs.

Conversely, an egalitarian rise of 5 per cent per annum in incomes for a period of more than ten years should make it possible for the goal of universal primary education in African countries to be reached. In any case, improving infrastructure, however necessary a task, will not be enough to put the majority of children back in school rapidly.

This leads us to underscore the danger of a uniform policy of cost recovery from families. Furthermore, education is unlike health in that it is much more difficult to offset cost recovery with quantifiable improvements in the quality of the service offered. In terms of equality of opportunity, we are led to prefer a policy of progressive pricing and conditional, targeted subsidies, such as the *Programa de Educacíon, Salud y Alimentacíon* ('Progresa') in effect in Mexico since 1997. The name of the programme is a reminder that the interactions between children's health and nutrition and the conditions of their schooling should be accorded due emphasis (Cogneau *et al.* 2002). Let us stress again that children cannot be held 'responsible' for their parents' behaviour. A policy of cost recovery for health, for example, should systematically differentiate between medication intended for adults and that targeted at children.

Reasonable redistribution of education costs amongst the richest and poorest households could greatly accelerate the process of enrolling poor children in school. Implementing such a policy does of course have exacting implications in terms of the management of both central administrations and local authorities.

Social mobility and dualism

Statistical knowledge concerning social mobility in developing countries is still very limited, but should increase once individual representative surveys recording information about interviewees' parents and the course of their own lives have been carried out. Another stimulating factor is the increasing amount of research on this theme in most developed countries, which ties in with the issue of equality of opportunity.

In the absence of long-term information about individual income, social mobility can be approached, via occupational mobility, as for developed countries (Erikson and Goldthorpe 1993).[22] Limiting their study to urban professions, Behrman, Gaviria and Székely (2001) show that in four Latin American countries,[23] the intergenerational permeability between white-collar and blue-collar professions is lower than in the US. For five African countries,[24] Cogneau, Maurin and Pasquier (2001) arrive at similar levels of permeability for intergenerational flux between formal and informal urban sectors. On the other hand, flux between agricultural and non-agricultural occupations is far lower, as well as more geographically dispersed, in the five countries studied, although neither the level of development, nor the political regimes in place, nor the role of regional/ethnic origin can explain this dispersion. The two countries with the highest intergenerational flux between agriculture and the other sectors are the same ones with the weakest income dualism, although it is not yet possible to tell in which direction the causality runs. They are the sample's two English-speaking countries, Ghana and Uganda, which are, moreover, both front-runners in structural adjustment policies.

More generally, the least-developed countries (LDCs) are characterised by their very high level of dualism, observable both in inter- and intra-generational mobility flux and in the level of income typical of the various sectors. This low individual mobility combines with large and persistent gaps in income between the three sectors, agricultural, formal, and informal, even for an equal degree of skill. And these intersectoral income gaps are themselves a non-negligible component of inequalities of income between households (Bourguignon and Morrisson 1998; Cogneau and Guénard 2002) and, consequently, an explanatory element for the spread of poverty.

There are many theories in the literature of economics and sociology to explain dualism. The main explanation of the rationing of formal jobs in the LDCs seems to us to be the unusual rarity of physical capital, both private and public, as well as of the technical skills that complement it. On the other hand, neither the regulations of the job market, nor the existence and/or level of a minimum wage, even if they were assiduously respected, seem to us to be the main problems; they are no greater than the problems of controlling workers' productivity (efficiency wages according to the 'shirking' model). Furthermore, discrimination in hiring on the basis of social origins does not seem to explain the low level of entries into the formal sector, no more than does gender discrimination. The rationing of formal hiring seems rather to concern uniformly those who entered the job market too late – that is, after the crisis of the 1980s. The rarity of formal physical capital, and the skills that specifically complement it (managers and supervisors), largely explains the rationing of formal sector jobs. The rarity of these skills, moreover, causes high turnover costs that are borne by the companies, resulting in the fixing of salaries and the likely increase in job rationing. Given the time it takes to look for a job, not only the level but also the low growth in the number of formal jobs are factors in the calculation of the expected income of a migrant or a candidate for mobility (Stiglitz 1974).

In 1999, the rationing of formal jobs in Antananarivo still concerned about 15 per cent of individuals aged 15 and over, even though, due to the development of the export processing zone and other private enterprises since 1995, this proportion had fallen by four points in five years. In 1995, over half of those excluded from formal employment could offer an hourly productivity superior to the current minimum wage. On the other hand, over a quarter of employees of companies with ten or more workers were paid at a rate inferior to the minimum wage. Simulations of a macro–micro model of the city's labour market showed that this job rationing was responsible for 6 points over 20 of income poverty (Cogneau 2001).

For the country as a whole, similar simulations show that a 10 per cent increase in formal employment results in a 5 per cent increase in average household consumption, and reduces poverty by 3 points, but has no effect on inequalities of income (Cogneau and Robilliard 2001). The weakness of rural infrastructures (roads, communications, irrigation) also partially explains the dualism between agriculture and the other sectors, as much in terms of mobility and joint employment as in terms of wages. Thus, a 10 per cent increase in productivity of agricultural activities would result in a rise of over 3 per cent in average household consumption and, more importantly, a 4-point decline in the rate of poverty. It is also vital that formal private investment be encouraged and public investment increased in sectors with strong externalities if the growth rates observed over the past few years are to be permanently maintained and are to translate rapidly into the reduction of poverty. The recent period partially makes up for the previous period of recession in terms of the utilisation of installed capacities, which is therefore limited. Macroeconomic calculations have shown that a 5 per cent yearly growth rate, based on an investment rate at least 3 points higher and reasonable growth in export, was consistent with the restraint of foreign debt and the necessary control of inflation (Cogneau 1998). The combined increase in private and public investment rates also involves stronger mobilisation of domestic savings, based on more efficient management of the banking system, an extension of micro-credit, and greater tax effort.

Policies for development of school enrolment and infrastructures, however indispensable, cannot be seen in isolation from development policies for jobs and urban income. Instantaneous observation of the territorial distribution of poverty by means of 'poverty maps' (Elbers, Lanjouw and Lanjouw 2001), a new and otherwise useful tool, tends to encourage a static view and a 'ruralist' obsession. But it is not because the poorest people are in the country that their individual prospects and their children's futures are not played out at least in part in cities. It is partly in the city that the future returns on education offered to country children are determined. What is more, urban income determines a major part of the demand for agricultural products in the marketplace. Finally, it is also around cities that the steps down the food processing chain for exportable agricultural products can be organised. This is the basis of part of the industrial take-off of South-East Asian countries. A dynamic view of the issue of poverty reduction should not emphasise a dichotomy between those in cities and those in rural areas, a dichotomy invoked all too often in the participatory debates concerning the PRSPs. Indeed, some rural zones are so remote and isolated that the cost of maintaining infrastructures is prohibitive. Instead, migration should be encouraged. On the other hand, the city is also where the entitlements of rural dwellers are determined in their absence, in particular by net buyers of agricultural products. It would be a positive development, therefore, if – in the context of justice considered as the reduction of tyranny outlined above – PRSPs were to be used to reinforce the influence of people cut off from access to political expression.

Conclusion

We conclude this chapter by asking three interrelated questions:

1   In what time perspective should poverty reduction issues be viewed, particularly in terms of intergenerational justice? Clearly, this is a difficult question, and one which John Rawls has particularly well understood. Let us imagine, following Jack Goody (1976), that some African societies are not ready to accept the immediate constraints of a growth strategy that, although it would benefit future generations, would disrupt the present generation's way of life. In other words, to what extent are participatory processes expected to respect an individual society's 'preference for the present' even if this inclination seriously compromises the reduction of poverty for the coming generations?

2   To what extent are the new policies of the fight against poverty willing to take on board the principle of dynamically efficient redistributions? In terms of evaluation, cross-section surveys produce an approach to poverty that greatly suffers from a static bias and frequently results in a misleading dialectic between urban and rural worlds. Further evidence of this static bias can be found in the omission in the current PRSPs of demographic and intergenerational themes – differential fertility, migration, social mobility, marriage and inheritance rules. Finally, in terms of social policies, the emphasis placed on the local provision of infrastructure and the financing thereof leads to the underestimation of redistribution policies likely to promote equality of opportunity in future generations efficiently.

3   Lastly, to what extent can PRSPs be used to spark a demand for justice addressed not only to the governments of the countries in question but also to the international community? It is absolutely clear that industrialised countries have a 'social responsibility' that goes beyond giving financial backing to policies deemed to be in accordance with their ideas. This responsibility applies particularly to the areas of international trade and the provision of global public goods. It is especially urgent to establish a strategic document for a worldwide fight against the Aids epidemic which is ravaging the African continent and constitutes one of the most extreme forms of deprivation of capabilities.

Notes

1   See John Rawls (1999), the only work by this author devoted to international problems. This is the meaning of the economic–philosophical work of Amartya Sen, who makes a distinction between international justice, which is settled on the level of the society of nations, and global justice, which is the basis for transnational movements like the feminist or anti-racist movements. See his lecture at the Collège de France: *The Idea of Social Identity*, 28 May 2001.

2　As chapter 6 of the World Bank Sourcebook (Ames *et al.* 2001) demonstrates for the macroeconomic level. The site created by the British NGOs, for example (http://www.brettonwoodsproject.org), puts Structural Adjustment and PRSPs in the same rubric.

3　The scope of distributive conflicts in developing countries is underestimated less than in the past. They were inaccurately reflected by inequalities of income alone (which were themselves very inaccurately measured in any case). In the case of Africa it has become clear that regional and ethnic violence usually involved conflicts centring around access to resources, particularly land. A dramatic illustration is afforded by recent examples as varied as the cases of Rwanda, Côte d'Ivoire and Zimbabwe.

4　For a certain number of fundamental concepts, see Fleurbaey (1998).

5　In the introduction to his well-known book, Rawls (1971) compares the question of social justice to that of scientific truth: 'The only thing that permits us to acquiesce in an erroneous theory is the lack of a better one; analogously, an injustice is tolerable only when it is necessary to avoid a greater injustice.'

6　See Sen (1992). Thus even the most liberal authors demand the equality of individuals in a certain number of basic rights – the right to own property, for example.

7　The practical impossibility of lump-sum transfers involves the use of distributive taxation and the 'distortions' associated with it. See Atkinson and Stiglitz (1980). Much literature has been devoted to the microeconomic and democratic bases of a social welfare function, subsequent to Kenneth Arrow's theorem of impossibility. Rawls's procedural approach resolves this impossibility in a way and leads to a borderline version of welfarism in his famous difference principle (principle 2a).

8　This idea does not necessarily accord with the abstract procedural logic (original position behind the veil of ignorance) advocated by Rawls. On this subject, see Habermas and Rawls (1997). The 'desocialised' character of Rawls's procedure is criticised by other authors like Pierre Bourdieu and Michael Walzer (see pp. 61–2).

9　If only to calculate the severity indices like FGT2, the only ones that combine satisfying axiomatic properties. See Foster, Greer and Thorbecke (1984). Distinguishing between the poor close to the poverty line and the poorest of the poor is all the more important in countries where the incidence of poverty is greater than 50 per cent.

10　This assessment is very apt to be conflictual, as the 'real parameters of the real law' that assign respective weights of effort and opportunity are unknown to the social players, and could be experimented by several generations through a bayesian learning process. See the last chapter of Piketty (1994).

11　Who underlines the point to which the state's monopoly on violence is coextensive with the generalisation of peaceful, lawful competition. See Elias (1987).

12　For this essential point, see Bourdieu (1980a).

13　'To fix ideas, let us single out the least advantaged as those who are least favoured by each of the three main kinds of contingencies. Thus this group includes persons whose family and class origins are more disadvantaged than others, whose natural endowments (as realized) permit them to fare less well, and whose fortune and luck in the course of life turn out to be less happy' (Rawls 1971: 83).

14　John Roemer's principle of equal opportunity (1998) represents this spirit of the 'Third Way'.

15　Here again the whole question is a matter of timescale and thus of generations. To support his well-known principle of difference, considered as a procedural argument, Rawls (1971) quotes a remark by Keynes admitting that the English Industrial Revolution eventually benefited the English proletariat.

16 Sometimes after economically disastrous socialist experiences, as in Madagascar and Tanzania for example.

17 Two fundamental elements pointed out by Goody (1976), together with specific rules of marriage and inheritance.

18 Sen (1992) quotes a declaration made by Haile Selassie which well illustrates this confusion of spheres of distribution characteristic of tyrannical reasoning: 'Those who do not work must starve.'

19 These paragraphs refer to and summarise the introduction to Cogneau and Guénard (2002). We refer the reader to this paper and to Bourguignon (1998) for the bibliography.

20 Which in fact raises other problems underlined by Bourguignon (2002).

21 A section on these developments can be found in Cogneau and Maurin's introduction (2001).

22 In virtue of the above remarks about individualisation, much research remains to be done on the boundary between anthropology and economics, in order to specify the criteria of mobility suitable for the societies under study. The study of the impact of matrimonial rules/strategies and inheritance on social mobility seems, analytically speaking, a particularly promising field.

23 Brazil, Colombia, Mexico, Peru.

24 Côte d'Ivoire, Ghana, Guinea, Madagascar, Uganda.

25 Bourguignon and Fields (1997) propose adopting a linear combination of the discontinuous indicator FTG0 and the continuous indicator FGT2.

26 On this subject see Chaudhuri and Ravallion (1994).

3 The lessons to be learnt from methods of regulating poverty in Europe

Serge Paugam

Over the last 20 years, all societies in Western Europe have seen a rapid increase in the population receiving state benefits, in most cases people who have been excluded or distanced from the labour market. Admittedly, this phenomenon has assumed differing proportions from one country to the next, but no country has really been spared, to a point where those systems for combating poverty which once seemed the most robust, the German and Scandinavian models for example, are now displaying their limits too. Each country is drawing on its resources to try and cope with this development and experimenting with various solutions which are currently being evaluated.

Comparing methods of regulating poverty means analysing at one and the same time how the question of poverty has been posed in different societies, the degree of importance bestowed on it, the resources which are being developed to eradicate it and, lastly, the solutions which are being put forward to tackle potential problems.

Methods of intervening to assist those considered disadvantaged have been shaped by the socio-historic traditions of the network of interdependence between the poor and the rest of society in the country in question. Such a network is not static. Although characterised by a certain measure of inertia on account of the strength of the institutions which make it up, it develops as a function of the economic and social situation and under pressure from the players involved in it. Its size differs too, ranging from that of an entire nation at a given stage in its development, to that of a local council whose methods of intervening to help the poor may be, to a greater or lesser degree, autonomous. In other words, a study of the regulation of poverty in European societies involves first of all taking into account what some like to call 'the stamp of history'; that is to say, the socio-historic foundations of national systems of intervention to help the most needy, and then tracing the way they have changed, with particular reference to recent experiments.

The sociology of the forms poverty takes in a given society at a given time in its history is, in fact, a sociology of social ties. The theoretical framework sketched out by Georg Simmel ([1908] 1967) in the early part of the twentieth century demonstrates that in the social relationship with poverty, the principle of assistance reveals not only the tensions, potential imbalances and even ruptures which affect and threaten the social system as a whole, but also a method of regulation which attenuates its effects and encourages interdependence between individuals and groups, even if these are based on relationships which are unequal and sometimes confrontational. The social status of the poor is strongly dependent on the method of regulation.

If, as our starting point, we adopt an approach which places the question of poverty in the context of the social system as a whole, an examination of the strategies adopted to deal with poverty in Europe may then be useful when trying to understand and analyse the current strategies of developing countries. When dealing with poverty wheresoever it occurs, four questions should first be answered: Who should help? Who should be helped? What principles should govern the giving of help? What resources should be used?

The foundations of the comparative analysis

The variety of ways in which the question of welfare may be tackled means that the comparative approach, which consists of starting with the specific definition of a policy such as France's basic guaranteed income and examining how other countries' policies are similar or divergent, runs the risk of rapidly ending in a methodological impasse. Indeed, this approach presents the disadvantage of analysing differences from a single perspective, perceived as the only legitimate frame of reference – a characteristic of national or cultural ethnocentrism – instead of trying to understand the socio-historic foundations of the institutions present in each country which conceive, define, and implement the policies in question. In other words, comparative research must try to go beyond questions arising from the social debate in such or such country to construct an analytical framework capable of taking into account the social principles behind it which generate both the philosophy and practical action. In order to understand the differences between the policies implemented in the various European countries, we must therefore engage in a socio-historic analysis of their respective representations of poverty and exclusion which are based on contrasting ideas on the relationship between state institutions proper, para-public organisations, and private bodies.[1]

The system of social protection as a whole

An analysis of methods of regulating poverty involves first taking into account the different welfare state models. Gosta Esping-Andersen's classification of welfare state systems identifies three different models: the liberal model, the corporate or continental model, and the social-

democratic or Nordic model (Esping-Andersen 1990). The first is characterised by the allocation of means-tested benefits, modest universal social
transfers, and a limited system of social insurance. The state stimulates the
market, limiting itself to minimal intervention to ensure basic social protection, and sometimes even tries to encourage the development of
private insurance. Typical examples of this model are the United States,
Canada, and Australia.[2] The continental model, on the other hand, is
founded on a system of compulsory insurance organised in a corporatist
spirit of defence of group interests and entitlements. This model fosters
the maintenance of differences in social status, but is also founded on a
traditional conception of the role of the family whereby women are
encouraged by a system of child allowance payments to remain on the
edge of the professional sphere and to make their prime responsibility the
bringing up of children. In this model, private insurance plays a modest
role in the system of social protection. Countries which adhere to this
model most closely are, according to Esping-Andersen, Austria, France,
Germany and Italy. Lastly, there is the Nordic or social-democrat model in
which the principle of the universality of social rights is applied systematically, enabling society as a whole, both middle and working classes, to
benefit from a very high level of social protection. This model, which is, in
a way, a synthesis of liberalism and socialism, favours the emancipation of
individuals both from the laws of the marketplace and from the role of the
family. Sweden is a typical example of the model.

This classification enables us to understand the way in which Western
societies organise social protection in general and the specific types of
social stratification which result. The form the welfare state takes, for
example, has an effect on the composition of the category of poor people
taken care of in the name of social assistance. In each welfare state system,
certain populations slip through the social protection net to swell, in
various ways, depending on the place and time, the category of state
benefit recipients. The steady expansion of the social protection system
during the prosperous post-war period of 1945–75 contributed to the
reduction of the traditional welfare sphere, but did not entirely eradicate
it. The number of poor people receiving benefits is therefore largely
linked to the ability of the welfare state system to maintain the most
vulnerable fringes of the population within the general net.

The example of unemployment benefit illustrates this. Most European
countries have undergone a similar development in the number of those
receiving the various minimum guaranteed social benefits; that is to say, a
very sharp rise in the first half of the 1980s, reaching a peak towards 1985,
followed by a period of stability and a decrease in several countries from
1988 onwards. The beginning of the 1990s saw numbers rising again everywhere. In actual fact, the overall rise in numbers in the 1980s and 1990s
was mainly linked to the erosion of the labour market. The unemployment curve, in particular long-term unemployment, and the minimum

guaranteed social benefits curve follow a very similar path. It should, however, be noted that this similarity in the development curves is clearly more pronounced in countries where cover for the unemployed through the contributory system of social protection is weak. The unemployed in Britain, for example, can only benefit from unemployment benefit at a very low universal flat rate and for a maximum of one year (reduced to six months as from 1995). Consequently, in 1992, 77 per cent of unemployed persons in Great Britain claimed to be living solely on Income Support. Under these conditions, the rise in the number of people receiving Income Support naturally reflects developments in the labour market. In the Netherlands, where there are two minimum benefits, the evolution of the number of people receiving the benefit especially created for the unemployed and in particular the long-term unemployed, also quite logically follow the unemployment curve. In Germany and Belgium, where social security cover for unemployment is much wider, the number of those receiving the minimum social benefits is, on the other hand, less sensitive to labour market trends. The increase in numbers in Germany was sharp and continuous throughout the period in question, although the evolution of the unemployment rate was not.

Moreover, the diversity of systems for ensuring a minimum guaranteed income means that caution should be exercised when comparing numbers. Should we wish, for example, to compare Great Britain and France, it is not enough simply to compare the number of those receiving Income Support with the number of those receiving the RMI (*Revenu Minimum d'Insertion* – minimum guaranteed income). In addition to these two minimum benefits, Family Credit in Great Britain, and the seven other minimum benefits in France, must be taken into account (Evans, Paugam and Prélis 1995). The growth in numbers from 1989 to 1993 then appears markedly weaker in France than in Great Britain: 4 per cent as against 37 per cent. In actual fact, trends differ from one benefit to another in France. The number of those receiving the minimum benefit for the elderly has dropped significantly as a result of the steady improvement in retirement pensions, whilst the number of those receiving the *Allocation de Solidarité Spécifique* (for the long-term unemployed), and above all the RMI, has shown a sharp rise. In Great Britain, the increase in numbers concerns both the unemployed, the sick, the handicapped, and the over-60s who receive Income Support, and families receiving Family Credit. The total number of beneficiaries of these minimum allowances was 50 per cent higher than in France in 1989, and around double in 1993. In addition, and to extend this comparison, we must also try to assess the number of eligible persons (spouses, children, dependants) and calculate the percentage represented by beneficiaries plus eligible persons in the population as a whole. In France, in 1993, there were around 5.5 million minimum benefit beneficiaries as against 11.7 million in Great Britain, representing 9.9 per cent and 20.8 per cent of the respective populations. This difference can, of course, be explained by differences in the way the social protection system in France operates, covering certain fringes of the population upstream of these minimum benefits to a greater extent than the British system.

The size of the population dependent on welfare can be partly explained by the overall conception of the welfare state in each of these countries. The typologies of the welfare states are therefore a useful support in an analysis of poverty in these two countries. It should be emphasised, however, that methods of regulating poverty do not issue directly and exclusively from these models. In Esping-Andersen's classification, for example, France, Germany and Italy are close to the same model, although welfare and reinsertion policies in these three countries are very different. In actual fact, the definition of the principles and ways of assisting the most needy is also linked to a heritage, but this is not the same as that to which we spontaneously refer to explain the creation of the welfare states.

National forms of the assistance relationship: four differentiating factors

Four differentiating factors may be adopted to help us understand the national particularities of the assistance relationship in Europe: the sharing of responsibilities between the state and the other players, the administrative definition of the population to be taken care of, the principle governing the definition of the help to be given and, finally, the type of social intervention. These factors relate back to the four simple questions mentioned in the introduction to this chapter and to which the various European countries give different answers: Who should help? Who should be helped? What principles should govern the giving of help? What resources should be used?

We will not, of course, be entering into details of social legislation in each of the countries, but will take each of the four factors in turn and identify the various contrasting structures which have resulted from their particular socio-historic tradition.

The sharing of responsibilities

Where welfare is concerned, the sharing of responsibilities between the state and the other players, in particular local councils, but also various associations, depends on the historical tradition of state intervention in each country. Although each welfare state represents a system of nationalised social protection in the sense of a set of social rights defined at the level of society as a whole and applicable wherever the place of residence may be, welfare has, in many countries, remained the responsibility of the local councils as far as the administration of benefits and sometimes even their definition is concerned. Very often, the extension of the system of social protection founded on the principle of insurance has rendered traditional forms of assistance obsolete and residual, to the extent that the state has preferred to leave responsibility for this, at least in part, to the local authorities, in particular in countries where they have shown themselves capable in this area. For historic reasons, the administrative organisation of welfare is very different from country to country in Europe. In certain cases the state is the principal player upon which all initiatives converge; in others, however, the principal player remains the local council. As a result, a great variety of situations exist and we might already venture the hypothesis that the social status of those receiving benefit is different in every country and sometimes even within a country, depending on whether the country in question has entrusted responsibility to the local councils or not. Moreover, it is worth noting that the visibility of the beneficiary category is not identical from country to country either, which may go some way to explaining the national differences that can be seen in the emergence and direction taken by social debate on this issue. Lastly, the sharing of responsibilities also concerns the division of initiatives between the state and non-profit organisations. The role of the latter also varies from one country to another (Salamon and Anheier 1997).

The definition of the 'target populations'

Defining the right to assistance means defining, in the administrative sense, the population liable to claim it. Two opposing ideas emerge. The first is based on a unitary definition; that is to say, the poor are defined in an overall fashion using criteria deemed to be legitimate by the institutions and society as a whole. The most classic criteria are monetary in character. This approach requires precise studies to be made on the poverty of households defined on the basis of a given income threshold. The first European countries to have recognised the right to a minimum guaranteed income for the most needy adopted this unitary principle and therefore defined a single legislation for the population considered poor. The second idea, on the other hand, is based on an assessment of the risks run by certain fringes of the population. Poverty is no longer seen as a homogeneous whole, but as a set of social categories in poverty to whom it seems legitimate to grant assistance in the form of a minimum income. This second approach leaves open the possibility of creating a hierarchy of the categories defined which depends on an evaluation of the severity of the difficulties or on the seriousness of the problems experienced. The categorial approach presents the disadvantage of leaving fringes of the population excluded from the right to assistance since they are required to fall into one or other of the categories in order to receive it. If none of these categories corresponds to the situation of the individual in difficulty, he or she cannot be helped unless it be through a form of optional, or extra-legal, assistance. Such situations were very common in France, for example, before the law on the minimum guaranteed income was passed; this now represents the last safety net for those who cannot be helped by any other category of minimum social benefit. The unitary idea avoids this problem, but has also often proved ill-adapted to individual cases. This is why countries which have adopted this principle have often, at the same time, left a large degree of latitude to the institutions responsible for its application to enable them to find solutions to fit the particular needs of individuals and households receiving assistance. Unitary and categorial ideas about the poor are, in fact, linked to two different philosophies of the definition of benefits.

The definition of benefits

In order to define the right to assistance, we must also, of course, define the benefits to which the population judged poor may lay claim. Two different approaches may also be observed in this area. The first is based on the 'principle of need', in the sense that the aim is to guarantee the survival of the most needy by giving them the means to satisfy basic needs, in particular food and housing. This ambition is at least partially at the origin of research into the living conditions of impoverished populations. A wealth of literature exists on the subject. Economists and statisticians of poverty in particular have always sought to provide a substantialist definition of this social phenomenon with the more or less avowed intention of replying to the questions posed by the social policy-makers.[3] The second idea, on the other hand, relates to the 'principle of status', in the sense that the aim is to help the most needy in the name of social justice and the community's duty towards the poor, whilst at the same time avoiding a substantial change in the existing social structure. In other words, assistance gives social status to those who benefit from it, but it must be defined with reference to other status in the hierarchy and, above all, must remain markedly lower than the salary awarded to the lowest-paid worker.

There is, of course, an underlying idea of need here, but it does not constitute the basic criteria on which the decision concerning the amount of benefit to be given is based. This is defined, above all, in accordance with the requirements of the classification of individuals into as many hierarchical statuses as there are needs for social distinction. In actual fact, it is the highly legitimate idea of social order which prevails to justify these inequalities in status. In this sense, assistance, as Simmel observed at the beginning of the century, is not so much a means of serving the interests of the poor as a roundabout way of maintaining the social *status quo*. Those European countries which have implemented a minimum guaranteed income all, to a greater or lesser degree, drew inspiration from one or other of these two principles to such an extent that even today they still constitute an essential dimension of national differences in the social relationship with poverty.

The type of intervention

The fourth factor of differentiation concerns ways of intervening to allow people access to the benefit set aside for them. The assistance relationship may differ radically depending on whether or not institutions and social work professionals are able to take autonomous decisions in relation to the standard framework designed to enable them to respond to those who approach them for help. Two forms of response can be identified in this particular area of social work.[4] The first is 'bureaucratic intervention' in the sense that the agent of social intervention, be it an institution or an individual, pays scrupulous attention to applying the law without taking individual circumstances into account. The response is always formal and immediate. The individual may either be helped because he or she corresponds to a situation defined in social law, or he cannot be helped and in this case must approach a more informal structure – in the charity sector, for example.

The second response is based on the interpretation of individual cases and the search for the most appropriate solution, depending on whether or not the demand is deemed legitimate. This may be termed 'individualistic intervention'. In this case, the role of the social agent involves real involvement in the evaluation of a situation. It also calls upon greater professional competence than in the case of strictly bureaucratic intervention. This type of intervention is easier when the prevailing social legislation has defined a wide variety of responses to particular cases. The agent then has to select, from among a wide range of possibilities, the solution which seems to suit the individual best.

One might ask which type of intervention best respects the dignity of the individual. Bureaucratic intervention would, at first sight, seem to avoid stigmatising individuals to too great an extent because their situation is treated in an impersonal manner. The social intervener does not judge, but simply checks whether conditions for obtaining benefit have been met, usually on the basis of an administrative file completed by the claimant. Individualistic intervention on the other hand, makes intrusion into the individual's personal life by the social intervener inevitable and may result in moralising on behaviour judged irresponsible or deviant compared to his or her own idea of how the needy should behave.

It can be seen, therefore, that these specific characteristics of the assistance relationship express four basic sets of opposing ideas: (1) centralism vs. decentralisation, (2) unitary approach vs. categorial approach, (3) the principle of need vs. the principle of status, (4) bureaucratic intervention vs. individualist intervention. They form a framework from which it is possible to draw up a typology of the methods of regulating poverty.

Three methods of regulating poverty

Societies adapt in many different ways to the development of poverty, depending on which particular aspect of their policies we choose to examine. A full description of these policies would lead to a never-ending comparison. But if we restrict ourselves to an analysis of the elementary factors of differentiation just described which, as we have seen, have their roots in historic forms of the relationship between the poor and the rest of society, it is possible to identify a more limited number. The only way to understand these socio-historic differences is to describe the ideal types and then analyse to what extent reality differs from, or reflects them. Table 3.1 lists three methods of regulating poverty: autocentred regulation, negotiated regulation, and localised regulation.

Table 3.1 Defining principles of the methods of regulating poverty

	Type of regulation		
	Autocentred	*Negotiated*	*Localised*
Main responsibility	State	Divided between state, local level, and associations	Local level
Definition of the populations	Unitary or categorial	Unitary	Categorial
Definition of benefit	Principle of need or status	Principle of need	Principle of status
Type of intervention	Bureaucratic	Individualistic	Bureaucratic (clientelist)

Autocentred regulation

This method of regulation is based on the principle of centralised power. The state has prime responsibility for welfare, even if it relies on local organisations and associations for the application of certain policies and to carry out specific tasks. The principle whereby support for the most needy is the duty of the nation as a whole, and consequently of the state, is, in this method of regulation, so legitimate that it corresponds to the expectations of society and institutions in general. Regulation is autocentred in that the state's traditional intervention methods are not only accepted, but continually reinforced by the very principle of the system which forces the players to conform to it if they, in turn, wish to obtain legitimacy and recognition in the welfare field.

This method of regulating poverty may also be expressed by either a unitary or a categorial definition of the target population. Similarly, a definition of the benefits available may follow either a need or a status principle. However, not all permutations are possible. The unitary approach corresponds more to the need principle and, conversely, the categorial approach is more closely linked to the status principle. The state will define the population in need of help in a unitary fashion if an institutional norm concerning the needs of the poor prevails, and will adopt a categorial definition if it favours the status principle. On the other hand, autocentred regulation is, in every case, expressed by a type of bureaucratic intervention which is the classic expression of the authority of the state and the way it operates. This type of intervention is not, moreover, specific to welfare. In more general terms, it corresponds, as Max Weber has pointed out, to a certain idea of the relationship between the state and the individual.

This method of regulating poverty has every chance of being the subject of national debate on the way in which the state is demonstrating support for the most needy. The bureaucratic method of intervention also gives a high level of visibility to the poor as a social group, or, in the case of a categorial approach, to the administrative categories upon which the definition of the poor is based. Statistics concerning those thus defined as poor are more easily obtained since it is the government of the welfare state which is compiling them for administration purposes. When this administration is the responsibility of local authorities, figures are more scattered and therefore less easily obtainable.

Negotiated regulation

This method of regulation implies above all a sharing of the responsibility between the different players involved in policy-making to combat poverty. This means that this type of policy is not primarily state policy and that expectations of it are not as high as for the previous type of regulation. The system of shared responsibility is more frequent in countries founded on federalist principles who generally grant more autonomy to regional or local authorities in the implementation of social policy. That said, all countries whose political and administrative organisation is based on this system do not necessarily follow the negotiated method of regulating poverty. The intervention of the social state is derisory in some cases, yet the prime characteristic of this method of regulation is the policy negotiated between the state and the other players. In other words, although the social state is not the sole player it is not absent from the negotiation either. It must also be stated that the sharing of responsibilities is only valid in the area of assistance and solidarity and does not therefore imply that the entire social protection system is based on this principle. A country may therefore have both a social insurance system which is uniform and centralised, and a diversified and decentralised benefit system.

In this method of regulation, the definition of 'target populations' is usually unitary. It is not easy to decentralise an entire categorial system since it generally involves fairly complex administrative procedures both regarding access to benefits and their management. Such a system can only really function if a limited number of players are responsible for it. The state may perhaps decentralise the administration of one or other of the categories, handing responsibility over to the local authorities, but it is unreasonable to imagine that they would take over the management of the entire system.

The negotiated method of regulation therefore corresponds more to a unitary definition of the poor and therefore to the principle of need. In this case, it is therefore sufficient to enshrine within a single law, valid for the entire country, the right of the most needy to obtain the means to live from the community and to define the general procedures for obtaining such benefit, leaving the task of applying, and perhaps complementing it, to the local authorities.

The principle of negotiation also then applies at local level, in particular in the relationship between social work professionals and the populations who apply to them for help. The flexibility of this system, and in certain cases the variety of the benefits available at local level as a complement to national legislation, means that this method of intervention is individualist. Social work professionals have, in fact, greater latitude to assess the needs of those who apply to them, and usually act on a case-by-case basis.

In this method of regulation, the social debate on the question of poverty is itself decentralised to the extent that it may seem non-existent at national level. It also has to be said that the sharing of responsibilities and the principle of the individualisation of benefit at local level makes an overall understanding of poverty and the category of the poor more difficult. In this case, collective expectations of the social state are only real when all local solutions, including those put forward by associations, have been exhausted.

Localised regulation

Unlike the preceding two types of regulation, localised regulation does not take the form of either direct or indirect state intervention. Most of the responsibility for intervention is taken at local level – that is to say, by the local council, which decides to provide for the needs of those judged to be in need of assistance. This method of regulation is more likely to be found in countries with a low level of social protection. The local councils take action because the state has not done so or because it cannot intervene adequately. This results in a great diversity of experiences and, consequently, glaring inequalities between regions within the same country.

In this method of regulation, the definition of the target populations is more likely to be categorial since local councils rarely have sufficient resources to take overall responsibility for poverty, particularly in countries where the level of social protection is already low. The population in need of help is so large and their needs so urgent that a unitary approach is almost impossible. The local councils are therefore forced to make choices based on priorities which seem to them legitimate. Both categorial definition and the status principle dominate through force of circumstance, which means that populations may be living in poverty without being able to obtain help. This type of regulation may well result in clientelist practices. It may also be bureaucratic in the sense that social work professionals theoretically have only to apply criteria defined by the local council to respond to the claims of the most needy. In practice, however, when this type of service is run exclusively by the local council – that is to say, with no state regulation whatever – there is room for a certain degree of adaptation to individual cases; this makes the introduction of vague and arbitrary criteria, favouring certain applicants to the detriment of others, almost inevitable. This is why the localised method of regulation is likely to result in a falsely bureaucratic intervention – that is to say one which is bureaucratic in principle but which effectively relies, at least partially, on practices which deviate in favour of particular interests.

This type of regulation also tends to hide institutional forms of poverty. In countries which practise it, the proportion of those receiving benefits is usually low and, in any case, very variable from one district to the next. In reality, the question of poverty is seen differently. Because the social protection system has not been developed, other regulatory mechanisms come into play, in particular support from the family and informal mutual aid networks which give poverty a different sense and social status from that which it takes on in countries where methods of intervention are more institutionalised.

As we have said, these three ways of regulating poverty correspond to ideal types. We will now analyse national experiences of minimum guaranteed income in greater detail and examine how they correspond to, or diverge from, this ideal-typical construction.

Contrasting minimum income policies

The eight case studies on which this chapter is based[5] constitute a body of historical and empirical material which can be used to test the concepts and ideal types described above (Paugam 1999). To prevent misunderstandings, we should point out that no national minimum guaranteed income policy corresponds exactly to the different types of poverty regulation drawn up as ideal-typical. A detailed analysis of each of them may very well lead to a result whereby only a few aspects correspond to one or other of the types of regulation, or even, in certain cases, to two at once. The method we have adopted is not a rigid classification. Moreover, policies to combat poverty are constantly evolving. The historical origins of the French system, for example, identify it as an autocentred method of regulation, but decentralisation initiatives have led to the steady transformation of social policies in favour of greater local autonomy, which in a sense makes it closer to the negotiated method of regulation. We finally decided to place France in the first type of regulation because of the maintenance of the state's primordial role in this field and the collective ambition to strengthen social cohesion with the central institutions of political life as a starting-point, but this decision does not prevent us from drawing attention to current developments. Identifying a country with a certain method of poverty regulation does not mean unreservedly identifying it with such a method. The deviations observed do not represent an error of interpretation but, on the contrary, encourage us to take the analysis further and in particular to try to find additional explanatory elements. France is not an isolated case. We have proceeded in the same fashion for each of the countries. The typology, such as we have designed it, is above all a tool with which to highlight the essential differences and to understand, through the bias of a socio-historic analysis, the specific dynamic of each of the systems.

Countries which practise a form of autocentred regulation

France and Great Britain, two countries which have very different systems for combating poverty, both practise a form of this first method of regulation. In line with the French social state's centralist and supposedly universal principle, initiatives to help the most needy are the duty of the entire nation. When French parliamentarians discussed the law on the *Revenu Minimum d'Insertion*, they began by reiterating the principles adopted two centuries earlier by the Revolutionaries in 1790 when the *Comité de Mendicité* was being set up (Paugam 1993). Even though this organisation was a failure, the spirit behind it did not disappear. One century later, the reformers instituted the right to assistance and encouraged the state to take charge of a sector hitherto more or less left to private benevolence. Several laws on assistance were passed: free medical assistance (1893), assistance to the destitute (1893), and for the old, infirm and incurables (1905). Although France was lagging behind Germany with regard to insurance and the organisation of a comprehensive system of social protection, this was far from being the case in the assistance field where state regulation appeared very early (Merrien 1994; Renard 1995).

Even today, it would be unthinkable to consider taking the risk of inequality occurring within the country by allowing local authorities to define the categories of eligible persons, the types of intervention, and the benefits. So keen has the state been to retain responsibility for overall administration that the desire to involve local players, in particular the *départements*, in the application of new social policies, such as the minimum guaranteed income, has not radically altered this principal. The French case, termed 'revolutionary centralism' by Max Weber, is an ideal-typical illustration of the rationale of successive state monopolisation of collective areas of competence, from the monopoly of legitimate violence to that of provident societies and insurance. The question of exclusion is formulated in France in accordance with this restorative principle from which the state cannot escape without provoking fierce criticism from its citizens. It is striking that the principle of state intervention is not often criticised, even by believers in economic liberalism who view it as a necessity in line with the Republican pact, on condition, however, that it does not unduly upset budgetary equilibrium.

The sharing of responsibilities between the state and civil society in the fight against poverty and exclusion is also significant. Whilst in Germany priority is given to the social services offered by non-state institutions, in accordance with the subsidiarity principle, French charitable associations define themselves in relation to the state. Because it is omnipresent in events and in people's minds, the state is, for them, an inevitable partner. They tend to put pressure on it to obtain subsidies and to be recognised as official players in social policy. They also try to encourage the public authorities to take direct responsibility. Charitable associations played a significant role in furthering the idea of a minimum guaranteed income before the presidential election of 1988. As a group, they are also behind many proposals for a law against exclusion.[6] In other words, they do not contest state intervention and would even like it to intervene more. In a sense, this amounts to a kind of inverse subsidiarity principle. They will act on condition that the state and the public powers have exhausted all possible solutions. However, expectations of the state where the fight against exclusion is concerned are legion.

Policy for combating poverty in Great Britain is also marked by its long historical development. National debate on the question has been going on for several centuries now. The first national poor law, guaranteeing all destitute persons financial help through a municipal tax, dates from 1601. It was criticised by many in the eighteenth century, not only because it had led to serious financial slippage but also because many saw it as an encouragement to laziness. A new law was voted in 1834 to eradicate voluntary poverty – notably by forcing the able-bodied poor to enter the workhouse – and above all to stimulate a market economy based on individual responsibility and the wage-earning class.

Because of the policy of stigmatising those receiving welfare, public assistance from this time onwards was considered by the working classes to be a symbol of degradation (Polanyi 1944). From then on, the status of welfare beneficiary was one of ignominy and so to prevent people suffering such a fate, several mutual aid societies were founded at the beginning of the nineteenth century. As François-Xavier Merrien (1994) has pointed out, from 1880 onwards a new representation of poverty emerged under pressure from several social reformers, generating the first social protection laws at the beginning of the twentieth century (state pension scheme in 1908, health and unemployment in 1911). The ideal of voluntary poverty progressively gave way to public discussion on the need to draw up a set of universal rights. The Beveridge Plan adopted during the Second World War completed this development in favour of centralised national solidarity organised by the state. The system of combating poverty is still founded on the principle put forward by Beveridge in 1942, whereby the state should take charge of, and standardise, the various aspects of social protection. The aim of this system is to guarantee the entire population a minimum income sufficient to cover basic needs and to compensate for a series of social risks: poverty, illness, handicap, and old-age. It includes non-contributory services financed through taxes and contributory national insurance and assistance services.

The French and British systems are based on the idea that poverty is first and foremost a matter for government policy. In both countries, current representations of poverty and methods of intervention have been structured by long-standing debate on the subject. For historical reasons which are different in France and Great Britain, this issue is still the subject of many a discussion, not only amongst researchers but also among political leaders who are usually judged on the results they obtain in this field. In both countries, access to a minimum income is obtained automatically on the basis of an administrative file filled in by applicants whose claims are based on nationally defined criteria. The French and British systems do not, apart from a few exceptions, allow for the individualisation of benefits on a case-by-case basis. The management of both these systems remains mainly administrative without any real assessment of the individual legitimacy of the claims. The bureaucratic formalism of the attribution of benefits is linked to the centralism of the state.

A fundamental difference nevertheless exists between the two countries. The British system is founded on a unitary approach to the population in question. The guaranteed minimum income, which as we have seen, is made up of two benefits, Income Support (for those who do not work), and Family Credit (a complementary benefit for people with children on a low income and who work at least 16 hours a week), serves to compensate for the gaps in the general insurance and assistance systems. It complements many other types of benefit and improves the level of social protection; but this second safety net is not categorial as is the case in France. It is addressed to the whole population irrespective of the type of need experienced by the different categories which make it up. It too is based on the principle of need, although since the Beveridge Plan the definition of the poverty thresholds, which were fixed so that the amount of benefit could be assessed, has been the subject of continual discussion.

In France, categorial intervention to help the most needy is a legacy of the social protection system. Legislation on the guaranteed minimum income for the most needy, for example, is founded not on a unitary principle – that is to say, one piece of legislation to cover all those judged to be poor – but on a series of minimum benefits set up for successive classes of people from the minimum invalidity pension created in 1930 to the RMI in 1988. Today, no fewer than eight such benefits exist to help people who have been excluded either permanently or temporarily from the labour market. The principle of this system is to cover different types of population with specific handicaps or exposed to particular risks. The RMI, of course, serves as a final safety net and as such cannot be defined as a categorial benefit, but, since it is a last resort for a population who cannot obtain the seven other minimum benefits, in reality it corresponds to an additional category in the social protection system.

The 'poor' category is therefore split into several administrative sub-categories and the categorial principle prevails as the legitimate framework for thought and action. In such a system, social work largely consists of finding the appropriate category for the person in difficulty. When their situation does not correspond to any established administrative category, they cannot be helped, except by occasional extra-legal benefits. This type of intervention has repercussions on access to benefits. In a categorial system, despite the variety of benefits available, there are always those who are excluded from aid, all the more so since the bureaucratic formality attached to it exacerbates its failings still further.

The recommended solutions for eradicating poverty are also very different. In Great Britain, unemployment and the widespread poverty associated with it have not resulted in an increase in benefits. On the contrary, attempts are even being made to decrease the amount of Income Support to encourage those who receive it, or who might receive it, to take responsibility for themselves. Inequalities between rich and poor have consequently become much greater (Barclay 1995) and disadvantaged populations depending on the minimum income payment whose status is already low are often suspected of taking advantage of the welfare system.

As in the nineteenth century, the social debate is therefore still centred on the potentially corrupting effect of aid to the poor. Foremost in the minds of politicians seems to be the need to lessen the social contributions weighing on employers, thereby stimulating the competitiveness of the productive machine which should in the long-term lead to job creation and enable the 'poor' to cease to depend on welfare – on condition, of course, that they are motivated by the idea of working again. It is a striking fact that many studies in Great Britain are devoted to the mechanisms of profit-sharing. Since individuals are supposed to be rational players, a welfare system must therefore be designed which encourages those who benefit from it actively to seek employment. The question of the 'underclass' is tackled – at least in part – in the same spirit, especially by the Conservatives. Indeed, this goes back to the traditional idea of a 'welfare class' into which the 'poor' have fallen and from which only incentive policies can rescue them.

In France, the question of poverty is approached, not in terms of an 'underclass', but as part of a general debate on national solidarity, the idea being that society as a whole has become more fragile. The debate on exclusion betrays a collective anxiety about the possibility of losing one's job and social advantages. Politicians, or those responsible for social policy, rarely put forward the idea that the 'poor' are taking unfair advantage of the welfare system and that benefits should be reduced to give them greater incentive to find a job. The idea most commonly expressed is that social spending must be increased in the name of solidarity.

Despite their differences in defining the priorities for helping the most needy, France and Great Britain are still marked by their past which makes the fight against poverty an affair of state. In other words, their policies are different, but the method of regulation, in the sense we have defined it, remains similar.

Countries which practise a form of negotiated regulation

The country which represents the negotiated method of regulation the most closely is doubtless Germany. As we know, the country is characterised by political and administrative decentralisation. The widespread division of political power amongst the regional institutions now gives the *Länder* a great deal of autonomy, both in taking legislative initiatives and in implementing social policies, to the detriment of central government. This tendency to distribute political and administrative powers is accentuated still further through the intermediary of the *Bezirke* (districts), who possess a significant amount of power in matters of social legislation.

The German system of social protection, in accordance with the Bismarckian principle, has been built on three pillars: a social security system financed by employee and employer contributions (sickness, accident, old-age, and unemployment), a state provident fund (war victims) financed by public subsidies, and a welfare system. The minimum income is a product of the latter. The system is characterised by the widespread individualisation of benefits. Article 3 of the 'Federal Act on Social Aid' of 1961 states:

> The form of welfare given should conform to the particularities of the individual case, and above all to the person, his needs, and the local situation. The wishes of the beneficiary must be taken into account insofar as they do not involve any extra costs.
>
> ('Federal Act on Social Aid', 1961)

This system presents the advantage of allowing basic benefits to be attributed to each person in need and at the same time ensuring additional benefits are paid which correspond to particular needs, since the analysis of each individual case by the welfare body may lead to the payment of one-off benefits, additional payments for additional needs, or housing benefits. Public welfare bodies must also provide support and advice to beneficiaries to help them overcome dependence on these benefits. This highly decentralised system seems far more flexible than those in France and Great Britain.

The principle of decentralisation also applies where insertion policy is concerned. Several experiments in helping people find work have been attempted. The law requires local councils to create job opportunities for people claiming benefit, in particular the young unemployed. The expenses incurred by the creation and maintenance of these activities may be paid by the social aid bodies. These measures are, in general, limited in time and their application is very variable since it depends on the local council in question.

It is interesting to note that the place occupied by social matters in public debate is much greater in centralised countries like France and Great Britain than in a country like Germany where decentralisation contributes to restricting debates to their local dimension. In Germany, the question of poverty remains secondary.[7] In the final analysis, negotiated regulation is founded on the obligation for the social players to try to find all the solutions possible using the institutional resources they have at local level, in accordance with national welfare principles. Social workers then assess the needs of the recipients case by case.

Belgium, the Netherlands, and the Scandinavian countries are also close to this method of regulation. The principle of local council intervention to deal with poverty is applied in each of these countries. In each case, the local authorities adopt a method of intervention which is more individualistic than bureaucratic. The definition of the populations is also most often unitary and benefits are granted in accordance with the principle of need.

Today, the Scandinavian countries still have a very traditional welfare system based on action by local councils in accordance with ancient national laws. Until recently, these countries were scarcely concerned by the question of welfare, this being intended for a residual fringe of the population. Nonetheless, the system of social protection seems increasingly threatened and the question of poverty is increasingly at the centre of social concerns. Whether in Germany, Belgium, the Netherlands or the Scandinavian countries, the negotiated method of regulation seems for the moment to correspond to the new challenges of poverty and to the difficulties encountered by the systems of social protection in vigour in these countries. It has to be acknowledged, too, that the rate of poverty there has remained lower than in the other European countries overall.

Countries practising a form of localised regulation

The countries of southern Europe come closest to this type of regulation. In Spain today, a distinction can be made between the social security system and the welfare system. Unlike the systems of the northern European countries, the Spanish systems are relatively recent. The present social security system was founded in the 1960s, but only really developed in the middle of the 1970s at the same time as the transformation of the political system. Despite the politicians' wish to cover the entire population through this and to limit recourse to the welfare system as far as possible, the number of people receiving several of the minimum social benefits rose sharply during the 1980s. There are now four of these: complements to the social security pension, minimal payments for the old and handicapped, unemployment benefits, and, lastly, the minimum guaranteed incomes grouped together under the term *Salario Social* which correspond to various regional programmes. The latter are recent. The oldest was created in 1989 in the Basque region. These programmes range from a real minimum guaranteed income (notably in the Basque region, Madrid, and in a more limited fashion, in Catalonia) to the much more restricted programmes of a minimum social benefit. So, unlike the RMI in France, the ultimate safety net in the Spanish system of social protection, the *Salario Social*, is not applied to the entire country and still relies on fairly disparate local initiatives and contrasting operating principles.

It is difficult to define any guiding principles for Spain since practices differ so greatly from one region to another. The absence of a homogeneous national idea of the guaranteed minimum income can also be seen in the wide variety of experiments being carried out in the sphere of social insertion policy. However, it should be noted that in the Basque region and Madrid, and to a lesser extent in Catalonia, the system which has been set up draws heavily on the principles of the French RMI, notably in the relationship of the right to welfare and the search for insertion solutions for its beneficiaries.

Lastly, in Spain, as in other southern European countries, the question of poverty does not mobilise the public authorities as much as in certain northern countries. The rate of unemployment is nonetheless very high, as is the percentage of households living below the poverty threshold.[8] Several factors are at play here. First, the institutional visibility of poverty – in the sense of being addressed through welfare – is less. An estimated 0.4 per cent of the population aged between 25 and 64 years – receive the *Salario Social* – which is very few compared to the numbers receiving Income Support or the RMI. Second, and doubtless this is the essential factor, poor living standards do not always imply severe social exclusion, mainly because of family solidarity amongst the disadvantaged classes, which we know to be more developed than in northern Europe. Similarly, the absence of employment may be partly compensated for by insertion into informal economic networks. Third and finally, the highly decentralised nature of social policy makes an overall perception of the problem of poverty difficult. It has, moreover, a tendency to become part of the more general question of regional inequalities in economic and social development.

The case of Italy is very close to that of Spain. The system of social protection is less effective there than in the northern countries. Welfare payments there are still attributed unequally over the country, which reinforces regional contrasts still further. But as in Spain, poverty does not mean a deterioration of social ties. Poverty is socially integrated, if only through the methods of resistance that the population as a whole has adopted in order to cope with it. Specialists on Italy highlight in particular the clientelism which seems to regulate access to benefit payments and public employment. This must be seen as the prolonged effect of the history of this country's institutions, during the course of which the central political and administrative system has not managed to really affirm its independence in relation to the various pressures exerted by categorial interests.

The localised method of regulation that can be observed particularly in Spain and Italy is very different from the method of negotiated regulation, even if the latter is also characterised by a search for solutions at local level. The difference stems essentially from the fact that the localised method of regulation is organised around a fragmented system of social protection which has not been greatly developed and in which welfare is left to the initiative of local councils, apart from a few exceptions concerning particular populations. The negotiated method of regulation is based, on the contrary, on a foundation of universal social rights enshrined in national legislation. The principle of negotiation is applied to determine the balance between national and local levels. Because of the individualist nature of intervention, it is also present in the relationship between local social aid institutions and the individuals who apply to them.

Conclusion: what lessons may be learnt?

Where the guaranteed minimum income is concerned, experiments being carried out in Europe have not, to date, brought forth any magic solution. Consequently, it is unlikely that a unified model will emerge for all the countries. Because of the weight of tradition and the relative inertia of current institutions and systems, and despite attempts at standardising legislation and policy, it is also probable that institutional forms of poverty and exclusion will continue in all their many and singular guises just as they have always done.

Because of their diversity, Western European policies for combating poverty may provide the perspective needed to enable us to ask the right questions about strategies currently being elaborated to fight against poverty in the developing countries. At first sight, some might say that action in developing countries is quite a different story and that any comparison with the realities of the Western world is doomed to failure.

However, international initiatives in this field, such as those launched in 1999 by the World Bank and the IMF, are often inspired in a non-explicit way by current models and their underlying philosophy in certain developed countries, even if only in part.

With regard to the question 'who should help?', it must first be pointed out that all countries in Western Europe rely on the role of the state. Those countries which seem the most open to economic liberalism, such as Great Britain, are in fact countries which set up an overall system of social protection and policies specifically aimed at combating poverty a long while ago, either on the basis of state intervention or in association with the state. As we have seen, many variations on the sharing of responsibility between the state and local authorities exist, but the principle whereby the state must be committed to this type of policy has never been challenged. On the other hand, it is interesting that the argument on state intervention is not a great incentive in the developing countries. Even though the World Bank's World Development Report, dedicated to the fight against poverty (World Bank 2000a), reminds us that the state plays an essential role, this argument seems innovative because international authorities previously placed such great emphasis on the development of the market economy as a means of eradicating poverty.

European countries continue to respond differently to the question 'who should be helped?' Although the principle of taking care of individuals who find themselves in a situation of poverty is now established in all European countries in the form of the right to welfare, the question of 'target' populations remains entirely unanswered. Nothing dictates that a unitary rather than a categorial approach should be adopted to define those in need of help because each approach relates to a particular representation of poverty and philosophy of social policy, and both are defensible. It is therefore probable that the diversity to be found within Europe will be even greater in the developing countries. The question which arises in these countries is to know whether policies for dealing with poverty are addressed above to all individuals with recognised personal rights or to families, lineages, or communities (see Chapter 2). Although the individualisation of benefits is difficult to imagine in societies where people are attached to units which are greater than their individual members and in which they do not always exist as autonomous persons, the priority targets for these types of policies must still be identified even if universal social cover cannot be provided in the immediate future. This question of the definition of the 'target populations' leads to another: that of the principles on which aid is to be based. Even if these relate both to general principles on the human rights and a universal idea of social protection, European countries, as we have seen, oscillate between the 'principle of need' and the 'principle of status' when it comes to a precise definition of aid for the needy. If the principle of need results from a unitary approach to the poor and a reference to individual rights, and the principle of status to a categorial approach, one might think that the second is likely to prevail in developing countries as a result of the weight of inequalities, hierarchies, and ethnic splits. In view of the urgency of the situation it is legitimate to clearly identify the most needy populations and to segment the benefits according to a statutory conception of the priorities and risks. But this approach risks leaving very poor people without help.

Finally, the question of resources, to which the European countries have not responded in an identical fashion, remains unanswered. Setting up a national policy for combating poverty means first identifying the resources to be attributed to the institutions and the staff in charge of them. Should we adopt a general system which allows institutions to apply the legislation to the letter at a risk of becoming very bureaucratic in the way they operate, or should we, on the contrary, facilitate the adaptation of the law to individual cases and local situations at a risk of rapidly developing forms of clientelism and the misappropriation of benefits? It is clear that recent pronouncements in developing countries on the forms of adaptation needed for local realities which respect the wish to remain close to the individuals themselves and to the legitimate commitment to listen to what that are saying, cannot really be conceived of without the existence of a formal institutional framework which is viable at national level. The danger awaiting many developing countries in attributing benefits to the most needy, is, as we know, that of clientelism both at state and local level.

The lessons to be learnt from European experiences do not in any case indicate a single system for dealing with poverty. Above all, they encourage us to seek answers in the developing countries to the four basic questions studied in this chapter, and in doing so to draw up the strategies best adapted to the particularities of each society, its history, its economy, and its culture.

Notes

1 For a presentation of the problems of international comparison in this sphere, see Schultheis and Bubeck (1996).
2 It would be tempting to identify Great Britain with this model, but the initial conception of the welfare state there does not correspond to it.
3 The English economist, B. Seebohm Rowntree, for example, made a great contribution at the beginning of the century towards steering research on poverty in this direction. The detailed study of the consumer budgets of poor households he conducted on the city of York in 1900 accompanied theoretical arguments on subsistence income and served, at least partially, as a basis for the elaboration of social policy on guaranteed income. The detailed results of each of these studies have been published in three books. See Rowntree (1902, 1941) and Rowntree and Lavers (1951).
4 We do not claim to define all aspects of social work here, but aim to limit ourselves to social intervention procedures in the field of access to rights.

5 The eight case studies concern Belgium, France, Germany, Great Britain, Italy, the Netherlands, Spain and the Scandinavian countries.

6 A draft bill on social cohesion was debated in the French National Assembly in April 1997, several days before its dissolution and the announcement of the early legislative elections. This project, which was subject to many amendments, was intended to satisfy the claims of the charitable associations. It was postponed and eventually voted in a year later in 1998.

7 Representations of poverty seem to conform to this statement. According to a recent poll, 50 per cent of Germans questioned considered that poverty no longer existed in their country, 30 per cent had no opinion, and only 20 per cent stated that it had not yet disappeared definitively (Schultheis 1996).

8 Out of 43 provinces in 1991, 11 had a percentage of poor families (calculated on the threshold of 50 per cent of the average annual family income) ranging from 30 to 41 per cent, whilst the national average was 19.4 per cent (Juarez 1994).

4 Urban poverty and recession in sub-Saharan Africa

Elements for an assessment

Mireille Razafindrakoto and François Roubaud

Sub-Saharan Africa is the region in which poverty is at once most acute and paradoxically at the same time least understood. This state of affairs can be explained to a large extent by the lack and/or doubtful quality of available data (see Chapter 11). For the most part, analyses of poverty based on statistical information are merely monographic and only very rarely take account of the temporal dimension. To go beyond merely anecdotal observations to obtain an overview of poverty in all its complexity it is necessary to produce an analysis of its evolution over time which takes into account the macroeconomic and social context of the country under consideration. We have therefore concentrated on African capitals in which the incidence of poverty has markedly progressed, and in which, concomitantly, a major restructuration of the socio-economic environment is taking place. On the basis of a certain number of factors derived from statistical data and illustrated by specific examples, we will attempt to draw up an inventory of the situation in the continent's major cities and evaluate the impact of the recessionary trend of national economies on their populations' living standards.

The first part of the study presents an overview of the situation, emphasising two major trends apparent in the countries of sub-Saharan Africa – prolonged recession and rapid urbanisation. The second part deals specifically with the evolution, extent, and characteristics of poverty in the urban context. The objective of the third part of the study is to attempt to understand the process which has reduced certain households to a state of complete destitution. Mechanisms at work in the African context following the economic recession will be explored. On the one hand, the effects of the deterioration of the labour market on the life of city dwellers will be explained, while on the other, the limits of individual and community strategies in the face of the magnitude of the shocks produced by the recession will be highlighted. Lastly, taking the example of Madagascar – which tends to confirm the influence of the macroeconomic context on the situation of urban households, despite the ingeniousness of their adaptation strategies – the question of a possible reversal of these trends, thanks to a recovery in growth, will be discussed.

Two major trends: prolonged recession and rapid urbanisation

Africa deprived of its inheritance

Since the wave of independence of the 1960s, sub-Saharan Africa's position *vis-à-vis* the rest of the world has been on a continual downwards curve. Unlike in other developing regions, per capita income has declined over the last 30 years. In constant 1987 dollar terms, it has dropped from $525 in 1970 to $336 in 1997; in other words, an average decrease of 36 per cent. During the same period, per capita income increased by 88 per cent in South Asia and by 355 per cent in East Asia. Even South America – where the 1980s were branded the 'Lost Decade', so severe was the crisis – enjoyed 55 per cent growth over the period (see Table 4.1). Of 30 African economies for which long-term figures are available, more than half have declined, and some have shrunk by more than 50 per cent.

Finding convincing long-term explanations for this phenomenon is not an easy task. At a time when the rest of the world economy is undergoing globalisation, Africa[1] is becoming sidelined. Most African countries still rely on a small number of primary commodities, and the fact that their economies are still characterised by limited diversification renders them extremely vulnerable (Berthélémy and Söderling 2001). Moreover, the unbridled growth of the population – in spite of the beginnings of a demographic transition – and the rapid degradation of the environment have effectively mortgaged the future. On the political and social front, the picture is almost as grim. Among 50 countries, there are no fewer than 14 armed conflicts, with their attendant loss of life, long-term injuries and refugees. After the enthusiasm engendered by the impressive wave of democratisation which began in the late 1980s, confidence is on the wane. Progress made has yet to be consolidated and the risk of destabilisation in various regions cannot be discounted. At the same time, the extent of corruption (with the dubious award for world's most corrupt country going to Cameroon in 1999, and Nigeria in 2000) highlights a generalised deficit of good governance and the failure of the state (Transparency International 2000).

While undeniable progress has been made in the fields of health and, particularly, education, Africa is still lagging behind. Around 250 million Africans do not have access to drinking water, and 200 million are deprived of basic healthcare. Once again, Africa is the only region in which nutrition has not improved – every year, nearly 2 million children die before reaching their first birthday. The terrifying effects of the Aids pandemic will surely be felt in the years to come, but its impact is still little understood. At the present time, Africa accounts for 70 per cent of the world's cases. Average life expectancy, which is presently just over 50 years, has already declined in southern Africa (the worst hit area), and some forecasts predict the appalling prospect of a drop in the figure of 20 years, a brutal collapse which would completely wipe out all the progress made since the 1950s.[2]

Evidently, these adverse economic conditions have had serious consequences in terms of poverty in Africa. Allowing for the scarcity of sources, it can be stated that, in 1998, nearly 50 per cent of Africans lived beneath the extreme poverty line, which corresponds to $1 per capita per day in purchasing power parity. It is estimated that, even if growth rates in the 1990s were relatively favourable compared to the preceding decade, the number of people in these circumstances increased from 240 million to 300 million in ten years (see Chapter 1). Consequently, nearly one in four of the world's poor is African, as compared to only 18 per cent in 1987. This is the result of a combination of poor economic performance and particularly high levels of inequality. Indeed, South America is the only region in which inequality is more pronounced.

The urban dynamics: cities suffer most

In this general context of recession, the very rapid development of cities in sub-Saharan Africa is one of the most important developments of the last 40 years. Urban growth was particularly marked between 1960 and 1975 (rising at an annual rate of 6 or 7 per cent). Since then, the rate has slowed considerably to between 4 and 5 per cent (ISTED 1998). More than the size of the urban population, which can still be considered moderate at the present time (at around 30 per cent in sub-Saharan Africa, as against 75 per cent in South America and 46 per cent in world terms), it is the speed of urban growth which gives cause for concern since it has not been accompanied by an equivalent economic dynamism. To take two precise examples: in West Africa, the number of people living in urban areas increased from 12 to 78 million between 1960 and 1990, with cities absorbing nearly two-thirds of total demographic growth (Snerch 1994). Today, the level of urbanisation is over 40 per cent, whereas in 1960 it was only 13 per cent. This substantial increase in the urban population is just as apparent in relatively 'rich' countries such as Nigeria and the Côte d'Ivoire – in which (in the same period) the urban population rose from 15 to 50 per cent – as it is in 'poor' countries such as Mauritania (9 to 42 per cent) and Chad (6 to 24 per cent).

The phenomenon is all the more worrying since sub-Saharan Africa is a unique case in world terms in that the region's rapid urbanisation has not been accompanied by economic growth (Hicks 1998). Between 1975 and 1998, the urban population increased at an annual rate of 5.2 per cent, while per capita GDP decreased almost continuously on average by 0.4 per cent per annum (see Figure 4.1).[3] While it is true that there was a reversal in the trend in 1995, this recent dynamic did little to compensate for the decline in per capita income, and seems, in any case, to have been

Table 4.1 Comparative performances of sub-Saharan Africa and other developing regions

	Sub-Saharan Africa			South Asia			East Asia			Latin America		
	1970	1997	%	1970	1997	%	1970	1997	%	1970	1997	%
Per capita GDP	525	326	−36	239	449	+88	157	715	+355	1,216	1,890	55
Per capita investment	80	73	−9	48	105	+118	37	252	+581	367	504	+37
Per capita exports	105	105	0	14	51	+264	23	199	+765	209	601	+188
	1987	1998	%*	1987	1998	%*	1987	1998	%*	1987	1998	%*
Poor people (%)	46.6	46.3	+34	44.9	40	+10	26.6	15.3	−33	15.3	15.6	+23

Sources: World Bank (2000a, 2000b). GDP, investment and exports are measured in 1987 US$. The poverty line corresponds to US$1.08 (1993) at PPP (purchasing power parity).

Note
*1987–98 increase/decrease in the number of inhabitants living in extreme poverty.

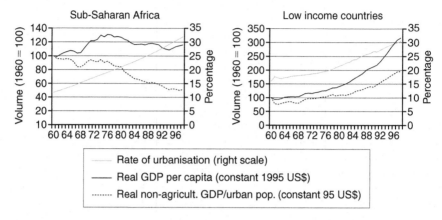

Figure 4.1 Evolution of the rate of urbanisation and per capita GDP.

Source: World Development Indicators, 2000, authors' calculations.

ephemeral. Improvements in macroeconomic management and structural reforms have encouraged recovery, but the upturn depended at least as much on exceptionally high world commodities prices between 1995 and 1997.

Non-agricultural GDP can be used to provide an overall idea of the development of economic activity in the urban context. The picture becomes yet bleaker for the cities of sub-Saharan Africa, in that the non-agricultural GDP divided by the urban population – which gives an approximation of per capita urban GDP – has decreased even more dramatically. Even though the latter was still 2.5 times higher than total per capita GDP for the region as a whole as late as 1998, it fell by 43 per cent between 1975 and 1998 (in other words, an average annual decrease of 2.4 per cent). The absence of economic growth in the urban context is thus wholly apparent.

In view of this recessionary trend, the future of cities in sub-Saharan Africa gives real cause for concern. The urban population is set to more than double by 2020. By that date, over 60 per cent of the region's population will live in cities. Taking into account the low living standards of city-dwellers and the limited development of urban infrastructures (see Table 4.2), the magnitude of the challenge to be met if cities are not to collapse into extreme poverty is clear for all to see.

The preceding analyses lead to an unambiguous conclusion: over the long term, Africa's poor economic performances have led to a fall in living standards and a growth in poverty of which city-dwellers have been the main victims. However, the reliability of the macroeconomic data used to measure the evolution of the real well-being of the population is open to question. First, due to the ongoing deterioration of national statistical

Table 4.2 Development indicators in various African cities

City	Country	Percentage of the urban population			% of households with access to electricity	% of households with access to running water	% of people employed in the informal sector
		1960	1980	1998			
Lagos	Nigeria	14	27	42	100	n/a	69
Abidjan	Côte d'Ivoire	19	35	45	73*	64*	65
Khartoum	Sudan	10	20	34	45	52	15
Lomé	Togo	10	23	32	51*	67*	n/a
Ouagadougou	Burkina Faso	5	9	17	41*	27*	60
Niamey	Niger	6	13	20	51*	33*	51
N'Djamena	Chad	7	19	23	9	17	38
Dakar	Senegal	32	36	46	80*	78*	n/a
Yaoundé	Cameroon	14	31	47	87*	16*	57*
Antananarivo	Madagascar	11	18	28	68*	16*	56*
Jakarta	Indonesia	15	22	39	99	n/a	33
Hanoi	Vietnam	15	19	20	100	n/a	n/a
Mumbai (Bombay)	India	18	23	28	90	55	68
Lima	Peru	46	65	72	76	70	49
Bogota	Colombia	48	64	73	99	99	54
Santiago	Chile	68	81	85	94	98	23

Sources: World Development Indicators, 2000 (for rates of urbanisation); UNCHS Urban Indicators program prototype database, World Bank (1998b).

Notes

* For access to water and electricity, DHS survey (Abidjan, 1994; Dakar, 1997; Lomé and Niamey, 1998; Ouagadougou, 1998; Ouagadougou, 1999) and 1-2-3 survey (Yaoundé, 1993; Antananarivo, 1999).

n/a = Data not available.

offices, official figures are to be viewed with caution. The international sources for Africa on which analyses are based are unreliable, incomplete, and often contradictory (Naudet 2000d). Second, living standards and, to an even greater degree, poverty, are difficult phenomena to quantify. For example, an indicator such as per capita GDP gives no more than a very vague approximation of the purchasing power of individual households. Faced with such limitations there is a great temptation to call into question the catastrophic vision evoked by official figures. The decline in living standards could merely be a product of the lamentable quality of national accounts.

However, by pooling over twenty surveys carried out over various periods in five African capitals (Abidjan, Bamako, Dakar, Antananarivo, and Yaoundé), the comparison of aggregated data from national accounts and the results of surveys on household consumption (two independent sources), widely confirm the conclusions described above (see Figure 4.2). On the one hand, in the five countries in question, and independently of their specific characteristics, the two kinds of sources converge. While they do not present exactly the same nuances, the trends point in the same direction; this is true not only for the long-term recession which lasted until the mid-1990s, but also for the subsequent recovery. On the other hand, it seems that the major cities (in this case, the capitals) have been by far the worst affected by the chronically poor economic conditions. Thus, a converging swathe of data confirms the hypothesis according to which living conditions in Africa, especially in the urban context, have declined dramatically.

One explanation for the less pronounced decline in the living standards of people in the country might be that the rural economy is less dependent on market fluctuations, largely due to the low rate of monetisation of agricultural activities and the very large proportion of food products consumed *in situ*. But in spite of this, average purchasing power is still systematically higher – and poverty less widespread – in the cities than in the country. A comparison of monetary poverty, based on data from surveys carried out in seven African countries shows that the incidence of poverty is twice as high in rural areas as in urban ones (Demery 1999), with a fairly high variations in ratio: from 1 to 1.2 in Nigeria in 1996, to 1 to 3 in Burkina Faso (1998), Uganda (1997), and Zimbabwe (1996). Sahn and Stiefel (2000) obtain figures even less favourable to rural areas based on non-income poverty indicators including quality of housing, possession of durable goods, and human capital in thirteen African countries.

Recession and poverty: case studies

The overall picture that has just emerged leaves no room for doubt about the catastrophic decline of the situation of households in African cities.

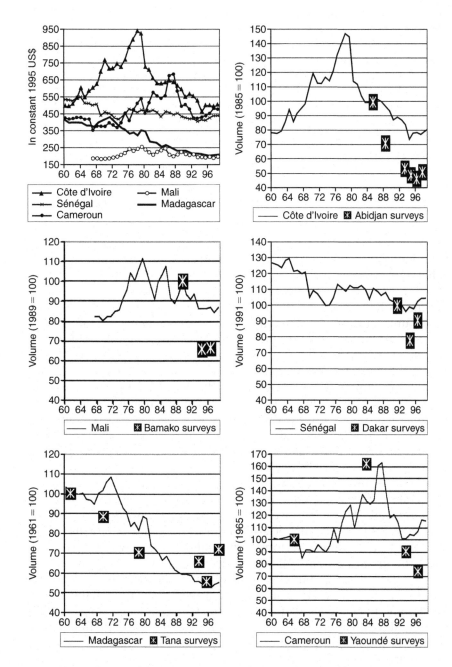

Figure 4.2 Evolution of per capita consumption.

Sources: World Development Indicators, 2000; various surveys on household consumption carried out in the capitals: DIAL (2000b) for Mali, Côte d'Ivoire, and Senegal; DIAL/DSCN for Cameroon; INSTAT/MADIO for Madagascar, our own calculations.

However, in order to present this assessment more clearly, and analyse the dynamic, the extent, and the characteristics of poverty, we will now concentrate on the specific cases of a number of capital cities. A first series of examples shows the marked increase of the incidence of poverty in three cities – Bamako, Abidjan, and Dakar (DIAL 2000b). The perspective is then widened to include all the capital cities of the West African Economic and Monetary Union (WAEMU) region. Lastly, the example of Madagascar – in which, according to the criteria employed, poverty appears in various guises and affects distinct groups – sheds light on the complexity and gravity of the phenomenon.

The dynamics of poverty in three capitals: Bamako, Abidjan and Dakar

Bamako

Over the last ten years, the capital of Mali, a country hemmed in by the Sahel and classified as a less-developed country (LDC) with one of the lowest human development levels in the world, has suffered a sharp decline in the living standards of its inhabitants. Characterised by a structurally unfavourable environment (notably a dependence on the climate and on fluctuations in cotton prices), the dramatic political, institutional and economic changes which have taken place in the country in a generally favourable context have not prevented an average annual fall in per capita consumption between 1989 and 1996 of around 1 per cent according to official figures. During the same period, the results of representative surveys carried out in the capital attest to a spectacular rise in income poverty (up from 33 per cent to 57 per cent in seven years), while the proportion of the city's inhabitants living in extreme poverty more than tripled (5 per cent to 16 per cent). This deterioration is solidly established and is not dependent on the criteria used.[4] It seems that Mali's encouraging macroeconomic performance since the devaluation of the CFA franc has had a positive, but limited impact on the situation of households. In fact, drivers of growth are to be found essentially in the agricultural and mining sectors (cotton and gold) and only indirectly affect the urban economy. While the decrease in the average income of households has had an influence on the rise in the incidence of poverty, this rise has been caused essentially by the worsening in inequality levels, which have, in fact, exploded. In 1989, the Gini coefficient stood at 0.27; by 1996, it had reached 0.38. Thus, two-thirds of the increase in extreme poverty in the Malian capital can be laid at the door of the increase in inequality.

Abidjan

With a population of 2.5 million, the capital of Côte d'Ivoire is one of the largest cities in Africa. Long considered a success story in the continent and classified as a middle-income country, Côte d'Ivoire enjoys one of the highest levels of development in sub-Saharan Africa. However, since the early 1980s the country's economy has been in long-term recession. Between 1980 and 1994 per capita GDP fell by 32 per cent to an estimated US$600. This assessment is corroborated by eight surveys on the living standards of Abidjan residents. The decline in per capita consumption over the period is calculated at 52 per cent, an annual average decrease of 5.5 per cent. The economic upturn observed since the devaluation of the CFA franc (an average annual increase of 1.5 per cent between 1995 and 1998), which gave rise to a certain amount of international enthusiasm concerning Côte d'Ivoire's economic prospects, is far from having effaced a decade of recession. Compared to official figures of negative annual growth of 2.6 per cent, it seems that the capital has been hardest hit by the crisis, with an average rate of decline in living standards twice that recorded for the country as a whole. The main causes of this situation are the contraction in public-sector employment, which accounted for 20 per cent of all jobs in 1985, but less than 7 per cent 13 years later (and this without the formal private sector having absorbed the difference), and the policy of cutting salaries. Moreover, as in Mali, the performance of cash crops, on which the Côte d'Ivoire economy is largely dependent, only marginally affects Abidjan, even if some of the income generated by them is recycled in the city. Evidently, the continuing decline in the overall purchasing power of households has been reflected by an upsurge in income poverty. Almost non-existent at the beginning of the period, the phenomenon affected nearly 40 per cent of Abidjan's inhabitants in 1995, only to retreat substantially (26 per cent in 1998). Extreme poverty reached a high point of 7.5 per cent in 1995. It should be stressed that if growth in the incidence of poverty is a solidly established fact up to 1995 (independently of any definition of the poverty line), any improvement after this date is statistically insignificant. The decomposition of the evolution of poverty between growth and inequality components, as in Bamako, brings opposite results (on a slightly different period): nearly all the increase in poverty between 1985 and 1998 can be laid at the door of the deterioration of average standards of living, whereas inequality remained relatively stable. However, it seems that periods of recession are linked to a rise in inequality, while periods of growth encourage its reduction. Thus, between 1985 and 1995, the Gini coefficient registered a sustained rise (from 0.34 to 0.44) (as in Bamako), before falling back to 0.38 in 1998.

Dakar

Senegal occupies an intermediary position between Mali and Côte d'Ivoire, with a per capita GDP of US$500 in 1998. The immense sprawl of the capital, Dakar, and its suburbs, which account for 2.1 million of the country's 10 million inhabitants and over half its urban population, as well as the majority of its modern activities and infrastructures, renders Senegal top heavy and unarticulated. Although the country is exposed to less dramatic variations than Côte d'Ivoire, its economic performance has been mediocre. In the last 30 years, the country has not enjoyed a single period of sustained growth, and at the end of the period per capita GDP was 7 per cent down on the 1970 level. As in all the other countries in the region, the devaluation of the CFA franc coincided with an upturn in the economy, but this upturn was nevertheless modest in the context of the long-term trend. Compared to other capitals, the period studied in the reports (1991–6) is shorter. In Dakar, as in the two other capitals considered above, living standards fell in the first half of the 1990s (by 22 per cent between 1991 and 1994), before rising after devaluation (by 17 per cent between 1994 and 1996). In total, per capita consumption in Dakar fell by almost 10 per cent between 1991 and 1996. The impact in terms of the incidence of poverty was great (46 per cent in 1991, 58 per cent in 1994 and 51 per cent in 1996), while extreme poverty doubled from 7 to 14 per cent. As in the case of the other cities, while a deterioration during the first pre-devaluation phase has been clearly established, the apparent improvement during the second phase is not robust. Since variations in inequality were small during the period as a whole (with a Gini coefficient of around 0.40), the increase in poverty levels can be explained, first and foremost, by a fall in income.

The magnitude of poverty in West African and Malagasy capitals

The examples provided above demonstrate that, in spite of relatively different contexts, none of the three capitals escape from the mechanism of deterioration of household living standards. While questions can be asked about the degree to which this assessment can be applied to other African cities, particularly as no comparable and reliable long-term time-series have been produced, the magnitude of the incidence of poverty is, nevertheless, irrefutable.

In the seven capitals of the WAEMU countries considered, and in Antananarivo, income poverty affects a large proportion of households (Figure 4.3). Even in Abidjan, one of the most highly developed cities in Africa, poor people account for over a quarter of the population. In four out of seven capitals, over half the inhabitants are affected by poverty, and in Ouagadougou (Burkina Faso) and Niamey (Niger) the figure is nearly two-thirds. If situations of extreme poverty corresponding to $1 a day in

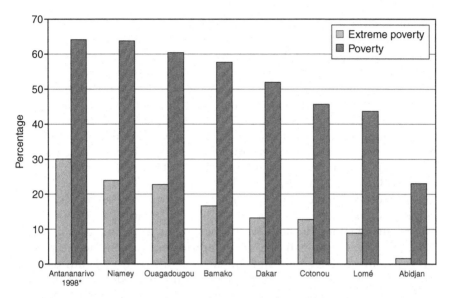

Figure 4.3 The incidence of poverty in eight African capitals in 1996*.

Source: Backiny-Yetna and Torelli (2001).

Note
The poverty line is defined $2 (1985 PPA) a day per capita. Extreme poverty is set at $1 a day.
* Data for Antananarivo refers to 1998.

purchasing power parity (PPP) – close to the minimum physiological sub-sistence level – are now considered, it is found that the incidence is by no means negligible, varying from 3 per cent in Abidjan to around 25 per cent in Niamey.

When an attempt is made to establish the profile of poor households, it becomes apparent that no section of the population is spared. House-holds directed by women are not always the worst off. While the probab-ility of becoming poor increases with the size of the household, the fact that small households are very much in the minority gives an idea of the difficulty of isolating a significant group of people totally safe from poverty. At the same time, while a tertiary education greatly reduces the risk of poverty it is by no means a guarantee against it. For example, in Bamako (Mali), over 30 per cent of households whose head has a univer-sity education are poor. Lastly, households whose head is a salaried worker in the public sector (public administration and enterprises) are more likely to escape poverty than others. However, they are far from being totally immune to it. Indeed, one household in two in this category in Niamey is affected by poverty. The ratio is one in three in Ouagadougou, Cotonou, Lomé and Bamako, and one in five in Abidjan and Dakar.

The many dimensions of poverty

The preceding analyses give some idea of the extent of poverty in African cities. However, the picture which has been painted provides no more than a partial image of the situation in that the assessment is entirely based on a monetary approach to the problem. Most studies undertaken in developing countries have this same weakness, even if the perspective is sometimes widened to include certain fundamental needs (health, education). Few studies have posed questions concerning the pertinence of this classical approach to isolating the poor part of the population and understanding its particularities. Nevertheless, the multidimensional nature of poverty is now universally recognised (World Bank 2000a). In the developed countries, a certain number of recent studies have used surveys to isolate other dimensions of poverty, based notably on scores for quality of life and more subjective measures of living standards (see Chapter 12). The results obtained, in both Western Europe and in countries in transition, show that, although analogies were made between these different facets of poverty, they were not sufficiently correlated and thus did not define the same categories of poor people. This methodology was applied for the first time in a developing country in a survey carried out in Antananarivo, the capital of Madagascar, in 1998.

Seven poverty indicators were developed, four of them based on objective criteria, and three on subjective ones. To verify the links between these different forms of poverty, the poverty line was defined in such a way as to consider as poor in all cases the least-well-off third of the population for each indicator, which corresponds to the incidence of monetary poverty derived from the internationally accepted figure of $1 a day per capita at purchasing power parity. The results are particularly interesting. While none of the seven groups of poor people defined above scored less than 32 per cent, only 2 per cent fell into all the categories (see Table 4.3). However, 78 per cent of the population falls into at least one category (Razafindrakoto and Roubaud 2000a).

The fact that the various categories of poverty do not overlap underlines the multidimensional nature of the phenomenon. First, this assessment belies the hypothesis according to which the approach chosen to measure poverty does not significantly alter the number of people defined as poor (Kanbur and Squire 1999). Second, it is clear that the weakness of the correlations made between various different dimensions of poverty acts as an encouragement to think more deeply about the nature and causes of the phenomenon – as well as the policies required to alleviate it – and to go beyond the purely monetary approach. Lastly, when figures derived from this methodology suggest that 80 per cent of the population is affected by at least one form of poverty – as opposed to 32 per cent in the monetary approach – questions about the real extent of the phenomenon have to be asked.

Table 4.3 Poverty: a multidimensional phenomenon

The various approaches to the problem of poverty	*% population*
Monetary poverty (consumption < 1$ a day per capita)	32.0
Non-monetary 'objective' poverty:	
in terms of living conditions (existential poverty)	35.0
in terms of human capital	32.6
in terms of social exclusion	34.6
'Subjective' poverty:	
General perception	33.0
Non-satisfaction of needs considered to be vital	34.5
Financial difficulties	33.9
Accumulating the various forms of poverty	2.4
Accumulating the four 'objective' forms of poverty	7.1
Accumulating the three non-monetary forms of 'objective' poverty	8.9
Accumulating the three forms of 'subjective' poverty	11.9
Presenting at least one form of poverty	77.7

Source: 1-2-3 MADIO Survey, Phase 3, Antananarivo, 1998, authors' calculations.

This situation is not specific to the capital of Madagascar. In fact, the lack of overlap between the approach concentrating on living conditions and the purely monetary approach can also be observed in Abidjan (Grimm, Guénard and Mesplé-Somps 2000). Using the two methodologies separately to identify two similarly sized groups of poor people, less than half of the households defined as poor in terms of living conditions were thus defined as such from the purely monetary point of view, and, reciprocally, only 44 per cent of households in the second group also figured in the first. These results support the idea that poverty can manifest itself in different forms which do not necessarily reflect household consumption levels. Furthermore, the extent of poverty seems even greater when its multidimensional nature is taken into account.

The mechanisms at work following the recession

This assessment of the extent of the incidence of poverty in African cities poses questions about the dynamic which led to the phenomenon. What are the mechanisms that caused the deterioration of living conditions in the urban context? How have households been affected, and who are the main victims? Have individual and community strategies been successful in limiting the effects of the fall in living standards? These questions are of central importance in understanding the evolution of poverty and isolating ways and means of significantly improving the situations of urban households in Africa.

The central role of the labour market dynamic

The evolution of standards of living and of poverty in African cities can be explained, primarily, by the dynamics of the labour market. In fact, in the countries in which the state is so weak that welfare (social security) and wealth redistribution (taxation, social spending) policies are either non-existent or badly targeted, households, particularly the poorest amongst them, are largely dependent on income deriving from jobs.

Contrary to an often-repeated idea, an adjustment has indeed taken place (and is still taking place) in urban labour markets in Africa. It is not, however, the kind of structural adjustment intended by present policies as a motor for renewed growth. Paradoxically, the adjustment observed is in fact characterised by effects entirely contrary to those expected. In particular, it has resulted in a growth in the number of people employed in sheltered, non-exchangeable goods sectors. During the last fifteen years, the labour market has undergone a marked upheaval, the principal characteristics of which are as follows: a freeze on recruitment in the public sector; an increase in the level of training of the labour force; a decrease in economic returns on tertiary education; a fall in real earnings and of per capita wages; a decrease in the proportion of salaried workers; the informalisation of labour; a rise in unemployment; and an increase in the women's labour force participation rates.

The perverse effects of public sector employment policy

Up until now, enterprises in the modern sector (both public and private), have adjusted principally through cutting the labour force, rather than by decreasing nominal wages. In private enterprises and the productive public sector, employees have been laid off, but substantial gains in productivity have not been made. However, it is probably in the public administration sector that recruitment policy has undergone the most dramatic changes. Even though, in effect, there have been no substantial cuts in the labour force (with the exception of Ghana, Guinea, and Benin), the freeze in recruitment has destroyed one of the central pillars of the previous system – the automatic link between tertiary education and employment in the public sector. In a context of very rapid demographic growth, this suspension of recruiting has automatically led to a dramatic fall in the percentage of jobs accounted for by the public sector. In Antananarivo (Madagascar), the figure declined from 26 per cent to 13 per cent between 1960 and 1995. In Abidjan, the phenomenon was even more brutal: over the ten-year period 1988–98, the figure decreased fourfold from 24 per cent to 7 per cent. Furthermore, salaries in the public sector are now, to a large extent, no longer index-linked and, in certain cases, have even actually fallen in nominal terms (like in Cameroon in 1993). All things considered, the purchasing power of public sector salaries has declined everywhere, in some cases by as much as 80 per cent.

Launched as a measure to right the unsustainable imbalance in public finances, the policy of massive cuts in the salaried labour force has had particularly negative repercussions. The fall in wages has affected productivity levels in the public sector. The ageing of the population pyramid resulting from the freeze in recruitment has, on the one hand, inhibited the expected upsurge in productivity, and, on the other, set in motion a process of exclusion of which young people have been the main victims. Civil servants – once the aristocracy of salaried workers and the spearhead of modernisation and development – have now been downgraded. Their accelerated pauperisation has been a part of the process involving the disappearance of a middle class created on the basis of academic meritocracy. A fairly large number of civil servants have joined the ranks of the urban poor.

A worrying increase in unemployment

The deterioration of the economic situation, sometimes aggravated by what appears to be a relative saturation of the informal sector, has caused an unprecedented growth in urban unemployment. Available data indicate an unemployment rate in African cities of around 20 per cent, a rate far higher than anything ever recorded in Latin America in the 1980s, even though the period was branded a 'lost decade' in the region (see Table 4.4). Contrary to the idea of 'luxury unemployment' proposed by Myrdal (1968) in the late 1960s relative to the Indian sub-continent, the absence of indemnification coupled with low income levels did not prevent a massive rise in the phenomenon. Moreover, while exclusion from the labour market affects all categories of the population, those with university qualifications are the hardest hit. Today, in Africa, degrees no longer guarantee jobs. This observation highlights a waste of human resources through a generalised underemployment of qualified labour, in spite of the relative rarity of this factor of production.

It nevertheless appears that, after a sharp rise in urban unemployment during the 1980s, the 1990s are characterised by a decline in the phenomenon, accompanied by a substantial increase in poverty and underemployment, both visible and invisible. For example, in Yaoundé, following a drastic 40 per cent cut in civil servants' wages and the devaluation of the CFA franc, the unemployment rate fell from 25 per cent to 18 per cent between February 1993 and May 1994. In Antananarivo, the rate of unemployment has not risen above 6 per cent during the second half of the 1990s. After a period of adaptation, the erosion of household purchasing power ended up taking its toll on support networks, as well as on the ambitions of those graduating from the education system, who are increasingly forced to work for low wages. Poverty is not so much the result of an

Table 4.4 Urban unemployment rates in Africa and Latin America (%)

	Latin America						Africa		
Country	1980	1984	1990	1995		Country	1980s	1990s
Argentina	2.3	3.8	7.5	18.6		Botswana (1984–5)	31.2	
Bolivia	7.5	13.3	7.3	4.6		Cameroon (1990–1)	29.3	24.6
Brazil	6.2	7.5	4.3	4.5		Côte d'Ivoire (1986)	20.0	12.5
Colombia	9.7	13.5	10.5	8.5		Guinea (1990–1)	19.0	
Costa Rica	6.0	7.9	5.4	4.3		Ethiopia (1981)	23.0	
Chile	11.7	18.5	6.5	5.7		Kenya (1986)	16.2	
Mexico	4.5	6.3	2.7	6.6		Madagascar (1989)	13.1	5.9
Panama	9.8	11.1	20.0	15.8		Mali (1989)	12.8	
Paraguay	4.1	7.4	6.6	4.8		Nigeria (1985)	9.7	
Peru	7.1	10.0	8.3	8.2		Senegal (1989)	18.6	
Uruguay	7.4	14.5	9.3	10.4		Sierra Leone (1988)	14.8	
Venezuela	6.6	14.0	10.5	10.3		Somalia (1982)	22.3	
						Tanzania (1984)	21.6	
						Zambia (1986)	10.0	
						Zimbabwe (1986–7)	18.3	
Average	6.9	10.7	8.2	8.5		Average	20.0	–
Median	6.8	10.5	7.4	8.4		Median	18.6	–

Sources: BIT, PREALC, various surveys.

Note

Averages and medians are not weighted.

absence of jobs, but of a sharp rise in the numbers of the salaried 'working poor' and, above all, of non-salaried workers.

A rapidly expanding informal sector

The freeze in recruiting in the public sector has not been accompanied by a marked rise in investment in the modern private sector. Thus, the stagnation in the demand for labour in the modern sector, and even, in certain cases, its decline, means that the informal sector plays an increasingly important role in the strategy of households looking for fresh sources of income. This phenomenon is all the more noteworthy in the urban context in that demographic pressure is still strong and the rural exodus is continuing, in spite of migration back to the country in certain nations. At the present time, the vast majority of jobs created in the cities can be characterised as casual subsistence-level labour. Thus, 85 per cent of jobs created in Yaoundé in 1993, and 60 per cent of those created in Antananarivo in 1994, were in the informal sector (Roubaud 1994a; Razafindrakoto and Roubaud 1999a). Moreover, the informal sector, which accounted for only 35 per cent of jobs in Yaoundé in 1983, was the source of employment for over half the labour force ten years later. In Antananarivo in 1995, informal sector jobs accounted for 58 per cent of the employment total.

The rapid informalisation of the entire productive system stems from two interlinking factors: a drift towards structurally more informal sectors and an informalisation of work within each individual sector. The lion's share of this intersector redeployment has gone to trade and services. It is in these low productivity sectors, which are ill-equipped to act as real drivers for economic growth, that most informal jobs are to be found (60 per cent in the case of Antananarivo; over 75 per cent in Yaoundé). Competition from cheap imported goods, mainly from Asia, smothers production activities and favours those linked to the distribution of commodities.[5] While it is clear that the informal sector plays a positive role as a shock absorber in periods of crisis, the growth in the number of informal units of production in a context of stagnation, or even reduction of opportunities, means that the jobs created are evermore precarious. The proportion of peripatetic and home-based activities is developing to the detriment of the localised informal sector. For the moment, the development of this sector is more closely linked to a logic of survival than to the emergence of alternative productive activities.

Lastly, deregulation and the flexibilisation of labour markets – due to pressure exerted by donor countries – have not been enough to create the conditions necessary for an economic recovery capable of creating high-quality employment. 'Less unemployment and more poverty', might be the phrase most apt to define the evolution of urban labour markets in Africa in the 1990s.

The difficult integration of young people or the risk of a rupture between generations

The negative trend of African economies, and, in particular, the deterioration of the labour market, has had a marked impact on youth employment conditions. Biographical surveys carried out in three African capitals (Dakar, Yaoundé and Antananarivo), allow for a precise assessment of the evolution of the situation from one generation to the next, and illustrate the constraints faced by young people today (Antoine, Razafindrakoto and Roubaud 2001; Antoine 2002).

In effect, by using three major events to define adulthood – first-time paid employment, residential autonomy, and the forming of a couple – it becomes apparent that the difficulties young people have in their integration manifest themselves primarily by the fact that their non-adult state is extended (see Table 4.5). On the one hand, the average age of joining the labour force is increasing. This phenomenon is particularly true of men in Dakar and Yaoundé. On the other hand, the delay in the forming of a couple – the second stage in the process of attaining adulthood – is very clear. Lastly, access to residential autonomy represents the area in which, taking into account the deterioration in economic conditions, all the difficulties endured by young people in the last generation are crystallised. This stage is reached increasingly later in life. The proportion of 25-year-olds who have left the parental home is decreasing everywhere. While various factors, including longer periods spent in education and various cultural changes, partially explain these phenomena, it cannot be denied that the economic crisis, by reducing the number of job opportunities and the level of income, exerts a major constraint on the ability of young people to become independent.

Second, the extension of their non-adult state does not enable the latest generation to enjoy better conditions of insertion into the job market than their forebears. In spite of a marked improvement in their education, young people are increasingly affected by unemployment and financial uncertainty. All the indicators agree on this point.

Table 4.5 Proportion of 'adults' at age 25 by city, sex and cohort (%)

	Dakar		Yaoundé		Antananarivo	
	Men	Women	Men	Women	Men	Women
Older generation	16	13	21	19	33	40
Intermediate generation	6	14	18	13	26	36
Younger generation	5	5	16	8	26	35

Sources: Biographical surveys, Antoine *et al.* (2001), authors' calculations.

Note
'Adults' are considered as those who are residentially autonomous, in paid employment, and who live as a couple.

Table 4.6 Insertion conditions at age 25 by city, sex and generation (%)

	Dakar		Yaoundé		Antananarivo	
	Men	*Women*	*Men*	*Women*	*Men*	*Women*
Unemployment						
Older generation	7	1	7	4	5	2
Intermediate generation	14	1	10	12	8	3
Younger generation	23	6	20	14	10	7
Informal employment						
Older generation	43	93	9	28	25	54
Intermediate generation	39	59	23	47	38	68
Younger generation	68	54	42	54	46	59

Sources: Biographical surveys, Antoine *et al.* (2001), authors' calculations.

Note

At age 25, of 100 young people in Dakar born between 1930 and 1944, seven were unemployed, and 43 per cent of those who worked are in the informal sector.

The unemployment rate for 25-year-olds is growing rapidly from one generation to the next (see Table 4.6). Even those who succeed in finding a place in the labour force do not escape from the deterioration in the situation. Less and less of them are gaining formal employment, and even fewer enjoying the benefits of public sector jobs, which offer the best conditions (salary, protection, etc.). The proportion of 25-year-old salaried employees in the informal sector has increased dramatically over the last 30 years. At the same time, the salary level for those entering the labour force fell over the long term, directly affecting youth poverty. In the case of Madagascar, in which it is possible to quantify their evolution precisely, comparative first job purchasing power fell by 75 per cent between the periods 1964–74 and 1989–97 (Antoine, Razafindrakoto and Roubaud 2001).

Third, to the extent to which the most highly educated of the younger generation have seen their conditions deteriorate most sharply compared to the previous generation, a downwards adjustment can be observed. This assessment runs contrary to the one in vogue in developed countries. Not only has the increase in the level of education of the most recent generation not produced a rise in its standard of living, but it is those with tertiary qualifications who have been hardest hit by the unfavourable economic conditions. The probability of being unemployed at age 25 has increased more sharply amongst this group than amongst the less qualified. While the hypothesis of a kind of 'luxury unemployment' resulting from a gap between the ideal professional requirements of young people and the reality of the labour market is not to be dismissed, it only partially explains the phenomenon. In effect, the quality of employment accepted by young degree holders has declined even more sharply than for those without university qualifications. The proportion of informal and unsalaried jobs is increasing everywhere, but, generally speaking, the phenomenon is most marked amongst those with university qualifications.

The powerlessness of households

In view of the substantial and, above all, continual deterioration in living conditions, questions can be legitimately asked about the strategies adopted by households to alleviate hardship. Households have two potential options: first, finding some alternative sources of income; second, changing their consumption habits and optimising their spending. As studies in Yaoundé (Roubaud 1994a) and Antananarivo (Ravelosoa and Roubaud 1998) have shown, both strategies have been employed.

The impressive growth in the women's labour force participation rate

During periods of crisis, especially a chronic crisis such as this one, households are obliged to choose which of their members will work. Faced with the decline in income from paid work, households are led to restructure their 'productive composition' in order to guarantee the reproduction of the domestic unit. The activity rates are a good indicator of the mobilisation of the household labour force. In Madagascar, over a period of 35 years, the percentage of economically active people in the capital leapt from 41 per cent (1960) to 60 per cent (1995). This was a massive and continuous phenomenon which could be observed in all age groups. In Yaoundé, over a shorter period (1983–93), during which the fall in living conditions was comparable (around 50 per cent), the labour force increased by 10 points.[6] In fact, a more detailed analysis shows that the increase in size of the labour force can essentially be explained by the rise in the rate of economically active women (see Figure 4.4). While the percentage of economically active people in Antananarivo has remained constant since the independence of Madagascar (69 per cent in both 1960 and 1995), the proportion of women in work rose from 15 per cent to 53 per cent. In Yaoundé, the percentage of working women almost doubled between 1983 (23 per cent) and 1993 (41 per cent).

It is, of course, not possible to attribute the increase in the number of economically active people, especially women, entirely to the recession. In effect, the rise in the number of people going through school, which renders entry into the job market increasingly natural, also encourages this change from a cultural point of view. But the mobilisation of labour reserves – including children – in households during times of crisis is a preponderant factor.

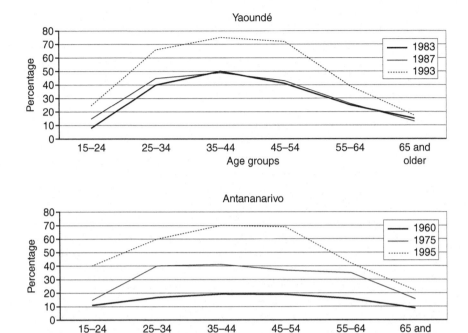

Figure 4.4 Long-term increase in the percentage of economically active women.
Sources: Roubaud (1994a), Ravelosoa and Roubaud (1998).

The limits of compensation strategies: multiple jobholding, private transfers, migration

Multiple jobholding is one approach to palliating the nefarious effects of low and/or falling wages derived from one's principal job. While, due to a lack of retrospective data, it is not possible to quantify the evolution of the phenomenon over time, its magnitude is much more limited than has long been thought. In both capitals, under 10 per cent of the active population held down more than one job at a time. Even civil servants, often stigmatised for their lack of assiduity in the workplace, are little affected (6 per cent in Yaoundé and 13 per cent in Antananarivo). In fact, there are few opportunities for secondary employment, which is hardly surprising in that a large proportion of those working in the informal sector are in a situation of invisible unemployment, and thus obliged to work as many hours as possible in order to increase income.

Another strategy available to households who find themselves in a critical situation is to mobilise inter-household support networks to exploit resources above and beyond job income. Some authors have underlined the importance of these inter-household transfers as a mode of socio-economic regulation in Africa (Mahieu 1990). In particular, it has been suggested that it is thanks to this generalised system of income and economic rents redistribution that the continent has managed to avoid several serious social crises which might ordinarily have been engendered by such long periods of recession. Nevertheless, our data shows that the weight of these inter-household transfers is marginal: thus, even if one were, in the absence of data on the past, to accept the not necessarily legitimate hypothesis according to which the practice of transfers developed as a result of the crisis, they cannot have played the cushioning effect suggested by the above-mentioned authors. While it is true that in 1993 90 per cent of the households in Yaoundé were either donors or recipients of transfers, the phenomenon is far from being generalised. For example, in Antananarivo, less than 50 per cent of households are involved in redistribution networks. Furthermore, the average net transfer is extremely small. In the capital of Madagascar, for example, it represents under 1 per cent of income generated by the primary activity, and practically nothing in the case of the poorest households.[7] And the mobilisation of familial and ethnic support networks has done no more than transfers in money or in kind to palliate shortfalls in income. In fact, it has had a contrary effect. In Yaoundé, for example, the level of 'communitarian pressure', which measures the average number of people not belonging to the nuclear family who are nevertheless taken in charge by the household (the practice of *confiage*, or 'placing' a family member with another family) diminished between 1983 and 1993. The decrease is even more marked for households at the top of the social pyramid (salaried workers, civil servants), rendering apparent more 'individualistic' defence strategies amongst the better off.

Lastly, migration is another possible strategy. However, opportunities remain limited. On the one hand, since rural areas have also been hit by the recession and still find themselves in a worse situation than cities, the rate of return migration is very low. On the other, the rate of international emigration has been partially slowed by the stricter entry conditions imposed by target countries (both within the region – for example, Côte d'Ivoire – and in Europe, for long-term migration).

Changes in consumption habits: narrow margins for manoeuvre

At the same time, households have attempted to modify their consumption habits and develop new purchasing strategies to cushion the impact of the fall in income. But here as well, their margin for manoeuvre is limited. Generally speaking, households have reacted to the decline in living standards by falling back on products of primary necessity and on the least expensive high calorie food products. In Antananarivo, the proportion of the household budget spent on food increased from 38 to 50 per cent between 1960 and 1995. In Yaoundé, per capita consumption was halved, while spending on food declined by 'only' 30 per cent. Diet is deteriorating everywhere, both in terms of quantity and quality. The most affected foodstuffs are meat and fish, dairy products, and fruit and green vegetables, while farinaceous and starch-based products are becoming predominant. However, even though these last are becoming increasingly important, households are, in spite of everything, obliged to reduce their consumption. For example, on average, inhabitants of Antananarivo consumed only 107 kg of rice per annum in 1995, as against 135 kg in 1960 (a fall of 20 per cent). During the same period, meat consumption collapsed (from 19 kg to 8 kg for beef, and from 9 kg to 2 kg for pork). Calorie intake provided by the six main food groups fell by 30 per cent and for many households the alimentary situation has reached a critical stage.

Furthermore, households are buying an increasing proportion of their provisions in the informal sector. But while this enables them to buy products at lower prices, the quality of these products is often poor. However, such is the generalisation of the role of the informal sector in households' food-buying practices that the phenomenon seems to have reached its peak. In the mid-1990s, three-quarters of the total consumption of Antananarivo's inhabitants derived from the informal sector. In terms of food consumption, the figure is 95 per cent. In spite of its much higher level of development, these percentages were of a similar order in Yaoundé (71 per cent and 93 per cent respectively).

In many countries, populations, particularly urban ones, were not content merely to react individually to what might appear to be a succession of bad economic policy decisions. In Madagascar, for example, people sanctioned their inadequate leaders through relatively peaceful political protest movements (in 1972, 1991, 1996 and 2002). More generally, the wave of democratisation witnessed throughout the continent can be interpreted as a more or less organised reaction on the part of citizens to the deterioration in their living conditions. But this political upheaval, which is perhaps still too recent and too fragile, has not significantly reversed economic trends in African countries. Lastly, households have not remained passive in the face of the difficult long-term economic conditions. They have employed every imaginable strategy at their disposition, but their ingeniousness has been to no avail when confronted by macro-economic shocks of such magnitude. Households have thus borne the brunt of the recession, and individual, familial and community strategies to counter the effects of chronically poor economic conditions have, ultimately, been derisory.

Causes for optimism: the Malagasy example

This overview of the powerlessness of households in the face of the inexorable deterioration of the economic situation leaves little room for

Table 4.7 Evolution of monetary poverty in the Antananarivo agglomeration, 1995–2001

	1995	*1996*	*1997*	*1998*	*1999*	*2000*	*2001*
Incidence of poverty (% of individuals)	39.1	35.6	28.2	28.4	27.2	18.9	19.4
Incidence of poverty (% of households)	34.9	32.4	24.3	25.4	24.0	16.3	17.1
Poverty line (in 1,000 FMG per month)	28.6	38.7	41.1	44.4	47.1	52.8	55.8
IPC (survey period: 1-2-3 Phase 1)	100.0	135.8	144.2	153.2	163.0	185.0	195.3

Sources: Employment surveys, 1995–2001; MADIO; authors' calculations.

Notes
Rates have been calculated on the basis of household income per member. The poverty line has been calculated on the basis of the consumption survey (Phase 3 of the 1-2-3 survey) in applying the 1985 $1 (PPP) per capita. This poverty line has been readjusted each year for the 1996–2001 period, taking inflation into account.

optimism concerning the future of African cities. Nevertheless, the example provided by the capital of Madagascar during the second half of the 1990s gives some cause for optimism. After a long period of stagnation-recession which produced a chronic downturn in household living standards, Madagascar has, since 1997, posted an unprecedented series of positive economic figures. The average annual growth of the GDP was between 4 and 5 per cent from 1997 to 2000 (which means an increase in GDP per capita of around 1.5 per cent per year). According to reliable microeconomic data for the five-year period 1995–9, these positive macroeconomic dynamics have had a favourable impact on living conditions of households in the Antananarivo agglomeration (Razafindrakoto and Roubaud 1999a). Substantial rises in purchasing power and an increase of 38 per cent in average income have been recorded during the period. The unemployment rate decreased by almost 1 point from 6.8 to 5.9 per cent between 1996 and 1999. Underemployment, which is still the major problem, is declining substantially.

At the same time, tensions in the labour market have been assuaged. The global rate of underemployment,[8] which affected 60 per cent of the active population in 1995, concerned 'only' 48 per cent in 1999. The decline in the number of family members 'forced' to work – which has been accompanied by a sharp reduction in the children's labour force participation rate (the figure for 10- to 14-year-olds fell from 13 per cent of children at work in 1995 to 5 per cent in 1999) – represents a positive result and has produced a concomitant rise in the number of children going to school (84 per cent in 1995 and 91 per cent in 1999). Lastly, in the same period, the incidence of poverty declined by over 10 points, falling from 39 to 27 per cent in terms of the number of individuals affected. It reached a new low in 2001 (19 per cent), with a fall of nearly 20 points between 1995 and 2001 (see Table 4.7).

This positive trend was originally triggered by the stabilisation of the rate of inflation and a wage increase (an increase in salaries in the public sector and of the minimum wage in the formal private sector). These macroeconomic phenomena sparked renewed vigour in the formal private sector, particularly in terms of the creation of jobs in the export processing zone. A virtuous circle came into being, the main consequences of which were an end to the process of informalisation of the labour market, and an increase in income levels in the formal and informal sectors due to a growth in demand. Even if the richest households seem to have benefited the most, every category of the population has gained something from the recovery.

The positive impact of the rapid upturn in the labour market on living conditions in the Malagasy capital during the second half of the 1990s gives a glimpse of a possible strategy for reversing present poverty trends in African cities. At any event, putting such a strategy into action is not as simple as might be imagined. Indeed, the recovery observed in Madagascar remains fragile (as the political crisis which occurred in 2002 showed). The recovery needs to be consolidated. In order to create a sustainable virtuous circle of real income growth, an increase in work productivity is vital. Gains in productivity, however, can only be achieved in an environment which is encouraging, or at least favourable, to both enterprises and salaried workers. And it will also be necessary to develop an adequate support policy to favour an egalitarian redistribution of the fruits of growth.

Conclusion

The preceding analysis has a certain number of implications in terms of economic policy. It appears that the fight against poverty in Africa should be waged on two fronts: in rural areas, obviously, where the incidence of poverty is highest, but also in the urban context. On the one hand, poverty levels are still very high, superior, indeed, to those registered in other developing regions. On the other, by 2025, over 50 per cent of Africans will be living in cities. If this evolution is not anticipated by developing a strategy to deal with the rapid growth of cities, the population of poor people in urban Africa might well explode. Lastly, the criteria of realism, efficiency, and the indirect effects of government policy all plead in favour of targeted interventions to combat urban poverty.

Taking into account the extremely low density of the rural population, the isolation of villages, and the massive shortcomings in public infrastructure, the reduction of poverty levels in the country can only be a very long-term undertaking. In the short term, the financial resources required to reduce rural poverty substantially – whether derived from national savings or international aid – are far beyond the reach of government budgets. Nevertheless, actions undertaken in the cities could have a much more rapid and efficient impact. By its very nature, the cost-effectiveness of a given programme (building a school or basic health centre, mending a road) is lower in urban areas because of concentration in demand. Furthermore, it is easier to create synergies between different aid projects in the urban context. For example, for the building of a primary school to produce an increase in the rate of student enrolment, a certain number of conditions – including transport infrastructure and market opportunities to exploit the investment in human capital – have to be in place. Evidently, these kinds of problems are easier to solve in the urban context.

A rise in the urban growth rate is a prerequisite. On the one hand, cities are places in which knowledge and skills are more easily expressed (exchanges of ideas, private initiative opportunities, etc.). On the other, the creation of dynamic urban markets generates solvent demand, especially in food products, which can be satisfied by rural areas. Lastly, high levels of migration to the cities increase the strength of the ties between the two sectors, reducing both land access pressures and the deterioration of the environment, and favouring an increase in agricultural productivity. The knock-on effects of urban growth on rural areas represent a major factor in the reduction of rural poverty. The challenge facing African countries is therefore not to keep people in rural areas, but to find a way to transform urban growth into a factor which encourages economic and social dynamism, as it is in most of the world's other regions.

Our analysis demonstrates that the future of households is intimately tied to reigning economic conditions. For as long as households can only sit back and endure the negative impact of a recession, any improvement in standards of living will depend largely on developments at the macroeconomic level. But while growth is an imperative, there is no miracle cure. In most countries, neither liberalisation, nor the opening up of trade, nor decentralisation, has created the proper conditions for a real reversal in the recessionary trends of the past. Moreover, growth is not enough. It must be accompanied by ambitious redistribution policies aimed at the poorest and at combating the rise in inequality. In order to meet these challenges, the reconstruction of the state, to which too little attention has been paid up until now, is an absolute priority (Englebert 2000). Its shortcomings have, in effect, largely contributed to the continual deterioration of the economic situation in African cities. Without being a panacea, the twin phenomena of democratisation and decentralisation open new horizons in terms of 'urban governance'. At the same time, since national savings capacity is insufficient in the immense majority of countries in the continent, a reversal in the downward trend in official development assistance is vital.

Notes

1 Throughout this chapter 'Africa' means 'sub-Saharan Africa'.

2 Life expectancy at birth has already declined in 12 of the 34 African countries in which censuses were conducted between 1980 and 1997 (Demery 1999).

3 The data on GDP per capita used here and in Figure 4.1 are not consistent with the ones in Table 4.1 because of different base-years for the volume/price decomposition.

4 The pauperisation of the inhabitants of Bamako is also corroborated by a deterioration in anthropometric indicators for child nutrition revealed in Demographic and Health Surveys carried out in 1987 and 1995–6. For example, while 10 per cent of children under 3 years old were affected by an acute form of emaciation in 1987, the figure had jumped to 28 per cent ten years later.

5 The best example of the perverse effect of the opening of economic borders is the clothing trade. Today, the stiffest competition for informal sector workers comes from the informal traders themselves, who are swamping the market with second-hand clothes imported from abroad.

6 This growth is all the more remarkable in that two structural factors exert downward pressure on the number of people who are economically active: on the one hand, the relative increase in the proportion of young people (15- to 24-year-olds) in the total population, this age group having lower labour force participation rates; and, on the other, the rise in school enrolment rates and the increase in the amount of time spent in education, which would normally have the effect of postponing entry into the workforce.

7 Furthermore, in Madagascar, transfers have a negative effect on redistribution. They are of most benefit to the most well-off households, who are the only ones able to send their members abroad. In 1995, the amount of total net transfers received (essentially from abroad) by the wealthiest 25 per cent of households in the capital (fourth quartile) was 40 times higher than that received by the poorest 25 per cent (first quartile).

8 The global underemployment indicator includes three forms of underemployment: (a) visible, comprising those who work less than 35 hours per week but who would like to work longer; (b) invisible, comprising those whose hourly wage is particularly low; and (c) the unemployed.

5 Do they really think differently?

The voice of the poor through quantitative surveys

Mireille Razafindrakoto and François Roubaud

For designing poverty reduction strategies the approach of collecting opinions from the various groups which make up a society, notably the poor, and involving them in a participatory process, is now promoted. The objective of this new approach is to enhance the ability of poor people effectively to influence public decisions affecting their lives. This chapter subscribes to this idea of giving opportunities to the poor, allowing them to express their opinion ('voice') and to participate in the decision-making process. By analysing data about people's views, collected from qualitative modules combined with representative household surveys, it presents and explores an original instrument, whose potential is as yet very largely underexploited in developing countries, for providing the poor with a 'voice' and studying poverty. It points the way to a very wide range of applications with a much more general scope. The wave of transitions to democracy throughout the world, and especially in sub-Saharan Africa, has made wider use of opinion polls as a source of information and a guide to policy orientations, alongside the traditional statistical tools used for economic analysis, both possible and necessary.

Paradoxically, the new democracies of the 'South' have as yet not fully exploited this extraordinary opportunity. Their slowness in doing so, which is extremely relative when one considers how new the democratic process is in these countries, can be explained on the one hand by the lack of financial and human resources, and, on the other, by the '*économiciste*' bias of the official statistical systems of information. The measurement of 'hard' economic variables such as growth, inflation and unemployment has always been their chief focus at the expense of qualitative, socio-economic or subjective indicators like electoral choices, preferences, opinions and values. However, even within the World Bank, this slant is beginning to be questioned, which is confirmed by the multiplication of studies on 'quality of growth' (World Bank 2000b) showing that the economic path of developing countries depends as much on what were formerly thought of as extra-economic factors (democracy, good governance, appropriation, etc.). A whole series of new databases (with indices of perceived corruption, civil and political freedom, ethnic and linguistic fragmentation, and so on) and a generation of new-style house-hold surveys, like CWIQ surveys launched by the World Bank (1999), are now being used (see Chapter 11).

Our aim in this study is to try to find out whether the specific objective characteristics and behaviour of the poor are linked to attitudes, opinions and values which distinguish them from the rest of the population. It should first be noted that the relationship of causality between the state of being poor and a given value-system is complex. The state of poverty, with its accompanying deprivations, sufferings and feelings of exclusion, can lead its victims to make requests, formulate demands or adopt a set of values as a direct consequence of their circumstances. Alternatively, it is possible that it is precisely these values and attitudes which have caused the poverty in the first place and that maintain the victims in a state of poverty. This chapter does not attempt to disentangle these connections, which are probably very closely intertwined; more modestly, it sets out to identify the views of the poor on a number of key issues which may have implications for the fight against poverty, to compare these views with those of other social groups and to draw attention to the attitudes which underpin them.

The first part of this chapter will deal with methodological considerations. We shall begin with a brief presentation of the methods traditionally used to record the 'voice of the poor' in developing countries, and the results obtained by these methods, before offering an alternative approach which makes use of representative statistical surveys. We shall then attempt to weigh up the advantages and disadvantages of each of these approaches. In the second and the third part of this chapter, drawing on an exceptionally rich corpus of household surveys carried out in Antananarivo, the capital of Madagascar, between 1995 and 2000, we shall go on to test out this original method of acquiring insights into the attitudes of the poor.[1] We shall make use of the data at our disposal, which comprise both objective quantitative information and qualitative perceptions, to study the opinions expressed by the poor on a number of topics. First, we look at the views of the poor on the main economic reforms implemented in the context of structural adjustment, before going on to examine wider ideological choices as to how society should be regulated (market economy, democracy).

Why and how to 'listen to' the poor

Qualitative participatory methods: a new approach

The approach using qualitative participatory methods, known under the general heading of PPA ('Participatory Poverty Assessment'), has evolved since the mid-1990s. The main objective of this new approach is to take into account the opinions of the various stakeholders, and especially the views of the poor. This approach is based on two underlying principles: on the one hand, the recognition that the poor are experts on poverty and are therefore in a better position than anyone else to say what poverty is, and to identify its causes and the means of extricating people from poverty; and on the other, recognition that poverty is a multidimensional phenomenon, many aspects of which are difficult to glean from traditional quantitative surveys, and that it cannot be reduced to the prevailing concept of poverty based solely on financial criteria. In general, approaches which lay the emphasis on participation aim to go beyond mere information gathering. They attempt to associate various stakeholders, and in particular representatives of the poor, with the process of monitoring the policies implemented.

PPA schemes have been set up in many countries (approximately sixty), largely at the instigation of the World Bank. They are based on surveys in the social anthropological tradition, which use a variety of techniques such as open or semi-structured one-to-one or group interviews, visual methods such as maps and diagrams, and participatory observations. They are part of a vast programme of consultation entitled 'Consultations with the Poor' intended to allow the 'voices of the poor' to be heard (Narayan, Patel *et al.* 2000; Narayan, Chambers *et al.* 2000). The aim is to collect their opinions in four main thematic areas:

- their perception of poverty (how they define poverty, what they see as its causes, and the difficulties experienced by the poor);
- what they see as the chief political problems and their political priorities;
- their experience of various institutions (local and outside their community);
- the issue of gender inequality within households and in the community.

Principal successes and limitations of Participatory Poverty Assessments

The principal successes of PPAs are mainly of two kinds. First, this approach has deepened our understanding of poverty, drawing attention in particular to the fact that poverty is a multidimensional phenomenon. In addition to familiar dimensions such as income levels, consumption and access to education and health, these assessments reveal other aspects such as vulnerability, insecurity, exclusion and the inability of the poor to influence the social and economic factors which determine their standard of living ('powerlessness'), as well as loss of dignity and self-respect. Second, they provide a broader and more solid basis for political reform. Participatory methods have set up a process of dialogue, and the fact that they involve a wider range of participants increases 'ownership'.

However, this approach has several limitations. To start with, the information gathered is too descriptive to be of much use in decision-making. Those in power usually prefer to make use of quantitative data when formulating policy, and in the case of PPA not only do perceptions vary and underline conflicts of interest but it is also doubtful to what extent the opinions expressed by interviewees are representative of the poor as a whole (the 'voiceless'). In addition, the direct consequences of participatory assessment may be limited, especially in the short term. Participants have extremely high hopes of these methods, seeing the time they give as an investment. Disappointment when these hopes turn out to have been unrealistic could rapidly lead to the population losing interest in such assessments and undermining the longevity of the participatory process. Finally, we should point out the fact that, usually, participatory approaches are not interested in monitoring and evaluating implemented reforms.

Qualitative thematic modules combined with statistical surveys: an alternative approach

PPA, which has resulted in 'the voices of the poor' being recorded by means of qualitative participatory methods, has clearly added to the body of knowledge about poverty (perceptions of poverty, its causes and the difficulties experienced by the poor). But the question now is how far this approach can be taken. It does not address two main issues: first, the representativeness of participants; second, the translation of the findings into information which can be used in drawing up concrete national measures, especially when the findings underline conflicts of interest.

An alternative or complementary approach can be suggested, which should soothe any qualms as to whether the opinions recorded are representative or not, thus solving the problem of having to choose between opposing arguments. In this approach, modules in the form of opinion polls, which highlight different topics from one year to another, are combined with conventional periodic quantitative surveys (which should preferably not be too detailed). The qualitative questions asked in participatory methods are standardised in these modules. The population, including the poor, are asked questions about their perceptions of poverty (definition of poverty and identification of causes), their needs and difficulties, and which policies would best satisfy their needs and wants (see Box 5.1).

Specific qualitative modules focusing on the cultural, social and political environments of households can also be added on to such surveys. It is ironical that very little information on these subjects is available in developing countries, especially in Africa, despite the fact that many analysts stress that the social, cultural and political contexts are determining factors in the organisation of African societies.

This approach has the advantage of simultaneously collecting objective data on the circumstances of households or individuals from the quantitative section of the survey (income levels, expenditure, housing conditions, and so on) and subjective qualitative data on the perceptions and attitudes of respondents (levels of satisfaction with living conditions, difficulties and needs, and opinions on policies and how well institutions function). Despite their qualitative nature, these data can be quantified because the percentage of the population that holds a particular view can be measured. Moreover, the opinions recorded can be analysed according to the characteristics of respondents. Lastly, they enable the opinions and the behaviours of the poor to be compared with those of the rest of the population when the survey is coupled with a traditional system assessing the living conditions of all households.

At a time when the concept of 'empowerment' has become integral to public policies, social-political surveys help provide a window onto the attitudes of social groups which have traditionally been excluded from decision-making processes, and thus increase their bargaining power. This contribution is especially vital in the poorest countries, where the bridging institutions of civil society are underdeveloped, and surveys are the only route by which the opinions of the underclass or 'voiceless' can reach the authorities (see Table 5.1).

Box 5.1 The 'voice of the poor' in the MADIO[2] surveys in Madagascar

The approach of adding qualitative modules to representative household surveys has already been applied in the capital of Madagascar via the periodic surveys 1-2-3 conducted under the auspices of the MADIO project in the years 1995 to 2000 (see Chapter 13). Generally speaking, these surveys were of a sufficiently flexible design to accommodate the objective of monitoring all aspects of poverty (DIAL 2000c). A number of thematic areas, which were varied from year to year, were dealt with in the specific modules added to one of the three phases of the survey 1-2-3:

- the inhabitants of Antananarivo and economic policy (phase 3, expenditure survey, 1995)
- education policy and structural adjustment (phase 1, employment survey, 1996)
- elections, political parties, ethnic groups and religion (phase 1, employment survey, 1997)
- administrative reform, privatisations and corruption (phase 1, employment survey, 1998)
- poverty via subjective assessment by households (phase 3, expenditure survey, 1998)
- saving patterns and use of bank accounts (phase 3, expenditure survey, 1998)
- unitary tax and land tax (phase 1, employment survey, 1999)
- changes in the economic situation (phase 1, employment survey, 1999)
- poverty, violence and exclusion (phase 1, employment survey, 2000).

Table 5.1 Comparison of the two methods: participatory vs. qualitative assessment combined with quantitative surveys

	Participatory methods (PPA)	Qualitative modules combined with traditional quantitative surveys
Method	An assortment of tools	Standard method
Main instrument	Semi-structured interview	Standardised questionnaire
Cost	Low or relatively low (depending on aims and geographical spread)	Relatively low or high, but very low marginal cost if quantitative survey already envisaged
Form of participation	Active participation through open discussions and analysis of situations	Opinion poll of population survey as sounding-board for the opinions of the excluded
Sample	Small or medium-sized centring on the poor but not really representative	Broad representative sample of all social groups
Type of information gathered	Qualitative and descriptive information (difficult to quantify)	Quantitative and qualitative information, can be quantified (offers possibility of detailed statistical analysis)
Findings	Detailed knowledge of the circumstances and attitudes of the poor	Better overview of the circumstances of the poor (compared to others); priorities and attitudes classified by their relative importance to the population
Principal limitations	Produces varied data on circumstances and attitudes; information difficult to use in decision-making	Predetermined questions; need for prior knowledge of the circumstances of the poor to avoid top-down practices and the risk of omitting important questions or factors

Clearly, some reservations might be voiced regarding opinion polls, such as the danger of imposing opinions on respondents, their artificial structure or even the manipulation of public opinion, etc. (as documented by Bourdieu 1980; Champagne 1990; Meynaud and Duclos 1996). But all in all, such reservations concern unscrupulous use of findings (naive and simplistic interpretations, tendentious conclusions or exploitation for commercial purposes) rather than their intrinsic legitimacy as a tool for gathering scientific information. Provided the requisite technical and ethical precautions are exercised in using opinion polls, as they would be in any other serious academic research, they can make a vital and irreplaceable contribution to the body of knowledge and the smooth running of democratic societies.[3] The fact that opinion polls are systematically forbidden by totalitarian regimes suggests that they are a by-product of democracy (Blondiaux 1998; Cayrol 2000).

The views of the poor on economic reform

For over a decade Madagascar has been engaged in a process of sweeping and profound economic and political reform. Of the various programmes of reform currently under way, we shall use the examples of three major strands of public policy which are central to the government's present strategy: reform of public services, privatisation of public or semi-public enterprises, and education policy. Although our choice of examples is partly governed by the availability of specific surveys on these reforms, it is justified by the influence these issues may have on the way society functions as a whole and on the living conditions of the poor.

The reform of public services

The inhabitants of Antananarivo are uncompromising in their assessment of public services. Less than 15 per cent think they are efficient, slightly under half give them the benefit of the doubt, and 36 per cent think they are inefficient. A direct consequence of this poor opinion of public services is the low level of confidence respondents have in them: almost 70 per cent of the population have no confidence that public services perform their function.

Paradoxically, the 'poorest' are also the most lenient in their judgement of public services (see Figure 5.1). Almost twice as many members of households in the poorest quartile think that public services are efficient (18 per cent compared with 10 per cent) and have confidence in them (36 per cent vs. 21 per cent) as members of households in the wealthiest quartile. In addition, fewer of the poor think there are too many state employees, that state employees do not work hard enough and that there is too much political toadyism in the administration (see Table 5.2).

These findings seem especially surprising in that the poor are the chief

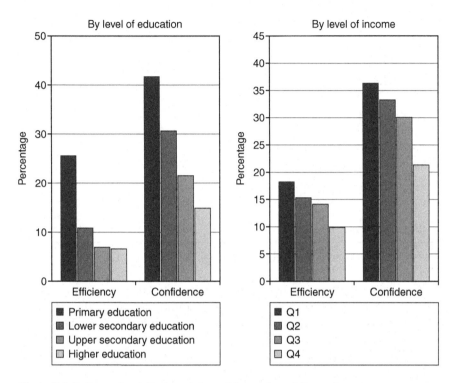

Figure 5.1 Indices of satisfaction and confidence in public services.

Sources: 1998 employment survey, authors' calculations.

Note
Q1, Q2, Q3 and Q4 are per capita income quartiles: from the poorest (Q1) to the wealthiest (Q4).

victims of inefficiency on the part of a state which has shown itself to be incapable of providing them with sufficient protection. Two explanations can be offered for this apparent contradiction. One is 'cultural': the low level of education of the poor means that their critical faculties are less developed and makes them less susceptible to prevailing free-market notions regarding the failings of the public sector and its supposed tendency to create distortions. Indeed, level of education emerges as the clearest distinguishing factor in answers to this question: a quarter of those who had received no secondary education said that they thought public services were efficient, compared with only 7 per cent of those who had been to university. On the economic side, the poorest respondents are probably also the most grateful for the protection afforded by the state, which, despite its flaws, does provide them with a number of services (education, healthcare, and so on) and regulatory safety nets of which they think they would be deprived in a deregulated free-market context.

Table 5.2 Poverty and public service reform

	Per capita income quartiles (%)				
	Q1	Q2	Q3	Q4	Total
Perception/assessment:					
Madagascar's public services are inefficient	33.7	32.7	34.8	44.3	36.4
Have no confidence in public services	63.2	66.5	69.9	78.5	69.5
Opinions on the origins of inefficiency:					
Too much political toadyism in the administration	71.0	72.9	74.2	75.7	73.5
There are too many civil servants	33.5	37.0	35.0	35.3	35.2
Civil servants do not work hard enough	52.4	52.8	54.6	58.3	54.6
Civil servants are overpaid	24.3	26.4	25.0	20.0	23.9

Sources: 1998 employment survey, MADIO, authors' calculations.

Paradoxically, although the wealthiest group judge the quality of public services more harshly, they are more optimistic about the changes observed during the second half of the 1990s (see Figure 5.2). This relatively favourable attitude on the part of the wealthiest can be observed with regard to each of the five public services identified in the survey (the civil service, security, education, health, urban infrastructures).

Although the poor are more lenient towards public services in their present state, they concur with the rest of the population as regards the measures which should be taken to improve their efficiency (see Table 5.3). There is consensus regarding the steps to be taken across all social strata. These are: linking salaries to performance; reinforcing the system of punishments for incompetent employees; recruiting young people to restore the balance between generations; and promoting decentralisation to make public services more accessible to the taxpayer.

Privatisation of public enterprises

The programme of privatisation of public enterprises is the second main strand of policies aimed at reshaping the role of the state in Madagascar. As in the case of public services, the population is very severe in its criticism of public enterprises. Two-thirds think they are badly run and almost 70 per cent are certain that they would be more efficient in private ownership (see Table 5.4). Although six out of ten poor people concur with this view, they are on average less critical of the management of public enterprises, which lends support to the notion that they are more attached to the public sector.

Despite harsh criticism of the management of public enterprises, plans

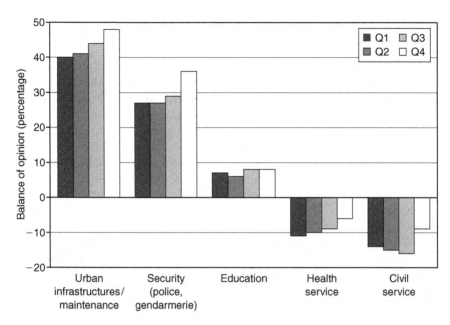

Figure 5.2 Balance of opinion on improvement in public services in 2000.

Sources: 2000 employment survey, MADIO, authors' calculations.

to privatise them by no means meet with universal approval. In 1995, 46 per cent of the inhabitants of Antananarivo were opposed to all forms of privatisation, whether partial or total. Three years later, the notion of privatisation in the abstract had gained some ground, but nearly a quarter of respondents were still totally opposed to privatisation. A further anxiety – and one which had not surfaced with regard to public service reform – concerned the way in which privatisations were being conducted: 40 per cent of respondents felt that the privatisations currently taking place were not being conducted in a sufficiently transparent manner.

Table 5.3 The consensus on the steps to be taken to reform public services

	Per capita income quartiles (%)				
	Q1	*Q2*	*Q3*	*Q4*	*Total*
Salary linked to performance	96.3	96.3	95.8	91.4	95.0
More severe punishments	90.3	91.8	90.6	87.5	90.0
Replace incompetent civil servants with young people	89.7	89.7	87.9	86.6	88.4
Promote decentralisation	89.0	89.4	87.4	87.9	88.4

Sources: 1998 employment survey, MADIO, authors' calculations.

But it is on the issue of opening up the economy to foreign investors that privatisations are most vehemently rejected. Six out of ten respondents favour some form of national preference, demanding that priority be given to Malagasy investors.

More broadly, the issue of relationships with the rest of the world is at the heart of opposition to liberalisation policies. Although Madagascar has one of the lowest levels of immigration in the world (0.2 per cent; see Razafindrakoto and Roubaud 1999b), two-thirds of the inhabitants of Antananarivo think there are too many foreigners living in Madagascar. Many of them also think that there is too much foreign investment in Madagascar; and nearly half feel that foreigners should not be allowed to buy or even rent land, although the system of 99-year leaseholds (emphyteotic leases) has been introduced specifically to encourage and stabilise foreign investment.[4]

Once again, the poor are most resistant to moves to reduce the role of the state and opening up the market. They subscribe to the prevailing view that there are too many foreigners and too much foreign capital in Madagascar, but hold still-more radical views on national preference, land access and the process of privatisation, despite the fact that they are not, a priori, the group which has most to lose from this operation since potential competition for the purchase of public enterprises or land is more likely to pit national investors against foreign investors. So economic interests are probably not the only factor in this closed attitude to the changes now taking place. This attitude on the part of the poor might reflect a

Table 5.4 Poverty, privatisation and opening up the market

	Per capita income quartiles (%)				
	Q1	*Q2*	*Q3*	*Q4*	*Total*
Public enterprises are badly run	59.4	63.9	69.4	74.8	66.9
Private enterprise would be more efficient	61.3	65.6	69.7	78.5	68.8
Against any form of privatisation in 1995*	54.7	49.7	42.4	38.1	46.1
Against any form of privatisation in 1998	31.2	25.9	25.5	11.6	23.6
Malagasy investors should be given priority in sales of public enterprises	60.4	65.0	57.6	51.2	58.6
Foreigners should have no access to property	48.8	46.5	45.0	37.1	44.3
Too many foreigners in Madagascar	63.8	71.2	66.1	62.2	65.8
Too much foreign capital in Madagascar	70.6	70.9	71.6	72.4	71.4

Sources: 1998 employment survey, phase 3 1995 employment survey (*), MADIO, authors' calculations.

stronger attachment to traditional Malagasy cultural values, which could be disrupted by globalisation.

Education policy

The third example we would like to use here to illustrate the notion that there are attitudes which are specific to the poor is the area of education policy.[5] Together with health policy, this is one of the cornerstones of the strategies currently used to combat poverty. Current policy is based on a substantial increase in public spending on education, and targets have been set for levels of school attendance, especially in primary education. Policy aims are well known. These are: renovating state school infrastructures; promoting education through other channels than central government (community and private schools); mapping regional requirements; improving the quality of education offered; recovering costs, and so on.

Having poor parents clearly affects an individual's chances of access to education: the percentage of children in school is lower in poor families, and they are likely to start school later and finish earlier as a result of financial pressures, poor educational performance, and so on. In addition, the cost of school fees restricts their choices in terms of the type of school, so that children from poor families mainly attend state schools, where quality has been worst affected by the budgetary crisis.

Despite these disadvantages, poor parents appear to be more attached to education and the state school system than parents in other groups (see

Table 5.5 Poverty, education and school policy

| | *Per capita income quartiles (%)* | | | | |
	Q1	*Q2*	*Q3*	*Q4*	*Total*
Net level of school attendance	78.3	85.7	90.1	93.2	85.0
Do not attend school for financial reasons*	45.3	35.5	36.2	0.0	39.3
Educated in private school (primary education)	36.7	53.9	67.4	85.4	55.4
In favour of free education for all					
primary	84.2	80.0	77.4	70.3	78.5
secondary	73.3	64.9	65.8	57.1	65.8
university	66.5	66.9	61.0	50.6	62.0
Private schools contribute to inequality	31.1	25.1	20.9	16.6	24.0
Graduates should be guaranteed jobs in public services	68.0	60.5	54.6	42.6	56.4

Sources: 1996 employment survey, MADIO, authors' calculations.

Note
* Applies to 6- to 10-year-olds.

Table 5.5). More of them see education as the best means of succeeding in later life, and they are more likely to be in favour of concentrating education spending on basic education, which is the current strategy of the government. Conversely, the rise of private education is a source of anxiety for poor parents, whose children would suffer most in the event of a two-tier system which would accentuate educational inequalities. Although they do not actually call for nationalisation of the entire education system, they differ from the rest of the population in being more likely to be in favour of free schooling and the spread of universal provision of state education. Moreover, a majority of poor parents are in favour of guaranteeing jobs in public services for graduates. These tendencies, which are out of step with current education policy choices, provide further support for the notion that the poor tend to rely on the state to satisfy their basic needs.

The views of the poor on major ideological choices

Poverty, economic liberalism and cultural liberalism

The last three examples (public services, public enterprises and education) showed that the chief characteristic of the attitude of the poor to the state is their attachment to the public sector and their reservations about reforms designed to reduce the role of the state. This begs the more general question of whether this characteristic reflects a coherent value-system as such which is specific to the poor and defines a preference on their part for a society in which the means of regulation is provided by the state and not by the market. The information collected in the various surveys clearly supports this hypothesis. The poor very widely reject liberalism in favour of interventionism in the economic sphere. Proportionally more of them than the other quartiles are in favour of an administered economy, in which the state plays a leading part in business. They argue for strong state intervention to correct the malfunctions and injustices they ascribe to the market: such intervention could include ethnic quotas at universities, in public services and government to combat discrimination, and subsidies on staple products to protect the standard of living. These findings are not specific to Madagascar, since they are mirrored in most developed countries (Richard 2000).

Let us now explore the reasons for these attitudes. Two alternative explanations can be offered. The poor may have objective reasons for rejecting liberalisation and, more broadly, globalisation, on the grounds that these processes would inevitably cause them to be marginalised and excluded. Their attitude could also be explained by a form of cultural atavism which goes beyond economic values, in which the poor would be less likely to subscribe to the values of individual freedoms – free enterprise, of course, but also the freedom to choose representatives or the moral freedom to choose one's way of life. If we pursue this line of thought, the poor, as being on the side of order, should emerge as being more conservative and more attached to traditional institutions (church, state and family) and the moral principles promoted by them (authority, discipline, and so forth). Post-modernist writers would seem to subscribe to this view, when they highlight the central role of education in spreading individualistic values and cultural liberalism in most Western democracies (Inglehart 1993, 1997). In the face of changes on a global scale, the increase in more rigid attitudes and closed concepts of identity (with the emergence of extreme right-wing groups and xenophobic attitudes), which affect the most vulnerable social groups in developed countries, would seem to be the direct expressions of this cultural atavism.

In Madagascar, this second explanation clearly does not hold water. The poor do not display especially repressive tendencies either in the area of domestic morality or in the area of democratic values. In the first place, in a climate where the level of ethnic and religious tolerance is generally high, the poor are by no means less tolerant than other social strata in terms of cultural liberalism.[6] On the contrary, they are more likely to agree to their offspring changing religions or marrying outside their own ethnic group (see Table 5.6). Fewer of them think that there is an ethnic problem in Madagascar, and they are less likely to belong to tribal or caste-based groups. Although very few people in any of the social strata see ethnicity as genetic, the well-off tend to ascribe specific qualities and faults to each ethnic group (lazy/hard-working, quarrelsome/peaceable, etc.), whilst the poor see them as more equal. Lastly, religious syncretism, which has been interpreted by some authors as a sign of openness to new spiritual ideas and de-institutionalisation of religious affiliations (Bréchon 2000), is more widespread amongst the poor.

These findings are especially interesting in that this weaker attachment to social norms inherited from the past does not stem from less involvement in religion. Post-modernist theorists have been able to demonstrate that although the more educated people are, the more culturally liberal they are likely to be, there is a negative correlation between cultural liberalism and the frequency of religious practices. In fact, it is the opposing influences of education and religion which partially blur the correlation between social class and cultural liberalism. In the case of Madagascar, the fact that the link with the area of religion is uniformly strong lends support neither to the body of received wisdom concerning the decline of moral values to discredit the proletariat that emerged from the Industrial Revolution during the nineteenth century (by means of associations of ideas such as '*classe laborieuse, classe licencieuse*'[7]) nor to the notion that the poor are more morally conservative on account of their religious affiliations (Roubaud 2000a). The fact that the poor tend to be Catholic rather than Protestant, which reflects the way Christianity was brought to Madagascar historically (Raison-Jourde 1991), constitutes Madagascar's second

Table 5.6 Poverty, religion and economic and cultural liberalism

| | Per capita income quartiles (%) | | | | |
	Q1	Q2	Q3	Q4	Total
Economic liberalism					
In favour of a regulated economy*	55.7	51.4	48.2	41.1	49.1
The state should play a leading role in business*	81.6	73.5	76.3	61.6	73.3
In favour of ethnic quotas (university, public services, gov.)	33.2	27.3	26.6	23.8	27.6
In favour of subsidies for basic necessities*	29.5	22.6	29.8	20.6	25.7
Cultural liberalism					
Had a religious wedding	39.5	43.7	53.8	64.5	51.0
Offspring can change religion	74.6	71.2	71.4	65.9	70.6
Not opposed to marriage between ethnic groups	61.5	64.8	59.9	51.1	59.5
Religious affiliations					
Religious practices: pray at least once a week	44.2	35.7	45.2	43.0	41.8
The message of the churches is relevant to today's problems	92.1	92.6	91.7	89.6	91.8
Protestant	33.9	44.6	55.2	45.6	45.5
Catholic	47.9	39.7	31.7	40.0	39.9

Sources: 1997 employment survey, phase 3 1995 (*), MADIO, authors' calculations.

peculiarity so far as the links between cultural liberalism, poverty and religion are concerned. The important part played by Protestantism in spreading a culture of individual freedom has long been demonstrated by sociologists. Indeed, it is offered as an explanation for the gap between a rich, Protestant, more permissive northern Europe and a poorer, Catholic southern Europe. Lastly, although the poor inhabitants of Antananarivo are Catholic and less educated, they are found to be more open than the wealthy to the values of cultural liberalism based on freedom of individual choice and an emphasis on personal fulfilment, and consequently, less prone to closed concepts of identity. The reason the well-off are less willing to adopt universalist values may be that they are seeking to promote strategies for perpetuating the family which might be compromised if there is too much mingling between social groups.

Poverty, democracy and involvement in politics

Although in terms of domestic morality the economic interventionism of the poor does not correspond to a more authoritarian, conservative attitude to individual modes of behaviour, their preferences in terms of political regulation have not yet been examined. Given that a free market economy and electoral democracy are closely associated, it is to be expected that where the former is regarded with suspicion, the latter will also be contested.

In the case of Madagascar, the upheavals in the relationship between citizens and the state in the economic and political arenas during the past decade have taken place almost simultaneously, since the country has been engaged in a dual process of change, on both the economic and political fronts. The liberalisation begun in the first half of the 1980s, with the first structural adjustment plans, was soon followed by a wave of popular protest which brought about the overthrow of the Socialist regime then in power and eventually to the Third Republic being established on democratic principles. Although the desire for democracy during the early 1990s seems to have been widely shared by all social classes, it was the middle and upper classes, and in particular state employees, who provided the impetus for the events of 1991 (Urfer 1993). It was with the working classes that President Ratsiraka scored highest in the 1992/3 elections, though he did not achieve anything like a majority even with this group (see Table 5.7).

During the second half of the 1990s, the poorest continued to support Didier Ratsiraka, and it was largely due to their support that he was re-elected in 1996. But this trend can no longer be interpreted as a rejection of democratic values, since President Ratsiraka had by that stage revised his views on the issue.[8] There is now no difference between the government and the opposition in economic or political terms: both claim to be strongly in favour of democracy and the free market.

More directly, and independently of their party-political allegiances, there is no evidence that the poor are especially likely to be against democracy. The level of involvement in politics is similar in poor households to that observed in households as a whole. First, very few people were not registered to vote – the most obvious sign of political exclusion. In 1997, only 5 per cent of the inhabitants of Antananarivo were not registered as electors. For comparison, the proportion of non-registered electors can be as high as over 10 per cent of the potential electorate in France (Héran and Rouault 1995). Another contrast with developed countries is that the poor are not marginalised by higher rates of non-registration, since the rate is constant across all social categories. Second, data on five recent democratic elections (the first and second rounds of voting in 1992/3 and 1996 and the 1999 local elections) all tend to point towards the same conclusion: the rate of abstention does not depend on the level of income. So, far from shunning elections, the poor exercise their political rights by voting in elections in as large numbers as other citizens.

This participation in itself provides evidence of support for democratic principles. But this support goes beyond mere electoral behaviour. It is also apparent in the opinions expressed by the poor regarding democracy as a political system, which are no different from those of their wealthier

Table 5.7 Poverty, the political class and democracy

	Per capita income quartiles (%)				
	Q1	Q2	Q3	Q4	Total
Political participation/involvement/voting					
Not registered (1996)	4.9	4.9	5.0	6.3	5.3
Rate of abstention (1st round 1996)	28.6	23.1	26.3	22.6	25.0
Rate of abstention (2nd round 1996)	47.1	47.1	42.1	50.5	46.7
Rate of abstention (local elections, 1999)*	37.5	30.5	34.2	37.7	35.0
Voting is always pointless (1996)	15.0	12.5	18.6	12.2	14.7
Support for democratic principles					
Opposed to the one-party system	88.3	89.0	90.2	90.8	89.6
Electoral democracy is appropriate for poor countries	70.6	70.6	77.5	69.2	72.0
In favour of more democracy	67.5	65.2	62.4	63.7	64.6
Democracy has a positive effect on development 1995*	62.9	64.8	63.6	64.9	64.1
Democracy has a positive effect on development 1997	35.8	42.5	38.7	35.2	38.2
Things that are wrong with democracy					
The political parties do not reflect your concerns	84.2	82.7	84.8	86.3	84.5
To embark on a political career = to achieve personal ambitions	81.7	78.7	75.1	76.1	77.9
Under-informed about politics	87.2	80.4	84.8	80.8	83.1
Democracy in moderation					
There are too many elections in Madagascar	86.1	88.3	82.2	83.1	84.9
Against total freedom of political association	71.6	66.2	70.7	65.4	68.2
Political involvement and votes					
Member of a political party	2.1	2.9	1.6	2.7	2.4
Feel close to a political party	10.6	14.7	18.2	15.8	14.9
Voted for Didier Ratsiraka (1st round 1996)	40.4	34.8	30.0	24.8	32.0
Voted for Didier Ratsiraka (1st round 1992)	26.5	28.5	29.0	16.1	25.1

Sources: 1997, 2000 employment surveys, phase 3 1995 employment survey, MADIO, authors' calculations.

Note
*Refers to heads of households only.

fellow citizens. They are as unenthusiastic as the other categories about a return to a one-party system and are equally unlikely to think that the electoral system is unsuitable for a poor country like Madagascar because the population is uneducated. In 1995, almost two-thirds of the inhabitants of Antananarivo, rich and poor alike, thought that democracy had a beneficial effect on Madagascar's development and were in favour of more democracy.

In fact, although there do seem to be the beginnings of a backlash against democracy in Madagascar, this is not true of the poorest categories in particular but of the population as a whole. In 1997 only 38 per cent still thought that democracy encouraged development, compared to 64 per cent two years earlier.[9] This regression implies a loss of confidence in the way democracy operates in Madagascar rather than in the democratic ideal. The vast majority of citizens are very critical of the way democracy operates in Madagascar – the lack of transparency in elections, the dearth of concrete measures, opportunism on the part of politicians who are only interested in furthering their own causes, toadyism, corruption, etc. These views, which are entirely supported by the facts (Roubaud 2000b), result in widespread rejection of the political caste and call for checks on democracy.[10]

A culture of consensus which encourages reforms

So far we have chiefly sought to draw attention to the differences between the attitudes of the poor and those of the other categories of the population, with the dual aim of defining what it is they really want and identifying spheres of intervention which are potentially divisive because there is a real or perceived conflict of interests between the poor and other groups. It might be thought that the more the 'voice of the poor' differs from the dominant view or that of influential groups, the more difficult it will be for them to make themselves heard and to achieve their goals. For example, opposition to proposals to channel more resources into basic education will be all the stronger because wealthy families benefit from higher education subsidies and feel that they have a right to do so.

But in general terms, it emerges from the foregoing analyses that, on the whole, the gap in opinions and values between rich and poor is relatively narrow. This finding confirms a Malagasy characteristic, since differences between social categories appear to be much more marked in other countries, notably in the developed countries for which we have been able to test the hypothesis.

This character trait gives the Malagasy a considerable advantage in the fight against poverty. As we have seen, it is possible to identify a number of areas or measures on which there is very wide consensus, and which should therefore be easier to implement. We have seen, for example, that there is agreement on the means by which public services should be reformed (performance-related salaries, decentralisation, etc.). Similarly, there is very widespread agreement that basic education should be free and public spending should be redirected towards basic education. In this area, the policy of cost recovering clearly presents problems. In the area of politics, improving standards amongst democratic intermediaries (the parties and elected representatives), which come in for very widespread criticism from the population, would be an effective way of increasing participation and hence reducing poverty. In another area, the need to eliminate corruption emerges as the biggest obstacle to development for over

95 per cent of the inhabitants of Antananarivo. They are equally unanimous in identifying inequalities between rich and poor as the chief source of injustice in Madagascar.[11] The fact that these opinions are very widely held does not mean that all policy decisions should be based solely on public opinion: however widespread the consensus may be, the fact that a reform is popular has never been a guarantee of its soundness. But universal support for a certain number of measures which have been proposed by the authorities can only reinforce the legitimacy of government action. The authorities should make use of this democratic tool in formulating and implementing their policies.

Conclusion

This chapter leads us to two types of conclusion, methodological and analytical. As regards methodology, we believe that we have demonstrated the usefulness of statistical surveys as a means of 'listening to the voice of the poor'. They provide an original and effective tool for formulating and monitoring policy. They make it possible for a vast range of questions to be asked and a whole series of indicators relating to the poor and poverty to be used (perceptions of poverty and its causes, attitudes and behaviours, needs and wants, indices of satisfaction, and so on). The concrete examples analysed in this chapter with reference to Madagascar are just a sample of the thematic areas which can be dealt with using this method. The standardisation afforded by survey procedures enables rigorous monitoring and evaluation to be carried out.

Finally, in countries where not only are the authorities not yet held substantially accountable for their actions and performance, but the bridging organisations via which the interests of the poorest groups in the population might be promoted (i.e. organised civil society) are almost non-existent, these representative surveys constitute a unique opportunity for the poor to express their opinions and influence public policy.

In broader terms, our findings lend support to arguments for wider use of opinion polls in Africa. Opinion polls can guide the authorities in formulating and implementing policy and provide an essential medium for public debate in developed countries, and there is no objective reason why they should not perform the same function in poor countries. Access to information is a vital component of democracy and the free market economy. Traditional indicators measuring the evolution of the economic situation (growth, inequality, rate of unemployment, level of poverty, etc.) are not sufficient in this respect. They must be completed by other indicators which monitor citizens perceptions of changes in the economic situation, together with their perception of the relevance and the effectiveness of reforms. They are the best possible gauge of 'ownership', which is currently considered as an essential factor in the success or failure of the implemented policies.

In many spheres, it is clear that the attitudes of the poor are not fundamentally different from those of the population as a whole. The same schisms and the same dividing lines can be found amongst the poor as in society as a whole. This overall conclusion should lead us to question the relevance (i.e. the sociological existence) of this group, which appears to be more a statistical aggregate than a fully fledged social group, with its own firmly articulated identity. The poor are therefore unlikely to exert autonomous, organised pressure to defend their shared interests (if indeed they have them), both because they are economically deprived and because their lack of cohesiveness as a group weakens their bargaining power in the political arena. In fact, this lack of homogeneity brings us back to a much wider problem – the difficulty of putting forward criteria for social stratification in Africa with any confidence, whether on the basis of age-group, ethnicity, social-professional or other categories: a meaningful sociology of class in mainland Africa has yet to be mapped out. However, from a political-economy point of view, this substantially heterogeneous character has interesting implications for strategies to combat poverty. It would seem that the failures to reduce poverty, or lack of enthusiasm of sub-Saharan states for measures designed to combat it, do not stem from opposition from the numerically strong landowning groups whose profits could be harmed by such measures. So the 'pro-poor coalitions' recommended by the World Bank in its World Development Report on this subject (see Chapter 1) should not encounter strong opposition. They should even be able to rely on strong popular support which will facilitate the task of building such coalitions.

If we now focus on those aspects of the views expressed by the poor which are specific to them, the firmest conclusion, and the one which deserves to be underlined, is the strong 'need for the state' they display. Not only are they much more lenient towards public services and those in positions of power, they are also the group least enthusiastic about democratic reforms, economic liberalisation and reductions in the role of the state (privatisation, opening up of markets, etc.). This attitude may seem paradoxical in the sense that not only ought they to be the most critical of the state, which is largely responsible for their marginalisation and impoverished condition, but, according to conventional economic theory, they should have most to gain from these policies. But in fact, their desire for more state intervention can legitimately be interpreted as a fundamental need for protection. Analysis reveals that the cultural hypothesis of a 'conservative' tendency amongst the poorest and least-educated classes, in which they are supposed to be structurally more resistant to change and innovation, can be rejected. The need for state intervention that they express is the result of a process of rationalisation of the economic and political history of the country over a long period. Since the setting-up of the structural adjustment programmes in the early 1980s, and the transition to a democratic regime at the beginning of the 1990s, their situation has steadily worsened. Under these circumstances, it is not surprising that the poor should have reservations about the gradual withdrawal of the state, which, despite its shortcomings, has managed up until now to provide them with a modicum of protection, and that they should feel unequal to the task of playing the free market game on their own. It is possible that Madagascar's spectacular economic recovery at the end of the 1990s (from 1997 to 2001), from which the poor have substantially benefited, had softened the most conservative attitudes. But the growth episode did not last and there is no guarantee that the trends towards greater inequality which had been emerging did not or will not leave some of them by the wayside (Razafindrakoto and Roubaud 2002). On a global scale, the last two decades have clearly shown that the removal of trade barriers, the increasing influence of the markets, and the weakening of national governments accentuate vulnerabilities in both the North and the South. Whilst the remarkable successes of emerging economies have played a part in reducing poverty, the financial crises in Asia and Latin America at the end of the 1990s and in the early 2000s show how fragile and easily reversible these gains may be. After all, loss of job security, devaluation and increased precariousness of unskilled work and/or mass unemployment in developed countries has resulted in increasingly radical conservative ideologies and reassertions of national identities (on France, see Bréchon *et al.* 2000).

However that may be, the fact that the poor are in favour of the welfare state, which is probably applicable outside the Malagasy context, presents those who have promoted strategies for combating poverty with a fundamental problem. Having made participation and 'listening to the poor' central to their policies, they are now faced with a genuine dilemma: how can they integrate an aspiration which seems at first glance to be incompatible with their own ideological positions? There are several possible answers:

- they can simply ignore this demand, in which case they would be flouting the principle they have just decreed, by turning the participative process into a mere token gesture, a sounding-board for policies conceived, formulated and implemented from above;
- they can attempt to bring the poor round to their own view, in the hope of demonstrating by example and persuasion that 'less state' is the best policy;
- more constructively, they can take note of this unsatisfied demand, accept that it is legitimate, and engage in the daunting task of reinventing (and in the case of African countries, inventing) a regulatory and protective form of state which does not interfere with economic growth.

It seems obvious to us that the third course of action is likely to be the most fruitful approach.

Notes

1 Given the multidimensional nature of poverty, defining the concept is a delicate task, the complexity of which has been stressed by many writers on the subject (see Herpin and Verger 1997a, Lollivier and Verger 1997). In this study we have continued to use the financial criterion (per capita income level) to define the notion of poverty, since it is the most accepted approach and the one which correlates best with the various forms of poverty (Razafindrakoto and Roubaud 2000a). In particular, there is no doubt about the correlation between individuals' subjective perceptions of their living conditions and their level of income, even though there is only partial correspondence.

2 MADIO (Madagascar-Dial-Instat-Orstom) was a project, the objective of which was to give support to the reinforcement of the national statistical system and to macroeconomic analysis.

3 Lancelot (1984) identified at least four benefits to democracy from opinion polls: selecting those in power (choice of candidates and elected representatives), monitoring the action of those in power (permanent vehicles for citizens' reactions), safeguarding the rights of the opposition (when all governing institutions are dominated by the same party, opinion polls reflect the diversity which would result from a proportional system) and contributing to a culture of freedom (i.e. the pluralism and spread of information without which democracy is merely a formal concept).

4 Since 1995, there has been a law prohibiting the purchase of land by foreigners in Madagascar. To offset this measure and reconcile it with the official policy of opening up markets and encouraging foreign investment, a system of leasehold which allows foreigners to lease the land for up to 99 years (emphyteotic leases) has been introduced. This measure was substantially imposed by donors and has met with huge obstacles in practice.

5 The module on schools incorporated into the 1996 employment survey provides an accurate picture of the demands of the population in this area (Roubaud 1999).

6 To define cultural liberalism, Grunberg and Schweisguth single out three elements: moral and especially sexual permissiveness; anti-authoritarianism; universalist values and a rejection of 'ethnocentrism' (in Bréchon 2000). The indicators at our disposal are most relevant to this third aspect, even if the two others are partially dealt with.

7 'the labouring class is a licentious class'.

8 Although the elections held in December 2001 have hardly been transparent, which led to the political crisis of 2002, compared to the situation prevailing in the 1980s, progress has been registered concerning press freedom and the right of association.

9 It is noteworthy that in 1995 the level of satisfaction with the way democracy operated in Madagascar was comparable to levels in European Union countries. The decline observed in 1997 would have placed it low on the list (only Italy scored lower, with 24 per cent), but the level of satisfaction was nonetheless higher than in new democracies in Eastern Europe (Toka 1995).

10 The movement of popular protest, which lasted nearly six months in 2002, was denouncing the fraud organised during the 2001 presidential election. More generally, it was condemning a regime where 'grand' corruption had become widespread. Marc Ravalomanana, whose slogan during his presidential campaign was 'Transparency, good governance and justice', was brought to the presidency in 2002 by this movement.

11 The other options offered were inequality on ethnic or religious grounds or gender inequality.

Part II

Scope and limitations of the new international initiatives

The World Bank and the International Monetary Fund launched two joint initiatives in 1999: the Poverty Reduction Strategy Papers (PRSPs) set the fight against poverty at the heart of development policies; the 'enhanced' Heavily Indebted Poor Countries (HIPC) Initiative is meant to bring effective debt relief to these countries, and to help finance their PRSPs. These Initiatives now channel all official development assistance (ODA) resources destined for low-income countries, which means all these countries' external resources; in a short period of time, PRSPs have become the key framework for development policies in poor countries. This part highlights the scope and limits of these international initiatives.

The new approach, which promotes *ownership, accountability* and *empowerment*, constitutes a watershed arising from the recognition of serious deficiencies in previous strategies. Three main innovations distinguish it from previous approaches:

- the fight against poverty (and not structural adjustment) becomes the priority objective, while implementation and success of these policies constitute conditions for debt relief and new funding;
- a participatory process links the donor community with the government and all branches of society to maximise the effectiveness of anti-poverty strategies during their design, monitoring and implementation;
- lastly, the new initiatives increase the overall coherence of aid, as debt relief granted within the HIPC Initiative is managed collectively, and the major donors are aligned on the PRSP framework.

Confronting these innovations and the goals set by the new poverty reduction strategies with their concrete development in the field nonetheless shows strong discrepancies, due both to intrinsic contradictions between their principles and to financial and human constraints endured by poor countries. It is too early to assess fully the chances of success or failure of these strategies, but this analysis emphasises the main challenges lying ahead.

The first three chapters of this part set down the guiding principles for drawing up PRSPs and the problems that arise in practice, both in terms of the actual content of the policies and their means of implementation. Chapter 6 analyses the stakes involved and the contradictions inherent to the participatory process (both in theory and practice), which is supposed to change the way economic and social policies are designed and implemented. It uses a form of flow chart that identifies the key stakeholders – the donors, civil society and the state – and helps us understand how they interact through converging interests, tactical alliances, power relationships, sources of tension, open conflicts, etc. Chapter 7 describes the contents of existing PRSPs, the shortcomings of which mainly reflect weaknesses in the strategies recommended by the Bretton Wood Institutions (described in detail in Chapter 1), and their difficulty in defining – or letting the developing countries define – alternative strategies. The focus that the BWIs (and to a certain extent the NGOs themselves) have put on participatory processes has meant that thinking on policy content has often been neglected. This chapter warns against the illusion that consists in thinking that changing the way in which policies are drawn up is sufficient to make them more effective, with no new thinking on their actual content. Chapter 8 is dedicated to a field study on the Mali PRSP, which illustrates the arguments presented in the previous two chapters with the concrete case of one of the world's poorest countries. It successively examines questions relating to policy content, the participatory process, and monitoring and evaluation. This chapter raises doubts concerning this country's capacity to design its own strategies to combat poverty, given the weakness of its institutions and its civil society, and its level of aid dependency.

The following two chapters analyse the inter-linkage between poverty reduction and debt relief. Chapter 9 highlights the incompatibility of the underlying principles of the PRSP and HIPC Initiatives, despite the fact that they were launched simultaneously. It also draws the conclusion from previous failed initiatives that it is essential not to raise excessive hopes, and to address the problems without trying to elude them. Based on an historical analysis, the findings highlight the wide gap between the initial ambitions of the initiatives launched by the BWIs and the actual results of their implementation, which generally give rise to a gradual lowering of the objectives. Chapter 10 demonstrates the highly un-equalitarian nature of the HIPC Initiative, and the uncertainty with respect to its potential impact, as it is decided on the basis of financial criteria of sustainability and not on the poor countries' needs in terms of development. Insofar as the countries in question depend entirely on flows of ODA for their external resources, and given the financial constraints that they suffer from, this diagnosis is central to the future of the PRSPs. The analysis also raises questions on whether debt relief is to be added to or substituted for traditional ODA.

6 A participatory process towards establishing new relationships between stakeholders

Jean-Pierre Cling, Mireille Razafindrakoto and François Roubaud

Since 1999, the World Bank and the International Monetary Fund require developing countries seeking concessional lending or debt relief under the Heavily Indebted Poor Countries (HIPC) Initiative to first prepare a poverty reduction strategy which should be described in a single economic policy document: the Poverty Reduction Strategy Paper (PRSP).

Three essential points distinguish it from its forebears:

- the fight against poverty becomes the priority objective; implementation and success of poverty reduction policies constitute conditions for debt relief and new funding, which are in turn meant to release the resources necessary for their application;
- a participatory process links the donor community with all branches of society (the 'stakeholders') to maximise the effectiveness of anti-poverty strategies during their design, monitoring and implementation;
- as the major donors have accepted this new framework, PRSPs tend to increase the overall coherence of aid – that is, both its objectives and its practice.

The new approach constitutes a watershed arising from recognition of serious deficiencies in previous strategies, which are mainly attributed by the World Bank to their lack of ownership by the countries supposed to put them into practice:

> One lesson from experience is that reform does not succeed without strong local ownership and a broad-based approach, which includes a consideration of institutions, governance, and stakeholder participation – a lesson that has provided the impetus for the Poverty Reduction Strategy Paper (PRSP) process.
>
> (World Bank 2002a)

PRSPs take this lesson into account. Their objective is to respect the following principles:

- 'ownership': government responsibility for conducting participatory process should increase its commitment to undertake efficiently the actions decided within the PRSP, while the participation of civil society, not only to the definition but also to the monitoring of policies, should ensure the whole population's support to reforms;
- 'empowerment': the participatory process is supposed to contribute to improving the quality of the political debate and to help to define a more adequate strategy meeting real social needs; by offering the poor a means to express themselves and to influence policies affecting their living conditions, this approach also aims at fighting social exclusion (which according to Sen is one dimension of poverty);
- 'accountability': through participation, all stakeholders are invited to discuss government policies, and government is now made accountable to all citizens.

Nearly sixty low-income countries (that is almost all the countries in this category, see list in Table 6.1) are currently engaged in PRSPs, while major donors have aligned on this new approach. For these countries, the participatory process is therefore supposed to change the rules of the game by transforming the way their economic and social policies are being designed and implemented. It is therefore especially important to make a first assessment of this process,[1] which is presented in this chapter. The first section describes the main guidelines of the participatory process as defined by the Bretton Woods Institutions (BWIs), which follow from the above-mentioned principles. The three following sections try to verify the extent to which these principles are being applied, as well as identify innovations and problems brought about by the new approach. The new missions of each stakeholder – donors, which now call themselves 'development partners', civil society and the state – are taken up in turn, while the new relationships between them are also analysed. A wide range of research (especially field research) is mobilised in order to evaluate the scope and limitations of the participatory processes.

A new approach for defining and implementing policies in poor countries

The new approach recommended by the PRSP framework provides for the establishment of a participatory process to define poverty alleviation policies. This is a distinct departure from previous practice, which in the main consisted of the definition by donors of policies that countries were subsequently required to apply, or risk financial sanctions. The process leads to the preparation of an economic policy document centred on the

Table 6.1 List of the countries engaged in the PRSP process

Africa	*Asia*
Angola	Armenia
Benin	Azerbaijan
Burkina Faso	Cambodia
Burundi	East Timor
Cameroon	Georgia
Central African Republic	Indonesia
Chad	Kyrgyz Republic
Comoros	Lao PDR
Congo Democratic Republic	Mongolia
Congo Republic	Nepal
Côte d'Ivoire	Pakistan
Djibouti	Sri Lanka
Eritrea	Tajikistan
Ethiopia	Vietnam
Gambia, The	Yemen Republic
Ghana	
Guinea	*Eastern Europe*
Guinea-Bissau	Albania
Kenya	Bosnia Herzegovina
Lesotho	Macedonia FYR
Madagascar	Moldova
Malawi	
Mali	*Central and South America*
Mauritania	Bolivia
Mozambique	Guyana
Niger	Honduras
Nigeria	Nicaragua
Rwanda	
São Tomé and Principe	
Senegal	
Sierra Leone	
Tanzania	
Togo	
Uganda	
Zambia	

struggle to reduce poverty: the PRSP. This paper is organised according to a general plan, the main aspects of which are defined by the World Bank in its sourcebook:

There are six core principles underlying the development and implementation of PRSPs. The strategies should be:

– country-driven, involving broad-based participation by civil society and the private sector in all operational steps;
– results-oriented, and focused on outcomes that would benefit the poor;

- comprehensive in recognising the multidimensional nature of poverty, but also
- prioritised so that implementation is feasible, in both fiscal and institutional terms;
- partnership-oriented, involving co-ordinated participation of development partners (bilateral, multilateral, and non-governmental);
- based on a long-term perspective for poverty reduction.

(World Bank 2002b)

The primary principle put forward in the above list concerns the participatory character of the policy definition process. The Bretton Woods Institutions (BWIs) overtly recognise the role of each individual country in the development of its PRSP, and the necessity of adopting a participatory process for which each is asked to set precise rules. They attempt thereby to respond to past criticisms of insufficient appreciation of the opinions and specificity of countries.

What is a participatory process?

The participatory process concept presumes the active involvement of all sections of society in the design, implementation and monitoring of the fight against poverty. It should thereby contribute to the enrichment of debate and to the definition of a more adequate strategy responding to real social needs. This approach, designated by the term 'empowerment', is meant to give the poor an opportunity to influence policies affecting their condition, and to allow better identification and awareness of their problems and expectations.

According to its advocates, management of the process by the state and the participation of civil society, not only in the definition but also in the monitoring of policies, should favour the degree of engagement by the administration. It should also promote the efficient introduction of intended actions, all the while soliciting support for reforms from the population at large and favouring their ownership by the country. Participation by all sections of society in what was previously the preserve of the state has at heart the principle of accountability, a principle frequently neglected until now in most poor countries. The World Bank provides the following definition of participation:

Participation is the process through which stakeholders influence and share control over priority setting, policy-making, resource allocations and access to public goods and services. There is no blueprint for participation because it plays a role in many different contexts, different projects and for different purposes.

(Tikare *et al.* 2001)

Apart from the donors, the panoply of civil society is involved in this process. In particular the public, notably the poor and vulnerable groups such as the youth, the handicapped, women's groups, and so on; the state, through central and local administrations, government (national and local), parliament and representative assemblies; civil society organisations and networks such as non-governmental organisations (NGOs), community organisations, trade unions and professional associations, academic institutions and research centres; the private sector, comprising all forms of business association and chambers of commerce.

The World Bank avoids setting too precise orientations that would contradict the philosophy it now seeks to defend. This attitude is also explained by the experimental nature of a process, launched with some precipitation and thus without thorough preparation, which constrains the institution to define guiding principles as it goes along. Despite this discretion, judgements of the participatory processes made by the BWIs in their Joint Staff Assessments (JSAs, which condition new funding and debt relief in the framework of the HIPC Initiative – see Chapter 10), are nevertheless based on a few fundamental principles. These criteria, set out in the general introduction to the sourcebook, are intended to ensure the effective participation of all the above-listed stakeholders in the process:

> To provide clarity and help structure its description of the participatory process, the JSA will focus on the following points in describing whether the PRSP has built country ownership through participation:
>
> – participatory processes within government (among central ministries, parliament, and sub-national governments);
> – other stakeholder involvement (for example civil society groups, women's groups, ethnic minorities, policy research institutes and academics, private sector, trade unions, representatives from different regions of the country);
> – bilateral and multilateral external development partners' involvement, including collaborative analytical work to support PRSP development;
> – mechanisms used to consult the poor and their representatives; and
> – plans for dissemination of the PRSP.
>
> (Klugman 2001)

It is useful to stress the permanent character of the whole process. If the participatory approach is considered a means to guarantee the effectiveness of anti-poverty strategies, its realisation is also an end in itself. It must appear among the goals of a PRSP. Progress in this direction, and any potential obstacles, should be the subject of evaluation and monitoring.

Why a participatory process?

With the launch of PRSPs, the BWIs have initiated a major change to previous practices. Formerly, even if national experts contributed to defining policies, and if these were subject to negotiation, poor countries had little weight and enjoyed narrow margins for manoeuvre. Information available to the public was more than limited as most documents used for negotiations remained confidential.

Widespread failure of structural adjustment programmes (SAPs) in low-income countries, especially in Africa, has its origins in social or political blockages to the implementation of programmes, as well as the inefficiency of intended measures even where they were really applied. Two weaknesses related to the mode of intervention by the BWIs largely explain this setback. On the one hand, it presumed that international experts were best placed to define adequate policies for the countries, following the principle of 'best practice'. On the other hand, despite being considered incompetent and marginalised in the design of strategies, national authorities were supposed to be willing and able to put them into efficient practice, without necessarily subscribing to them.

The development of the governance concept has been put forward as a major condition for the success of policies, while the wind of democratisation has stressed the need to grant additional weight to the 'voiceless' both on the national and on the international stages. In consequence, a better understanding of the economic, socio-political and institutional conditions specific to each country is now considered an imperative. Moreover, there is now a consensus concerning the primordial character of support for policies, not only by governments but also by the population, which defines the ownership concept.

Figure 6.1 synthesises the main innovations introduced by the principles guiding the PRSP process, compared to policies previously recommended by the World Bank in its Economic Policy Framework Papers (PFPs). As the figure shows, PRSP principles represent a fundamental rupture with past practice, both in terms of the way policies are designed and in their content, their funding and performance indicators. In all these aspects, the failure of previous strategies required the BWIs to formulate policies based on largely opposing principles.

Once the principles of the participatory process, as outlined by the World Bank, have been described, we are led to question the affected countries' interest for this new apparatus. In other words, what do the new means of defining economic policies bring to beneficiary countries compared with former arrangements, not only in principle but also in practice? It is clearly premature to attempt a precise reply to this question. PRSPs are just being established and the process has not really started in the majority of countries. The guide used here to analyse the participatory process adopts a double dimension: from the point of view of the PRSP

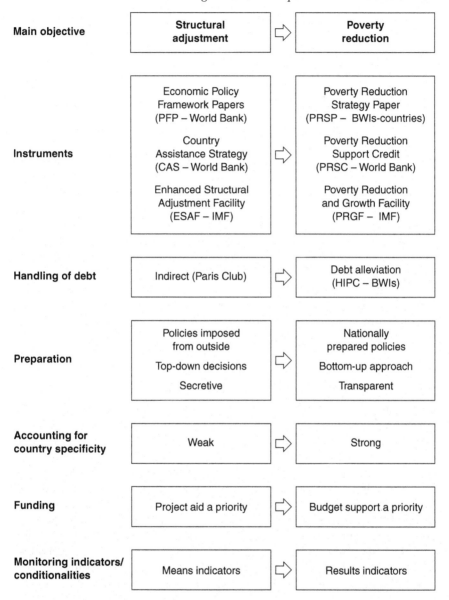

Figure 6.1 Innovations brought by the PRSPs

actors (mainly the donor community, civil society and the state) and their interrelationships (Box 6.1). In the PRSP logic, the simultaneous participation of these three actors is crucial for the success of the strategy, as summarised by the image presented by a participant in the regional forum on this theme organised in Dakar (World Bank 2001c): 'You cannot cook well if the three legs of the pot are missing'.

From this perspective, our analysis aims to appreciate better the potential impact on development policies from the innovations brought by the PRSP approach, as well as the difficulties inherent in the process, and thereby investigate the chances for success.

The donors' new position

The traditional determinant weight of donors in financing developing countries with no access to private capital flows has been increased with the introduction of PRSPs. These now become essential instruments in relations between developing countries and the donor community, as a necessary condition both for debt relief and for access to new concessional BWIs' lending.

At the same time, the launch of PRSPs consecrates the broad failure of policies previously promoted by the BWIs, characterised in particular by a multitude of conditionalities imposed on countries benefiting from their loans (Devarajan, Dollar and Holmgren 2001; Collier 1997). The BWIs now adopt, in principle at least, a more humble attitude concerning the countries where they intervene. In parallel, they also seek better coordination between the different donors, to put an end to the frequent incoherence of their interventions.

Less donor intervention to promote ownership

Since the 1980s, the BWIs have multiplied conditionalities imposed on developing countries. The number of 'structural' conditions included in IMF facilities (engagements linked to structural reforms in LDCs) grew from an average of two in 1987 to 17 in 1997, before falling to 13 in 1999 (Chavagneux 2001).[2] It is accepted that these conditionalities failed due to a lack of local ownership of policies imposed from abroad, without real support in the countries concerned. This led to an 'instrumentalisation' of the BWIs as, facing public opinion, governments identified them as being responsible for the policies (Chambas and Kerhuel 2001). From a technical viewpoint, numerous anomalies arose from the fixing of conditionalities to the measures to be adopted, and not to policy results.

PRSPs promote establishing a new relationship between donors and beneficiaries, aiming to make recipient countries more aware of their responsibilities both in the definition of policies and in their application. This new position of the donors raises three types of contradiction.

The first, and the foremost, is inherent to the nature of the process. In effect, conditionalities do not evaporate in the PRSP framework, they are merely 'internalised' as, in order to obtain desired debt relief, countries are supposed to define a home-grown economic strategy that is subsequently validated by the BWIs. As such, the principles of ownership and

Box 6.1 The new relationships between stakeholders

The major novelty of the new strategies to fight poverty is their recognition of the central role and expanded scope for stakeholders to be involved in the definition and implementation of policies, thereby ending the purely techno-cratic approach previously favoured. In consequence, analysis of the PRSP processes underway, as well as their chances of success, may be guided by a diagram, based on the identification of key stakeholders in the procedure, which stresses the modalities of their interaction (convergence of interests, tactical alliances, power relationships, sources of tension, open conflicts).

As a first approximation, three generic categories merit distinction. Each may be split into two sub-groups, the one dominant and the other dominated:

- the state, in its broadest sense, differentiating between the Ministry of Finance and other public institutions (technical ministries, local admin-istrations);

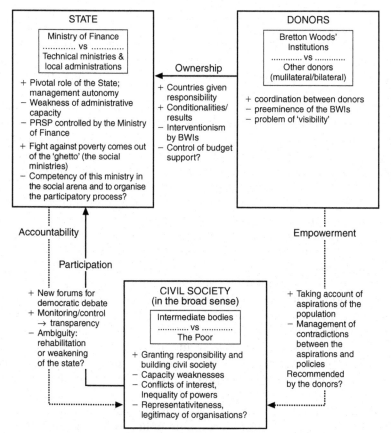

Figure 6.2 The relationships between the state, civil society and the donors.

Note
(+) positive points; (−) weak points, problems.

- civil society at large, differentiating between organised intermediate groups and the citizenry (whose opinions are supposed to be relayed through 'public opinion'), most especially the poor;
- the donor community, separating the BWIs from other donors (multi-lateral and bilateral).

Figure 6.2 attempts to synthesise the intensity and the nature of relationships (both inter and intra) which generally characterise these three poles today. We have sought to determine the factors that work, in concrete terms, in favour (+) or against (−) an efficient and balanced coordination of poverty alleviation policies. The interest of this diagram is not simply heuristic. It may also be applied (and eventually refined) to specific national contexts and consequently mobilised in a prescriptive perspective to reduce contradictions that threaten the realisation of objectives set by the PRSPs. In effect, the presentation of this tri-polar model is not fixed, but the result of a social construct in permanent flux.

conditionality would appear antithetic. The principle extolling national sovereignty thus remains, in fact, largely illusory: the means of intervention by the international financial community remain dependent on coercion to a large degree.

PRSPs are, above all, conditions imposed by the BWIs for the granting of new financial aid. This puts a bias on the process of local ownership from the start. As the strategy must be ratified by these institutions, the respect for conditionalities and policies suggested by the latter takes precedence over those judged adequate by national actors. But, how can there be some ownership without freedom of choice? As argued by Stiglitz (2002), freedom means the right to make choices, and to accept their consequences.

As an example, in several low-income countries the poor are wary of liberal economic reforms and disengagement by the state (see the case of Madagascar in Chapter 5). Nevertheless, most often the divergent positions on this orientation are not only ignored in the elaboration of policies, but also they are not even considered a topic for debate in seminars and workshops grouping various stakeholders. In sum, for as long as the negotiating power of national authorities remains limited compared to that of the BWIs, which is the case with most low-income countries, the participatory process appears largely an alibi. A lack of technical capacity in most of these countries, together with the foregoing, explains why several PRSPs have in fact been directly prepared by the BWIs or by external consultants (Habbard 2002).

This procedure, which nevertheless constitutes the principal innovation of PRSPs as ways of designing economic policy, is where the distance is probably greatest between laudable objectives claimed and what pertains in practice. Observation of the PRSP design processes shows that, until now, BWIs' intervention remains generally very marked.

The PRSP logic also leads to a growth of budget support at the expense of project aid.[3] Whereas project aid precludes all policy appropriation, it could be thought this would become easier with budget support. This is justified first by the fact that funds liberated by debt relief within the PRSP framework lead to public debt service savings and, as such, constitute budget support. In addition, the desire to obtain aid 'ownership' by recipient countries has as its corollary the granting of greater management control over these funds, which is inherent in budget support.

This is a contradictory evolution from the donors' point of view. It may be less costly in management terms, which ties in well with the trend to reducing official development assistance (and the human resources available for project management – particularly true of the World Bank), but it presents the inconvenience of reduced visibility. Funds disbursed into the budget are no longer identifiable whereas those earmarked for projects allow donors to claim a role in the fulfilment of such projects. This characteristic explains the reticence of certain countries faced with this development (Booth 2002).

For recipient countries, project aid poses several unresolved problems, widely studied in recent years, notably regarding fungibility, accountability and transparency in aid management (Naudet 2000a, 2000b). The two latter problems are even more acute in the case of budget support. In the end, reinforcement of the managerial capacity of states and greater accountability are clearly indispensable (see pp. 176–7). In the short term, the BWIs propose greater aid selectivity to compensate for reduced conditionalities and to limit the risks associated with the relative growth of budget support. This involves the channelling of aid in priority to those countries that manage development aid correctly and transparently (World Bank 1998a; Chavagneux and Tubiana 2000). Nevertheless, experience shows that the amount of debt relief granted to poor countries is allocated according to purely financial criteria connected to their debt sustainability; these criteria neither take into account their financial needs in order to conduct their poverty alleviation strategies (see Chapter 10), nor the quality of their governance. Overall, debt relief to poor countries within the HIPC Initiative has privileged political considerations, encouraging the rapid disbursal of promised sums because of international pressure. Nothing indicates that the political and geostrategic goals that in large part underlie the geographical allocation of development aid, regardless of selectivity principles, play any less a part than before.

Finally, conditionality criteria have changed. They no longer concern only the measures to be adopted, but also and above all the outcomes regarding poverty reduction (see in particular the link with the Millennium Development Goals presented in Chapter 11). The evolution of conditionality and the relative growth of budget aid are intimately linked. In effect, the establishment of results-based indicators is also a means of controlling a posteriori the use made of external funds, because permanent monitoring as applied to project aid is no longer feasible.

The extent of the changes should not be underestimated. Rather than encourage developing country governments to act out a pantomime, inciting them to stress the formal aspects of their respect for their commitments, for the first time emphasis is placed on the fundamentals; that is to say, policy results. We may say this is a sensible principle for the evolution of any policy, whatever the field. However, it will be more difficult to put these principles into practice than it seems. Box 6.2 describes some of the implementation problems experienced with the new approach in Burkina Faso.

The emphasis put on policy results also raises some analytical problems. What would happen if, for example, the trajectory followed by a country differs from its goals for exogenous reasons, such as the Aids epidemic which has reduced life expectancy in several African countries (see Chapter 1), or a prolonged slump in the prices of primary export commodities? Such questions touch the limits of understanding of the links between growth and poverty, or the impact of the international environment on the poor (see Chapter 1), and more generally the difficulty of evaluating the impact of policies (see Chapter 14).

Reinforcement of donor cohesion or of BWIs' hegemony?

Conceived as a holistic development strategy, PRSPs aim to improve coherence between donor interventions. Insofar as all donor countries are also shareholders in the BWIs, approvals of programmes naturally lead a priori to their incorporation in each country's aid policy. This is exactly what has happened progressively over recent years, the OECD contributing to this harmonisation process by defining its guidelines for poverty reduction to be followed by its member countries (OECD 2001). However, the risk remains that greater practical cohesion masks an alignment of all donors, whether bilateral or multilateral, behind a strategy defined and applied by the BWIs through their new financial instruments without consultation with the others.[4]

The European Commission (EC) considers that PRSPs should serve as bases for the definition of its aid policies (Box 6.3). Programming directives for the ninth European Development Fund (EDF) destined for the ACP countries (Africa, Caribbean and Pacific) within the framework of the Cotonou Convention, state (European Commission 2001): 'for countries involved in the definition and the implementation of poverty reduction strategies within the context of the World Bank initiative, it is automatically presumed that the EDF departure point will be preparation of a PRSP'. This desire also poses the question of European participation in the definition and implementation of PRSPs in the field: in spite of the fact that the European countries contribute to more than half of inter-

Box 6.2 Implementing the new approach to conditionality in Burkina Faso

Under the umbrella of support for structural adjustment and of the Strategic Partnership with Africa, Burkina Faso was chosen to conduct a test on a new approach to conditionality. This European Commission initiative began in 1997. The aim was to improve government ownership of the policy planning, monitoring and evaluation processes, and to improve aid effectiveness by introducing measurable performance indicators defined prior to the test. The indicators used to assess and disburse budget support related to budgetary orientations and procedures, management of public contracts, health (attendance rates at health centres, cost of medical treatment, vaccination rates, etc.) and education (primary school enrolment rates, average cost of primary schooling, etc.).

All the stakeholders were disappointed by the initiative. Factors such as difficulties in controlling the information provided, insufficient thought concerning the monitoring tools to be used, the issue of joint responsibility and how much freedom the government had to choose the appropriate actions to reach the goals set, were all used to explain this part failure. However, although it was aware of the system's shortcomings, the European Commission recommended that the experience be continued under the PRSP process, as an incentive to accelerate the reforms aimed at adopting the results-monitoring approach, and to make it clear to the government of Burkino Faso that it approved of the policies that it wished to implement. This continuation of the new approach to conditionality within the PRSP was backed by the World Bank and the other donors.

According to a field study aimed at assessing the budget policies monitoring system, the instruments for the new conditionality can be criticised with respect to the monitoring system itself and to the donors' practices (Malgoubri *et al.* 2002). The main points highlighted in the study are outlined below.

The monitoring system was not sufficiently thought through. For example, all the indicators, whether they concern input, output, outcome or impact, are monitored on an annual basis (except for income poverty indicators, obtained from household surveys to be carried out every four years). This periodicity does not suit all the indicators, or the administrative services' monitoring capabilities. The impact of a public intervention can be felt over a longer time span than a financial year. The preparation of such indicators depends on several factors, some dependent and others independent of government action. The link between budget policies and results in terms of poverty reduction has not been clearly identified. This requires better targeting of the actions to be undertaken, the introduction of surveys capable of estimating the impact of public intervention policies and a significant increase in an administration's analytical capacities. Also, there is insufficient control over the information collected. For example, all too often it is the public service providers who are required to provide the data on take-up levels for public services, although they often lack motivation or have little information on the overall aim of the operation. This method provides no information on the factors that explain the level of demand for public services other than the level of supply.

Despite the joint protocol for PRSP support signed by the World Bank and the European Commission, the two institutions continue to disagree about the monitoring of the PRSP. The World Bank continues to formulate conditionalities on the instruments, not only on results, contrary to the European position. The World Bank expects the government to introduce a better monitoring system. It adds a legal argument whereby, as it is granting loans and not donations, the contract requires that the borrower commits itself to actions and not to attaining results, which are by nature uncertain. Similarly, the document that sets out the measures required to reach finalisation of the HIPC initiative demands reforms that are not necessarily in agreement with the PRSP's goals. It demands that a new plan be adopted to recruit teachers on a contractual basis, rather than as part of the civil service, and with a lower salary scale. These measures are not mentioned in the PRSP. Actions are also demanded with respect to governance, but are not included in the PRSP either. In addition, HIPC funds are currently managed in a way that is closer to project management than to budget support. The donors' practices and the messages they are giving are therefore ambiguous. This casts doubts on the government's ownership of the reforms but also, at the end of the day, on the donors themselves. Finally, it is a shame that, although the indicators and the monitoring systems have been studied since 1997, the resulting system is just as 'imperfect' as in the other countries under the PRSP system. Also, putting the focus on the indicators has disposed of the very necessary debate on the content of the reforms. Possible ownership of the indicators tells us nothing about the ownership of the reforms!

Source: Mesplé-Somps, derived from Malgoubri *et al.* (2002).

national development aid (and that the EC, through its delegations, is represented in most developing countries), the BWIs appear reticent to accept European participation when this is proposed (see Chapter 8). In addition, France, who figures among the principal bilateral donors of development aid, finds difficulty in making its position felt.

For such coordination to function effectively, the BWIs need to consider the experience of other donors. Although the UNDP has long experience in the fight against poverty (Kankwenda *et al.* 1999), the BWIs have taken very little account of it, either in terms of concepts or country strategies (see Box 6.3).

A participatory process, to strengthen democracy

One of the main innovations in the PRSP approach consists in associating civil society in the definition and monitoring of policies, with the goal of

Box 6.3 The views of the European Union, France and the UNDP

If all aid agencies have unanimously engaged in the battle against poverty, and accepted to align behind the new strategy conceived by the BWIs, recurrent lines of tension running through this community have not miraculously disappeared. This box considers the positions of three strategic donors: the European Union and France, two of the largest aid donors (notably regarding Africa), and the United Nations Development Programme (UNDP) for its intellectual contribution.

The European Union: its giant wings impede it from walking

The European Union fully adheres to the new international consensus surrounding poverty alleviation. The priority accorded to this question is long standing and largely institutionalised. Article 130 of the Maastricht Treaty already made poverty reduction an obligation for European cooperation. The European Union has played a precursory role on numerous fronts in the reorientation of official development assistance (budget aid, ex post results-based conditionalities, donor coordination within countries, management of public finances, and so on). It has furnished itself with financial instruments and procedures that are perfectly integrated in the global architecture initiated by the BWIs (such as with the establishment of Poverty Reduction Support Grants – PRSGs). The principles underlying the ninth EDF and Country Strategy Papers insist on the need for articulating European aid and the PRSP process.

The European Commission's diagnosis of the current PRSP framework (essentially based on interim PRSPs) is highly positive. The European Commission nevertheless underlines a number of shortcomings that highlight its own priorities. Principles of ownership, of accountability, of transparency and of participation are highly valued.

In particular, the principle and the quality of the participatory process are considered a central aspect of the preparation, implementation and monitoring of PRSPs, and consequently of the EU's interventions. Europe proposes to guarantee the reality of consultations and the taking into account of the wishes of civil society, especially the poor themselves ('voicing' and 'empowerment').

On the other hand, less stress is placed on questions of economic policy content, in the strict sense (with the exception of regional integration and, less importantly, equity), for which the European Commission is comparatively poorly equipped, than on their links with questions of governance (including the fight against corruption), respect for human rights and democracy. Furthermore, in 2001 the IMF (in a remarkable way and for the first time to our knowledge) conditioned its aid programme to the Côte d'Ivoire on Europe resuming its aid to that country (which depended on improvements to the respect of human rights by the government).

France: difficulties in making its small voice heard

To a certain extent, the stress international cooperation put on poverty alle-viation at the end of the 1990s caught France unawares. After a period of vacillation, while French cooperation sought to avoid its marginalisation by claiming it 'engaged battle against poverty without explicitly stating so (without knowing so?)', it ended by officially embracing the consensus on aid policy. Today, if France is entirely involved in different international initiatives (PRSPs, HIPC, Paris 21) and has realigned its instruments in this sense, it is no less seeking to make its voice heard.

In a general way, the French position remains distinguished from the 'post Washington' consensus by the importance it attaches to the mechan-isms and instruments of public regulation to counterbalance an overly liberal orientation where the 'market' dominates (DGCID 2001). It consists of reinforcing the role of the state in poor countries, improvement of the functioning of administrations, promotion of active redistributive policies, and the protection of social and political, as well as economic rights. The aim is to fight not only poverty, but also inequality and exclusion. It also comprises the consolidation of international regulatory bodies charged with improving the production and availability of global public goods, all the while favouring greater participation by poor countries in negotiations.

While strongly put forward, the particularity of the French point of view and its contribution are largely ignored by the BWIs. The Development Committee (IMF and World Bank 2001a) makes significant mention of the excellent participation of other donors and cites numerous activities and initiatives underway or foreseen: the British (DFID), regarding statistics and impact analysis; the Dutch for capacity building activities; Switzerland, Germany and the Nordic countries, the European Union, Japan for aligning their aid instruments to the generic PRSP framework; the OECD Develop-ment Assistance Committee (DAC) for donor coordination; UN agencies (UNDP, ILO, etc.), notably in the field of international development indic-ators, and so on. Paradoxically, no mention is made of the French contribu-tion. The reason for this silence is no doubt to be found in the implicit competition for leadership in the field of development aid towards poor countries, especially in Africa, and in France's structural difficulties to promote its interests. It should be noted that, unlike the BWIs which can base their strategic options on a substantial stock of high-level expertise, France's means for research and reflection are sparse (like those of most other donors, including the European Union). From this point of view, comparison with the United Kingdom is illuminating: their capacity for influence is much greater than their financial contribution.

UNDP: how to exercise influence with ideas, but no money?

As in several other fields (governance, capacity building, programme approach, donor coordination), the UNDP plays a leading role in poverty alleviation. Following its famous criticism of structural adjustment in *Adjust-*

ment with a Human Face (Cornia, Jolly and Stewart 1987), the UNDP took up the torch and has demonstrated remarkable perseverance in promoting the theme of poverty: establishment of the Dimensions of Social Adjustment programme with the World Bank and the African Development Bank; institutionalisation of the Global Human Development Report (HDR), published each year since 1990 and giving rise to the publication of national reports on Sustainable Human Development (NHDRs) prepared by local specialists in several developing countries.

The UNDP was the first to take up the work on poverty by Amartya Sen, future Nobel prizewinner, and played an important role in developing the theory behind the phenomenon; the concept of sustainable human development; the development of indicators of human development (HDI) and of human poverty (HPI), and so on. In the political arena, the UNDP, together with UNICEF, originated the 20/20 initiative according to which donors and governments in developing countries should devote 20 per cent of their resources to basic social services. The organisation, following the Social Development Summit (Copenhagen 1995) received a mandate to coordinate the UN's operational assistance for poverty-centred development.

The PRSP initiative launched by the BWIs in late 1999 telescopes with efforts towards developing national poverty alleviation strategies already engaged on the ground by the UNDP in numerous countries (the Poverty Strategies Initiative), strategies the principles of which are astonishingly close to those advocated today (notably the stress placed on ownership and the involvement of civil society). The hegemonic power of the BWIs and their incomparable financial muscle has relegated the UNDP to a secondary place in a field where it can claim a certain comparative advantage. A sign of this unfavourable balance of power in the competition between donors is that certain Poverty Strategies Initiatives initiated by the UNDP have been simply swept aside, and the process restarted from zero despite the considerable waste of resources (see Chapter 8 for the case of Mali).

Today, and while seeking harmonious collaboration against a universal plague, UNDP operatives eat humble pie and are reduced to finding niches to demonstrate their expertise, with the meagre consolation of a memory of having been at the origin of this movement.

strengthening the democratic debate and, as such, the legitimacy and efficacy of policies. Organisation of the participatory process poses a number of difficulties that, depending on the case, may be intrinsic or, on the contrary, specific to the low-income country concerned. The difficulties examined hereafter touch on the criteria necessary to allow civil society representatives to contribute to the determination of economic policies, as well as the real influence of the exercise on political decision-making.

Despite numerous difficulties and imperfections, there is no doubt that this initiative should be encouraged (see Box 6.4). Few of the countries

Box 6.4 Poverty alleviation: the World Bank between two stools

For several years, the World Bank has been subject to criticism from both wings of the political stage. The first, largely relayed by anti-globalisation movements, comes from the Left. It is based on a rejection of liberalisation, the founding principle of structural adjustment policies promoted by the BWIs, which is blamed for originating a growth in inequalities and the marginalisation of poor countries. The second criticism, more discrete but no less effective, comes from the conservative American Right. They argue for greater isolationism, stigmatising the failure of development aid policies, a waste of resources and their diversion to the profit of authoritarian or corrupt governments ('aid fatigue', 'trade not aid'). Ironically, they apply the same 'bureaucratic tests' to the BWIs (which they consider as costly parasites) that the latter impose on developing countries (see in this regard the famous Meltzer report 2000).

The placing of poverty alleviation to the fore has not reduced this twin assault, despite the consensus surrounding the subject. We summarise the arguments of former US Treasury Secretary Larry Summers (Summers 2001) which epitomise those of critics on the Right (although he was part of the Clinton democrat administration). His administration exercised great pressure during preparation of the 2000/2001 World Development Report, pressure that resulted in the resignations of Joseph Stiglitz and Ravi Kanbur as well as reformulation of the report re-establishing the role of growth as central (Wade 2001):

- Nothing (no economic study) proves that participation brings an improvement to growth policies. Asian experience shows that authoritarian regimes favoured growth that in turn facilitated pressure for a democratic transition.
- According to this technocratic economic approach, the Bank would do better to rely on 'scientific' studies showing the solid foundation of policies (which, according to Summers, constitute its comparative advantage) rather than base its arguments on suggestions from non-specialists and their populist drift.
- Larry Summers takes offence: how could the Bank promote an expression of citizens other than that of the democratically elected government, which is an emanation of the people and which represents its natural or sole interlocutor ('No U.S. city mayor would begin to tolerate from the federal government the kind of practices that the Bank regularly imposes or seems to impose in the context of democratically elected countries.'). According to him, such a detour via 'civil society' cannot but fragment young democracies. Summers nevertheless recognises the analogy is less pertinent for undemocratic regimes.

Paradoxically, the incursion of the BWIs into the political arena and the institutionalisation of new means of intervention (promotion of the participatory process, reinforcement of dialogue with non-state actors) are also denounced by the Left. The two criticisms converge on this point: 'stuffed with economists and engineers, development aid institutions do not have adequate competency for this type of activity' (Chavagneux 2001). It is nevertheless necessary to underline the fact that, beyond appearances, the motivations are radically opposed. On the one hand there is a refusal of the political implications; on the other there is an affirmation of the strictly political character of all forms of intervention (even when this is presented as strictly economic), but denial of the technical capacity of the BWIs to form a consensus, or suspicion as to the real intentions of what may be just a slogan.

Some Left critics also consider that poverty measurement will be politically slanted to justify the treatment of the less poor among the poor, to drain the social protection debate, or as a smokescreen for the stage appearance of governance or decentralisation which merely displaces forms of clientelism and corruption from national to local elites (Lautier 2001).

In effect, the two criticisms mobilise the rhetoric of 'perverse effects', magisterially described by Hirschman (1991), to disqualify poverty alleviation strategies, and notably the participation of civil society as proposed by the BWIs. Clearly, the criticism of Summers appears out of court, at least in the political context of poor countries. Effectively, elections are the high point in a democratic regime when citizens delegate powers to representatives, whom they may unseat at the next election should they wish. From this standpoint, the participatory process may appear to contradict these principles in part. Why should the government be accountable to intermediate institutions (civil society) not subject to any procedure ensuring representativeness (unlike elected assemblies)?

Nevertheless, it is demagogic and illusory to think that formal democracy (elections, as practised in Africa) is enough to ensure a thorough representation of the hopes of the citizenry, even if the poor constitute a majority:

- for the small minority of countries undergoing democratic consolidation (Benin, Madagascar, Mali, Senegal, etc.), newly elected regimes have not radically changed the state's predatory nature. At best, elections ensure a more rapid rotation of elites bent on the capture of rents granted by access to public resources ('a place at the trough'). In these cases, citizens' control and the accountability of authorities and the political class are always deficient. Nothing indicates that corruption has declined. The link between policies applied and those voted for is not necessarily clear, as political parties present no precise manifestos;
- for most countries, democratic transition has not taken place and governments remain authoritarian or semi-authoritarian (Togo, Cameroon, Gabon, and so on).

In any event, and unlike historical democracies, intermediate civil society bodies (parties, trade unions, associations, NGOs) are extremely fragile, if not absent. Yet it is they who are supposed to ensure democratic control between elections (lobbying groups, petitions, demonstrations, etc.). There is thus little or no mediation between the elected powers and the people, especially the most disfavoured among them (for the case of Madagascar, see Roubaud 2000a).

In such conditions, the participatory process principle is a potentially positive factor. It may contribute to the reinforcement of intermediate institutions (social capital), weigh on the accountability of the state, enlarge the democratic debate and improve the circulation of information. This is clearly not to say that the way participatory processes have been established is satisfactory, nor that the sidelining of elected assemblies in several cases is acceptable.

Regarding criticism from the Left, we share some of their arguments: underestimation of the question of inequalities and the role of the state (despite its partial recognition), disqualification of some economic policy tools (policies of redistribution) or certain actors (trade unions) for ideological reasons, the masking of conflicts of interest, ignorance of the risks of decentralisation, and so on.

Nevertheless, it appears to us that the reproach of systematic duplicity by the BWIs in their adoption of the basic principle of poverty alleviation is in large part unfounded. For example, Lautier (2001) interprets imposition of the poverty incidence indicator as central to poverty measurement, by which interventions may be judged, as the result of a political calculation by the World Bank. This choice is meant to convey the supposed desire of the Bank to seek the 'least poor among the poor', because that would allow the rapid publication of results at least cost and limit the chances of an eventual social dispute (the poorest among the poor are rarely sufficiently organised to act or to make their voice heard). In reality, previous and current policies of the BWIs incite thinking to the contrary. On the one hand, such a strategy would have led to the establishment of indicators of basic needs and of the social services (education and health), factors that have recorded far better performances than growth over the long term and depend on the evolution of monetary poverty (they are, on the other hand, more directly guided by public policy and thus more 'controllable'). On the other hand, the Bank traditionally signals a marked preference for rural development. Indeed, it is exactly in the countryside that the immense majority of the 'poorest among the poor' are concentrated.

engaged in the definition and implementation of PRSPs are democratic (some are overtly autocratic) or afford their populations alternative opportunities to express themselves. It would be naive to think that PRSPs alone can generate a civil society if it does not already exist. It nevertheless contributes to structuring it, and also provides a forum that was previously absent for the expression of problems and opinions. An eloquent example comes from Benin where the participatory process undertaken in the provinces allowed government representatives to 'discover' that the main problem for schools was teacher absenteeism (Booth 2002).

The criteria for legitimacy, representativeness and civil society capacity

The World Bank considers three criteria as essential for ensuring effective civil society participation at the national level:

- legitimacy: the group is registered, is recognised by the public and has functioned effectively according to its stated objectives;
- representativeness: the group represents the interests and the needs of its constituency;
- capacity: the group has the organizational and analytic capabilities necessary to carry out its objectives, it is able to articulate the group's demands and interests, and is able to represent its members in multi-stakeholder dialogues.

(Tikare *et al.* 2001)

Somewhat surprisingly, despite its essential role in the process, civil society is not precisely defined by the World Bank. This 'catch-all' term comprises very diverse definitions, according to source and epoch. Civil society, in its most accepted form, may be defined by exclusion; neither is it the state, nor is it the merchant community. We will accept the following definition:

Civil society is a political space within which non-profit organisations seek to influence rules applied to such or such aspect of social life. In this context, the term 'rules' can refer to specific policies, more general standards, or deeper social structure.

(Scholte 2002)

In reality, while non-governmental organisations (NGOs) are generally considered as the only representatives of civil society, they frequently lack representativeness, legitimacy and capacity. The central role played by NGOs (by default, in the absence of other representative organisations) risks to increase the normal perverse effects arising from their function as 'development brokers' (seeking development 'rents') or as 'fronts' for the administration (Bako-Arifari and Le Meur 2001; Lautier 2001; Raffinot and Roubaud 2001). According to Hoddinott (2002): 'In fractionalised communities, or where trust and/or social capital are weak, there is a risk that community participation may result in the capture of benefits by local elites, to the detriment of the poor.'

Trade unions are often excluded from the process. This weakens them further, considering the fact that (where they previously existed) they have been sapped by several decades of crisis and structural adjustment. The private sector is considered *de facto* a part of civil society (Chambas and Kerhuel 2001), despite the World Bank considering it a stakeholder in its own right alongside civil society, parliament, the general public, and so on. Furthermore, it should be noted that representatives of the private sector are not always explicitly involved in the participatory process (see Chapter 8 for the example of Mali). This may be explained by the frequent atrophy of employers' associations in low-income countries (taking account of the weak contribution of the formal sector), and also by the fact that enterprises (at least the largest among them) have their own means of lobbying government.

Does this mean that the participation of civil society is useless, or even that it introduces bias to the functioning of democracy? To be sure, parliament is often marginalised in the PRSP framework: in several cases it is not consulted on the PRSP content – which nevertheless constitutes a multi-year framework defining the country's economic policy – or, alternatively, its opinion is insufficiently taken into account (McGee, Levene and Hughes 2001). However, parliament considers itself the only truly representative institution. 'I am the civil society', says the speaker of the Malian parliament (see Chapter 8), which is largely abusive considering the democratic weaknesses of these countries. Despite the foregoing, it is clearly desirable that parliament fully participates in the process (European Commission 2001; McGee, Levene and Hughes 2001). The tension between democratic legitimacy (based on elections) and representativeness and participation, in connection with the increasing weight of the civil society and of the governance concept, is far from being restricted to poor countries. This tension is also increasingly acute in the old historic democracies in the North (Capdevielle forthcoming).

It is clear that the lack of coordination and organisation of civil society in poor countries is a serious handicap for the success of the process. It appears that few among them have a civil society sufficiently organised to meet the various conditions required by the World Bank to participate in the exercise: Ghana might be the exception that provides the rule (Booth 2002). In most others, the process must above all be seen as a motor for strengthening civil society, in the knowledge that results will not be instantaneous and that the process can only be effective over the long term, given national traditions and democratic weaknesses.

The participatory process: a utopian ideal?

Implementation of the principle of accountability leads us to question the management of conflicts of interest within civil society and the way in which policy definition takes into account the outcome of the participatory process. In addition, the PRSP process signals, for the BWIs, an incursion into the political arena that they have attempted to avoid until now, at least officially (Chavagneux and Tubiana 2000). This incursion is partial, however, insofar as PRSPs do not take into account conflicts of interest within society and the need for arbitration, nor all the implications of the process for the state.

As outlined in the World Bank World Development Report *Attacking*

Poverty, which eludes the question in large part (see Chapter 1), the principle of the participatory process does not permit the resolution of conflicts of interest. In this sense, according to Lautier (2002), the participatory process concept is 'utopian'. The choice between a purely consultative character of the process or, to the contrary, the granting of decisional power is not explicit, even if there is a trend in practice towards the former alternative, which in turn generates frustrations among participants who hope to contribute to policy-making (McGee, Levene and Hughes 2001). In this regard, the function of the participatory process is fundamentally different from that of the participatory municipal budgets established in Porto Alegre (Brazil) by the Workers' Party, cited as an example by the World Bank (Tikare *et al.* 2001). Unlike the PRSPs, the adoption of these budgets reflects choices between various projects presented by constituents.

Shortcomings in the participatory process may lead to two alternative outcomes:

1   It is probable that those exercising the greatest power impose their point of view. In Nicaragua, the privatisation of water distribution services was incorporated in the PRSP despite opposition from civil society and parliament (Habbard 2001). The obligation to allocate funds released by debt relief to health and education services, rather than to other sectors, equally raised questions from certain sections of civil society. The pertinence of the option was subject neither to debate nor to real justification. Such practice limits the involvement of various national stakeholders to a simple consultative role.

2   The alternative is that difficult and socially divisive issues will be avoided during the participatory process, thus making the poverty reduction strategies less successful. In some countries, such as Bolivia, governments attempt to please all stakeholders and discussions centre on the distribution of development aid rather than on the definition of a true strategy (Habbard 2002). More generally, while the question of priorities is essential, given the constraints of public finance, it is a source of potential conflict (excluding those imposed by BWIs' conditionalities) and is left aside in most PRSPs.

In other respects, the interest of the approach is manifest only where it leads to the preparation of a feasible PRSP, which is ultimately successfully put in practice. Civil society frequently blames the failure of previous strategies on weak implication by national authorities, rather than policy content. But the participatory process principle, even where it favours national support and adhesion by civil society, does not necessarily lead to a stronger involvement by governments in the realisation of PRSP targets.

While admitting that an effective monitoring system may be established, it will not be operational unless the system of accountability functions as it should. According to this concept, those who govern have a duty to inform, to justify and to explain their actions to their citizens, and the latter must have the possibility to sanction their leaders and to force them to take decisions. It is nevertheless rare that such a framework effectively surrounds political life in poor countries (Bratton and van de Walle 1997). Democracy, which may guarantee a respect for such principles, frequently presents numerous dysfunctions. Public opinion has little weight compared to the power of those who govern, and little influence on the conduct of national affairs (see Chapter 5).

Defining economic policies to alleviate poverty is a difficult exercise, both for national leaders and for civil society. For most of them it is a first experience. Capacity weaknesses, a lack of training and inadequate information prevent them from proposing concrete policies that can withstand rigorous analysis or be defended against donor prerogatives. Ownership, as an objective, risks coming up against this problem of inadequate capacity with, as a result, a return to the practice of externally defined policy-making, although this is supposedly a thing of the past.

Weakening or rehabilitating the state?

What is the impact of the donors' new attitude and calling on civil society for the state and for its vocation? The start of the PRSP process and the priority given to poverty alleviation undoubtedly involves changes to the role of the state, as signalled by the World Bank in its 1997 World Development Report *The State in a Changing World.* Some ambiguity remains. Rehabilitation is of course partial, as it does not question liberalisation policies introduced with structural adjustment that effectively reduced the state's field for intervention. It can also be argued that promoting the concept of governance (that means all institutional, formal and informal decision-making procedures) seems to dilute responsibilities and to weaken the role of the state. In fact, the state has to conduct the participatory process and at the same time share the responsibility with a growing number of collective and individual, public and private actors (Banegas and Meyer 2002).

As remarked by Haubert (2001), it is nevertheless surprising that the promotion of civil society accompanies a convergence of criticism of the state by liberal thinkers and by left-wing NGOs: 'The necessity for a vigorous civil society, acting in partnership with market forces and with a reduced and purged state, reappears as a leitmotiv in the discourse of the donors as well as of progressive militants.'

This increased role raises a major question. To be sure, PRSPs confer a pivotal role on the state as the pilot of the participatory process, and as being responsible for the conduct of poverty alleviation policies. But, after several decades of crisis and structural adjustment ruled by the 'less state' philosophy (the impact of which is compounded by the devastating effects of the Aids epidemic in several African countries), we may ask if the state is capable of assuming these new responsibilities. In this respect, structural adjustment policies have not only failed, but they have also paradoxically contributed to a severe weakening of the state (Razafindrakoto and Roubaud 2001a). The World Bank considers this problem to be especially acute in Africa:

> The adjustment decades also saw a substantial deterioration in the quality of public institutions, a demoralization of public servants, and a decline in the effectiveness of service delivery in many countries. Together with falling incomes, these effects – which cannot be speed-ily reversed – translated into falling social indicators and capabilities in many countries and to losses of human capital, especially (though not exclusively) in the public service.
>
> (World Bank 2000c)

Definition and implementation of poverty alleviation policies: the state's responsibility

Structural adjustment policies tended to reduce the role of the state through external and internal liberalisation of the economy, as well as by eroding the responsibility of countries charged with applying largely exter-nally defined policies. PRSPs, on the contrary, claim to increase national autonomy; similarly, they reinforce the public sector's role in defining and applying economic policy.

The state is thus conferred with the responsibility for establishing a heavy and complex mechanism. This mission demands not only time but also financial and human resources. Its success depends on a number of preconditions rarely met in the current circumstances of low-income countries, more so because various pressures militate for the attainment of rapid results. First and foremost, institutional capacity limitations and the exorbitant costs of managing and maintaining the mobilisation of stake-holders over the long term will restrict the scope of the process. Deficien-cies of organisational capacity appear from the early stages of consultation and policy definition.

In countries with limited experience, the establishment of efficient pro-cedures for participation and programme monitoring by the public is far from easy, particularly when linked to strict timetable constraints.[5] In such conditions, participation can only be partial. Furthermore, for local authorities to shoulder the process, as envisaged by the World Bank, such authorities need to possess the capacity of organising the participatory process at their level. This financial and time constraint, coupled with the lack of experience of responsible administrations, explains difficulties experienced with the circulation of information, which is essential for the establishment of a truly participatory process.

For participation to be real, PRSPs must be available to the public. In Cambodia, the full PRSP was only made available in Khmer in the final version, all earlier drafts being written in English (Eurodad 2001a). More generally, the scope for debate is limited by the weak availability of information, not only about the strategy being developed but also about past policies and their impacts. Previous strategies and existing analyses should be taken into account as inputs to the preparation of PRSPs. In some countries (such as Bolivia, Honduras, Mozambique and Nicaragua), interim documents incorporated previous poverty reduction policies, but such cases are far from widespread.

Budget management reform

The three-year framework for economic policy defined by a PRSP includes estimates of costs and associated resources for the envisaged policies, which increases the state's budget programming responsibility. The BWIs have recommended multi-annual budget planning for several years, in the context of Medium Term Expenditure Frameworks (MTEFs).

The World Bank claims that strengthening public expenditure management in low-income countries is also an urgent priority, so as to identify the development aid circuit as well as the resources allocated to poverty alleviation:

> A major issue in Burkina Faso and Zambia is the need to capture fully foreign-financed capital expenditure in the budget and fiscal reporting system. Benin and Burkina Faso face additional challenges in tracking poverty-reducing spending at the subnational level.
>
> (IMF and World Bank 2001a)

The state, in order to meet its new responsibilities, assumes greater autonomy in the management of foreign aid flows. This runs counter to the project aid logic where parallel structures used to be established to bypass and compensate for the state's inefficiency (Booth 2002), resulting in the inevitable supplementary weakening of national institutions. While apparently positive in terms of cohesion and ownership, the impact of this change to the form of aid depends, in fact and above all, on the quality of public institutions in the recipient country. If a large part of public aid is purely and simply diverted by a predatory state, or if it is managed within a clientelist system (two common occurrences), then the growth of budgetary support will eventually have a negative impact on the overall efficacy of aid.

In sum, therefore, PRSPs encourage accelerated reform of the state and reinforcement of its capacities. On the other hand, blockages to reform may constitute an obstacle to the implementation of policies under optimal conditions (Overseas Development Institute 2001). This worry is expressed by the BWIs' review (IDA and IMF 2002): 'In many countries, current PEM [Public Expenditure Management] systems are too weak to support a meaningful presentation of the overall public expenditure program in the PRSP and to monitor implementation.'

Results-oriented expenditure management is one good example of the above-mentioned difficulties. This approach to public expenditure management is strongly supported by the World Bank and the donors in order to improve the efficiency and accountability of the budget process. But its implementation – often without due preparation – is confronted with serious difficulties; this should not be a surprise, considering the difficulties met in developed countries for putting in place this approach (see the example of France, in spite of the five-year span between the actual decision and its implementation in 2006).

The eventual incapacity of the state to fulfil certain of its allotted functions risks a particularly regrettable retreat. This is especially the case with budget aid. If a financial surplus realised through debt relief is diverted, or simply badly utilised, great will be the temptation to return to habitual practices of project aid. Yet, it will be too late. The sometimes-substantial surplus brought by debt relief would have been squandered already.

A new distribution of power within the administration

PRSP preparation is accompanied by institutional change and a redistribution of powers in local administration. In most countries, the job falls to the Ministry of Finance, reflecting the strong link between the PRSP and external funding, traditionally under this ministry's remit.

This is a positive evolution to a certain extent, in that sectoral ministries previously in charge of these policies generally had few means and little authority. Bringing the fight against poverty out of the 'ghetto' where it was previously confined means that it is more likely to receive greater resources (Habbard 2002).

However, the Ministry of Finance is not necessarily the best-placed authority to contribute to strategic thinking on a subject where it has no obvious competence compared to technical ministries. Nor does it have greater competence for organising a truly democratic dialogue for the transparent definition and implementation of policies. On the contrary, Ministries of Finance are more often reputed for their opacity and their technocratic character; they are more familiar with secretive bilateral negotiations with the BWIs or the Paris Club than with discussions with other ministries and civil society.

Conclusion

Weaknesses of the process under way are clearly illustrated by confronting the goals set by the participatory process for the definition and the implementation of the PRSPs with their concrete development in the field. As shown in this chapter, the following difficulties and contradictions are especially evident:

- the hegemonic power of the BWIs, relative to national actors, is contrary to the participatory approach; their role is ambiguous insofar as, while vaunting the control of the process by the countries, they impose conditionalities;
- various constraints and limits due to the current circumstances of different countries have not been taken into consideration; this is particularly true of difficulties in managing the process (organisation and resolution of conflicts of interest), as well as with shortcomings affecting some actors, notably their capacities to coordinate, analyse, criticise and propose policies, and effectively to influence final decisions.

The principle of the participatory process creates democratic demands that developing countries, like the BWIs, are neither necessarily ready nor equipped to satisfy. Moreover, effective realisation of the consultation process is trapped between two opposing objectives: the appreciation of everyone's point of view, and rigour and efficiency. It is hardly surprising that populations, even national leaders, are to a certain extent sceptical about its real purpose. This scepticism may have a demobilising effect, especially if allowed to take root. To be sure, it is an evolving process intended to improve with time. But time is against the poor countries. Disappointment and a loss of confidence arising from failures, not to speak of damage caused by the inadequacies of precipitously implemented policies, risk sucking the countries into a vicious spiral of poverty.

Despite its inadequacies, however, the process engaged with the preparation of PRSPs has already had positive repercussions, even though these remain limited. Apart from the encouragement to orient policies in favour of the poor, impacts differ according to circumstances. Substantial advances noted in some countries merit particular mention:

- the creation of new forums for public debate and the implication of different actors within society;
- improvements in budget management, especially greater transparency;
- the fixation of precise and measurable goals permitting concrete policy monitoring and evaluation, even though the interest demonstrated by countries in this aspect remains limited for the present.

In sum, the risk of failure by the PRSP process is real. It could arise both from the weak quality of a participatory process that limits its impact on the effective range of policies that result, and from the incoherence and lack of innovation of proposed policies – the latter being analysed in the next chapter. However, whereas previous structural adjustment policies were fixed from the start by the BWIs, the field is now more open. The formal conditions for developing public policies, backed by international aid and targeted on poverty reduction and development, have never before been so favourable. All now depends on the capacity of stakeholders, especially within the developing countries, to seize the opportunity.

Notes

1 This assessment is very preliminary, as less than twenty countries out of around sixty had completed their participatory process and finalised their PRSP at the time of writing this chapter (October 2002).

2 But a case study conducted on six poor countries (Albania, Ghana, Kenya, Mozambique, Vietnam and Zambia) concludes that the streamlining of conditionality within the new instruments put in place within the PRSP Initiative is limited to the IMF. It is narrowly conceived and restricted to structural, but not macroeconomic conditions; according to this study, what may happen is that many of the more important structural conditions dropped by the IMF will be taken up in World Bank programmes (Killick 2002).

3 Budget aid corresponds to funds directly attributed to the state, with no precision as to the destination of investments. To the contrary, project aid comprises a fixed envelope allocated to a specific project, subsequently undertaken under the control of the country or of the donor institution.

4 For example, Panos (2002) considers that the macroeconomic framework was not open to debate during the participatory process held in Nicaragua, partly because the PRSP was largely determined by a PRGF programme being negotiated at the same time.

5 According to the Zambia PRSP: 'In an ideal situation, and time allowing, the process of I-PRSP preparation should have involved as many stakeholders as possible. Unfortunately, there has been need for urgency for government to prepare I-PRSP so that it quickly becomes an input in the country's quest for HIPC debt relief at the earliest opportunity possible. Zambia expects to enter a period of heavier debt servicing in the coming few years and quick debt relief is urgently required to moderate this burden. Under the circumstances, consultations for I-PRSP have been limited to government institutions.'

7 Poverty Reduction Strategy Papers

Old wine in new bottles?

Jean-Pierre Cling, Mireille Razafindrakoto and François Roubaud

Around sixty low-income countries are engaged in the PRSP Initiative, which has become the key framework for development policies in these countries. The BWIs have mobilised considerable human and financial resources to implement this new approach and to ensure its success. All the major donors rapidly decided to follow suit and link their aid policies to the PRSP Initiative. Given the enormous efforts made to introduce these programmes, their increasing importance for the countries concerned and the strong mobilisation of the international community, their success or failure will undoubtedly have not only a determinant impact for the populations of the countries concerned, but also on the future of international development aid.

Having presented the general principles of PRSPs, which constitute a coherent and precise programme to fight poverty, this chapter seeks to establish a first diagnosis of their content. The analysis rests on the examination of interim and final PRSPs prepared at the end of 2002, paying particular attention to those of the countries to have finalised arrangements[1] as well as to assessments undertaken by various outside observers, and by the BWIs themselves, notably their Joint Staff Assessments and the review of the PRSP approach completed by both institutions (IDA and IMF 2002). Our goal is not to undertake an exhaustive review of the strengths and weaknesses of the documents. Rather, we seek to highlight a number of oversights that have implications for efficient poverty reduction, and which appear inadequately stressed to date. We argue that their inadequacies reflect, above all, those of the policies promoted by the BWIs, analysed in the first two chapters of this book.

We demonstrate that the invariable accent on previous strategies, with relatively minor changes to treat the poverty question, leads many PRSPs (final and interim) to present several gaps and inconsistencies. These weaknesses apply equally to the pertinence and to the range of policies, to the uncertainty surrounding their sustainability, and to the negligence of monitoring and evaluation procedures that would allow corrections to be made in an iterative process. The difference between the language employed and reality is equally stark. The translation of general orientations into concrete operational measures raises several difficulties due, in particular, to human and financial resource constraints imposed in the field.

The PRSP: a coherent and precise programme integrating the multiple dimensions of poverty

Even if the content of a PRSP should depend on the prevailing context in each country, its formulation is guided by a number of basic principles. According to the World Bank sourcebook, definition of a poverty reduction policy requires several obligatory stages, described below (Tikare *et al.* 2001).

Performing a poverty diagnosis taking its different dimensions into account

Establishment of a summary picture of the economic context and of the state of poverty is necessary in the first place (see Box 7.1). The nature and the determining factors of poverty, as well as poverty profiles of the affected populations, should be subjected to precise and detailed analysis. This is a precondition for the conception of an effective strategy for poverty reduction.

This procedure adopts a multidimensional approach to poverty, corresponding to that defended by the World Development Report on this theme (see Chapter 1).

> Participation in poverty diagnostics allows for the collection and analysis of quantitative and qualitative data. Quantitative data provides both aggregated and disaggregated data on poverty which can help guide broad policy decisions. However, without qualitative data to explain certain issues and to fill in gaps that quantitative measures miss, governments and civil society will not be able to address specific issues for reducing poverty.
>
> (Tikare *et al.* 2001)

A strategy for fighting poverty

Having described the characteristics and determinants of poverty, each PRSP should list the components of the strategy proposed for its alleviation. According to the World Bank, every PRSP should cover the four foregoing themes and BWI evaluation of the document should centre on the quality of their treatment by the countries:

- macro and structural policies to support sustainable growth in which the poor participate;

- how to improve governance – including public sector financial management;
- appropriate sectoral policies and programmes; and
- realistic costing and appropriate levels of funding for the major programmes.

(Klugman 2001)

Taking into account the complexity of the phenomenon, the interconnection of causes, and the multiplicity of handicaps suffered by the poor, poverty alleviation cannot be approached through specific projects only. What is necessary is a global, coherent programme, stressing policies that favour improved living conditions for the poor ('pro-poor' policies), taking into account the eventual negative impacts of certain measures and establishing safety nets.

A PRSP should thus present a wide range of actions in a holistic framework:

- financial stabilisation measures (reduced public deficit, fiscal reform, monetary control, and so on);
- structural reforms designed to facilitate market mechanisms and favour growth (liberalisation, privatisation, institution of a stable enabling environment to promote development of the private sector);
- sectoral reforms (in the areas of rural development, health, education and infrastructure, notably with the co-management and participation of beneficiaries to improve the quality and provision of basic services);
- institutional reforms such as decentralisation, bringing decision-making closer to the concerned population, capacity building of the state, improved functioning of institutions, and more generally promoting good governance and democracy.

If these axes of intervention are together supposed to have positive effects in reducing poverty, particular attention is given to measures directly targeting the least-favoured cohorts of society. Other than the growth of revenues of the latter (through employment policies, micro-enterprise promotion, and so on), three specific goals should guide the precise definition of policies, as set out in the World Bank Development Report devoted to poverty alleviation (see Chapter 1):

- to facilitate access by the poor to 'opportunities' and to resources (increased spending on education, health, basic infrastructure, and so on);
- to favour their 'empowerment' and their participation in social activities (decentralisation, information dissemination, participatory processes, etc.);
- to increase their 'security' (establishment of insurance systems, facilitating access to credit, targeted aid, food security, etc.).

Box 7.1 Typical structure and content of existing PRSPs

The principle of policy ownership implies that PRSPs should be country-specific. However, if the World Bank's sourcebook is wary of proposing a normative plan, the orientations proposed and elements underlined as essential in this document, as well as in the JSAs, lead to uniformity in PRSP content. The order of chapters, as well as the stress placed on specific measures or on particular sectors, varies according to country, but most final (and interim) PRSPs contain the same strategic axes. Thus, the documents frequently adopt the following structure:

1   *Current situation:* economic and social context, review of past and present policies (occasionally with outcomes – Bolivia, Honduras, Mozambique, Nicaragua), poverty profile (characteristics and determinants).

2   *Description of the participatory process* (essentially organisational logistics, with in some cases a summary of recommendations drawn – Bolivia, Honduras, Nicaragua, Tanzania).

3   *Goals and strategic axes for poverty reduction.* The various axes proposed are, generally:

   • developing an adequate pro-growth macroeconomic framework (macroeconomic stability, competitiveness of the economy and particularly key sectors, private investment incentives);
   • developing basic social services (education, health, potable water, etc.);
   • promoting employment opportunities and increased incomes for the poor (rural development, promotion of micro and small enterprises, micro-credit schemes, transport and communications infrastructure);
   • social protection for the poor (especially the installation of safety nets, but also natural resource and environmental husbandry);
   • institutional strengthening and good governance (administrative efficiency and transparency with stress placed on the improvement of public resource management, corruption, judicial reform, decentralisation).

4   *Cost assessment and resource allocation:* precise definition of actions and measures envisaged accompanied by an assessment of the resources required; HIPC resource allocation. Despite efforts realised in this area, cost assessment remains frequently very general and incomplete.

5   *Monitoring and evaluation.* In theory, this aspect comprises the development of a set of indicators and definition of a system of adequate monitoring and evaluation (means to be applied, responsible organisations and institutions, expected results). It should be stressed that this aspect is the weakest and least structured in most PRSPs. It is frequently limited to a list of surveys and indicators, with no appreciable understanding of or interest for a coherent and solid system for measuring and assessing policy outcomes.

An action plan with precise, measurable goals

An action plan should be defined, together with a precise calendar taking into account priorities and measurable objectives. The order of introducing reforms is of some importance; the hierarchical organisation of public interventions is necessary, according to their immediate and long-term impacts. In addition, the precision of goals, and above all their publication in a PRSP, constrains governments to produce concrete programmes and honour their engagements, which results in increasing government accountability. This procedure also allows linking the level of aid provided to results obtained by countries engaged in the fight against poverty.

Monitoring and evaluation procedures

Definition of an action plan comprising goals quantified in terms of results has as its corollary the establishment of a system for monitoring and evaluating policy outcomes. Three phases broadly describe the setting up of a results monitoring system:

* setting goals and targets corresponding to the main objectives defined in the poverty reduction strategy;
* identifying indicators and required levels of disaggregation;
* determining a procedure for monitoring the evolution of indicators (identification of sources, whether survey results or official data, frequency of monitoring and so on).

(Rubio, Prennushi and Subbarao 2001)

Countries must set medium and long-term goals for poverty reduction in order to ensure that policies are well conceived, efficiently implemented and effectively monitored. Nevertheless, given that policies often produce real results only over the medium and long term, PRSPs should list intermediate indicators allowing milepost assessments of progress (see Chapter 11). The PRSP sets out a three-year programme. It must nonetheless be subject to annual reviews that assess results obtained relative to set goals and analysing the way in which policies are implemented. Revisions may be considered following such reviews.

Pertinence and range of proposed policies

The content of PRSPs is of unequal quality, according to the country concerned. This is true of the quality of analyses as well as for the preparation of policy proposals. Countries where poverty alleviation programmes have been in preparation for several years (Honduras, Mozambique, Uganda and to a lesser extent Nicaragua), and/or those to have received significant external technical assistance (Bolivia, in particular) are distinguished by more elaborate PRSPs.[2] To the contrary, strategy papers are more superficial for countries that prepared them under a time constraint and that lack adequate poverty alleviation experiences (Burkina Faso, Mauritania and Tanzania).

Despite the differences, the analysis of PRSPs leads to two conclusions:

- proposed strategies are relatively uniform with weak consideration of each country's individual conditions (Box 7.1);
- in most cases they consist of a simple recycling of previous policies, with marginal adjustments to establish a link with poverty.

The assessment of PRSPs by the BWIs in their Joint Staff Assessments (JSAs) is based on some general principles reaffirmed in its sourcebook (World Bank 2001a). This conditionality explains why, in practice, PRSPs are relatively uniform and eventually, at least as far as the macroeconomic policies are concerned, not so much different from the traditional SAP recipes (macroeconomic and financial stabilisation, external and internal liberalisation). We are thus confronted with a real homogenisation process: in order to obtain the international funding they badly need, poor countries adjust their strategies to what they know is expected from them by the BWIs. This 'calibration' is reinforced by the wide availability of PRSPs and JSAs (notably on the World Bank website), which generates a cascading mimetic effect.

Given that PRSPs are inspired and validated by the BWIs, their inadequacies reflect, above all, those of these institutions. Two of their analytical shortcomings are discussed in detail hereafter: the lack of articulation between macroeconomic policies and sectoral programmes, and the gloss over the question of links between poverty and inequality. The inadequate appreciation of the multidimensional nature of poverty – which is formally stated but with no realisation of the consequences – and the absence of a realistic strategy for global insertion are reviewed more briefly.

Macroeconomic policy and poverty relief: two unconnected fields?

Each PRSP insists that macroeconomic stability constitutes a primary condition for ensuring poverty reduction. By making this requirement appear as important, if not more so than specific measures designed to alleviate poverty, eventual incompatibilities between the two types of approach are completely ignored. Emphasising at the same time financial stabilisation (as required by the BWIs), and the investment necessary in social sectors (for example), constitutes a difficult exercise. In Tanzania, assessment of basic health needs leads to the observation that budget allocations to the sector should be doubled. This poses an evident difficulty for resources. Similarly, in Uganda, the PRSP assessment document (JSA) notes that the forecast programme cost, otherwise adjudged consistent and pertinent, is incompatible with the goal of macroeconomic stability. In parallel, structural reforms aimed at liberalising and opening the economy still assume a major place. An accent is placed on PRSPs' medium to long-term benefits for growth, even though they fail to examine explicitly the possible negative impacts on the living conditions of certain population categories, in the short term at least (see Chapter 1).

Other than the basic assumption that strong growth and macroeconomic stability are required to reduce poverty, the section covering macroeconomic policy is frequently presented separately in PRSPs, without mention of precise links with the goal of alleviating poverty. This weakness is rarely underlined in JSAs, which in most cases simply support the stress placed on the goal of macroeconomic equilibrium. The similarity between final and interim PRSPs regarding macroeconomic policy indicates this has not been a subject for discussion in the participatory process. It is implicitly presumed that financial stabilisation and liberalisation will necessarily benefit the poor, by eliminating market distortions, without the need for further explanation or discussion of the fundamentals. Nevertheless, various studies show the uncertain impact on poverty of reforms previously introduced, with structural adjustment programmes results depending on the particular context of each country (Eurodad 2001a).

For example, the impact of trade reform on poverty is generally overlooked, as it is recognised by the BWIs' review:

> While all full PRSPs have supported the desirability of trade openness in broad terms, the majority has dealt with the underlying issues in a fairly limited way. Only in Honduras and Mozambique was there an attempt to clarify the link between these reforms, and growth and poverty reduction.
>
> (IDA and IMF 2002)

Cambodia's PRSP is a good example of this neglect. This is a country with widespread rural poverty, and which neighbours one of the world's lowest-cost rice exporters (Vietnam). Cambodia's commitment to reduce import restrictions for this commodity before joining the World Trade Organisation could therefore have a major impact on rural poverty (Oxfam 2002). Nonetheless, this aspect is completely ignored, both in the Interim PRSP and in the JSA established by the BWIs.

While recognising this general shortcoming, the World Bank refuses to use trade policies to support the fight against poverty and, rather, promotes using other instruments. The chapter of its sourcebook entitled *Trade Policy Reform and Poverty Alleviation* thus considers:

> It might appear tempting to design a pro-poor trade reform by identifying sectors that are important to the poor – either on the consump-

tion side or the income side – and singling out these sectors for differentiated cuts in protection ... A better approach is to focus on developing two different sets of instruments – one, trade policy, focused on providing the incentives appropriate for efficient production and use of goods and services, and another, distributional policy, focused on alleviating poverty.

(Hoekman *et al.* 2002)

This approach is supported by two arguments: first, according to a well-known principle, one instrument can only aim at one objective at a time (that is, trade policy cannot both fight poverty and increase efficiency); second, political economy of reform shows that a differentiate trade regime increases lobbying and eventually distortions.

These arguments are somewhat simplistic if one takes into account the market imperfections in developing countries, as well as the important redistributive impact of trade policies (but the sourcebook only suggests using safety nets in order to limit this impact). This is the reason why the redistributive impact of trade liberalisation measures, as well as the questions of pace, design and sequencing of reform should imperatively be discussed by PRSPs:

The approach to PRSPs reflects a broader problem in IMF–World Bank thinking about trade reform. It is rooted in the received wisdom that trade is inherently good for growth and good for the poor. Until that is challenged, the new poverty rhetoric of the Bretton Woods agencies will remain at variance with the reality of their policies.

(Oxfam 2002)

The question of inequalities, conflicts of interest and the need for arbitration

By emphasising the primacy of growth for poverty alleviation (*Growth is Good for the Poor* is the title of the widely quoted paper by Dollar and Kraay 2001), the World Bank tends to underestimate some other important factors at the macroeconomic level, especially old impact of inequalities:

Part of the ongoing debate on poverty reduction strategies bear on the issue of the actual contribution of economic growth to poverty reduction. There is no doubt that faster economic growth is associated with faster poverty reduction. But what is the corresponding elasticity? If it is reasonably high, then poverty reduction strategies almost exclusively relying on economic growth are probably justified. If it is low, however, ambitious poverty reduction strategies might have to combine both economic growth and some kind of redistribution.

(Bourguignon 2002)

In practice, the impact of growth on poverty depends to a great extent on initial inequality. Higher income inequality reduces the impact of growth as the poor are further away from the poverty line and their income increases start from a lower base (Ravallion 2001). Because of this relationship, income redistribution has a dual pay-off in poverty reduction. It reduces poverty instantaneously by giving the poor a higher income. In addition, it also contributes to a permanent increase in the elasticity of poverty reduction with respect to growth and therefore to an acceleration of poverty reduction for a given rate of economic growth (Bourguignon 2002).

One would expect poverty reduction strategies to take into account these conclusions, especially as their PRSPs assign very ambitious objectives as far as poverty reduction is concerned, such as halving extreme poverty by 2015 (which is the first of the eight Millennium Development Goals – see Chapter 11). The distributive justice theory developed by Rawls and Sen, also emphasises the link between inequalities of chances, poverty and future inequality (see Chapter 2).

In fact most PRSPs do not really address the question of inequalities and redistribution: a detailed analysis of available PRSPs (when this chapter was written) reveals that they often prefer the concept of disparity to inequalities and that they hardly ever use the word 'redistribution' (Bolivia excepted, whose PRSP mentions this expression seven times). More generally, our analysis shows that inequality related concepts[3] are used very irregularly: the four Central and South American countries, which are also the most inegalitarian, use these concepts every other page on average, whereas the eight African countries, which are much poorer but also generally less inegalitarian, use them only once every three pages; Vietnam, whose socialist regime makes it more 'inequality conscious', mentions these concepts frequently (every 1.5 pages), whereas Albania, in spite of high and rapidly increasing inequalities, is very reluctant to mention this subject (once every five pages). By reaffirming that 'growth is the main instrument for the reduction of poverty', the latter implicitly refuses any active redistribution policy. No doubt most PRSPs wish to avoid head-on conflicts of interest between different categories of the population, but also to avoid questioning the social cohesion that the participatory process is meant to build or to reinforce.

This lack of interest for the inequality issue (with only few exceptions) is all the less surprising, as the concept of social inequality is very neglected by the World Bank. This institution seems to consider the fight against inequalities as a simple means and not as an end. No matter whether the question is to promote a policy aimed at reducing inequality or not, PRSPs always follow the above-mentioned instrumental approach; the Guyana PRSP goes as far as arguing:

With per capita income of less than US$3 per day, there is very little scope for income redistribution as a mechanism for poverty reduction ... Given the evidence of a strong correlation between growth and poverty reduction, income redistribution is not a viable option.

(Guyana PRSP 2002)

Like Guyana, and although they are among the countries with the most unequal income distribution world wide, Honduras (which like Guyana is a middle-income country) and Nicaragua base their opposition against redistribution policies on technical arguments related to their inefficiency, and explicitly consider that their development level is insufficient to finance a redistribution policy having a significant impact on poverty. Instead of this, their PRSPs aim at accelerating growth in order to reduce poverty. On the contrary, the PRSPs of Bolivia, Mauritania and Zambia use the same instrumental approach to suggest improving income distribution in order to accelerate growth and ultimately to reduce poverty faster.

Overall, the process of state disengagement that PRSPs hope to continue is not propitious for pro-poor redistribution policies. The recommendation of a system of beneficiary cost recovery in the health services provides proof. This system risks not only to deepen inequalities but also to induce the perverse effect of reduced state effort in social infrastructure. The principle of community participation may also encourage the state to withdraw from its role of supervision and support in promoting equity between the regions, and also within districts (Serra 2001).

The differential treatment of public services, in cost-recovery terms, is proposed without any justification. In Tanzania, while the PRSP foresees the abolition of primary school fees, it proposes to resolve financial constraints in the health sector by the participation and involvement of the private sector and civil society. Part of the costs will thus be supported by end users, without regard to the difficulties such a policy choice creates for the poorest. In those countries which have introduced such practices, the appraisal of health sector cost-recovery systems is very mixed. In Mauritania, the PRSP notes that despite a modest improvement in the general situation, the problem of medicine availability has not been resolved and access to healthcare by the poorest had not been taken into account. This observation encouraged revision to make the system more flexible (reducing costs to a sustainable level and the free provision of certain treatments).

In parallel, with few exceptions (notably Burkina Faso, Mauritania and Uganda), fiscal policies are not mentioned as instruments to be used in promoting income redistribution in favour of the most impoverished. Poverty alleviation strategies necessarily imply arbitration that is almost never explicitly stated. For example, the principle of universal social protection is implicitly queried (Lautier 2001), which raises questions about the position to be adopted regarding the non-poor, or the less poor among the poor.

In the same way, in many countries access to land by the poor would require the application of a land redistribution policy to the detriment of more favoured categories. Nevertheless, Table 7.1 shows that measures foreseen in PRSPs in this regard are generally limited to guarantees of tenure.

The only arbitration clearly ratified is that between urban and rural communities; the latter, where most of the poor are concentrated, is given priority. The limited interest attached to urban poverty is particularly marked in African PRSPs, where specific actions targeting the affected population are almost non-existent. The pertinence of such an option nevertheless merits analysis. The incidence of urban poverty is rising and risks increasing greatly in coming years. Furthermore, given the potential synergies and the availability of infrastructure, poverty reduction strategies are more efficient in urban settings (see Chapter 4). Trickle-down effects from the urban regions onto rural communities are also to be considered (increased demand, migration), whereas the inverse is clearly less pronounced (Sahel and West Africa Club 2001).

In the end, policies aiming at fighting sexual and ethnic discriminations and reducing regional inequalities, which are probably less conflictual than the fight against social inequalities (although they are obviously interconnected), are the only strategies on which there is a relative consensus, and which are mentioned by many PRSPs.

Implications of a broader concept of poverty

The principles of the new strategic directions in fighting poverty must take account of the multidimensional nature of the phenomenon and thus mount an attack on all its forms. Nonetheless, it does not appear that the policy implications of a conceptual broadening of the notion of poverty have been appreciated. Thin, Underwood and Gilling (2001) stress that diagnoses identify different categories of poor, whereas proposed strategies almost always consider them indifferently. The difficulty of arbitration, and more precisely of target choice, becomes more acute. Which form of poverty should be attacked first? How can the eventually contradictory effects of policy on the different dimensions of poverty be managed?

As an illustration, policies of insertion and protection are foreseen to correct the short-term negative effects of macroeconomic reforms on some vulnerable groups (safety nets and insurance schemes). However, taking into consideration implementation capacity constraints (notably financial), such policies are not very ambitious and are relegated to a lower priority level.

In reality, the difficulty of targeting different categories of the poor has been resolved by adopting classical approaches.[4] Typically, monitoring indicators are centred on monetary poverty, health and education

Table 7.1 A sample of PRSPs' stance on inequalities

	GNI/ capita ($)	Gini index	Diagnostic on poverty and inequalities	PRSP main focus to fight inequalities
Africa				
Burkina Faso	210	55.1	High regional and gender inequalities	Fiscal policy; equitable access to education
Mozambique	210	39.6	High inequality between the capital city area and the rest of the country; gender inequalities	Regional disparities
Uganda	300	37.4	Increasing regional inequality; land inequalities	Strengthen land rights of the poor and women; equitable tax system
Zambia	300	52.6	High and increasing income inequalities; gender inequalities	Access to basic services; safety nets; land rights; Aids
Europe				
Albania	1,580	0.43*	High poverty and rising income inequalities, especially between urban/rural areas	Safety nets; stimulate employment and investment in rural areas
Central and South America				
Bolivia	990	44.7	Very high poverty and income inequalities	Land redistribution (idle land) and improved land rights; equity in gender access to education
Guyana	860	40.2	Geographic inequalities.	Redress geographic imbalances (access to basic services, land policy)
Honduras	860	56.3	Very high inequalities, especially between urban/rural areas	Access to land rights and to support services for farmers; land redistribution (idle land, size exceeding the limit fixed by law)
Nicaragua	400	60.3	High income inequalities; gender inequalities	Access to basic services and safety nets; decentralisation
Asia				
Vietnam	390	36.1	Poverty halved since 1990; high income inequalities between urban/rural areas; gender inequalities	Narrow the gap between the rich and the poor; improve gender equality; public welfare system; fiscal policy

Sources: World Bank Indicators 2002, Gross National Income per capita (GNI) in 2000 and Gini index of inequalities for various recent years; countries' PRSPs.

Note
*PRSP Albania.

(Overseas Development Institute 2001). If, however, non-participation in the political process were a facet of poverty, improvements to electoral procedures (registration, abstention) would contribute to its alleviation. More generally, respect for human rights and good governance, criteria underlined by all donors as consubstantial to development, are treated superficially – and then only via a few specific themes (such as gender inequality in access to education, malfunctioning of the judicial system and corruption).

Limiting poverty to its economic dimension, the basic assumption stressing the link between macroeconomic equilibrium, growth and poverty builds on a number of empirical analyses, even where their pertinence may be in doubt. The relationship between growth and macroeconomic stability on the one hand, and democracy and the respect for human rights on the other, is much less understood (see Chapter 5). In general, PRSPs do not investigate the possible antinomies between these various goals.

The integration into the world economy: a neglected factor

Few PRSPs treat the question of the international environment profoundly. The only measures envisaged may be summarised as the simple pursuit of liberalisation as initiated in the past, accompanied by limited supports for export promotion. In most cases, these options have not sufficed to influence a country's trajectory significantly.

Perceptions of the notion of governance, as presented in PRSPs analysed here, appear confined to the conduct of domestic affairs. The stress placed on the participation of civil society, which has little to do with international questions, has contributed to a neglect of the external dimension of programmes. This is even more regrettable as the living conditions of some sections of the population are strongly dependent on international circumstances (fluctuations of primary commodity prices, variations in aid flows, etc.). Furthermore, countries must seek to participate in global dynamics and to draw profit from eventual opportunities offered at the regional or world levels (see Box 7.2). In the current context of globalisation, poor countries risk to enhance their marginalisation by limiting their horizons to their borders (while LDCs represent less than 0.5 per cent of world exports).

The fact that PRSPs propose no coherent policies for international insertion is all the more paradoxical as, with few exceptions, the generally reduced size of most of the countries concerned excludes a growth strategy based primarily on expanding domestic markets. Promoting the growth and diversification of exports of labour-intensive products was central to strategies proposed in the 1990s (see Chapter 1). While this remains the only real option envisaged by PRSPs for global economic integration, it is probably not applicable in the majority of countries

Box 7.2 The Monterrey consensus

The United Nations International Conference on Financing for Development was held in Monterrey, Mexico, in March 2002. We present hereafter a critical analysis of its final declaration, entitled 'Monterrey consensus', which is supposed to bring about a new approach to development, replacing the so-called 'Washington consensus'.

The Monterrey consensus begins by promoting a new partnership between developed and developing countries, with a view to achieving the Millennium Development Goals (MDGs). With the emphasis put on ownership by the BWIs within the PRSP Initiative, the consensus consistently reaffirms each country's responsibility for its own economic and social development, and that the effective use of trade and investment opportunities can help countries fight poverty. It also supports regional initiatives such as NEPAD (New Partnership for Africa's Development), which shares the same philosophy. Without neglecting the new efforts committed by the international community (such as additional funding to aid), there is a real risk that the emphasis put on developing countries' responsibilities allows developed countries to forget their own responsibilities towards the rest of the world.

Good governance (fighting corruption, effective administration, etc.) and sound macroeconomic policies are considered as essential in order to promote growth, poverty eradication and sustainable development. Although the macroeconomic recommendations (apart from general objectives such as price stability, sustainable fiscal and external balances) are rather vague and the appropriate role of government in market-oriented economies is recognised to vary from country to country, these recommendations do not distinguish themselves clearly from the 'Washington consensus'.

The emphasis is placed on the role of investment and trade for development. The need to encourage more direct investment to developing countries, particularly Africa and the less-developed countries is affirmed. The priority is given to trade liberalisation to stimulate development. The questions of market access and agricultural subsidies are briefly mentioned, as well as the need to mitigate the consequences of the erratic fluctuations of commodity prices for developing country exporters (through financial compensations or risk insurance).

The trade and investment recommendations are probably the most frustrating for the least developed, especially African, countries. These countries hardly attract any foreign direct investment and the Monterrey declaration will not change this situation much. Their access to developed country markets (at least to the European Union) is much easier than for other developing countries and this is therefore far from being the main issue. The agricultural subsidies, which have indeed had a disruptive impact on their own farmers, are here to stay (see the increase adopted by the United States in 2002). One of the most acute issues for them, commodities prices, is barely touched: when a coffee-producing country sometimes loses half of its export revenues from one year to another, making its farmers starve and sending the whole economy into a slump, poverty reduction strategies become a pantomime. But as pointed out by UNCTAD (2002), the BWIs (and most donors) refuse to address this problem, first and fore-most for ideological reasons (one would need to establish international reg-ulatory mechanisms).

Lastly, the Monterrey declaration contains a commitment by developed countries to increase official development assistance (reaffirming the target of 0.7 per cent of GNP launched in the 1970s, which has only been reached by a few Nordic countries). The traditional slogan 'Trade not aid' is some-what replaced by 'Trade and aid'. Prior or during the conference, the major donors announced some additional funding for the future: the European Union committed itself to reach an average of 0.39 per cent of GNP (from the current 0.33 per cent) by 2006 (an increase by an extra $7 billion per year by 2006); the United States pledged to increase their funding by $5 billion from 2006 (that is a increase of 50 per cent). The US additional funds will go to a new 'Millennium Challenge Account' (MCA); the alloca-tion of the grants will be based on criteria of 'good governance' and 'sound economic policies'. Priority will be given to the health and education sectors. If these commitments are fulfilled (but they will be hard to retract), the ODA declining trend observed during the 1990s could be reversed in the next few years.

involved. According to Wood and Mayer (1998), the comparative advant-age of African countries derives mainly from the abundance of their primary natural resources. Experience shows, however, that the export of mineral products is of little benefit to the populations of these countries, while the export of agricultural produce is also frequently the domain of large-scale productive farms.[5] In this regard, as in so many others, the weaknesses of PRSPs are, above all, those of the understanding of mechan-isms of development and, in this case, of the potential role of foreign trade.

Are poverty reduction strategies sustainable?

Recognition of the serious efforts accomplished by most countries in the preparation of a global development strategy should not mask major uncertainties about the possibilities of realising set objectives. This is insuf-ficiently stressed at present, these uncertainties being explicitly under-lined in a few studies only (especially Gunter 2002; Lalmant 2001).

Most JSAs (Bolivia, Honduras, Mauritania, Mozambique and Nicaragua) repeatedly note the ambitious nature of programmes, sometimes with ambiguity: is this a warning or a compliment (or both)? Considering the apparently neglected capacity constraints of poor countries, however, the question may be posed: are the new poverty reduction strategies sustain-able? Despite the introduction of cost evaluation techniques and of a fixed timetable, the documents do not seem to measure clearly the amplitude of resources needed to implement policies and attain the established goals, which are frequently over-ambitious, if not unrealisable.

A lack of priority ranking

Examination of several PRSPs leads to doubts as to whether greater priority is really accorded to poverty reduction. To be sure, several axes of intervention are necessary to combat the various forms of poverty. However, by stipulating poverty reduction as the primary goal, we might have expected the definition of concrete and realistic strategies focusing on measures directed at some precise spheres or sectors. Instead, the PRSP preparation process appears to stop at an almost exhaustive list of recommendations for actions to be taken. There is neither prioritisation nor apparent reflection regarding the most efficient measures to be adopted, taking into account the human and financial resources of beneficiary countries. With the exception of Bolivia, which made a realistic choice by focusing its proposals on a limited number of sectors, more often PRSPs make no ranking of priorities. It should of course be recognised that the fixing of priorities constitutes a difficult exercise for low-income countries.

First, it presumes that the most urgent and fundamental pro-poor policies have been identified previously. This is far from being the case in most of the countries concerned, due to a lack of data, of analysis and of in-depth reflection. Spheres identified as priorities in PRSPs are invariably the rural sector (comprising from 60 to 80 per cent of the population), the social sectors and, eventually, the informal sector. These sectors involve different categories of the population, however, and require a broad range of actions that need to be ranked according to priority.

Countries are also subject to a multitude of directives from the BWIs. This does not provide a propitious context for arranging policies according to priority. In addition to the requirement to consider the multiple deficiencies and needs of the population (the different dimensions of poverty), there is a more or less explicit obligation for countries to examine different economic policy areas so as to respond to the evaluation criteria of international institutions (stability and macroeconomic growth, security, empowerment, environment, gender equality, and so on).[6] Different types of intervention, which in some cases should be undertaken in parallel to be of effect, are thus required to respond to the various objectives.

Finally, as already stated, introduction of the participatory process presumes that the interests of all sections of society are taken into account. This is difficult to reconcile with the need to establish priorities. How can a government, which often suffers a lack of credibility and legitimacy, tell certain categories of the population they are not a priority? For this reason, rather than deny conflicts of interest between various actors, the goal of poverty reduction and its underpinning principles of justice should be clarified (see Chapter 2).

An ambiguous need to rehabilitate the state and to strengthen its capacities

The accent placed on the participatory process has led to ambiguity regarding the effective responsibilities of the state and to neglect of the imperative for its rehabilitation (Whaites 2002). Yet, as previously underlined, the state must play a major role in implementing the participatory process. Despite the rhetoric on the importance of institutions reaffirmed by the World Development Reports 2002 and 2003 (World Bank 2001d, 2002c), it appears that the degree of effort needed to reform and reinforce the state has yet to be fully appreciated. This is necessary to permit the state to fulfil not only its regalian functions but also those of redistribution. The primordial character of the tasks falling on it for the success of policies is underscored in several studies (notably Haan *et al.* 1997). Management of poverty reduction strategies is, in effect, even more complex than that of earlier programmes of stabilisation or adjustment (Chambas and Kerhuel 2001).

The goal of remedying the dysfunction of institutions to ensure good governance is not absent in PRSPs. It is tackled, in the main, by three linked spheres of action: the pursuit of ongoing reforms to improve public service efficiency; a heavy accent on the fight against corruption and the means of managing public finances; and decentralisation. The proposed strategies, nonetheless, seem too limited compared to the magnitude of the tasks.

In the first place, administrative reform focuses essentially on the management of public finances. Precise measures mobilising specific tools are envisaged to improve expenditure management. This comprises one of the major advances induced by the preparation of PRSPs (Booth 2002).[7] Nevertheless, other than this aspect which cannot by itself ensure the success of policies, options foreseen for reinforcing the administration remain vague or partial, and above all lacking ambition. It is significant and surprising that, among the frequently cited constraints poor countries must tackle, hardly any mention is made of implementation capacity problems (notably those linked to the qualification and number of civil servants[8]). Corruption and administrative inefficiency are stressed, however. The implicit hypothesis is that the pursuit of previous reforms, confined to restructuring the administration, will suffice to remedy such difficulties. Yet results from such reforms have until now been widely judged disappointing or negative. No fundamental effort to rehabilitate the state is perceptible (recruitment policy, adoption of incentive/sanction systems, inculcation of a democratic culture or of a sense of organisation). PRSPs do not tackle questions of human resource shortcomings concretely, in the short to medium term, to ensure policy implementation. Capacity weaknesses nevertheless constitute a recurrent and constrictive problem, not only at every stage of defining the PRSP but also for the effective application of the proposed measures. By placing an accent on basic education to combat poverty, the ineluctable question of the qualification requirements for managers remains unanswered. Improvements to the training of young graduates to remedy the shortage of qualified people in the public service (in the private sector as well), implies specific policies that go beyond limited courses and training schemes of modest amplitude. The same is true for the retraining of established personnel in the various branches of the administration, at intermediate and upper echelons.

In second place, the stress placed on decentralisation, initially favoured by the BWIs with a view to limiting the prerogatives of the central authority, is not without danger. Indeed, not only is it uncertain that local authorities respond to the aspirations of the poorest, but also the delegation of responsibilities to organs (or structures) whose institutional and technical capacities are even more limited than those of the central state raises significant doubts. Otherwise, the record of decentralisation in developing countries is to date mixed. Positive effects remain partial and in any case vary according to the country (OECD 1997). Results strongly depend on the local context: degree of cohesion of the population (notably the absence of ethnic conflicts), accountability demonstrated by local institutions and politicians (or lack thereof), and the degree of organisation and lobbying power exercised by the poor at the local level (Roubaud 2000a).

PRSP evaluation documents (JSAs) almost systematically note uncertainty regarding the capacity of countries to implement policies. This major weakness is stressed in the cases of Bolivia, Honduras, Mauritania, Mozambique, Nicaragua and Tanzania. Nevertheless, this difficulty is mentioned merely in passing, with no precision as to the policies and concrete means foreseen or needed to be reinforced to remedy the situation. Implicitly or explicitly (as with the examples of Bolivia and Nicaragua), strong foreign technical assistance is envisaged to overcome the obstacle. Doubts as to the efficacy and the viability of such solutions are nevertheless recognised.

Building civil society capacities: an underestimated condition

Similarly, and despite the rhetorical accent placed on the role of civil society, PRSPs as a whole do not cover the question of empowerment (reinforcing civil society capacities) in a rational way. PRSPs are often seemingly content with the establishment of a participatory process, without envisaging meaningful measures to provide training or technical and financial supports to associations. The structuring of civil society and the strengthening of its capacities are nevertheless essential conditions for the participatory process to be effective, and for a system of accountability to develop locally and nationally. What is more, this constitutes a short-term means of compensating for deficiencies in the judicial system, where reform has proven lengthy and complex.

Financial constraints remain in place

PRSPs are supposed to encourage beneficiary countries to devote a maximum of their means to the goal of poverty reduction. Funding for programmes should be ensured through an appropriate use of resources, notably by the priority allocation of funds released from debt relief to social expenditure. Despite this advance, however, countries risk to face continued financial constraints (see Chapter 10). This doubt is particularly mentioned in JSAs for Bolivia, Honduras, Mauritania, Mozambique and Tanzania. The volume of global aid is on a declining path. New debt relief measures are intended to stimulate the arrival of private capital, but past experience disavows the hypothesis. With few exceptions, private and public capital flows destined for heavily indebted countries have tended to decline since adoption of the HIPC Initiative (Gunter 2002). Several analyses consider this initiative will not bring a significant increase in future net resource flows (Severino 2001a). Even accepting the thesis according to which the simple reallocation of available financial resources will allow countries to mobilise additional funds for poverty relief, the amount likely to be freed will remain a priori feeble, particularly in comparison with what is required to undertake the programmes. Admitting that debt servicing by heavily indebted poor countries falls to a sustainable level,[9] the overall approach does not question the sustainability of PRSPs. For many countries, financial constraints that limit governments' room to manoeuvre in the implementation of ambitious policies and reforms remain unresolved.

Policy monitoring and evaluation: a neglected aspect of the PRSPs

Policy monitoring and evaluation is one of the main weaknesses of most PRSPs. There is, especially, a striking imbalance between the ambitions of both evaluation policies and the scope of indicators, and the lack of attention given to the reliability of data-collection mechanisms (Habbard 2002). We summarise hereafter the main lessons drawn from the existing PRSPs, these aspects being analysed in depth in Chapters 11 and 14 of this book.

The lack of proper poverty assessment and monitoring

The preliminary presentation of a review of poverty and of the factors determining its presence is a purely formal exercise in most PRSPs, and is rarely exploited in the definition of strategies. On the one hand, to conform to such practice requires a significant effort by administrators more familiar with day-by-day management. On the other hand, short-term obligations leading to the rapid preparation of documents do not allow in-depth reflection. Finally, analyses do not always respond to the required criteria of quality and, above all, pertinence to be of use to decision-makers (see Chapter 11). In effect, they need to be based on reliable up-to-date information, and to bring elements of response to essential questions regarding poverty. Killick (1998) insists on the fact that data and analytic weaknesses in African countries are such that knowledge about these countries remains extremely limited. It is thus impossible to establish a clear picture of the efficacy or not of policies.

In such conditions, as underlined in JSAs, the weaknesses of PRSPs regarding the determinants of poverty and the impact of past policies on household living standards are unsurprising. A logical corollary is the absence of linkages between diagnoses established and strategies proposed. The introduction of an adequate system to monitor policies and their impact on living conditions of the poor could help remedy this deficiency. Nevertheless, the interest accorded to the monitoring/evaluation function remains secondary in most PRSPs, for the present. It is limited to the listing of indicators and surveys, without the objective of building a coherent and solid plan of action to monitor, assess and recommend policy directions (range of pertinent indicators, survey programme, institutional arrangements, and so on). In passing, it is significant that those countries suffering the most from an absence of pertinent up-to-date data (Mauritania, Mozambique and Tanzania) are also those where proposed measures for monitoring and evaluation are judged particularly inconsistent.

A critical review of the indicators proposed in final PRSPs completed at the end of 2002 of 11 African countries gives evidence of existing shortcomings (Gubert and Robilliard 2002):[10] the monitoring system is neglected in the papers; the list of indicators proposed for tracking the progress of suggested policies/actions and evaluating their results is extremely poor; PRSPs put more emphasis on final indicators than on intermediate ones, although the latter are easier to measure; according to Booth and Lucas (2002), 'this is a serious deficiency, as rapid feedback on this level of change is what matters most for accountability and learning'; they also put too much focus on monetary poverty, on access to health and education services indicators neglecting those dealing with the population's level of satisfaction; the study also highlights the absence of indicators to measure the political clout of rural areas, or that could gauge the state's effort (share of public spending affected to rural areas); the lack of available data, and the human and financial constraints affecting the collection of indicators are not taken into account, etc.

A fundamental challenge for the definition of policies and for their implementation

The importance of the monitoring and evaluation function actually goes beyond the assessment of progress (or retreat) in meeting PRSP objectives. The range of policy evaluations contributes to the identification of efficient policies to combat poverty, resolution of problems of arbitration and ranking, good management of funding constraints, and precise determination of obstacles to and factors promoting growth. In this respect, impact analyses of policies (not only *ex post* but also *ex ante*) are supposed to play a major role, in particular the Poverty and Social Impact Analysis (PSIA) already recommended by the BWIs in some countries. These should be undertaken to aid PRSP definition, but are difficult to implement due to poor capacities (or competency) and data.

Two conditions must be satisfied for this to happen. First, the approach must not be limited to a technical exercise, inaccessible to all stakeholders. Second, means must be mobilised for diffusing information and reliable pertinent data, so that practical lessons may be drawn for the definition or reorientation of policies (see Chapter 11).

It is rather characteristic of JSAs to list, at the end of the review, numerous constraints and risks (in most cases major), but to make few comments as to their implications or to the precise means contemplated for overcoming them. Mentioned in this vein, according to the country, are risks of exchange rate slippage, political risks, institutional weaknesses, risks of natural disasters, risks of reduced external funding, etc. The classification of these different constraints under the heading 'risks' indicates an admission of powerlessness to define and recommend adapted and effective strategies to control the key factors conditioning policy success. To a certain extent, such problems are put to one side for as long as no assessment of their precise impact has been realised, pending the arrival of real pressure before they are seriously addressed and appropriate solutions proposed. The debt constraint was treated in a similar way before the enhanced HIPC Initiative was proposed. This may also be a means of preparing excuses in the event that poverty reduction strategies fail.

Conclusion

Weaknesses of the process under way are clearly illustrated by confronting the goals set by new poverty reduction strategies, crystallised in PRSPs, with their concrete development in the field. Shortcomings in the content of policies themselves merely reflect weaknesses in the strategies proposed by the international institutions. These include the elusive character of poverty and of the poor as social actors, uncertainties about arbitration procedures in conflicts of interest, ambiguity surrounding the role of the state, selective amnesia regarding some redistributive policies, allusive treatment of questions of inequalities and the international environment, and a lack of priority ranking in a context of strong financial and human resource constraints, despite the resources released by the HIPC debt relief initiative.

The emphasis placed on the fight against poverty and the establishment of a participatory process, while supposed to promote appreciation of the needs of the population and of the specifics of each country (see Chapter 6), eventually appears to be of marginal influence on the content of programmes. In a way, PRSPs are 'old wine in new bottles', to answer the question asked by the title of this chapter. Does this mean that past policy orientations were broadly appropriate, but that their failure resulted essentially from the fact they were not really implemented? According to this apparently favoured hypothesis, a change to the methods of elaborating and applying policies would be enough to ensure their success, without necessarily reviewing their pertinence. Such an assertion is far from proven and merits being questioned,[11] which has been done in this chapter.

These shortcomings prevent us from considering that PRSPs are defining new development policies. In a period when development aid is increasingly based on compassionate motives, which is especially the case of poverty reduction policies (Severino 2001a), is it surprising that the main difference between PRSPs and the previous Structural Adjustment Policies concerns the focus on poverty?

Notes

1 At mid-2002, 15 countries had finalised their PSRP: Albania, Bolivia, Burkina Faso, the Gambia, Guinea, Guyana, Honduras, Mauritania, Mozambique, Nicaragua, Niger, Tanzania, Uganda, Vietnam and Zambia.
2 Uganda and Bolivia were among pilot countries for the establishment of Comprehensive Development Frameworks.
3 That is, the following words: equity/inequity; equality/inequality; equal/unequal; equitable/inequitable; redistribution.
4 The Bolivian PRSP, which explicitly raises the question of human rights and democracy, again constitutes the exception that confirms the rule.
5 For example, Zimbabwean horticulture is cited as an example in the World Bank Handbook on PRSPs, but it neglects to mention that the sector was traditionally under the control of rich white farmers, descendants of settlers in the former Rhodesia (Cling 2001).
6 While the JSAs mention priority ranking as a weakness, they centre essentially on underlining spheres not covered, or treated inadequately, in the PRSPs. It is, however, rare that evaluations question the potential efficiency of a measure in fighting poverty, or suggest whether policies are of greater or lesser priority.
7 Several countries, such as Ghana, Malawi, Tanzania, Rwanda, Mozambique

and Kenya, have engaged budgetary reforms and reinforced the organs of budgetary control (Booth 2002; Foster *et al.* 2002). In Mali, parliament votes the budget and the Supreme Court undertakes necessary verifications (see Chapter 8).

8 The number of civil servants per capita is on average particularly low in Africa, where poor countries are concentrated (Razafindrakoto and Roubaud 2001b).

9 Several analyses discuss the realisation of this goal. Notably underlined is the fact that debt sustainability assessments are based on over-optimistic projections of GDP growth and exports (Gunter 2002).

10 This review focuses on rural indicators, but its conclusions also apply to urban areas.

11 The debate concerning the failure of SAPs opposes researchers, but a certain consensus exists that it is due to the combination of three types of factor: the partial application of policies; the insufficiency, organisational inadequacy and the short-term focus of policies; the unfavourable external environment (Klasen 2001). Accepting the consensus, the content of previous policies should at least be completed and take greater account of longer-term objectives. It is clear, however, that the pertinence of certain measures is the subject of controversy (liberalisation, trade opening, and so on).

8 Poverty reduction in Mali

Will the PRSP process make a difference?

*Idrissa Dante,[1] Mohamed Ali Marouani
and Marc Raffinot*

Mali is a landlocked Sahelian country, which ranks among the ten poorest countries worldwide according to UNDP's Human Development Index and in terms of GDP per capita. It is also one of the Heavily Indebted Poor Countries (HIPCs) eligible for debt relief. Since September 2000, it has benefited from debt relief under the original HIPC Initiative, and partly from relief granted under the enhanced HIPC Initiative. The Interim Poverty Reduction Strategy Paper (PRSP) was completed in July 2000 and the final paper was adopted by the cabinet in May 2002.

As the Bretton Woods Institutions (BWIs) imposed the preparation of a PRSP as a requirement to obtain debt relief, it is legitimate to suspect that Mali, like other countries confronted to the same constraint, has not been fully implicated in the process. One could even expect it rather to have prepared the requested document as quickly as possible so as to obtain both debt relief and access to new funding. This is a paradox as one of the PRSP Initiative's main objectives is precisely to increase ownership of development policies. This particularly implies changing the relationships between the various stakeholders (donors, governments, civil society) through the participatory process implemented for the definition of the PRSP; it also implies institutional changes in order to put in practice the PRSP principles (the PRSPs are supposed to be a permanent new framework), and to establish an adequate system of monitoring and evaluation (see Chapter 6 for a detailed presentation of these new relationships and principles).

This chapter tries to observe how these new principles have been applied along the participatory process conducted in Mali. By doing so, it aims at assessing whether a true 'institutionalisation' of the PRSP process is taking place, or whether it remains a new conditionality only, as it was initially perceived in this country. The analysis is based on numerous interviews conducted with the various stakeholders: civil servants, members of civil society organisations, members of parliament, and representatives of donor agencies and of the BWIs.[2]

The first section shows that the definition of a poverty alleviation strategy predates the PRSP (called locally *Cadre Stratégique de Lutte contre la*

Pauvreté or CSLP). However, the PRSP progressively replaced previous strategies because of the financial weight of the BWIs and of the strong aid dependency of Mali. The second section examines changes induced in the government's relationships with the BWIs and other donors, and between donors themselves. This latter aspect is particularly interesting as Mali was chosen as a pilot country to attempt improvements to donor coordination, before the PRSP Initiative was even started. The third section highlights the human and institutional constraints prevailing in Mali, which hinder the implementation of a successful participatory process. Finally, we ask whether the PRSP process could encourage a new way of designing development policy in Mali.

Definition of a poverty alleviation strategy predates the PRSP

The ground was already prepared for the PRSP when it was proposed to Malian authorities as a new BWIs' conditionality. Former President Konaré had placed his second term of office under the sign of poverty reduction. A National Poverty Alleviation Strategy was completed in 1998 with UNDP's support right before the launch of the PRSP Initiative. After a period of coexistence, the latter progressively replaced the former due to the overpowering weight of the BWIs and especially because of the financial windfall expected from the completion of the PRSP.

From the National Poverty Alleviation Strategy to the Poverty Reduction Strategy Paper

The UNDP has deployed considerable efforts during the second half of the 1990s to support preparation of a National Poverty Alleviation Strategy (*Stratégie Nationale de Lutte contre la Pauvreté* or SNLP). The NPAS comprised:

* qualitative and quantitative analyses of poverty (based on the 1994 National Survey);
* evaluation of 34 pro-poor projects covering the whole country;
* national consultation (November 1997) to define the principal axes of the strategy, bringing together representatives of the administration, civil society, universities, development partners, and elected bodies.

The NPAS was validated by a series of national and regional consultations. Finally, the strategy was adopted by the cabinet in July 1998, and ratified in September 1998 at a Round Table Donor Conference in Geneva, when funds were pledged (more than those sought). Nevertheless, few new projects were announced. In essence, it comprised old projects refurbished for the occasion to stress poverty relief. Despite this, the NPAS was rapidly implemented (Diallo and Raffinot 1999).

In 1999, the NPAS was 'operationalised'. A network of 30 'focal points' (key people identified in ministries and other bodies) was charged with monitoring. The NPAS was under the responsibility of a specially created ministry, the Ministry of Social Development (Ministère du développement social or MDS). While opinions diverge regarding the level of ownership of the NPAS (Serra 1999, citing criticism by some NGOs), most of the people interviewed in October 2000 referred to the NPAS and not to the PRSP (Dante *et al.* 2001). When the PRSP was proposed, the World Bank wanted to start from scratch:

> The Malian PRS [Poverty Reduction Strategy] was initially considered by the World Bank to be inadequate for the purposes of the PRSP. As a matter of fact, the work required to produce a PRSP was considered so important, given the timetable, that Mali was obliged to go through an interim PRSP phase before being able to propose a final PRSP.
>
> (Lok Dessallien *et al.* 2001)

This resulted in a conflict with UNDP. The main reasons given by the World Bank were the following:

- the lack of a recent household survey for the elaboration of the NPAS;
- the lack of macro and structural-adjustment elements in the first document;
- the length of time for the PRSP initiative did not allow for grass-roots participation in the process of drawing up the final PRSP;
- the fact that the NPAS is only focused on a few points – some sectors like energy, transportation and industry were only partially covered by it.

Little by little, however, tension reduced and the NPAS was accepted as a basis for the PRSP (in conjunction with a prospective study, *Vision 2025*, also supported by the UNDP). It would have been difficult to do otherwise. Human resources are limited in Mali and largely the same people were mobilised for the NPAS and the PRSP.

The two processes nevertheless continued, piloted by two different ministries, the Finance Ministry (*Ministère de l'Économie et des Finances* or MEF) being responsible for the PRSP. Even though there have been no major problems at this level, the two processes appeared to advance more in parallel than be coordinated. Thus, for example, the 'focal points' of the NPAS were not used as such in the elaboration of pro-poor sectoral strategies during the final preparation of the PRSP. The end of the NPAS in 2002 removed this duality.

The PRSP is seen as an additional conditionality imposed by the BWIs

Introduction of the PRSP as a condition for debt relief was rather sudden. Malian authorities appeared surprised by the new approach. Aminata Traoré (1999), former Minister for Culture and Tourism, wrote: 'The engagement of the World Bank in the fight against poverty should not distract us. It merely represents a further conditionality designed to render budgetary austerity supportable and acceptable.'

Debt relief granted under the HIPC Initiative was initially conditional on pursuance of a classic IMF-backed programme in the framework of the Enhanced Structural Adjustment Facility (ESAF). This programme experienced some difficulties, notably due to delays arising in the privatisation of the state electricity company (*Electricité du Mali* or EDM) and restructuring of the cotton sector (privatisation of the *Compagnie Malienne de Développement des Textiles*, CMDT). These problems led to the suspension of several PRGF (Poverty Reduction and Growth Facility, which replaced ESAF) disbursements by the IMF.

Preparation of a PRSP, as a condition for debt relief, only arose after September 1999. This conditionality was applied retrospectively to Mali. So as not to penalise countries already engaged in the original HIPC framework, the BWIs declared they would be satisfied with an Interim PRSP to grant HIPC debt relief. The final PRSP would thus become one of the conditions to obtain debt reduction under the enhanced HIPC Initiative.

Reality is a little different. To avoid criticism, the BWIs granted enhanced HIPC debt relief, in a provisional form, as from their acceptance of an Interim PRSP. Technically, this involves a cancellation pending forgiveness which would come, year by year, after the completion point (see definition in Chapter 10, p. 241). The Paris Club has granted a 70 per cent cancellation, pending 90 per cent forgiveness after the HIPC completion point.

The PRSP was introduced in a less than clear manner; the BWIs for a long time gave the impression of not knowing exactly what they wanted. This created a certain sentiment of disarray, reflected by this declaration by former President Alpha Konaré: 'Whatever the programme, they tell us we must go to the HIPC. I frequently ask myself just what is inside it.'[3]

The Interim PRSP has been criticised by the BWIs in their Joint Staff Assessment (JSA), but these criticisms have been judged too secondary to justify further delays to debt reduction.

What is really at stake?

Before debt relief was granted in 2000, Mali was a heavily indebted country. At the end of 1997, its debt represented 119 per cent of GDP according to official figures, despite several reductions already granted by the Paris Club and other bilateral donors. However, this clearly excessive burden was overstated for two reasons. First, it was highly concessional in nature (its Net Present Value – see definition in Chapter 10, p. 243, Box 10.1 – represented just 56 per cent of GDP). Second, a significant part of the debt was 'passive': debts to the former Soviet Union were suspended, pending agreement, and those to China were not subject to effective repayments. For such reasons, Mali has been capable of honouring its debt service due since 1994 without difficulty.

Debt relief granted by the HIPC Initiative has been the subject of much speculation. Under the original Initiative, the Net Present Value (NPV) of Mali's debt should have fallen from 221 per cent to 200 per cent of exports (a fall of just 9.5 per cent). Reduction under the enhanced HIPC Initiative is more substantial: the NPV of the debt should not exceed 150 per cent of the value of exports, implying a reduction of 32 per cent. The BWIs largely broadcast the global volume of debt reduced (US$870 million, according to IMF 2000). They have been far more discreet about the fact that this sum represents debt service reductions of a limited amount (of the order of FCFA 24 billion per year – around US$3.8 million – once all agreements have been signed). This sum represents but a low share of public expenditure, of the order of 4 per cent.

Despite this, the allocation of money released by debt reduction represents a not to be neglected occasion for the Malian government. Spending on education and health represents, in effect, a very small share of the budget (and is otherwise little known). Debt relief could thus permit significant growth of this spending, although increased fiscal pressure could have produced the same result, as mentioned by managers of the *Projet d'Appui à la Mobilisation des Recettes Intérieures* (PAMORI – Domestic Revenue Mobilisation Support Project), commissioned to identify the main fiscal 'reserves'. Debt reduction has already allowed large-scale recruitment of teachers (rising from around 700 per year to 2,000 in 2001).

The BWIs' relationships with the Malian government and other donors

Mali is one of the most aid-dependent countries in the world (about 16 per cent of GDP in 2000). This massive inflow of aid introduces some large distortions. It is attributed through various channels and remains largely opaque. Even the overall amount differs significantly according to source (Naudet 2000c). For such reasons, Mali was chosen by the OECD and the UNDP as a pilot country to attempt improvements to donor coordination (OECD and UNDP 1998, 1999). Because of this strong aid dependence, the new relationships with donors that PRSPs wish to establish are especially crucial. The success or failure of this new approach in Mali will depend a lot indeed on the development partners' behaviour and on the coherence of their interventions.

The final PRSP is close to the desires of the BWIs

The BWIs made a considerable effort in Mali to avoid direct involvement in the PRSP preparation process. Their intervention was limited to expressions of opinion on documents submitted to them and to discussions with Malian authorities in the field or in Washington. This clearly represents a significant difference from previous practice, where Policy Framework Papers (PFPs) were frequently prepared in Washington and submitted to governments for approval after short 'negotiations' with a few officials.

In spite of this new approach, in the eyes of the Malian administration the PRSP remains above all a tool to obtain debt reduction and new funding. This is why the final document corresponds broadly to the wishes of the BWIs. The fact that the process is piloted by the Ministry of Economy and Finance (MEF) is already a guarantee for these institutions (even if this ministry occupies a lowly position in the official hierarchy of ministerial departments in Mali). It is without doubt the ministry that most closely reflects the views of the BWIs, and it is certainly not the one with greatest legitimacy in poverty relief. This opinion must be nuanced, however, as the MEF is not homogeneous. It is the result of a fusion of the former ministries of Finance, of Planning, and of Regional Integration, the various units of which have different preoccupations and are still poorly coordinated.

There has also been an evolution in public opinion which reconciles the country's official position with that of the BWIs. For example, massive fraud in public enterprises (notably the CMDT) encouraged disillusion among informed public opinion and allowed the privatisation paradigm to gain ground. Nevertheless, civil society organisations are strongly opposed to the privatisation process, mainly fearing lay-off of workers (Société Civile du Mali 2001).

Concretely, standardisation of PRSPs comes from the fact that teams charged with their preparation have access to documents already accepted by the BWIs (notably through the electronic publication of accepted PRSPs on World Bank and IMF websites, in the legitimate spirit of transparency) and thus seek to conform so as to guarantee a favourable joint staff assessment.

Are the World Bank and the IMF conducting the same strategies?

In their discourse, the BWIs associate the introduction of the PRSP process with a transformation of their own practices. One of the most important concerns the tight coordination of the IMF and the World Bank in their interventions under the HIPC Initiative. Another should be the change in funding, now oriented more towards generalised budget support. A third concerns the introduction of *ex-post* evaluation criteria, stressing the impact of measures and not only the means produced.

For Mali, it appears that coordination has improved, even if some limited sources of friction appear occasionally. The cotton crisis, for example, posed a problem: as a sectoral policy issue it fell to the World Bank; but the IMF became involved because of its macroeconomic implications.

IMF missions linked to the Poverty Reduction and Growth Facility are limited to the traditional framework (budget and the balance of payments), and may be likened to the management of current business over the very short term. They refer to the PRSP for the general context and the rest of the programme. PRGF documents, while strongly insisting on the importance of poverty alleviation, are IMF 'classics', notably concerning criteria and benchmarks. Since July 2002, the IMF decided to use the PRSP as the sole reference document. It stated, however, that it wanted to 'operationalise' it, without specifying explicitly how.

The way the BWIs will prioritise the new conditionalities linked to poverty reduction and classic macroeconomic conditionalities is as yet unclear (there is talk of 'conditionality cascades'). It does not seem that BWIs' staff has a clear position on the question. Some insisted on the importance of ownership, even if this implies some bending of orthodoxy. Others, to the contrary, placed an accent on the programme already outlined in the PRGF (which contains government commitments), and hoped the PRSP would scrupulously take up the elements of the programme. This posed a difficulty, insofar as the programme is very detailed for 2001 and the first half of 2002, and that it is otherwise incorporated in quarterly forecasts extending until 2004. The room to manoeuvre given to those preparing the PRSP was thus limited to the period 2004 to 2006, and essentially to the budgetary distribution of funds liberated by debt reduction (these funds are already taken into account in the programme, but globally and for a reduced amount).

The World Bank appeared initially to hold to its former Country Assistance Strategy. The most favourable interpretation of the PRSP process rhetoric leaves some room for doubt. Here too the PRSP is supposed to take up faithfully programmes and reforms already underway, which cover a wide field of economic policies.

As regards poverty reduction, the Bank puts forward its project in support of local initiatives (*Projet d'Appui aux Initiatives de Base* or PAIB), a project very popular with NGOs, to which it grants funds, but which bypasses local elected bodies. In a more general manner, it remains difficult for the Bank to break out of the project optic, which remains its *raison d'être*. As jokingly stated by one of the European diplomats following the PRSP process in Bamako: 'Despite everything, the Bank remains a lender of first resort', stressing the pressure to release funds that characterises this organisation (practices of the African Development Bank, totally absent from the PRSP process, are even more of a caricature).

The PRSP process is supported by bilateral and other multilateral donors

After an initial period of mistrust, other donors have invested massively in the process underway. They wanted to support the PRSP preparation process financially (but frequently remained stuck in procedural payment problems) and followed it in a close and collaborative manner. In effect, the PRSP gave new vigour to an aid coordination programme jointly launched in 1996 by the OECD Development Assistance Committee and the UNDP. This programme identified the absence of a unique Malian reference document as a major obstacle to aid coordination. This does not signify, however, that the donors are ready to change their established procedures radically. In particular, the move to generalised budget support is not judged opportune by all.

In practice, the PRSP has been followed by donors during periodic meetings coordinated by the Dutch Embassy (long involved in questions of debt relief and poverty alleviation). Donor representatives participated in the meetings of working groups constituted for preparation of the PRSP. These discussions on macroeconomic and sector strategies have allowed profound exchanges of views with the government and between donors. This improved knowledge of the points of view and activities of the partners is seen in a very positive light. The same positive reaction was observed in Burkina Faso in 1997, when the European Commission proposed a negotiated exercise to reform conditionality (Leandro, Schafer and Frontini 1999).

The principal support of donors consisted of appointing four international consultants to the PRSP Committee, in addition to one local consultant, and several other consultants specialised in sectoral issues. This evidently posed delicate problems of ownership (one of the consultants has been commissioned by the World Bank), even if the process remained driven by Malian authorities. Consultants limited their interventions, as much as possible, to technical aspects or to the synthesis of documents already elaborated during the process. Some international institutions or donors provided funds to support work in a PRSP group close to their domain of expertise. Thus the International Labour Organisation (ILO) funded diverse activities of the 'employment and training' group, and sought by this bias to bring the theme of employment to the fore in the final PRSP (and more precisely the theme favoured by the ILO: 'decent employment').

Problems of coordination between the BWIs and other donors

This strong implication by donors generated tensions. Indeed, if the PRSP is a framework for coordinating policies and aid in general, it is difficult to understand why it is validated only by the BWIs.

For this reason, local representatives of European Union (EU) states made an official request to participate in all negotiations between the Malian government and the BWIs. This request was refused by the latter. The reason given was that bilateral donors were represented by their administrators sitting at the boards of the BWIs, through whom they were informed and could intervene to influence programmes.

It is nonetheless unclear as to whether the *status quo* can be maintained. To be sure, BWIs' disbursements weight relatively little in the total amount of foreign aid going to Mali, and to HIPC countries in general. In Mali, the World Bank (through its subsidiary, the International Development Association or IDA) represented just 16 per cent of the total in 1997/1998 and the IMF 5 per cent, compared to 14 per cent for France, 7 per cent for Germany, 4 per cent for the Netherlands, 6 per cent for Japan and, at the multilateral level, 12 per cent for the EU and 10 per cent for UN agencies (UNDP 1999). Furthermore, these figures overvalue the support of the BWIs as they refer to loans, and not to grants as is the case for other donors.

The lack of national capacity to work out strategies

Preparation of the PRSP experienced great difficulties due to the weak national capacity to programme development, above all in a participatory context. With Mali being one of the poorest countries worldwide, acute human and organisational constraints affected all the national stakeholders: within the administration, the PRSP process was a one-man project for a long time, while the civil society was not structured enough to bring a valuable contribution to the process. These constraints also prevented the implementation of a proper monitoring and evaluation system, which is supposed to be one of the main innovations of the PRSP Initiative.

The administration's weak capacity to react

Preparation of a PRSP is a complex process that brings together numerous bodies from within and outside the administration. The Malian government reacted slowly. Although the interim PRSP was completed in July 2000, work on the final version did not really start until February 2001. The process was for a long time steered, almost single-handed, by a technical adviser in the Ministry of Economy and Finance. It was not until April 2001 that the organisation of the process was 'institutionalised' through a decree. Only after that date were 11 groups constituted and set to work, with the goal of producing a draft version of their report before May 2001. Creation of a coordinating unit was not made official until June 2001.

Not all the 11 working groups were capable of supplying a document at the required date. Some groups waited to receive promised funding before starting work. Work produced by the different working groups was of uneven quality. This demonstrates the profound state of disorganisation of the Malian administration. The low level of salaries and the absence of sanctions explain why several senior civil servants spend the bulk of their time undertaking paid work outside their essential mission. Donors have a large responsibility in this state of affairs, as they continue to propose paid training courses, missions and consulting work to these same people, introducing major distortions in the labour market of highly skilled workers.

Organisational problems to define development policies

Technically, preparation of the PRSP certainly falls on the National Planning Directorate (Direction Nationale du Plan or DNP). This is recognised, formally at least, by the institutional arrangements established. However, the duality introduced by the institutionalisation of the PRSP Committee complicates matters, even if this Committee is charged only with coordinating functions. In practice, the DNP is marginalised. It has few means and its personnel have very few advantages compared to their colleagues at the MEF. Furthermore, the DNP has lost much of its technical capacity since, in 1982, the National Plan was supplanted by structural adjustment programmes (Coulibaly, Diarra and Traore 1999). It has concentrated on preparing the Public Investment Programme, without disposing of the means to monitor and assess projects.

This weak capacity of conception is also explained by the multiplication of administrative entities, causing wastage of human resources. Thus, part of the available resources is found in the economic analysis unit attached to the Prime Minister (*Centre d'Analyses et de Formulation des Politiques de Développement*, funded by the African Capacity Building Foundation (ACBF)). The UNDP funds the National Capacity Reinforcement Programme for the Strategic Management of Development (*Programme de Renforcement des Capacités nationales pour une Gestion stratégique du Développement* or PRECAGED). The World Bank funded the *Cellule Croissance Accélérée et Développement* which worked out interesting analyses, but was enventually set apart and closed. Its documents have never been used by the Malian administration. These structures are outside the formal administration, which prevents a good valorisation of human resources.

Technical constraints on the analytical side

In a country like Mali, where 70 per cent or thereabouts of the population is considered as poor, poverty relief is above all a struggle to accelerate development in general, even if distribution issues are also important. However, how to enhance growth and promote pro-poor growth remain unanswered questions. The difficulty becomes all the more important, as in the absence of recent and reliable data the relationship between poverty reduction and growth is far from clear in the case of Mali.

The Malian economy has grown at a sustained rate since the 1994 devaluation (5.7 per cent on average between 1995 and 2000), due to strong recovery of the cotton sector, stimulation of gold production (linked to promulgation of a new Mining Code and favourable world prices), and good rainfall. Nevertheless, this steady growth appears to have had little influence on poverty according to the Annual Report of the Sustainable Human Development Observatory (*Observatoire du Développement Humain Durable*): whereas the incidence of poverty (using a national threshold based on basic caloric needs) rose considerably at the beginning of the 1990s prior to the CFA Franc devaluation (1994), it only fell slightly thereafter from 68.8 per cent to 64.2 per cent between 1994 and 1999 (ODHD 2001). But these estimates of poverty incidence result from a simple extrapolation from growth aggregates based on the 1994 household survey, which is a debatable methodology, and therefore are highly questionable.

It is necessary to have relevant sectoral analyses and studies of the relations between policies and their impact on the economy and on society before starting to prepare development policies. Also necessary are studies of the international environment and the principal shocks susceptible to affect the national economy (see Chapter 7). Few in-depth analyses are available in Mali. Most of the available studies are dispersed and somewhat specific. There is no systematic mechanism for their collection, and even less for periodic synthesis, notably in the field of rural development policy that remains marked by much imprecision and a weak capacity to quantify objectives and means.[4] This is even more regrettable as the situation evolves more rapidly than new solutions appear, which is particularly the case with the epidemic of Aids in Mali, the prevalence of which seems to have been much underestimated until now.

An attempt to reflect on the theme of accelerating growth was made in 1998, with the establishment of a small group funded by the World Bank, using its Revised Minimum Standard (RMSM) of that institution. The report based on their work (Cellule Croissance Accélérée et Développement 1998), despite its interest, was never really taken up by the Malian administration. A large number of similar studies have been realised on the initiative of one or another donor, without any real capitalisation of the resources produced. For this reason, the World Bank organised a forum, in the PRSP context, to present a wide variety of work concerning poverty analysis in Mali. This allowed circulation of information until then little available in Mali (but at a relatively high cost).

Civil society difficulties to participate fully in the process

Malian civil society comprises a large number of sometimes very small entities. There are more than a thousand NGOs (non-governmental organisations) and associations. In addition, there are several labour and employers' associations, churches, and so on. Formally, representatives of Malian civil society participated in PRSP working groups. However, the capacity of these organisations to participate in the preparation of national strategies is generally technically weak.

Moreover, civil society was uneasy in a process essentially managed by the administration. The process was judged too rapid and too technical. This is why civil society organised a parallel process including national and regional workshops, financed by USAID. This rapid exercise (one month) resulted in a report critical of those responsible for the PRSP process (Société Civile du Mali 2001). The report advanced few concrete elements and insisted, above all, on the need for a tighter association of civil society groups. Malian NGOs nevertheless had previous experience, as Mali was retained as a test case for the SAPRIN (Structural Adjustment Participatory Review International Network) exercise, an evaluation of structural adjustment realised by NGOs and funded by the World Bank. This assessment, which was rather disappointing technically, concluded that with structural adjustment programmes 'the Malian economy followed the right path towards reducing poverty and improving the living conditions of the population' (SAPRIN-Mali and IREPAS 1999). This gives little insight as to on what the recommendation for greater future consultation with Malian civil society was based.

The PRSP process illustrates the difficulty of ensuring a deep implication of citizens. The first issue is evidently one of representativeness. Several NGOs have no legitimacy other than to be interfaces between the population and donors. Most of them depend in large part on external funding (each donor thus has 'its' civil society) and have frequently been constituted by local dignitaries, civil servants, or opportunists.

The problem of representativeness is all the more critical as the Malian PRSP made no room for elected assemblies – a situation otherwise widespread and criticised by Summers (2001), who reproached the World Bank and considered that this type of behaviour weakened democratically elected representatives. The only role considered for the National Assembly consists of validating the prepared document by its vote. The Speaker of the National Assembly protested against this exclusion by saying: 'I am the civil society.'

The private sector participated in working groups in an almost totally passive way. It remains profoundly dependent on the administration and has no desire to appear opposed to it in public. It is also interested in the regular growth of foreign financing. The cotton crisis placed representatives of producer groups to the fore, and they contributed indirectly to the process by their participation in a 'General Assembly' (*Etats Généraux*) devoted to cotton that established the broad lines of a negotiated settlement. This raises a more general problem, which consists of defining a place for opposition in the PRSP context. In a certain way, the PRSP project in itself presupposes unanimity, or at least hypothesises that it would be possible to convert the whole population to supporting 'good policies and best practices'. Even if this were the case, the size of the task in providing information and education seems to have been clearly underestimated. In Mali, for example, the IMF was astonished that provisional versions of the PRSP repeated already 'rejected' measures, as if the agreement obtained by the IMF in the PRGF framework had involved more people than the dozen or so high-level negotiators with whom the missions habitually work.

It may be retained that all this underlines, above all, the risks that this call to 'civil society', comprising NGOs in the main, might undermine a still-fragile democracy at the national level, and above all locally (because of decentralisation). A more optimistic approach puts the accent on the eventual reinforcement of civil society capacities and of its powers of questioning and proposition.

Weak capacities to ensure an effective monitoring of the PRSP implementation

The institutional setting for poverty monitoring is still vague. The statistical office (*Direction de la Statistique et de l'Informatique*) has the legitimacy for this task, but currently lacks the capacity.

The weakness of the Malian statistical system, characterised by a serious lack of basic economic and statistical data, constitutes a major drawback to the effective monitoring of poverty reduction policies (indeed, for development in general). As mentioned before, there is no reliable data on poverty;[5] also, no input–output table has been prepared since 1987; household revenue data is essentially extracted from the consumption survey of 1989, etc.

This situation results from three principal factors: above all, lack of technical capacity (mainly for results analysis), the low diffusion of available data, and shortcomings in funding the Malian statistical system from the domestic budget. This last factor is crucial, as it encourages dependency on donor funds to perform surveys, hence their irregularity and low degree of ownership.

The main criticism directed to the UNDP-initiated NPAS, which was its use of a dated household survey, equally applies to the PRSP. Indeed, the household consumption survey undertaken in 2001 (*Enquête Malienne sur l'Evaluation de la Pauvreté*, or EMEP) was supposed to provide recent information for the preparation of the PRSP, but provisional and partial results were only made available in June 2001 (after the preparation of provisional reports by different working groups). Only the first part of EMEP was available before the completion of the PRSP elaboration.

In addition, the goals for poverty reduction have yet to be defined, other than for the sectors of education and health where the PRODEC (*Programme Décennal pour l'Education* – Decennial Programme for Education Development) and PRODESS (*Programme Décennal de Développement Socio-Sanitaire* – Decennial Programme for Socio-Sanitary Development) projects already define objectives (although until 2004 only). Nevertheless, the links between targets and budget resources have yet to be established. Furthermore, macro and sectoral databases (such as social accounting matrices) and modelling tools (such as applied general equilibrium and microsimulation models) would be useful for analysing the impact of public policies on poverty (see Chapter 14).

The PRSP progressively transforms into a medium-term development plan

Progressively, the PRSP has evolved into a sort of medium-term development plan covering a period of five years (2001–5 then 2002–6). This approach caused the resurgence of classic problems associated with development planning, but within a new context.

Going beyond an inventory of current programmes and projects?

In the first place, it is inevitable that a plan of this nature can do little more than embrace projects and programmes already financed or underway in its early years. As such, it is difficult to target policies and programmes on poverty alleviation based on projects designed with a different priority. This is especially the case in a country like Mali, characterised by strong aid dependence and thus by choices for cooperation by different donors who rarely shared the same orientations regarding development.

Ensuring an effective link with the budget

In the second place, the initiative is handicapped by weak linkage between development planning and the budget process. There have been significant advances nevertheless, notably in the sectors of education and health, where ten-year sector programmes have been established in 1997 (see above). In the health sector in particular, PRODESS describes the objectives and actions to be undertaken by the administration and its partners, the funding required and the annual tranches. It does not go so far as to constitute a common fund or to filter all the resources through the budget and Malian procedures. Elsewhere, an evolution towards programme budgets was initiated in 1997. The PRSP helped make this process more effective. A medium-term expenditure framework (MTEF) has been implemented for the first time. This represents a major step forward, even if it is still not in line with sectoral policies and objectives.

Programming in a global environment

A significant obstacle to the realisation of the PRSP comes from the multiplicity of procedures to be taken into account. Indeed, the Malian government has been simultaneously absorbed by domestic political issues (elections in 2002, combating corruption, etc.) and by major events (such as hosting the African Cup of Nations football tournament in 2002, the cost of which was close to the amount of debt relief for that year). Economically, it has to undertake negotiations for external funding (notably the PRGF), restructuring the cotton sector (demanded by the BWIs), various projects, regional integration within the West African Economic and Monetary Union (WAEMU) and the African Union, the Cotonou agreement with the European Union, the WTO agreements, and so on. This is a lot to do for an administration that is small in number, lacking resources and little motivated.

Conclusion

Despite all the difficulties associated in part with the novelty of the process, the PRSP appears as an opportunity to renew the national debate on development strategies. If there were a real will to seize this occasion, this could be the start of a permanent process. This supposes that certain conditions are fulfilled.

First is the clarification and simplification of the institutional machinery. A body that normally undertakes coordination of government actions must guide the government's economic policy. In Mali, the only such body is the office of the Prime Minister. External partners must do all they can to avoid imposing the creation of yet further entities to resolve each immediate problem. Moreover, the problem of motivation and work ethics in the civil service must be tackled.

The second condition is to provide the bodies involved in the process with the tools to perform their task. This would allow them to analyse and develop their own perceptions of the situation, define actions deemed desirable, monitor their implementation, and assess their impact. Development partners should avoid limiting themselves to funding emergencies or provoking thousands of occasions which divert local managers from their tasks. It is necessary to invest in basic information and to ensure the motivation of people involved in strategic planning to accomplish their work.

One of the reasons for the absence of initiatives from the Malians is the implicit sharing of tasks between bilateral and multilateral donors, which leaves little room for the definition of national public policies. Bilateral donors, the World Bank and specialised United Nations agencies, prepare and finance programmes and projects, and the IMF controls public finances. As for the Malians, their role consists, above all, of trying to maximise external aid by accepting everything proposed to them. Even the debate that has taken place between bilateral donors and the BWIs for participation of the former in missions of the latter refers to the distribution of roles between them, rather than to a reduction of external influence on public decisions.

The PRSP could be the occasion to reform the system of cooperation with Mali, if donors accept to help Malians realise their own objectives rather than make crucial choices in their place. Greater transparency in the management of public funds and increased vigilance to fight corruption could further encourage donors to favour budget support. This would not only allow reinforced construction of the state (contrary to structural adjustment, which had its weakening as an objective), but also the creation of closer links between Mali's goals and the means it has available, so that poverty alleviation does not remain simple rhetoric.

Notes

1   Idrissa Dante died in July 2002.
2   This chapter is a synthesis of a study undertaken within a wider eight-country programme coordinated by the Overseas Development Institute (ODI) and financed by the Strategic Partnership for Africa within the framework of SPA PRSP Process and Poverty Monitoring Task Teams' study to investigate the extent to which poverty reduction policies, programmes, practices, and monitoring systems are being institutionalised in selected African countries. Various missions in Mali have taken place between September 2000 and July 2002.
3   Speech at the launch ceremony for the 2000 UNDP Report in Bamako (*Les Echos*, Bamako, 14 July 2000).
4   The absence of reflection on rural development strategies in the PRSP exercise was also denounced in other countries (see Chapter 7). In this context, it is not sufficient to stick to an approach aimed at increasing agricultural production. Analysis is required of the different types of farms, in particular those of the poorest producers.
5   In the absence of reliable data, both the level and the evolution of poverty differ widely according to various studies. According to the Annual Report of the Sustainable Human Development Observatory (ODHD 1999), the incidence of poverty rose considerably between 1989 and 1996, from 40.8 per cent to 71.6 per cent. A study by DIAL (2000b) confirms this increase: according to DIAL, urban poverty grew from 33 per cent to 57.2 per cent between 1989 and 1996. A study by Sahn and Stifel (2000), using a methodology based on household assets (declared in demographic and health surveys, or DHS), produced totally contradictory results on almost the same period. According to them, poverty fell significantly in Mali between 1987 and 1995 (from 23 per cent to 16 per cent), and the reduction applied to all regions of the country, rural as well as urban.

9 Debt relief or aid reform?

Jean-David Naudet

In the space of three years, between 2000 and 2002, some 60 countries, at the instigation of the Bretton Woods Institutions (BWIs), have prepared, written and validated a Poverty Reduction Strategy Paper (PRSP) responding to common characteristics and standards: centred on poverty alleviation, using a participatory process, with the simultaneous and prioritised incorporation of sectoral aspects, the determination of a battery of outcome indicators and a system of monitoring and evaluation, etc.

This enormous mobilisation and channelling of energies and competencies again bears witness to the formidable power of the BWIs over poor countries, in a way more rapid and weightier than with structural adjustment, to which many recipient countries and some donors resisted for a long time. Naturally, a PRSP is above all a conditionality or, more exactly, according to the new BWIs' vocabulary, a 'trigger'; in other words it is a requirement for access to funding and to the HIPC Initiative (debt Initiative for Heavily Indebted Poor Countries). This explains why, of all the concerned countries, just one has so far refused the offer of joining the exercise: the Lao Republic.[1]

The purpose of this chapter is to study the characteristics of the PRSP and HIPC Initiatives. It starts with the analysis of different factors that have progressively influenced their gestation and development. In the first section, the conditions and the context within which the initiatives were conceived by the BWIs are briefly recapitulated. The political handling of the PRSP and HIPC Initiatives is the subject of the second section, which describes the various forms successively adopted by these initiatives. These analyses lead to a third section that compares the current state of PRSPs with the expectations of their initial promoters, and proposes some elements for future reflection.

This chapter does not pretend to cover all the international questions contributing to building political institutions like the World Bank. In this sense, it is somewhat different from other contributions in this volume: it presents the reflections of an involved actor, and not a state of knowledge about the subject.

Trends at the end of the 1990s: the terminal phase of structural adjustment

The late 1990s correspond to a period of doubt, of challenge and of intellectual agitation in the world of development institutions. The 'aid crisis' was in full swing, fed by the continual decline of resources over the decade. Prolonged economic failure by several poor countries, especially in Africa, posed questions for the efficacy of development policies. Development institutions, confronted by new problems, were seeking a renewal of their analyses and practices.

A capital problem: poor country debts due to the World Bank

J.-M. Severino (2001a) concluded that the economic mission of structural adjustment, based on debt management and reducing barriers to trade, was a success as the growth of poor countries was only a secondary preoccupation.

Decades of adjustment have effectively allowed the international financial system to avoid a crisis, particularly through the management of significant debt flows to the large developing countries. However, the absence of sustainable growth in the poorest nations caused another (mini?) debt crisis, consequent on 20 years of multilateral lending that could not be rescheduled. The World Bank had become the primary creditor of all less developed countries and, for the poorest, the only creditor to count in annual servicing.

Figure 9.1 clearly shows the rise in power of the international financial institutions in the external debts of low-income countries. Between 1970 and 1999, the stock of bilateral debt owed by heavily indebted low-income countries was multiplied by nearly 15 (in current US dollars). At the same time, however, multilateral debt increased four times as quickly – it multiplied by more than 60. The share of private debts (officially guaranteed) fell following the debt crisis of the 1980s. Annualised flows show a more radical evolution. In 1970, and excluding officially guaranteed private debts, multilateral institutions provided 14 per cent of new borrowing whereas the 86 per cent remaining came from bilateral donors. Twenty years later, the proportions have almost inverted, with 62 per cent and 38 per cent respectively.

These trends are not specific to heavily indebted countries. They are almost the same for all low-income countries, as well as for sub-Saharan Africa. This continent is nevertheless distinguished by a severe drop of drawings since the start of the 1990s, and an even more pronounced 'scissor effect' between bilateral and multilateral obligations, the latter representing almost 85 per cent of the total in 2000.

This situation certainly poses little threat for the international financial system, as the sums involved are modest. In the long run, it is nevertheless unsustainable for the following reasons:

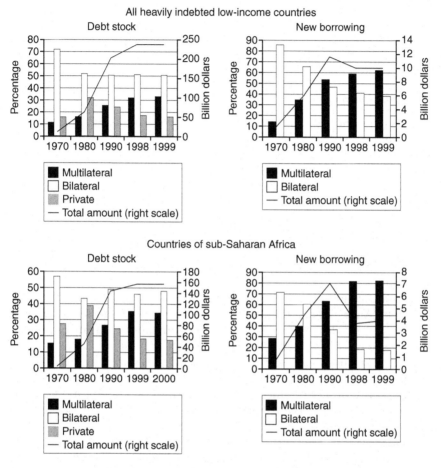

Figure 9.1 The rise of multilateral debts of poor countries, 1970–2000.

Source: World Bank, *Global Development Finance* (2001).

Note

Data refers to long-term external public debt. The group of heavily indebted low-income countries does not correspond exactly to those of the HIPC Initiative.

- financially, as there is no apparent issue for the rapid rise of such debt without a change to the rules of the game (moratoria are often for 20 years);
- politically, net flows are due to resume quite rapidly for many of the world's poorest nations;
- even morally, as seeking quarterly payments from countries that are bleeding to death, which sometimes cannot pay teachers' salaries, is one of the more painful tasks recently undertaken by some World Bank resident representatives.

It was easy to foresee that the question of multilateral debts owed by poor countries would explode in the first decade of the century and create an intolerable situation for the BWIs. The problem required urgent treatment, implying a change to the partnership rules initiated in 1996 with the start of the HIPC Initiative.

The critique of aid efficiency

Criticism of the efficiency of development aid mounted progressively throughout the decade of the 1990s, which no doubt comprised one of the factors (among others) contributing to the weakening of financial contributions by donors. In 1998 the World Bank published a major report entitled *Assessing Aid: What Works, What Doesn't, and Why*. This report synthesises the institution's reflections and thinking on the aid theme. It stresses four principal theses, each illustrated by numerous research studies:

- the impact of aid on growth is only positive in the context of 'good policies';
- classic 'conditionality' based on promises of future reforms, is inefficient. An *ex post* conditionality system would be preferable, linking the release of aid resources to results obtained and the quality of policies pursued;
- aid is far more fungible[2] than is generally presumed and the allocation of resources, notably project aid, is either illusory (by the liberation of resources destined for other uses) or an attempt more or less bound to fail (if the foreseen allocation is not among the government's priorities);
- differences between developing countries are important, notably with regard to the quality of institutions and policies. Therefore, these countries should receive different treatment.

From these broad and abundantly illustrated factors, the report concludes that the conditions for success in poor countries are above all tied to the nature of policies pursued and to the quality of public institutions. In consequence, the destination and the nature of aid should above all depend on the institutional conditions and policies of the host countries. More precisely, three types of country may be distinguished:

- those where the quality of policies and institutions is satisfactory, where sizeable and efficient aid should serve to finance an overall public expenditure programme, established in partnership;
- those where policy qualities are satisfactory, but institutions are weak, where the continuation of aid mainly linked to projects may be justified to ensure an efficient environment for some priority preoccupations;

- finally, those where policies and institutions are deficient, where neither conditional aid nor project aid is efficient, and where it would be more appropriate to encourage the 'circulation of ideas' (improvements to the context and to institutions, circulation of knowledge, promotion of dialogue and reflection, demonstration of anecdotal but reproducible innovations).

This new doctrine is today designated by the term 'aid selectivity'. It consists of reserving the rare resources transferred by international donors in priority for destinations where the conditions for its efficient use are the best.

From the poverty of nations to the poverty of citizens

Two long-term trends have influenced the ways of thinking about development for several decades: the passage from a largely economic optic to a vision more concentrated on the individual, and the evolution from a uniquely national reference point to a multiple one (global, national and local). These changes, of course, are but the echo within the development community of more profound changes in Western society at large, such as the decline of nationalism and the development of liberalism or of globalisation.

Amartya Sen (1999) provided concepts to transpose these evolutions to the realm of international aid. He identified three types of solidarity: 'grand universalism', based on consideration and on equal rights given to each citizen of the world, as an individual; 'national particularism', where the exercise of equity is applied to each country taken separately; and, 'plural affiliation', linking not individuals or states but all representative institutions of a transnational character.

In practice, each of these broad frames of reference corresponds to a particular type of aid. The globally humanist pole linking individuals is most directly associated with humanitarian aid, but also with all direct action by NGOs or aid agencies (representing the taxpayer) targeting poor populations. Inter-state aid corresponds naturally to the framework of international justice between nations. The intermediate case of multiple linkages may be associated with multiple acts of cooperation linking international institutions of a similar nature (decentralised cooperation, for example, between regions or communities, professional associations, and so on).

The growing accent placed on poverty alleviation and on the role of civil society clearly arises from the drift from 'national particularism' to 'grand universalism' and to 'plural affiliation'. The duty for solidarity by aid institutions is being addressed less and less to states, and more to individuals and civil institutions. The result is a 'humanitarianisation' of development aid as the frontier between the two poles of intervention becomes less and less clear.[3]

The redirection of development aid towards the fight against poverty was promoted and facilitated by the World Bank (coming after the UNDP and some bilateral donors). The institution has again demonstrated its capacity to retain leadership in development thinking, and to work for international mobilisation around the cause of poor countries. Nevertheless, this new situation raises real difficulties for the institution.

In effect, since the end of the 1970s the World Bank has established a recurrent diagnosis according to which the causes of underdevelopment and of poverty are above all the responsibility of government actions in the affected countries. This diagnosis previously stressed bad economic policies; these weighed more if there was also poor governance. A glance at the World Bank Report *Attacking Poverty* is sufficient to see the extent to which solutions are being sought, almost uniquely through reforms to the modes of governance and policies in the countries concerned (see Chapter 1). However, statutorily the World Bank, like other multilateral financial institutions, can only grant resources to states. As such the World Bank faces a dilemma: how to relieve the poverty of citizens, the responsibility for which is essentially incumbent on governments, all the while being limited to granting resources only to the latter?

Indeed, 'grand universalism' places cooperation institutions in a difficult position: how to assist the 'poor but badly governed citizen' (Naudet 2000b)? Two approaches were attempted in the 1980s and 1990s:

1   Conditionality, which consists of inciting governments to adopt and implement policies favouring their citizens, especially the poor, through the granting of aid. This approach, which frequently led to constraints, was criticised within the international institutions due to a lack of ownership of defined policies, and hence of their efficiency.
2   Circumventing weak governments and institutions by offering services directly to citizens, using externally funded institutions. This widespread practice, particularly but not exclusively for humanitarian aid, sometimes resolved short-term difficulties but encouraged interference, a lack of ownership and non-sustainability.

At the end of the 1990s a third way opened: selectivity proposed the concentration of actions, as a priority, on well-governed poor citizens who were the only ones liable to be assisted efficiently. This politically awkward 'solution' led to the adoption, in the PRSP framework, of a fourth alternative favouring the participatory definition of policies. The idea was that if policies slanted in favour of poor citizens came from those affected and were not externally imposed, then neither foreign interference nor lack of ownership should constitute obstacles.

New multilateral debt reduction contracts

The foregoing factors led to a need to design a 'new contract' between the BWIs and poor countries. This should incite greater responsibility, be more open to all sectors and actors, and be directed in particular to populations (unlike structural adjustment). The relationship between the BWIs and the low-income countries, however, is above all that of a creditor to a debtor. The 'new contracts' should also allow re-establishment of the regularity of a relationship strained by multilateral over-indebtedness.

The effect of these different constraints gave rise, in separate ways, to the HIPC and the PRSP Initiatives. Their later convergence gave birth to the sought-after contractual renewal, which was subsequently proposed to all poor countries.

The timid appearance of the HIPC Initiative

The World Bank and the IMF launched the HIPC Initiative in September 1996. The Paris Club refined the Initiative and fell in line, developing facilities to grant forgiveness of previous debt (Naples terms, then Lyons terms; see Chapter 10). The basic difference is that, for the first time, multilateral debt was concerned.

The Initiative had a prudent start, due to fears raised by the abandonment of multilateral debt intangibility. Conditions were highly restrictive: they required very low per capita incomes (less than US$750), unsustainable external debt (between 200 and 250 per cent of GDP at Net Present Value; see definition in Chapter 10), a high budget deficit, and qualification as a 'model pupil' of structural adjustment during IMF scrutiny of eligibility.

Above all, the calendar of the Initiative was extremely constrictive. Before reaching a 'decision point', an eligible country must have successfully followed an IMF-supported programme for at least three years. Subsequently, it must repeat this success during a further three-year programme before arriving at a 'completion point'. Only then would debt relief become effective.

The Initiative was a direct descendant of structural adjustment. It was destined to be a supplementary 'facility' (the term is perhaps not best chosen) granted to poor countries that best succeed in their IMF-backed macroeconomic reform programmes.

These conditions were too restrictive to tailor the original HIPC Initiative solution to the problem of poor country multilateral debt. Until 1999, when the HIPC Initiative was transformed, only seven of the 41 countries potentially eligible for relief benefited from a start to debt relief (that is Bolivia, Burkina Faso, Côte d'Ivoire, Guyana, Mali, Mozambique and Uganda).

The search for a mechanism to succeed structural adjustment

During the second half of the last decade, meanwhile, top management at the financial institutions was preoccupied with preparation of a follow-up to structural adjustment. It was necessary to design a new conceptual framework for development, a new contractual instrument for partnership and a new financial tool.

The Comprehensive Development Framework (CDF) is a vast multi-actor development plan presented in matrix form. Promoted by President Wolfensohn himself, and made official in July 1999, it seemed for a short time to become the new working instrument of the World Bank in developing countries. The CDF attacks two weaknesses of previous adjustment programmes in particular:

- it has a global vocation, as its name implies, allowing action in every sector and is not restricted to macroeconomic reforms alone;[4]
- through its extended field of application and its multi-actor character, it is destined to become the prime instrument for coordination between donors, and more generally between all stakeholders (government, civil society, private sector, financial partners).

Full-scale trials of the CDF were even undertaken in a few developing countries. Almost at the same time, in September 1999, World Bank departments developed and presented the idea of a strategic framework for partnership centred on poverty alleviation. It is this instrument, the PRSP, which is both more operational and more 'modern', that finally emerged as the successor to structural adjustment.

The PRSP concept was created in direct response to the trends described above, regarding the central thrusts towards poor citizens and aid efficiency. It is conceived primarily as a tool in the service of populations, and particularly the poor. Institutions play but an instrumental role to the benefit of these populations.[5] The question of badly governed poor citizens is treated, as mentioned above, by the introduction of participatory preparation and monitoring, giving a voice to the poor. PRSPs also seek to adopt recommendations arising from studies of aid efficiency.

In the first place, it must be the product of a consensus between local actors around development strategies. In this respect it is an instrument 'owned' by local institutions, and donors should be largely absent from its elaboration.

Second, a PRSP should not give rise to classic conditionality constraints. It should intervene in countries presenting acceptable policies and be based on a measurement of results obtained, compared to goals fixed in common, according to the precepts of the conditionality reform exercise undertaken through the Strategic Partnership with Africa (SPA).

Third, a PRSP should result in vast programmes of public spending jointly funded by various sources. It should coincide with budget reinforcement at the national level, and its rehabilitation as the leading instrument for development, as outlined in recommendations arising from the observation of aid fungibility and project dispersal.

Conceived to integrate the supports of new reforming trends in development aid, the PRSP will progressively take on (or approach) a more and more elaborate technical content: poverty analyses, participatory surveys giving a 'voice to the poor', monitoring and evaluation systems based on a battery of results indicators, medium-term public spending programme, multi-donor, multi-sector programmes, and so on.

In its first phase, the PRSP framework was defined as an appropriate response to the requirements of partnership, as outlined in the first example envisaged by the *Assessing Aid* study cited above: that of countries where policies and institutions are satisfactory and where central budget procedures are sufficiently efficient and transparent to become the main vector for international aid.

The 'enhanced' HIPC Initiative

The 'enhanced' HIPC Initiative was born at the G7 summit in Cologne in 1999. Modifications to the initial Initiative were of three principal types:

- entry conditions were relaxed and debt forgiveness deepened;
- the calendar for the Initiative was slightly shortened and simplified;
- the PRSP became the framework for the strategic partnership of the HIPC Initiative.

Enlargement of the Initiative evidently resulted from its previous excessively prudent character. By 1999 it was becoming obvious that the original Initiative, which benefited only seven countries in three years, did not respond sufficiently to the problem of low-income countries' debt.[6] Policies were also driven by international public opinion that seized on the question of poor country debts.

It is nevertheless necessary to note that the shortening of the period is relative. The interim period, between the decision point and the completion point, becomes more flexible instead of being fixed at three years, and debt relief is granted from the start. However, the precondition of a three-year programme remains. Above all, the new condition imposed by the need to prepare a PRSP to reach the decision point constitutes a real constraint. This complex exercise is a complete novelty for the countries involved, and preparation of a PRSP, if done in good faith, can only be the result of a lengthy and difficult process.

The essential innovation brought by the enhanced HIPC Initiative comes from the link it established with the PRSP process. This linkage marks the real end of structural adjustment. The PRSP becomes the obligatory framework for partnership between poor countries and donors.

Apart from the 'modernity' of PRSPs, and notably their concentration on the question of poverty, removal of the HIPC Initiative from the adjustment paradigm represents an essential step to enable the proposition of real new solutions to the treatment of debt. The explosion of multilateral debt is a direct result of structural adjustment. It was barely convincing to seek to treat the long-term sustainability of this debt within the same mechanism that was the cause of insolvency, if only for a tiny number of 'model pupils' which resolutely changed their ways. Without doubt, enlargement of the Initiative to all low-income countries and its greater ambition compared to previous exercises, necessitated the adoption of a new framework for partnership.

Partial forgiveness of multilateral debts should also be accompanied, in a more symbolic way, by a change of position by the financial institutions (particularly the World Bank). The World Bank was primarily a 'project Bank' before adjustment, in the 1980s, and even, to a certain extent and in a way similar to the IMF, a 'managing agent' for states taking in charge, with them, their problems of insolvency regarding third-party creditors.

Treatment of multilateral debt puts the BWIs in the simultaneous position of being the managing agent and creditor of states, an uneasy combination of roles. The position sought by the World Bank as 'banker to the poor'[7] allows partial resolution of this difficulty. The BWIs now seek a solution to previously contracted sovereign debt through a contract concluded with society as a whole.

The accent placed on participation allows the PRSP process to appear as such a contract, the general terms of which are as follows: states are not excused from reimbursing their debts, rather they must do so to the profit of their poor populations in the form of greater social spending, in exchange for which the BWIs grant partial debt relief.

Enlargement and standardisation

The spirit, the architecture and the technical content of the HIPC and PRSP Initiatives are now well defined. But the mechanisms remain extremely complex, tied to multiple and constrictive conditions for entry into a lengthy evolving process. Furthermore, these are very new procedures for the countries supposed to adopt them. The enhanced HIPC Initiative is always conceived in an optic of selective accompaniment to countries presenting favourable conditions for the success of the process.

This does not tally with the political orientations given to these initiatives, and which result from the desire of rich countries to achieve real progress on the debt question, to reverse net BWIs' transfers from some low-income countries, and to respond to civil society pressure as epitomised by the Jubilee 2000 campaign. Following the Cologne summit, the goal established was that three-quarters of eligible countries would reach their decision point during the year 2000.

There is manifest incompatibility between the principles of the mechanism and the quantitative goals of interventions; an incompatibility made even more insoluble by the inclusion of ownership and the absence of conditionality from the principles. This contradiction will be resolved by relaxing HIPC conditions, by lightening the content of PRSPs and by permanent tension between conditionality and ownership (see Chapter 6).

The first relaxation measure consisted of 'inventing' the Interim PRSP stage. This document (the I-PRSP, which really requires none of the essential elements of a PRSP – participation, poverty surveys, monitoring and evaluation, programme budgets), is now enough to reach the decision point. In addition, the requirement to have followed a three-year programme was lifted in an *ad hoc* manner for some countries.

This conversion, which allowed the great majority of affected countries to enter the process, effectively postponed debt repayments to a later date. In the meantime, debt relief often started in the absence of solid programmes for additional social spending. HIPC funds are sometimes curiously under-used due to a lack of absorptive capacity, or used without real concern as to their efficacy.

It is too soon to undertake a precise analysis of the consequences of this 'softening' for the Initiative as a whole. However, political and institutional pressure remains strong and will not diminish. To the contrary, once the decision point has been reached, the requirement in principle for one year's application of the PRSP before reaching completion point will become more significant.[8]

Progress with the preparation of final PRSPs already provides some guidelines as to the 'softening' trends underway, both with regard to the participatory process (where simple wide consultation appears sufficient), and to technical instruments (where monitoring and evaluation systems and programme budgets could be considered as targets to be reached at a later stage of the process).

As such it is hardly surprising that donors appear unanimous in considering that the HIPC Initiative will not have fundamental consequences for their policies (Killick 2000, citing a OECD Development Assistance Committee paper). Acceleration and enlargement of the Initiative will singularly weaken whatever is left of its reforming character (see Box 9.1).

What remains of the reform?

The primary objective pursued throughout the process, as mentioned above, has been to find a solution to the problem of multilateral debt. It appears that this solution is now underway. Without knowing the duration of the re-established 'solvency' of poor countries, it is nevertheless true

Box 9.1 Innovation and standardisation: The PRSP example – from 'Ali Baba's cavern' to purgatory

The major international development aid institutions evolve in a critical universe. They are required to present new initiatives at regular intervals to re-mobilise public opinion, and even that of their own administrators, and hence secure funding (it happens that several initiatives start at almost the same time, as with the case of the CDF and the PRSP; in these cases, the most seductive wins the day). Through the PRSPs (more widely included in the HIPC Initiative), it is possible to attempt to retrace the classic stages of the process of innovation, then of the diffusion of a technocratic instrument.

1   The favourable context is that of a critical environment where previous instruments have reached their limits of adaptation and amelioration. The PRSP approach builds on the repudiation of conditionality, of structural adjustment and of project aid.
2   A new instrument is devised to respond to earlier criticisms. In fact, on closer inspection it becomes apparent that the reasoning is based on a comparison of operational problems experienced by the previous approach (not its initial concepts) and the concepts of the new approach. This has the effect of artificially swelling hopes that may be placed in the latter. An intense marketing campaign is then undertaken in all international gatherings.
3   The tool is designed to operate under conditions of favourable technical and institutional capacities, a communality of values with recipient countries and a partnership of quality.
4   The initiative is launched on one or two pilot states more or less matching the above conditions. The pilot experience benefits from a particular attention to the capacities and means made available, the suppleness of experimentation, and widespread diffusion of 'good practices' and the like. For PRSPs, Uganda was the model pupil chosen for a full-scale trial.
5   The instrument is then calibrated for standardisation. The conditions for entry and departure are precisely defined. Timing of the HIPC Initiative was thus determined in liaison with that of PRSPs: first a three-year programme and a PRSP to reach a decision point, then three years of PRSP application until completion point. Guidelines are written (particularly voluminous in this case). Consultants and experts are mobilised. The initiative is ready for publication. It is time for the technical content to be equipped with appropriate and seductive tools: quantitative and qualitative surveys, poverty profiles, participatory strategic reflection, overall strategic framework, medium-term programme budgets, results-based programme aid (mainly budgetary), real-time monitoring of results and impacts. In other words, a rich content with restricted entry conditions: it is the 'Ali Baba's cavern' phase.
6   The initiative is widely diffused through intensive 'sensitisation' in all

countries (donors and recipients) by teams heading the initiative. It becomes progressively apparent that few countries meet the objective conditions for application and that the initiative, as constructed, could encourage only modest financial flows and not attain the heart of the matter (in this case the multilateral debts of poor countries).

7   Conditions of access to the initiative are softened both objectively (a simple I-PRSP suffices to reach the decision point and just one year of application is required to attain completion) and by a benevolent appreciation of specific conditions. Several countries slip through the rule of a previous three-year programme, and interim and final PRSPs of mediocre quality are accepted.

8   Technical content of the initiative is revised downward. For example, programme budgets are postponed to a later phase. The programme serves, in fact, to define in part the path leading to more-elaborate technical instruments – budgetary statistics, monitoring/evaluation. Many things do not happen as foreseen in the progress of the initiative. The PRSP is often received as a new conditionality. Documents are rewritten by consultants after the participatory phase. Participation by the poor is often symbolic or staged.

9   Almost all the countries concerned are part of the initiative, financial flows are active but the over-ambitious technical content has been watered down compared to initial expectations. PRSPs are now considered the start point for establishment of technical content. We are in the 'purgatory' phase of a largely open process, which merely serves as a transitional passage to somewhere else (ultimately to attain the initial targets). The initiative undergoes a series of improvements and adaptations. Operational weaknesses in implementation progressively reappear (problems of conditionality, lack of ownership, lack of political will, overly strong technocratic constraints, and so on).

Have we turned full circle? Not exactly. A significant amount of poor country debt, mainly multilateral, has been erased and/or redirected to social service budgets along the way. This amply justifies a bit of gymnastics. PRSPs have indeed filled their main goal, which is to provide an international framework to convince and to provide proof to financial institutions of the imperious and necessary reduction of multilateral debt to poor countries.

that no previous debt relief initiative for the poorest has gone so far. In this respect, the HIPC Initiative represents real progress.

It is also legitimate, however, to question the motives that governed the birth of the HIPC and PRSP Initiatives and to measure the extent to which observed evolutions have followed previously established recommendations.

The complex relations between donors, citizens and states

Preparation and adoption of a PRSP probably signify a new stage in the slide of donors towards 'grand universalism'; that is to say, solidarity with citizens rather than with states. At least it has encouraged the BWIs, closely linked statutorily to states, to open a door that some donor countries have already entered.

To what extent do PRSPs provide a new tool for action in favour of 'poorly governed poor citizens'? The growth of resources available for social spending is without doubt a direct response to this question. The filtering of these resources by the state budget naturally limits their efficiency, especially in the case of 'bad' governance. A perfect example comes from the case of some countries failing to consume resources liberated by the HIPC Initiative. Are poor populations really managing to influence policies during the participatory process? Some elements of reply to this question are provided elsewhere in this book (notably Chapters 6 and 7).

The incentive to reduce donor-held debts has helped to open a breach between the state and its poor citizens, allowing the descent of resources held by the one and the mounting of opinions held by the other, even if early results remain modest. It constitutes a new mode for action to the profit of poorly governed citizens, following the evident failure of previous strategies.

The new relationship between states and the World Bank that results is more problematic. Recent literature stresses the BWIs' rehabilitation of the role of the state and the progressive engagement of these institutions in politics (Chavagneux 2001). However, some elements demonstrating an opposite trend may be discerned. The state is no longer considered the natural locale for policy formulation. Essentially, it is an actor implementing policies, hence the accent placed on strengthening its budget. Implementation by the state (designated by the term 'governance') is nevertheless widely diagnosed as the main obstacle to development and to poverty relief. If the operational role of the state is reinforced, compared to other operators (projects), it is at once enclosed in this domain and also sternly criticised.

For this reason, the trend of politics to disappear has taken a further step. The PRSP process, representing the consensual vision of society as a whole, seeks to be placed above politics. It is symptomatic to see political parties and elected assemblies consulted on an equal footing with any other group in the PRSP's participatory framework. This represents the height of the 'Anti-Politics Machine', brilliantly illustrated by Ferguson (1990): an idealised world where needs and means dominate, and where institutions are considered as simple managers of the means and all that is asked of them is efficiency and transparency. The difference between the consensual apolitical vision of the PRSP process and the reality of the interactions of actors and institutions risks being a source of misunderstanding and ambiguity.

Towards new disillusions about aid efficiency?

Rarely has an institution been so contradicted, in so short a time, as has the World Bank on the theme of selectivity. The appearance of this doctrine resembles a ground swell. It was clearly present from 1995, with the report entitled *A Continent in Transition*, and subsequently reinforced with numerous studies by World Bank researchers (Burnside and Dollar 1997; Collier and Dollar 1998; Devarajan, Dollar and Holmgren 2001).

Finally, it was affirmed as policy in the report *Assessing Aid* in 1998, and regularly reiterated since then by the highest authorities at the Bank. In 1997, for example, President Wolfensohn declared there was 'no escape from the facts'. According to him, more people will escape poverty if aid is concentrated on countries following good policies, than if allocations make no distinction.

Three years later PRSPs, which constitute the new unique framework for partnership with poor countries, are everywhere developed and implemented according to the same principles. The example of Zambia illustrates this retrograde step regarding selectivity. *Assessing Aid* affirms:

> Suppose that development aid only financed investment and investment really played the crucial role projected by early models. In that case, aid to Zambia should have financed rapid growth that would have pushed per capita income above $20,000, while in reality per capita income stagnated at around $600.
>
> (World Bank 1998a)

The report compares the actual growth of Zambia with that which ought to have resulted from the productive use of investment resources transferred. The obvious divergence of the two curves over the long term highlights Zambia as an example of countries where the 'return' on aid was particularly weak. Despite this, two years later and without major changes, the country reached a decision point granting it admission, like others, to the HIPC Initiative and normal access to external resources; this did not prevent the World Bank from integrally repeating the Zambian example in its World Development Report 2000/2001 on poverty, to justify the principle of aid selectivity.

There is little doubt that the selectivity doctrine is politically inapplicable by multilateral institutions, and even more by creditors,[9] as has been signalled by various authors (DIAL 1998). The World Bank insists, in its analyses, on the need to define a new form of aid for countries where classic preconditions for its efficient use are not fulfilled. *Assessing Aid* proposed to finance 'ideas' rather than budgetary expenditure programmes in these countries. But the definition of aid programmes specially conceived for 'difficult' countries has never been precisely outlined. The idea of ranking all client countries according to the quality of their policies, of their institutions and of governance has proven too delicate both techni-cally and politically.[10]

Finally, the wish to differentiate the instruments and the objects of aid according to recipient country remains more or less moribund. For example, the increased use of budget aid is universally presented as a desirable evolution in the PRSP framework, whatever the quality of institutions, budgetary processes and governance. The powerful mechanics of standardisation have dominated the perhaps too subtle idea of adapting aid practices to the contexts where they were to be applied.[11]

With the abandonment of the selectivity doctrine, the prime elements of reforming aid to achieve greater efficiency were, in practice, either brushed aside or diverted from their original principles.

The ownership principle has often been placed in difficulty both by the standardised framework of the PRSP exercise, the strong time constraint and variable capacities of structures responsible, and also by the fact that definitive adoption of a PRSP took place within BWIs' boards. These twists to the principles of ownership should not cause underestimation of the real progress achieved, compared to Economic Policy Framework Papers where states were frequently little involved in the preparation (see Chapter 6).

The constraint of having to prepare a PRSP resembles a classic condi-tionality, based purely on declarations of intent such as was criticised in the structural adjustment paradigm. Objectives set in the document and the intended system of monitoring and evaluation (often for a later stage) should allow, in principle, a move to an outcome-based conditionality. Nevertheless, the assessment of results obtained, and above all the estab-lishment of causalities, contains significant amounts of subjectivity (to what extent does the quality of policies pursued explain the results obtained?). The BWIs were frequently reproached for failing to ensure that adjustment conditionalities were respected in reality (for example, Kanbur 2000), even where these were based on reforms where results could be assessed objectively (such as privatisation). How may we hope that the same will not happen with new conditionalities based on assess-ments that are even more ambiguous?

Nothing allows us to think that efficiency of resource allocation, notably aid flows, will be increased in the new partnership framework fixed by the PRSP process. Thanks to debt relief, there might be an increase in aid flows, provided that debt relief is not compensated by a further reduction in other forms of official development assistance. Ownership will be improved but within the context of more complex rela-tions between the state and other stakeholders, and with a certain ambigu-ity regarding contractual relations with the donors.

Not surprisingly, the New Partnership for Africa's Development (NEPAD), launched by five African Heads of State, which is based on several of the BWIs' new principles (ownership, selectivity, etc.), risks to be confronted by the same implementation problems (see Box 9.2).

Box 9.2 Can the NEPAD fit in with the current poverty reduction system?

The new Initiatives are, to a certain extent, fundamentally biased. Whatever one might think of their validity, from the very outset they depart from the founding principle of ownership that they set themselves. They were initially conceived and then promoted by the BWIs, and although most governments in poor countries entitled to benefit from them have formally adhered to them we cannot rule out the possibility that they were obliged to do so, as the PRSPs are a prerequisite, a new conditionality, for access to international aid resources. From this point of view, the NEPAD (New Partnership for Africa's Development) is an endogenous initiative that reverses the situation. The question is to see whether it is credible and compatible with the new international poverty reduction strategies.

The NEPAD, proposed by five African heads of state (Algeria, Egypt, Nigeria, Senegal and South Africa) was adopted by the OAU at its summit in October 2001. It results from a merger of two previous initiatives, the South African President Thabo Mbeki's 'Millennium Partnership for the African Recovery Programme' and the Senegalese President Aboulaye Wade's 'Plan Oméga'. The NEPAD was given a favourable reception when it was officially presented at the G8 summit in Genoa in July 2001, and was the object of a detailed response from the eight countries (and the European Union) in Kananaskis in June 2002. In particular, the G8 Africa Action Plan contains a commitment to direct half of supplementary ODA (official development assistance) to Africa in the coming years. The NEPAD has also been officially recognised by the United Nations and is now systematically referred to in all international documents.

The NEPAD is more of a general statement on the continent's needs than a real development strategy. It has three parts: (a) the essential prerequisites of development (peace, political governance, human rights; economic governance, cooperation and regional integration); (b) the priority sectors (investments in infrastructures, new information technologies, health, education, agriculture, market access); and (c) the mobilisation of resources (increasing national savings and capital flows, both in the form of foreign direct investments and international aid). It sets out an action programme based on these elements.

The concern shown by the international community to support this initiative can be explained for two main reasons: first, it shares its general philosophy; second, the initiative stems from the African countries themselves and therefore fits in, at least partially, with the principle of policy ownership. Whilst pleading for a more balanced long-term partnership between the north and the south, the latter intends to assume full responsibility for its own future. The NEPAD asserts 'the determination of Africans to extricate themselves and the continent from the malaise of underdevelopment and exclusion in a globalising world'. But, paradoxically, it is also on the issue of ownership that the NEPAD is most criticised. Although it finds a new balance in relationships between the poor country governments and the donors, it neglects relationships between these governments and their people.

The NEPAD's approach is not approved of throughout the continent. Contested by several African governments, who accuse its five promoters of attempted hegemony, it is above all severely criticised by a large number of organisations from the civil society, which complain that they were not made part of the process and that the populations are totally excluded. The excessively 'top-down' approach gave rise to a whole series of recriminations, which can be summed up as follows: 'promoted by a small group of political elites, the NEPAD is an African plan without society, aimed at the recolonisation of Africa'.

Although the NEPAD was doubtless wrong not to invite local civil society to take part in its elaboration, we do not believe that the accusation made against it that it is too close to the 'Washington consensus' is justified. Although the economic content of the NEPAD is relatively classical, it is more original on the question of governance where, particularly as far as politics is concerned, it goes further than the PRSPs. Although the BWIs recognised the central role of political participation and democratic representation in drawing up poverty reduction strategies, particularly in the World Development Report 2000/2001, in the field, they intend to confine themselves to a narrow, instrumental view of governance, reduced to its economic dimension alone (sound management of public finances, fight against corruption). Most of the PRSPs reflect this reorientation. In contrast, the NEPAD tackles the question of political governance head on, as an essential prerequisite of its implementation. It even goes as far as to advocate the promotion of direct, participatory democracy. The innovative African peer review mechanism will be responsible for making sure that any countries that wish to benefit from the NEPAD actually meet these conditions. In this way, it reintroduces the principle of selectivity in aid allocation, which was partially abandoned with the PRSPs and the HIPC Initiative.

Fundamentally speaking, the NEPAD is directly in line with the 'post-Washington consensus' (reasoned liberalisation, re-evaluation of the role of the state and the institutions, etc.) and appears to be working in the same direction as the new international poverty reduction strategies. There remains the question of its relationship with the PRSP/HIPC process and its financing. This issue is not covered in the NEPAD. To avoid confusion or harmful competition between the two initiatives, it would be wise to draw up a precise definition of their respective areas of competency, insisting on their complementarity. This architecture should be based on the principle of subsidiarity. The NEPAD seems to be the better equipped to deal with policies on the supranational scale – for which the essentially national and infranational PRSP approach is not well suited – for example, for regional projects (regional integration infrastructures, the digital divide, research networks), but also as a privileged interlocutor for promoting the voice of Africa in international negotiations (opening developed countries' markets, global public goods, etc.)

As it is the case for the BWIs' Initiatives, the challenge now consists in designing and implementing development policies that match the general principles laid down in the NEPAD and really involve the populations concerned.

One of the major issues will be the effectiveness of the peer review mechanism. Much remains to be accomplished on this level. The results obtained by the regional institutions, amongst which the NEPAD should find its place, are far from satisfactory. In addition, recent examples of regional initiatives relating to conflict prevention (Côte d'Ivoire) or election monitoring (Zimbabwe, Madagascar, etc.) are far from encouraging.

Conclusion

Like most aid system initiatives, the characteristics of the PRSP process may be deduced, almost integrally, from the constraints, currents of thought and objectives of the BWIs, without necessarily referring to the situations of poor countries themselves. The BWIs have a formidable capacity to mobilise the entire international community, other donors as well as the recipients, around the initiatives that they define.

Once again, the mobilisation is in a 'good cause': that of maintaining financial flows from the rich countries to the poor, and of international solidarity in the fight against poverty. It is perhaps more true this time, as debt reduction granted within the HIPC Initiative framework goes much further than ever before and for once brings hope of durable relief to the debt burdens of poor countries.

Strong international mobilisation also brings costs, however. In the first place, the development of a discourse that diverges from reality as the process advances (and even from the mobilising doctrine), and which systematically lauds advances and eludes problems, contributes to raising exaggerated hopes for the PRSP process. Second, mobilisation relies on the simultaneous treatment of all poor countries. The resulting standardisation seriously weakens an aid reform process that intended different modes of intervention according to the conditions in recipient countries.

The game is probably worth the candle, but progress realised in treating the debts of the poorest countries will have to compensate for the disillusion that the new partnership, judged on its results (as it claims), risks to cause.

Notes

1 Ghana also initially refused the Initiative, but accepted to participate after the change of government.
2 The fungibility concept applied to budgeting means allowing the reallocation of expenses from one budget sector to another. By analogy, the fungibility of development aid means that foreign aid allocated to a particular sector (for example, to building schools) might conduct the government to reallocate its

receipts (initially supposed to finance schools in our example) to other sectors. This effect reduces (or even cancels) the final impact of aid on the sector considered (education in our example).

3 A possible definition for the essential objective of development aid could be, over the long term, the alleviation of poverty within nations.

4 Even though adjustment programmes also showed a rising trend to 'occupy' a wide range of sectors.

5 Traces of investment in 'sovereignty', common in the 1970s, are hard to find in PRSPs. Also absent from primary preoccupations is promotion of the private sector, unlike certain programmes of the 1980s. In the same way, rarely mentioned are 'elitist' investments (universities, airports, etc.) that are of direct benefit to a small part of the population only.

6 This was the case with previous debt reduction initiatives which only made the debt situation of the poorest countries more 'sustainable', and thus finally more 'enduring'.

7 Which corresponds to a passing stage between 'national particularism' and 'grand universalism'.

8 Internal discussions have already taken place at the IMF to see whether it is possible to gain time by dating the intermediate period not from the definitive adoption of a PRSP but from the start of the first budget that incorporates the PRSP.

9 Some bilateral donors have modified their policies to favour selectivity (The Netherlands, Germany), even if this may be considered a cover to managing resource reduction.

10 The World Bank adopts such a classification in constructing its *Country Policy and Institutional Assessment,* but this indicator remains purely for internal use and does not automatically trigger differential treatment. Debate surrounding the classification of countries in receipt of aid has also been one of the subjects of greatest controversy in the EU–ACP Cotonou agreement.

11 Equally due to the difficulty for donors to define, unilaterally, contextual categories and to classify countries in an objective way.

10 The HIPC Initiative and poverty reduction

Anne-Sophie Bougouin and Marc Raffinot

The original HIPC Initiative (debt relief initiative for Heavily Indebted Poor Countries) was launched at the end of 1996 by the Bretton Woods Institutions (BWIs) and the Paris Club, which groups bilateral public creditors (Boote and Thugge 1997; Andrews *et al.* 1999). It aimed at making the debts of low-income countries sustainable. No explicit link was made between debt relief and poverty reduction. Its highly complex mechanisms sought to promote good utilisation of resources released by debt relief. Implicit in 'good utilisation' was the continuation of structural adjustment programmes established in conjunction with the BWIs (Moisseron and Raffinot 1999).

Under pressure from the global campaign by non-governmental organisations, the G7 meeting in Cologne (1999) decided a deepening and an acceleration of the Initiative. The importance of fighting poverty was placed at the centre of the debt reduction plan only after the launch of the 'enhanced' Initiative in September 1999. Preparation of a Poverty Reduction Strategy Paper (PRSP) became a condition of eligibility to the Initiative.

The link established between debt relief and poverty reduction within the enhanced HIPC Initiative framework was simultaneously transformed into a general principle to be applied to all new concessional funding by the World Bank and IMF. Thus PRSPs replaced the former Economic Policy Framework Papers (PFPs) and in principle became the reference document for the entire donor community. In addition, the approach was extended to low-income countries as a whole, whether they benefited or not from debt relief under the HIPC Initiative.

This chapter aims to present the original and enhanced HIPC initiatives, as well as bilateral initiatives that have been grafted onto them. It involves analysis of their mechanisms and their true impact. This allows identification of the leeway opened for poverty relief, but also of the limits set by the HIPC Initiative to the preparation of poverty reduction programmes and their implementation.

The origins of the HIPC Initiative

The rapid build-up of debt arrears by low-income countries explains the early appearance of debt relief initiatives for this category of country (notably at UNCTAD, as from 1978). After various bilateral initiatives, and despite strong hesitancy (Huw 1999), the Paris Club started to grant debt reduction in a systematic way. Relief was initially granted on 33 per cent[1] of rescheduled flows (G7 summit in Toronto, 1988), then 50 per cent (London, 1991). The Naples meeting of the G7, in 1994, was not satisfied with merely raising this percentage even higher (to 67 per cent), it also took a decisive step in deciding that in order to release countries from the rescheduling cycle, relief granted could henceforth be applied to debt stock (and not only to its servicing over a given period). This trend was pursued at G7 meetings at Lyons (1996, with 80 per cent reduction) and Cologne (1999, 90 per cent). Finally, in Tokyo in January 2000, certain G7 countries (notably France) announced a 100 per cent reduction.

Added to the foregoing were purely bilateral debt reduction initiatives and private debt repurchases funded by groups of public donors. France, in 1989 and 1994, undertook to reduce the debts of Franc Zone countries. Switzerland, in 1991, has launched a Swiss Debt Reduction Facility (*Facilité Suisse de Désendettement*, or FSD) capitalised initially at US$360 million. This facility was granted on the basis of bilateral agreements and jointly managed, with the involvement of civil society (Stöckli 2000). China also significantly reduced its bilateral claims on HIPC countries in the year 2000.

Discounts recorded on the secondary market conferred public development aid with an important leverage. The commercial debts of Bolivia, Côte d'Ivoire, Niger, Senegal and so on, were thus almost completely extinguished at minimal cost. Other bilateral measures were adopted to expunge debts with established procedures, such as those granted to El Salvador, Guatemala, Honduras and Nicaragua after the passage of hurricane Mitch in November 1998.

Despite the multiplication of these forgiveness operations, their real impact should not be exaggerated (Raffinot 2000). In effect, for a long time such reductions applied only to amounts liable for rescheduling in the Paris Club, amounts that reduced mechanically with time following the first rescheduling (which generally corresponds to the cut-off date[2]). The IMF and the World Bank, in turn and with prudence, proposed a multilateral debt reduction initiative at the end of 1996 (the HIPC Initiative). Until then, debts to these institutions were 'intangible' and various expedients were used so that countries avoided default on payments to these institutions. The argument advanced was that any debt reduction could cast doubt on the World Bank's solvability (affecting its credit rating), which would imply an increase to the cost of resources it borrowed on international markets and hence of its loans.

Poor countries considered as 'heavily indebted' in the context of this initiative comprised a group of some 40 states with low per capita GDP, and access to resources at concessional terms from the World Bank and the IMF (see Box 10.1). The HIPC Initiative constitutes a significant step forward compared to previous practices; it breaks the taboo of the intangibility of multilateral debt and is buttressed by general rules defining debt reduction, even if assessment continues on a case-by-case basis.

Faced with modest results over three years (Joseph 2000), and under pressure from a coalition of NGOs, the G7 countries' meeting in Cologne in June 1999 decided to deepen and accelerate the process. In September 1999, the Joint Development Committee of the World Bank and the IMF approved new measures raising the ceiling for debt sustainability, speeding the granting of relief, and reorienting the Initiative around poverty reduction. This new slant aimed to increase the Initiative's impact, notably through a sizeable increase to the number of countries eligible for debt relief. Nevertheless, the general logic remained as fixed by the 1996 initiative: to make debt more sustainable – a logic subject to criticism for various reasons analysed hereafter.

The HIPC Initiative, a three-stage process

The HIPC Initiative unfolds through several stages. To be considered, a country must first attain a 'decision point', which is to say it is declared eligible by the BWIs and thus must respond to various criteria. At this stage, creditors decide the amount of relief that may be granted once the process is completed. The amount is measured in a way to bring debt to a sustainable level. The country must then introduce a number of reforms and programmes negotiated with the BWIs, during a fixed period (two years on average). This is the 'transition' period. The candidate country only benefits from irrevocable debt relief on reaching the 'completion point'.

The criteria for decision point eligibility

To become eligible for the HIPC Initiative, countries must satisfy the following criteria:

- be eligible for loans from the International Development Association (IDA), a subsidiary of the World Bank that grants concessional loans to countries with a per capita GDP of less than US$885 in 1999;
- be faced with an 'unsustainable' level of debt (in accordance with the criteria imposed by creditors, which are presented in the following section), after having benefited from 'traditional' debt treatment mechanisms in the Paris Club under Naples terms, which cancels 67 per cent of the country's publicly guaranteed commercial debts;

- have successfully followed reform programmes approved by the BWIs for at least three years. This includes pursuit of a structural adjustment programme and the implementation of sectoral reforms backed by World Bank funds;
- have defined an overall poverty reduction strategy presented in a Poverty Reduction Strategy Paper (PRSP), prepared by national authorities. This document must be formulated through a wide consultation with civil society, in order to ensure transparency of the process and participation by the population. Being a government document, acceptance of the PRSP by the BWIs does not imply that the latter are completely in agreement with the text. Contrary to former practice, the BWIs perform a common assessment of the document (Joint Staff Assessment) in which they express their potential reservations.

Debt sustainability

The sustainability of debt owed by HIPC countries is essentially defined in a financial logic. The aim of the exercise is to determine the capacity of a country to repay its debt, in terms of its export receipts and/or, its public revenue devoted to annual debt servicing. Debt Sustainability Analysis (DSA) builds on ratios that make wide reference to the Net Present Value (NPV) of debt, rather than its nominal value (see Box 10.1).

The three indicators used are as follows:

- Net Present Value of debt stock/exports of goods and services; for a given year, this estimates the relative weight of a country's total debt compared to the value of exports in the same year;
- debt service/exports of goods and services: for a given year, this assesses the relative weight of debt service payments compared to the value of exports in the same year;
- Net Present Value of debt stock/government revenue: it measures, for a given year, the relative weight of a country's total debt compared to the value of budget receipts collected in the same year.

Creditors use these three indicators to assess, on the one hand, the capacity of a country to release the financial resources necessary to meet its debt reimbursement obligations, and on the other hand the burden of these reimbursements on the state's financial capacity. The third indicator is used only where a country, highly open to the exterior, risks disqualification under the two first criteria. Note that the ratio of debt service to government revenue is not used, which is surprising given that the HIPC countries' external debt is almost completely public.

Within the HIPC Initiative, creditors defined ceilings for these indicators so as to provide a numerical definition of the notion of a country's external debt sustainability. The various ceilings defined within the

Box 10.1 Nominal value and Net Present Value

Most loans granted to low-income countries are concessional (interest rates are well below market rates). For the same amount, their debt 'weighs' less than one contracted at market rates (which is the case for countries like Mexico, Korea, and so on). From a financial standpoint, these loans may be analysed as the sum of a loan at market rates and a grant. Let us consider, for example, a loan of 1,000 granted to a developing country for ten years, with a five-year period of grace (no capital repayments) and an interest rate of 0.5 per cent. The calculation of debt service is done in the classic manner, and repayments may be actualised at market rates (supposed here to be 5 per cent) and added. The sum of the repayments (711) is known as the Net Present Value of the loan. In this case, the grant element is equal to 290 (1000–711), which simply reflects the fact that the interest rate is much lower than that of 'the market', and that a grace period is provided. The loan of 1,000 (nominal or face value) at 0.5 per cent over ten years (five deferred) is thus finally equivalent to a loan of 711 (at 5 per cent over ten years) and an immediate grant of 290.

Loan example:

Year	1	2	3	4	5	6	7	8	9	10
Capital repayments (1)	0	0	0	0	0	200	200	200	200	200
Interest (2)	5	5	5	5	5	5	4	3	2	1
Debt service = (1) + (2)	5	5	5	5	5	205	204	203	202	201
Actualised debt service (at 5%)	4.8	4.5	4.3	4.1	3.9	153.0	145.0	137.4	130.2	123.4

original and the enhanced Initiatives are presented in Table 10.1. The ratios were less favourable in the original Initiative, which in part explains why only seven countries qualified for admission to the Initiative before the international campaign by civil society groups encouraged less stringent ceilings.

The use of the NPV is the only way to get a fair burden sharing between creditors. However, the HIPC framework uses currency-specific discount rates to calculate the NPV debt, which is unclear, entails some flaws and has led to arbitrary uses in some cases (Gunter 2002).

The HIPC beneficiaries

Applications by 42 countries[3] should be examined within the HIPC Initiative framework: these low-income countries have external debts

Table 10.1 Sustainability criteria for external debt

	Original HIPC Initiative (%)	Enhanced HIPC Initiative (%)
Debt stock (NPV)/exports	< 200–250	< 150
Debt service/exports	< 20–25	< 15
Debt stock (NPV)/budget receipts	< 280	< 250

considered, a priori (before profound examination), as unsustainable according to the above criteria (Table 10.1).

Among these 42 countries, 38 are eligible for the HIPC Initiative (Table 10.2). These countries have a level of indebtedness considered unsustainable after application of traditional means of debt treatment in the Paris Club (Naples terms). They have already partly benefited, or will benefit from relief under the HIPC Initiative. The four ineligible countries have returned to sustainable levels of debt after applying Naples terms by the Paris Club (Angola, Kenya, Vietnam, and Yemen). Lao Republic and Ghana both refused initially to apply for relief under the HIPC Initiative, but the latter has revised its position since.

The debts concerned

Two types of debt are covered by forgiveness decided within the HIPC Initiative: multilateral debts and officially guaranteed commercial debts (bilateral public debts other than those arising from official development assistance, ODA).

Commercial debts (private non-guaranteed) are also treated within the HIPC Initiative (under the principle of equal treatment for different types

Table 10.2 Countries engaged in the HIPC process

Countries potentially eligible for the enhanced HIPC Initiative (42)	Angola, Benin, Bolivia, Burkina Faso, Burundi, Cameroon, Central African Republic, Chad, Comoros, Congo-Brazzaville, Congo (RDC), Côte d'Ivoire, Ethiopia, The Gambia, Ghana, Guinea, Guinea Bissau, Guyana, Honduras, Kenya, Lao Republic, Liberia, Madagascar, Malawi, Mali, Mauritania, Mozambique, Myanmar, Nicaragua, Niger, Uganda, Rwanda, São Tomé, Senegal, Sierra Leone, Somalia, Sudan, Tanzania, Togo, Vietnam, Yemen, Zambia
Of which countries not admitted to the enhanced HIPC Initiative for reasons cited above (4)	Angola, Kenya, Vietnam, Yemen

of creditor), but in a marginal way as the HIPC countries have relatively few commercial claims. This nevertheless raises occasional legal disputes, with some private creditors refusing a reduction to the amounts outstanding, as in the case of Nicaragua. Different creditors intervene in the following ways:

- bilateral official creditors, members of the Paris Club, cancel up to 90 per cent of 'officially guaranteed commercial debts', which they estimate for each HIPC (see Table 10.3);
- bilateral public creditors, not members of the Paris Club (China, Kuwait, Libya, and so on) are supposed to provide a similar reduction ('at least as favourable treatment');
- multilateral creditors (IMF, World Bank, Development Banks) complement relief granted by bilateral official creditors, if the initial exercise fails to make a country's debt sustainable;
- commercial creditors should grant 'at least as favourable treatment' as the members of the Paris Club.

In addition, some creditor countries decided to go further and cancel the remaining 10 per cent of bilateral officially guaranteed commercial debts and official development assistance debts not taken into account by the HIPC Initiative. France, in particular, the second-largest creditor of the HIPC countries after Japan, intends at completion point to convert claims on ODA loans owed by HIPC countries into grants.

The enhanced HIPC Initiative and the accent on poverty reduction

The re-centring of the Initiative on poverty alleviation has led to the introduction of a new condition for HIPC countries to obtain debt relief: preparation by national authorities of a Poverty Reduction Strategy Paper

Table 10.3 Strengthening the HIPC Initiative

	Original HIPC Initiative (1996)	*Enhanced HIPC Initiative (1999)*
Bilateral debt (Paris Club)	Lyon terms (cancellation of 80% of officially guaranteed commercial debts)	Cologne terms (cancellation of 90% of officially guaranteed commercial debts)
Multilateral debt	Further debt relief to attain a sustainable debt	Supplementary relief, with lower sustainability ratios
Debt relief timing	At completion point	At decision point, through 'intermediate' aid granted by different creditors

---

Box 10.2 Concessional BWI loans

The World Bank, like other development banks, normally grants loans at market rates. However, a subsidiary called the International Development Association (IDA) was created in 1960 to fund projects in low-income countries. Conditions for IDA loans are highly favourable; today they are free of interest (but a commission of 0.75 per cent is charged). They are of 40 years' duration, of which ten are deferred. The IDA, therefore, cannot be a permanent structure; its funds have to be replenished periodically and the thirteenth such operation was completed in 2002. Loans accorded by the IDA are not only project-based. They have also been used to support structural and sectoral adjustment programmes. Today, the IDA can lend to finance poverty reduction programmes (Poverty Reduction Support Credits, or PRSCs).

The IMF was not created to finance development, but to oversee the stability of the international financial system. As such, it was not originally provided with mechanisms allowing it to provide cheap credits. Nevertheless, the first sales of gold allowed the institution to create a Trust Fund in 1976, which was used to offer less onerous loans to low-income countries. After repayment, these funds allowed creation of the Structural Adjustment Facility (1986), then the Enhanced Structural Adjustment Facility (1987), and in 1999 the Poverty Reduction and Growth Facility (PRGF). PRGF loans are at an interest rate of 0.5 per cent, and for a period of ten years of which 5½ are deferred (IMF 2001).

This arrangement has been criticised as it leads the IMF to play the part of a development institution, which is not its role. Conversely, the World Bank has expanded its role of project finance to granting loans linked to macroeconomic programmes. Since the HIPC Initiative, the World Bank and the IMF act in concert in the HIPC countries (joint missions, same conditionalities, joint PRSP assessment, etc.).

The Meltzer Report to the US Congress (2000) proposed to follow the BWIs' logic to the end, institutionally at least. It sought stricter distinction of the roles of each: the IMF would regulate capital flows to middle-income developing countries, while the World Bank would look after the poorest countries. This radical reform was not adopted.

(PRSP). In the same way, this condition was simultaneously extended to cover access to all new resources provided by the BWIs (see Box 10.2): the IMF's Poverty Reduction and Growth Facility (PRGF), and Poverty Reduction Support Credits (PRSCs) granted by the World Bank (IMF 2000). This potentially extends the PRSP approach to the 77 countries eligible for the PRGF.

For the BWIs, PRSPs must present the macroeconomic, sectoral and social programmes that the government intends to adopt to stimulate growth and contribute to absorbing poverty. The BWIs also insist on the importance of good management of public affairs with a view to poverty reduction and debt relief. PRSPs are said to be 'interim' (I-PRSP) during a transitional phase. They must be finalised and implemented for at least one year before a country can attain the completion point.

How the process unfolds

Reaching the decision point marks the first stage of the HIPC process. To do so countries must not only have unsustainable debts (after traditional Paris Club rescheduling), but also have followed a three-year structural adjustment programme (as agreed with the IMF) and prepared a poverty alleviation strategy, presented in a PRSP or interim PRSP established in concert with civil society (see the eligibility criteria listed on p. 241).

At the decision point, the BWIs decide what debt relief will be granted a country at its completion point. The amount is calculated in such a way as to make a country's indebtedness sustainable (based on debt data available at the decision point – see Box 10.3).

The country then enters a transition phase. During this it must prepare a final PRSP (if it has presented an I-PRSP at the decision point stage), implement the reforms negotiated at the decision point in its PRSP or I-PRSP, and continue macroeconomic stabilisation efforts with introduction of a new BWIs-backed programme. At this stage of the process, the BWIs provide interim assistance, notably disbursements under the new loan mechanisms and from foreseen multilateral debt relief. Other multilateral and bilateral creditors also grant a first part of relief, at their discretion.

The transition period is said to be 'floating' in the enhanced HIPC Initiative: its duration depends on progress achieved by the country. It was set at three years in the original HIPC Initiative then shortened to less than two years in the enhanced Initiative; it now seems to be on the increase again. Having regard to economic performance and progress realised by countries in the implementation of a poverty-relief-driven development programme, the BWIs decide when a country reaches its completion point. At this stage of the process the debt relief foreseen at the decision point becomes effective.

Where are we now?

In June 2002, 26 countries had embarked on the process and had attained the decision point under the enhanced HIPC Initiative. The integration of countries within the Initiative was accelerated at various moments, for example, in late 2000 the BWIs undertook to incorporate 20 countries before the year-end (see Table 10.4).

Only six countries reached their completion point by June 2002 (Bolivia, Burkina Faso, Mauritania, Mozambique, Tanzania and Uganda) and consequently obtained the totality of debt reduction definitively. Besides, seven countries have started to benefit from debt relief under the

Box 10.3 Ways of calculating relief to be granted

At the decision point the different creditors decide the amount of relief to be granted at the completion point. The method used to determine the amount is as follows:

- relief intended under the HIPC Initiative is calculated from the debt stock once it has been treated in the Paris Club (Naples traditional terms);
- the new debt stock, relative to a level considered sustainable for the country, is calculated using debt indicators that must be within ceilings defined by the creditors as sustainability criteria. Indebtedness indicators must be reduced in such a way as to respect sustainability criteria.

Example of calculation in the case of Cameroon
Cameroon's debt stock after traditional treatment by the Paris Club (Naples terms), base year: 1999

Indebtedness indicators	
Debt stock (US$ million, NPV)	4,691
Exports (US$ million)	2,287
Government revenue (US$ million)	1,424
NPV debt stock/Exports	205.1%
NPV debt stock/Government revenue	329.5%

For most countries, the criterion in use is the NPV of debt stock/exports. But for countries like Cameroon, that are very open (exports/GDP > 30 per cent) and performing in revenue collection (revenue/GDP > 15 per cent), the ratio used is the one that provides the most important debt relief (see Table 10.1 for sustainability criteria). In the case of Cameroon, debt reduction is more important if the debt stock/export ratio is taken into account. Debt relief due under the HIPC Initiative framework would then amount to 1,260 million dollars (= 4,691 – 150 per cent of 2,287), that is, roughly 27 per cent of the amount outstanding, and thus a reduction of the same degree (approximately) may be expected for all annual payments.

original HIPC Initiative: Bolivia, Burkina Faso, Côte d'Ivoire, Guyana, Mali, Mozambique and Uganda.

What are the amounts at stake and what should they be used for?

Two main questions are raised: are the sums involved really significant? What are the mechanisms for their distribution and what uses are they destined for?

Table 10.4 Progress with the 38 countries eligible for HIPC relief

(a) Countries entering the process (26)

Countries having reached their decision point at 30/06/02 (26)	Benin, Bolivia, Burkina Faso, Cameroon, Chad, Ethiopia, Gambia, Ghana, Guinea, Guinea Bissau, Guyana, Honduras, Madagascar, Malawi, Mali, Mauritania, Mozambique, Nicaragua, Niger, Rwanda, São Tomé, Senegal, Sierra Leone, Tanzania, Uganda, Zambia
Among which, countries having reached their completion point at 30/06/02 (6)	Uganda (May 2000), Bolivia (June 2001), Mozambique (September 2001), Tanzania (November 2001), Burkina Faso (April 2002), Mauritania (June 2002)

(b) Other eligible countries (12)

Countries still due to reach their decision point (9)	Ethiopia, Comoros, Burma, Burundi, Central African Republic, Congo-Brazzaville, Congo (RDC), Côte d'Ivoire, Togo
Countries in conflict excluded for the moment (3)	Somalia, Liberia, Sudan

The amounts at stake: relief spread over the long term

Debt relief accorded to the 26 countries which had reached their decision point by June 2002 amounts to US$41 billion, in nominal value (US$25 billion in NPV), according to the joint IMF–World Bank Development Committee (IMF and World Bank 2002; see Table 10.5). Altogether, including Paris Club reductions and additional bilateral relief that has been promised, the total reduction of debts for 42 HIPC countries, in nominal terms, should amount to US$100 billion.[4] This represents US$63 billion NPV (IMF and World Bank 2001b).

Table 10.5 Relief due under the HIPC Initiative

Nominal value of total debt stock		*Nominal value of likely total debt relief*	
The 42 HIPC qualified countries (US$ billion)	*The 26 countries having reached a decision point (US$ billion)*	*The 26 countries having reached a decision point*	
		US$ billion	*% of Debt Stock*
180 (141 in NPV)	84 (58 in NPV)	41 (25 in NPV)	49

Source: IMF and World Bank (2002).

Despite these impressive figures (representing two to three times the annual aid flows from OECD countries), Cohen (2000) underlines that this reduction is perhaps less generous than it appears. In effect, the 'market' value of HIPC debt is very much reduced. Cohen, using an econometric model estimated for middle-income countries, estimates the market price of HIPC debt at 28 cents for each dollar of nominal debt. In other words, about two-thirds of the external debt of the HIPCs would not have been repaid anyway.

The announced amounts of relief are stock figures. The reduction signifies in practice that, during a greater or lesser period (from a dozen to 40 years or so according to donor), repayments that ought to have been made for debt servicing will not be transferred.

A specific study is necessary to know precisely what this represents in annual terms for each particular case. This is all the more complicated as the annual amounts are not constant. They have a natural tendency to diminish with time (but in an irregular way, according to the calendar for future payments).

Table 10.6 presents estimates of future debt service reduction prepared by the IMF for a sample of HIPC countries (where data could be assembled). For the others, figures in italics are indicative estimates.

Two elements are presented for comparison: debt relief is compared to population size, and to GDP. These ratios show, for the sample countries, a mean annual debt reduction of slightly less than US$5 per person, which is far from representing a financial windfall. Furthermore, this relief is extremely unevenly distributed. Benin and Burkina Faso, indebted to lesser degrees, benefit from slightly more than US$3 per person and per year, whereas Guyana and São Tomé will receive 20 times as much. The inequitable aspect of the HIPC procedure is highly visible. It has already been signalled, and could have been avoided (DIAL 1999). It results from the fact that the Initiative was not destined to reduce poverty, but to make debt more sustainable and thus, in large part (insofar as debts were not repaid) to resolve the problems of the creditors and not those of the indebted countries. The same diversity may be seen comparing debt relief to GDP.

Will this debt forgiveness be enough to create the incentives to implement new poverty alleviation policies? This is what is supposed to happen according to the 'debt overhang' hypothesis developed in the late 1980s (Krugman 1988; Sachs 1988). This states that debt, beyond a certain level, reduces private investment and the interest for reforms (from which in such cases, creditors may envisage debt reduction in their own interest).

Nevertheless, it is far from clear that this approach may be applied to the HIPC countries, as transfers to these countries have been positive (Raffinot 2000). Birdsall, Claessens and Diwan (2001) stress this fact, but argue that the HIPC Initiative would encourage positive incentives among the donors for the priority treatment of development problems, without

Table 10.6 Debt and debt servicing relief for the 26 countries having reached their decision point

	Nominal debt relief (US$ million)	Average annual debt service relief in the early years (US$ million)	Total HIPC relief in $ per person	Annual HIPC debt relief in $ per person	Annual debt relief as a % of GDP
Benin	460	20	75	3.3	0.8
Bolivia	2,060	120	253	14.7	1.4
Burkina Faso	930	*47*	85	*4.2*	*1.8*
Cameroon	2,000	80	136	5.4	0.9
Chad	260	*13*	35	*1.7*	*0.8*
Ethiopia	1,930	*97*	31	*1.5*	*1.5*
Gambia (The)	90	10	72	8.0	2.5
Ghana	3,700	*185*	197	*9.9*	*2.4*
Guinea	800	*40*	110	*5.5*	*1.1*
Guinea-Bissau	790	*40*	669	*33.5*	*18.1*
Guyana	1,030	*52*	1,198	*59.9*	*7.6*
Honduras	900	*45*	142	*7.1*	*0.8*
Madagascar	1,500	62	100	4.1	1.7
Malawi	1,000	50	93	4.6	2.8
Mali	870	44	82	4.2	1.7
Mauritania	1,100	36	423	13.8	3.8
Mozambique	4,300	92	249	5.3	2.3
Nicaragua	4,500	215	915	43.7	9.5
Niger	900	40	86	3.8	2.0
Rwanda	800	*40*	96	*4.8*	*2.0*
São Tomé	200	*10*	1,333	*66.7*	*21.3*
Senegal	850	*43*	91	*4.6*	*0.9*
Sierra Leone	950	*48*	192	*9.6*	*7.1*
Tanzania	3,000	*150*	91	*4.6*	*1.7*
Uganda	1,950	87	91	4.1	1.4
Zambia	3,850	260	390	26.3	8.3

Source: Estimations and calculations based on IMF documents, notably the decision point documents.

Note
Estimates based on a linear extrapolation of debt relief over 20 years appear in italics.

being permanently slowed by debt-related discussions. Berthélemy (2001) shows that the HIPC Initiative will not be effective unless governments have already adopted good policies as, if not, incentives to do so would be insufficient.

Debt and debt servicing relief: a gift for debtors – or creditors?

The situations of HIPC countries differ. For some, the debt relief represents a real support, insofar as they have punctually met reimbursements in recent years (Burkina Faso, Mali, Uganda, etc.). Such countries will repay less than previously forecast. Unfortunately, this does not always mean they will pay less than today as some, such as Mali, will have a rapidly climbing debt service profile in coming years.

For states that have not been able to honour their obligations, however, the HIPC Initiative merely represents a means of formalising their *de facto* situation. This does not generate new resources, however; it may, in fact, reduce them in some extreme cases if countries that previously paid practically nothing resume due reimbursements after relief. In every case, it imposes a constraint on these countries, which are required to devote supplementary funds to poverty alleviation.

Table 10.7 presents data for the country sample retained in Table 10.6. As it is difficult to obtain data for the amounts of debt service actually paid, we have adopted an indirect approach that gives approximate results. Column 1 presents 1998 forecasts of debt service payments due in 1999. Column 2 gives the amounts really paid. Column 3 shows the relationship between the two. The average rate of reimbursement is 71 per cent, but encompasses wide disparities: some countries reimburse very little (less than 20 per cent) while others pay more than was foreseen. This somewhat paradoxical latter result should not surprise, as actual debt servicing naturally differs from the amount forecast for several reasons (new borrowings, exchange rate variations, and so on). The comparison is also imperfect due to the significant 'sleeping' debt of HIPC countries. Debt is thus termed when creditor countries more or less explicitly accept not to be reimbursed (China), or when a moratorium is in vigour pending global renegotiations (Russia). In this way, Mali appears in the table as reimbursing 75 per cent of debt service falling due but, in fact, it accumulated no further arrears in 1999.

Debt reduction accorded covers very different percentages of debt servicing due in 1999 (mean is 37 per cent). For some countries, it represents a very small proportion: such is the case for Honduras and Senegal (a country considered not sufficiently indebted to qualify for the first HIPC Initiative). To the contrary, relief is significant for countries such as Rwanda or São Tomé.

The figures in Table 10.7 also make it possible to estimate, very roughly, whether countries will pay more or less than in 1999 after debt relief. Supposing that the amount of due debt servicing is close to that of 1999, after relief this should vary according to the difference between columns (1) and (3). If this difference is greater than the figure in column (2), it signifies that payments after relief will be even greater than the sum actually reimbursed in 1999. This is the case for Chad, Guinea, Honduras, Mauritania, Mozambique, Niger and Senegal. For these countries, it is likely that creditors will be the winners from the operation. Of course, this is a rough approximation as it is possible that debt servicing due in 2001 and thereafter will be less than that in 1999.

Table 10.7 Debt servicing and debt relief (US$ million)

	Debt service due in 1999 (1)	Debt service paid in 1999 (2)	Repayment rate (%) (2)/(1)	Annual HIPC relief (IMF estimate for 2001 and thereafter) (3)	Annual relief as a % of 1999 service due (3)/(1)
Benin	63	56	89	20	32
Bolivia	394	389	99	120	30
Burkina Faso	51	53	104	*47*	*91*
Cameroon	419	470	112	80	19
Chad	43	27	63	*13*	*30*
Ethiopia	622	147	24	*97*	*16*
Gambia (The)	21.6	16.6	77	10	46
Ghana	452	409	90	*185*	*41*
Guinea	173	114	66	*40*	*23*
Guinea Bissau	44.5	8.6	19	*40*	*90*
Guyana	82	79	96	*52*	*63*
Honduras	537	335	62	*45*	*8*
Madagascar	170	147	86	62	36
Malawi	84	44	52	50	60
Mali	113	85	75	44	39
Mauritania	158	88	56	36	23
Mozambique	266	86	32	92	35
Nicaragua	320	179	56	215	67
Niger	109	44	40	*40*	37
Rwanda	32	20	63	*40*	*125*
São Tomé	7.2	3.9	54	*10*	*139*
Senegal	262	186	71	*43*	*16*
Sierra Leone	41	7	17	*48*	*116*
Tanzania	268	155	58	*150*	*56*
Uganda	116	126	109	87	75
Zambia	385	425	110	260	68

Source: World Bank, *Global Development Finance* (2000 and 2001).

Note
Estimates based on a linear extrapolation of debt relief over 20 years appear in italics.

The amounts at stake: additionality or substitution?

Table 10.8 restates debt relief data and compares it with the amount of official development assistance (ODA). At this level as well, extreme disparities between countries are evident. Situations vary according to the amount of ODA provided. For some countries such as Benin, Chad, Honduras and Senegal, HIPC debt relief represents less than 10 per cent of aid received in 1999. For others, to the contrary, the increase should be appreciable (more than 50 per cent of aid for Guinea Bissau, Guyana and Sierra Leone, and more than 40 per cent for Zambia). Nothing

Table 10.8 Resources released by the HIPC Initiative and ODA (US$ million)

	Average annual debt service relief in the first years	Annual amount of ODA (1991)	Annual amount of ODA (1996)	Annual amount of ODA (1999)	Percentage of debt reduction compared to 1999 ODA
Benin	20	266	288	211	9.5
Bolivia	120	506	831	569	21.1
Burkina Faso	*47*	420	415	398	*11.7*
Cameroon	80	517	411	434	18.4
Chad	*13*	264	296	188	6.9
Ethiopia	*97*	1,095	817	633	15.2
Gambia (The)	10	101	37	33	30.3
Ghana	*185*	881	649	607	*30.5*
Guinea	*40*	379	299	238	*16.8*
Guinea Bissau	*40*	115	178	52	*76.0*
Guyana	*52*	130	142	80	*65.0*
Honduras	*45*	300	357	817	*5.5*
Madagascar	62	456	357	358	17.3
Malawi	50	523	492	446	11.2
Mali	44	452	491	354	12.4
Mauritania	36	218	272	219	16.4
Mozambique	92	1,069	888	804	11.4
Nicaragua	215	837	931	675	31.9
Niger	40	373	254	187	21.4
Rwanda	*40*	361	467	373	*10.7*
São Tomé	*10*	51	47	28	*35.7*
Senegal	*43*	635	579	534	*8.0*
Sierra Leone	*48*	104	184	74	*64.2*
Tanzania	*150*	1,080	877	990	*15.2*
Uganda	87	665	676	590	14.7
Zambia	260	883	610	623	41.7

Source: World Bank, *World Development Indicators*, 2001.

Note
Estimates based on a linear extrapolation of debt relief over 20 years appear in italics.

guarantees that the resources are, in effect, additional; that is to say, that they will supplement resources habitually available to the country.

Nevertheless, in the majority of cases it appears that debt relief obtained under the HIPC Initiative is far from compensating for the reduction to ODA in recent years (even when expressed in current dollars): this is the case for Benin, Cameroon, Chad, The Gambia, Guinea, Guinea-Bissau, Madagascar, Mali, Mozambique, Niger and Senegal. Even if HIPC resources eventually succeed in being additional, they risk not re-establishing total ODA to the levels of the early 1990s.

Table 10.9 Resources released by HIPC relief and government revenue (US$ million and percentage)

	Average annual debt service relief in the first years	Government revenue in 2001 (IMF estimates)	Relief as % of receipts
Benin	20	380	5.3
Bolivia	120	1,754	6.8
Burkina Faso	47	314	14.8
Cameroon	80	1,788	4.5
Chad	13	123	10.6
Ethiopia	97	1,235	7.8
Gambia (The)	10	65	15.4
Ghana	185	886	20.9
Guinea	40	356	11.2
Guinea Bissau	40	36	109.3
Guyana	52	221	23.3
Honduras	45	1,143	3.9
Madagascar	62	536	11.6
Malawi	50	322	15.5
Mali	44	431	10.2
Mauritania	36	210	17.1
Mozambique	92	428	21.5
Nicaragua	215	570	37.7
Niger	40	182	21.9
Rwanda	40	189	21.1
São Tomé	10	11	93.6
Senegal	43	822	5.2
Sierra Leone	48	101	47.2
Tanzania	150	1,128	13.3
Uganda	87	600	14.5
Zambia	260	680	38.2

Source: Calculations from IMF and World Bank (2002).

Note
Estimates based on a linear extrapolation of debt relief over 20 years appear in italics.

Debt relief and government revenue

Comparison of these two aggregates is particularly pertinent, as HIPC debt relief is in fact a reduction of public debt. Table 10.9 shows that, on average, debt relief amounts to 13 per cent of public revenues for the sample, which is far from being considerable. Such an increase to public revenues is certainly possible from domestic sources, with a slight increase to tax pressure, which is usually very low in HIPCs.

Nevertheless, the differences between countries are significant for this comparison as well; debt reduction represents less than 6 per cent of government revenue for countries like Benin, Honduras or Senegal. For Guinea Bissau and São Tomé, however, the percentage is greater than 90 per cent of revenue.

Debt relief and increased public spending

The foregoing applies even more strongly to public expenditures, which are generally higher than revenue. HIPC debt reduction represents a weak share of public spending (of the order of 6 per cent for countries like Mali or Burkina Faso). This marginal character disappears, however, if social 'pro-poor' spending is taken for comparison. In effect, such expenditure represents a small part of the budget.

Debt relief could have a major impact on these priority sectors. Indeed, their budget allocations are frequently less than that allocated to debt servicing. This represents an important engine for additional growth – so much so that one may wonder whether beneficiary countries possess the necessary capacity for absorption. In Mali, for example, debt relief has allowed teacher recruitment to grow from 700 per year to 2,000 in 2001, which evidently poses problems of qualification and teacher training.

Table 10.10 illustrates the impact of debt relief on social expenditures. Here again, the impact is significant in some cases (more than 100 per cent in São Tomé, Sierra Leone and Zambia, and between 50 and 100 per cent in Ghana, Guinea and Nicaragua), but almost negligible in others (less than 20 per cent in Benin, Bolivia, Chad, Ethiopia, Honduras, Senegal and Uganda). This again raises the question of the inherent logic of the Initiative, which does not clearly target poverty reduction (Ranis and Stewart 2001).

Supplementary relief granted by France

After a period of dithering, French Co-operation (now included in the Ministère des Affaires Etrangères, or Ministry of Foreign Affairs) has 'converted' to the PRSP paradigm. It participates in the formulation process and equally provides financial support. It accepts to collaborate in this framework with other donors, notably the UNDP. The French development agency (Agence française de développement, or AFD) has also joined the poverty reduction crusade (AFD 2001). It is as yet too early to see what concrete changes this will bring to project design and evaluation, other than the new accent on social projects. Evidently, it remains possible to support traditional projects (roads and so on) that could have a significant impact on the well-being of beneficiaries, if not on poverty as such (which in any case remains difficult to verify).

French Co-operation has tried to distinguish itself through mechanisms of debt relief. At the Cologne summit, the G7 countries decided to cancel, bilaterally, public development aid debts (due on ODA loans) owed to them by the eligible countries, and which were not taken account of in the HIPC Initiative. Within this framework, France took a stance in favour of the establishment of a mechanism guaranteeing control over the use of funds released by annulations. This argument led to adoption of the principle of converting scheduled service repayments into grants: beneficiary

Table 10.10 Resources released by HIPC and public social 'pro-poor' spending (US$ million and percentage)

	Social expenditure				Average annual debt service relief in the early years	Average annual relief as % of social spending in 2001
	1999	*2000*	*2001**	*2002**		
Benin	115	110	161		20	12.4
Bolivia	882	921	918	956	120	13.1
Burkina Faso	141	121	143	207	*47*	*32.5*
Cameroon	264	287	336	437	80	23.8
Chad	190	186	231	298	*13*	*5.6*
Ethiopia	268	534	694	1,007	*97*	*13.9*
Gambia (The)	24	22	23	23	10	43.5
Ghana†	345	358	246	285	*185*	*75.2*
Guinea	85	73	68	72	*40*	*58.8*
Guinea Bissau	70	89	82	92	*40*	*48.2*
Guyana	87	105	104	124	*52*	*49.5*
Honduras	488	601	750	769	*45*	*6.0*
Madagascar	156	188	230	298	62	27.0
Malawi	208	167	205	226	50	24.4
Mali	103	105	123	136	44	35.8
Mauritania	85	95	84	117	36	42.9
Mozambique	259	312	343	336	92	26.8
Nicaragua	343	344	379	342	215	56.7
Niger	104	88	95	122	40	42.1
Rwanda	75	73	90	96	*40*	*44.4*
São Tomé	8	8	9	10	*10*	*111.1*
Senegal	254	226	293		*43*	*14.5*
Sierra Leone	15	15	25	46	*48*	*190.0*
Tanzania	289	352	622	837	*150*	*24.1*
Uganda	306	401	438	569	87	19.9
Zambia	166	149	205	231	260	126.8

Source: IMF and World Bank (2002).

Notes
Estimates based on a linear extrapolation of debt relief over 20 years appear in italics.
Data refer to 'pro-poor' social expenditure comprising health, non-university education, basic sanitation, and certain rural development and urban development programmes.
* IMF estimates.
† Data reported for Ghana do not cover all the expenditure, as some donor flows are missing.

countries would continue to make payments servicing their debts to France, which would return the same amount to a national Treasury account in the form of conditional grants (requiring the twin signatures of the French and beneficiary governments before withdrawals). These measures also anticipated the definition of a 'debt reduction and development contract' (*Contrat de désendettement et de développement,* or C2D) with beneficiary country governments, setting priorities for fields of intervention susceptible to receive these funds (Ministère des Affaires Etrangères and Ministère de l'Economie, des Finances et de l'Industrie 2001).

France thus decided to adopt a dual approach. On the one hand, it respects procedures initiated by the BWIs, consisting of placing debt relief in the framework of the normal budgetary process. On the other, it decided to cancel its claims in an alternative way. A first experience with debt relief funds, attempted with middle-income countries in 1992 (Côte d'Ivoire, Cameroon, Gabon, Congo), appears inconclusive however. The complex mechanism seems to have discouraged administrations from presenting eligible projects (Ministère des Affaires Etrangères 1999).

Is it not likely that countries entitled to re-financing through grants, and otherwise having access to HIPC resources, would be similarly reticent to finance programmes within the new, equally complex arrangement: signature of a C2D with France; payment of due debt servicing before receipt of an equivalent amount as a grant; allocation of expenditure subject to the twin approvals of the local administration and French authorities; project/programme implementation under the supervision of French development institutions (AFD and Ministry of Foreign Affairs)?

According to French authorities, these specific mechanisms should allow to: (a) safeguard the room for manoeuvre created by debt relief; (b) ensure the fitting of annual refunding flows to scheduled debt service payments; (c) involve the population, through the definition of targets for funding and sustainable reciprocal promises as contained in 'debt relief contracts' and PRSPs.

The precise significance of this duality is not yet clear: is it a mistrust of the HIPC process, or a desire to conserve a Gallic means of exercising pressure? It may also be asked whether the advantages (funding of well-targeted projects) have really been weighed against the inconveniences (dispersal of budgetary management techniques, subdivision of public finances).

Except for a few countries, like Côte d'Ivoire and Cameroon (which should benefit from US$80 million each year under the HIPC Initiative and US$100 million through refunding by grants over the short term), resources brought by C2D grant conversions will be relatively weak compared to HIPC relief, as illustrated in Table 10.11.

The allocation of funds released through debt relief

The core of the fight against poverty, as with the Social Dimensions of Adjustment programmes of the early 1990s, was initially considered as a reinforcement of social sectors (essentially education and health). In the enhanced HIPC Initiative the BWIs have stressed the wish that the amounts released (public resources) are not wasted. As such, it is required that they are allocated to priority social sectors, comprising basic healthcare and primary education, and also some variable secondary sectors according to specific needs. In any event, allocations pass through the

Table 10.11 Stock of French ODA to be converted to grants (US$ million)

Country	Amount of French ODA to be converted to grants	Annual average flows (2002–2020)*	Annual amount of French ODA (1999)	Forecast completion date
HIPC countries having reached a decision point:				
Cameroon†	1,007	56.0	134.8	2002
Guinea	174	9.7	37.4	2002
Mozambique	73	4.1	34.0	2001
Madagascar	71	3.9	79.3	2002
Mauritania	65	3.6	23.1	2001/2002
Rwanda	36	2.0	5.4	2002
Bolivia	26	1.4	13.8	2001
Malawi	12	0.7	0.2	2002
Uganda	12	0.7	1.6	Reached
Tanzania	10	0.6	4.9	2001
São Tomé & Principe	7	0.4		2002
Honduras	4	0.2	18.6	2003
Nicaragua	2	0.1	6.9	2002
HIPC countries yet to be examined:				
Côte d'Ivoire	1,282	71		2003
Congo-Brazzaville	393	22		2003
Congo (RDC)	176	10		
Burundi	52	3		2003
Myanmar	10	1		
Sierra Leone	2	0.1		2003

Sources: Ministère de l'Economie, des Finances et de l'Industrie, Report presented to Parliament on the activities of the IMF and the World Bank, August 2000 (provisional amounts).

Notes
Original figures were in Euros; conversions at an exchange rate of US$0.93 per Euro.
* Estimated by linear projection of grant conversion over 18 years. In reality, the amounts will be greater in early years and diminish thereafter.
† Cameroon should benefit from amounts closer to US$100 million than the US$56 million mentioned for early years.

budget, which does not preclude that part of the funds transit local authorities, associations or NGOs for project implementation.

The deeper the process, the more it appears evident that it builds on a very limited vision of poverty. Listening to declarations made by the poor, it is clear that their demands go beyond these fields (they touch on public security, roads, for example) and that they do not always place health and education at the same level of priority.

Increasingly, budgetary allocations from debt reduction are diversifying (rural roads and water schemes, fight against Aids, and so on). It may be asked just where this trend will end before it submerges the 'poverty alleviation' paradigm in a loosely defined 'pro-development' strategy.

Furthermore, social services that are developed need to be accessible by the poor. Cost recovery policies elaborated by the BWIs are thus thrown open to question (together with the pricing policies of global pharmaceutical laboratories).

Projects to be funded: what are they and who will undertake them?

PRSPs present sector strategies to which HIPC resources are channelled, and the goals to be met in terms of poverty reduction. It remains for the country to define the projects to be funded within these strategies, and which will reach the intended goals.

After PRSP definition, countries that benefit from HIPC relief need to buckle down to project preparation. Some have already been tempted to repackage old projects that failed to secure funding (largely because they were poorly conceived). Most of these have been refused by the BWIs (notably the case in Cameroon).

Is it possible that projects prepared in haste can really respond to needs, or will have an impact on poverty? If projects are not rapidly identified, funds will not be released. Thus, for example, Mali budgeted CFA Francs 2 billion for health in 2000, based on HIPC resources, but less than CFA Francs 1 billion was paid out.

This raises again the old but persistent problem linked to the capacities of beneficiary countries to absorb these new resources (which may seem ironic in the HIPC process, as a sizeable part of the amounts made available comes from undrawn European Development Fund resources). The absence of administrative means, the little-advanced process of decentralisation in many countries, the evident lack of capacities by NGOs and local associations to participate in the implementation of the projects, rapidly risk establishing limits to the good use of the resources. To be sure, difficulties in absorbing funds may cause frustration. In some countries, announcements of sizeable sums to be released through debt relief have already raised hopes for improvements to civil service salaries.

Faced with this, a process of HIPC resource capture is emerging through the creation of false NGOs, as in Cameroon where the authorities recently voted a decree authorising one-man NGOs, and opened the door to a potentially dangerous drift. It is difficult to see how good-quality projects, based on a participatory approach, could emerge in this context and foster the poverty reduction.

The consequences for poverty reduction strategies

The HIPC Initiative is supposed to improve the conditions of the poor in beneficiary countries. The way it has been organised, however, generates some distortions to the global poverty relief strategy (Eurodad 2001b). It may be noted, in particular:

*   The broad logic of the HIPC Initiative is to bring assistance only to

poor countries with a debt burden greater than a fixed level. Those, like Haiti, which are unfortunate to be insufficiently in debt, do not qualify for this supplementary aid. This clearly inequitable situation could easily have been avoided by allocating the funds released according to 'debt neutral' criteria, such as population or GDP for example (DIAL 1999). This was not done and the distribution of debt cancellations between countries (eligible and ineligible) does not correspond to criteria of poverty reduction. Some of the countries classified among the poorest according to the United Nations failed to qualify for the HIPC Initiative. Such is the case of Afghanistan, Bangladesh, Bhutan, Cambodia, Comoros, Djibouti, Haiti, Lesotho, Nepal, etc. Conversely, countries not among the poorest have attained HIPC status: Angola, Cameroon, Congo-Brazzaville, Côte d'Ivoire, Ghana, Kenya, Vietnam, Bolivia, Guyana, Honduras and Nicaragua. As a result, the majority of the world's poor people live in countries (like India) that are not eligible for HIPC debt relief (Ranis and Stewart 2001). To fight poverty, a modification of sustainability criteria should promote an approach based on fiscal sustainability taking into account the Millennium Development Goals (Gunter 2002).

- To avoid exposure to civil society criticism, BWIs have sought to accelerate the process (such as in late 2000). For this reason, debt reductions have been obtained as soon as a country presented an I-PRSP. This pressure, in some cases, probably implies a reduction to PRSP quality standards (Severino 2001b) and may explain why the BWIs insist that PRSPs are documents that present a general framework, and not precise or costed strategies.
- The arbitrary selection of HIPC Initiative beneficiaries has been frequently denounced, especially at its beginnings (Chavagneux 1998; Raffinot 1999). Some countries were included whereas, in reality, they bore little debt (Burkina Faso). Others, despite clearly unsustainable debts, were included only later (Mozambique, Nicaragua). Consequently, resources released and dedicated in priority to poverty relief will be very unequal, according to country.
- The special treatment of resources released by debt reduction, and the close surveillance of their utilisation, is highly questionable. No doubt it allows better 'marketing' of the Initiative to public opinion, but it takes no account of the fungibility of public funds and presents the flaws of all allotted funds. Either the amounts released by debt reduction will be too small to permit funding of a real programme to reduce poverty, or they will be too vast, which risks, to the contrary, creating problems of absorption or inducing wastage on a greater or lesser scale. Furthermore, these amounts do not constitute permanent funding; they will reduce with time, even if the final horizon exceeds a generation. Finally, polarisation around the amounts liberated by debt relief risks to mask the global strategy. As noted by Gupta *et al.* (2001):

In this context, all spending on poverty reduction needs to be tracked, not just that associated with the Initiative. The objectives are increases in spending on poverty reduction programs and in the share of total public spending devoted to these programs.

Switching to generalised budget aid, to the contrary, allows a means of overcoming the parcelling created by the HIPC Initiative.

- Debt reduction stretches over several decades. Countries thus engage in a very long-term process, which poses potential problems of lassitude both by the beneficiaries and by the donors. Severino (2001b), notes:

  This Initiative risks to place developing countries under long-term tutelage: every year ... beneficiary countries must discuss their budgets in Washington and with the main bilateral donors. Are we ready to assume this long-term political reality? Finally, we may ask whether the donors are equipped to handle the situation: are they capable of following global programmes of institutional support for such a long time?

- HIPC Initiative aims at achieving debt sustainability, avoiding new rescheduling of debts. This aim is likely to be attained, according to DSAs presented by the BWIs. This assertion has been criticised, because of over-optimistic growth assumptions used in these DSAs (United States GAO 2000). However, it is difficult to understand how countries borrowing at 0.75 per cent or less and receiving mostly grants could default, except in the case of a generalised mismanagement. DSAs based on fiscal sustainability and assuming the mere continuation of the past trends show that the debt ratios are likely to decrease in some West African countries (Moisseron and Raffinot 1999).

Conclusion

The HIPC Initiative launched by the IMF and the World Bank in late 1996 constitutes important progress, which experienced significant acceleration in June 1999 (the Cologne G7 Summit). For the first time, the totality of debts owed by the poorest countries (including multilateral debts) were subject to a global study and relatively generous treatment. The Initiative concerns 42 countries, and the forecast amount of debt relief is close to US$100 billion. The marked wish, since 1999, to link debt reduction and poverty relief is a major innovation. Preparation of a PRSP has become, in this context, a precondition that is extending to all countries seeking the benefit of concessional lending from the BWIs, and not merely those benefiting from debt reduction.

Nevertheless, the amount corresponds to reductions in debt service payments due over several decades. Annual amounts liberated are, as such, limited and above all variable according to the country concerned. In per person terms, the amounts are extremely disparate and much the same is true when annual relief is compared to public receipts or expenditures. For many countries, the stakes are low and there is a risk they will fail to produce expected improvements in the management of public finances.

It is also necessary for these amounts to be truly additional, and not to substitute for aid provided until now. States and international institutions have so promised, but this is a matter where declarations of intent have rarely been followed through. For several countries, debt reduction will not compensate for the cut in official development assistance during the past decade.

The situation is complicated by the fact that prior to the Initiative, some countries repaid all their debts before benefiting from reduction (Burkina Faso, Mali, Uganda, etc.) while the performance of others was far lower (Guinea Bissau, Mozambique, etc.). For the former, the Initiative re-establishes a clear room for manoeuvre, which is not the case for the latter.

Furthermore, the sums released will be subject to strict monitoring; they must be allocated to public expenditure susceptible (in principle) of alleviating poverty, and in the first place to sectors of education and basic health. The HIPC Initiative will thus have a significant impact in these areas, sometimes so great (because of the weakness of current spending) to create a strong risk of wastage. This impact concerns the augmentation of social spending, and not the utilisation of sums received from abroad that may be used freely by states. This is why the HIPC Initiative leaves the question of deficit financing intact.

Bilateral donors have adopted debt reduction programmes going beyond the HIPC Initiative. France has established 'debt reduction and development contracts' (C2D) which permit further debt relief, but at the cost of a potentially cumbersome parallel procedure.

Most procedures concerning the reduction of public debts naturally involve public administrations. The hoped for intervention of civil society appears problematic, notably because of a reduced capacity to engage dialogue on such questions and to take in charge programmes or projects aimed at reducing poverty.

Notes

1   Rate of forgiveness applicable only to bilateral non-ODA public loans; that is to say, to publicly guaranteed commercial debts. ODA debts were rescheduled.
2   Debt treated in the Paris Club is not the complete bilateral debt of a country but the pre 'cut-off date' debt (the debt stock at the time of the first passage

with the Club). This cut-off date is rarely changed for successive reschedulings granted to a country. Borrowings after the cut-off date do not qualify for consolidation.

3   There were originally 41 heavily indebted countries. Comoros was added to the list in 2001.

4   Excluding Liberia, Somalia and Sudan, absent from BWIs' projections (IMF/World Bank 2001b).

Part III

Monitoring and evaluation systems

Unlike the previous development strategies that focused on policy content, the new international poverty reduction initiatives widen the perspective by taking into account two further dimensions – namely, planning and implementation processes, and policy monitoring and evaluation (M&E) systems, which are now deemed to be vital components of development strategies.

Generally speaking, how successful these new strategies prove to be will of course depend on the relevance of the options selected in each of the three areas. But it will also depend just as much on the combination of the three aspects and how they are linked together, although the overall architecture of the system is yet to be set up. We are forced to recognise that, although progress has been made on the first two fronts, as shown in the first two parts of this book, M&E systems are currently the weakest link in the chain. There are great ambitions: not only to introduce M&E systems for all poverty reduction strategies but also to ensure that the systems themselves are in line with the basic principles of the PRSP Initiative in terms of ownership, empowerment and accountability.

It is quite clear that everything is still to be done, and even still to be invented, in this area. Although policies – not necessarily good or effective ones – have indeed been implemented by the poor countries, they have seldom been monitored and even more rarely rigorously evaluated. In many countries, the statistical system is in ruins, political demands insignificant and there are problems in providing the general public with economic and social information. As for policy evaluation, it is faced with intrinsic methodological problems that are not specific to developing countries, but also with serious deficiencies in even the most elementary of the information systems mentioned above. At a time when work is underway to draw up new indicators to monitor governance, it is important to stress the fact that statistics and economic surveys are in themselves an essential component of good governance: the market economy and democracy go hand in hand with greater access, in real time, to economic and social information.

This part of the book obviously does not claim to look at the entire issue of M&E systems. First, it focuses more on the instruments than on the institutional systems that need to be introduced (coordinating statistical systems, matching supply/demand, role of civil society, etc.), whose organisation is part of a complex alchemy that is only touched on briefly. Second, for the monitoring systems, it puts the accent on results indicators rather than other types of measurements (means indicators, intermediate indicators). These choices in no way mean that we underestimate the importance of the other dimensions, in fact in some cases we are convinced that solving the institutional aspects is more important than any technical shortcomings. However, we have adopted an angle giving preference to thinking that highlights a certain number of original contributions, where DIAL's researchers and their partners have well-proven experience and a recognised comparative advantage.

The first three chapters deal with the question of monitoring, whereas the fourth looks at the issue of policy evaluation. It is quite clear that if nothing is done, the proliferation of surveys launched urgently at the finalisation stage of the PRSPs will do nothing to solve the failures of past systems (quantity and quality of information, human constraints, etc.). These failings are all the more harmful as they will directly affect the monitoring systems, but also the evaluation systems that will come up against the insurmountable problem of data availability. Chapter 11 focuses on one of the components of the monitoring systems, household surveys, which are the main statistical instrument used to measure poverty evolution. The chapter is a critical analysis of the systems existing in poor countries, from a conceptual standpoint and above all with respect to their actual implementation in the field. Following a diagnosis of why past experiences failed, we are able to put forward a number of proposals designed to overcome the failures, both on a technical and an institutional level.

On the basis of European experience of poverty monitoring in statistical surveys, Chapter 12 attempts to draw useful lessons for poor countries. It shows that, even in a context where human and financial resources are far more favourable, a large number of difficulties still subsist, and the scientific debate is still very open. (Which poverty? Which indicators? How can they be measured?)

Chapter 13 presents two original survey systems, developed by DIAL and successfully implemented in the field in several developing countries: '1-2-3 surveys' and 'Rural Observatories'. Empirical examples are given to illustrate the type of results that can be obtained. They are compared to the main surveys traditionally used on an international level, highlighting the potential complementarity of their different features. Apart from the methodological aspects, the authors show how an active policy of communication and dissemination of results can be mobilised to respond to social demands and stimulate democratic debate in countries where statistics have not played a role in the past.

Finally, Chapter 14 takes stock of the different methods used for evaluating poverty reduction policies. The idea is to propose instruments that not only look at the policies' effectiveness (in terms of growth), but also help measure their distributive impact (in terms of inequalities and, consequently, poverty). Using the latest developments of economic research in this field, it highlights the analytical challenges underlying this type of exercise. It also demonstrates that what the BWIs refer to as Poverty and Social Impact Analysis (PSIA) are still at the drawing-board stage, given that the toolkits designed by economists are incomplete and still being developed. In this context, the authors look towards the future and, amongst possible paths (incidence analysis, poverty maps, micro-macro modelling, etc.), choose to focus their attention on micro-simulation techniques, which are particularly well suited for this type of evaluation. They explain the basic principles and explore the potential, adopting a clear approach, backed up by concrete examples, on this eminently technical subject. By removing the aggregate models' traditional hypothesis of the representative agent through explicit modelling of individual behaviour, micro-simulations open up new possibilities that tie in well with the principles of the new Initiatives. They move towards better integration of the micro and macro levels and endeavour to take more account of the players' freedom of choice with respect to economic policies.

11 The existing systems for monitoring poverty

Weaknesses of the usual household surveys

Mireille Razafindrakoto and François Roubaud

Following the end of the structural adjustment era, the reshaping of development policies in the fight against poverty poses a formidable challenge to statisticians whose job it is to monitor and evaluate the policies. It is no longer just a question of considering the major macro-financial indicators (growth, inflation, debt, etc.) – special attention must be paid to the levels of well-being of populations, with all the complexity that this implies. Clearly, appropriate methods are called for. These must satisfy three major objectives:

- measuring and analysing poverty to support the definition of anti-poverty strategies;
- real-time monitoring of changes in living conditions, in order to provide feedback on the impact of reforms, to judge the effectiveness of the policies and to suggest any adjustments that may be needed;
- making information available to all, thereby enabling all those concerned in society to play an effective part in the decision-making process and in checking and evaluating policy, and, as a corollary, making governments feel accountable for the effects of their actions on the population.

This means that we need, on the one hand, a reliable, up-to-date and effective system for gathering statistical information, and, on the other, a policy of systematic and regular dissemination of the results. The emphasis placed on reducing poverty and improving the well-being of the population implies that the monitoring and evaluation systems should be based on a central module of household surveys, enabling the measurement of changes in their living conditions.

In many poor countries, particularly those in sub-Saharan Africa, these objectives are far from being achieved. In most cases, the statistical data – and the analyses based on them – when they exist, are either incomplete or of little relevance to the real needs of decision-makers and civil society in general. What is more, the statistical data have until now been reserved for the almost exclusive use of decision-makers, if they are used at all. The actual results of policies remain unknown to the public, who have no means of scrutinising, checking and applying pressure on their leaders.

Making it compulsory to carry out a prior poverty assessment, and to set up monitoring and evaluation systems, as one of the basic principles in the drafting of the Poverty Reduction Strategy Papers (PRSPs) should help to remedy the weaknesses of economic and social information systems. However, while this exercise is essential for validating the PRSPs, those with national responsibility at varying levels, not to mention the donors, do not seem to have any real awareness of the importance and the implications of these principles in conducting policy. Drawing up 'poverty profiles' often appears little more than an exercise in style, imposed from outside. Converging indicators testify to a poor understanding of the structural weaknesses of the information systems: for the most part, the diagnoses made in the PRSPs are based on unreliable data, without questioning their validity; the analyses go no further than observing the scale of poverty, without trying to emphasise elements that could be used to define policy. In addition, many countries are opting to continue with existing monitoring systems, and, realising that they do not really provide what the decision-makers require, are complementing them with occasional evaluation projects. As in the past, this is likely to lead either to the production of analyses with little relevance due to the lack of appropriate data, or to multiple surveys with no effort at coordination. In the latter case, severe financial and human constraints characterising poor countries will limit the quality of results. So although the drafting of the PRSPs is an opportunity for (re)constructing a suitable information-gathering mechanism, the urgent need to complete them has not encouraged real inquiry into the various causes of the current system's failings and ways of correcting them. In fact, an in-depth field study of the institutionalisation of PRSP processes, covering eight African countries, concluded that the monitoring/assessment proposals reflect the main weakness in the strategies being developed (Booth 2002).

This chapter aims to contribute to the construction of an appropriate survey system able to fulfil the goals of poverty measurement and monitoring, as well as making information available to a wide public so that poverty reduction policies can be defined and evaluated. The first section will be devoted to presenting the principal monitoring indicators and the form in which they need to be produced to satisfy the needs of the new poverty reduction strategies. We shall then look at the characteristics of the most common living conditions surveys. In the second section, after pointing out the shortcomings regularly observed in practice, particularly in Africa, we shall attempt to identify the causes of this state of affairs, in order to arrive at a number of concrete corrective proposals.

Measuring and monitoring poverty

Monitoring and evaluation indicators

The need to reinforce the statistical information system in order to improve the availability and quality of data in developing countries is no longer in doubt, even if the human and financial resources available are not yet equal to the challenge. Following resolutions made at various international conferences during the 1990s (Copenhagen, Jomtien, Beijing, Cairo, Rio de Janeiro, New York), it was recommended that eight goals on poverty, and more globally on human development, be monitored to evaluate progress relative to the Millennium Development Goals (MDG, see Table 11.1). The international initiative PARIS21 (PARtnerships In Statistics for development in the 21st century), launched in November 1999, aims to reinforce the capacities of poor countries to collect and analyse statistical data, in particular so that these indicators can be monitored.

The indicators presented in Table 11.1 are given here for reference and as examples. They have been selected by international institutions in order to provide global monitoring of how the development situation is evolving across the world. But it is clear that these indicators cannot be enough, and that they should not all be applied in every country (see Box 11.1).

Within the framework of the drafting of the PRSPs, the choice of indicators must depend in part on each country's specific objectives. It must result from the identification of needs and priorities (areas judged to be of highest priority, or where the problems of poverty or inequality are the most acute). In addition, monitoring systems must take local capacity into account, and specifically the existing human and financial resources. The choice must be realistic, so that the chosen indicators are available regularly and in real time, enabling the information to be used effectively to monitor the progress made and evaluate policies (and, if necessary, reshape them). Furthermore, following the aim of participatory monitoring, the indicators must be accessible to everyone. This implies not only that they be communicated to a wide public (decision-makers and society in general), but also that emphasis be given as far as possible to the most significant indicators, those that are the most meaningful for the large majority of people involved. In particular, it cannot be enough to publish documents containing nothing but tables of synthetic indicators, comprehensible only by specialists or experts in the field.

As a general rule, we can distinguish between two types of monitoring indicators: intermediate indicators, and final (or outcome) indicators. But in certain circumstances, four levels of monitoring might be advisable in order to fulfil the objectives both of measuring the progress that has been made and of evaluating policies (see Table 11.2). Among the intermediate indicators we can distinguish between:

Table 11.1 Millennium Development Goals: goals, targets and indicators

Goals and targets	Indicators for monitoring progress
Goal 1　Eradicate extreme poverty and hunger	
Target 1. Halve, between 1990 and 2015, the proportion of people whose income is less than $1 a day	**1** Proportion of population below $1 (PPP) a day[*] **2** Poverty gap ratio (incidence × depth of poverty) **3** Share of poorest quintile in national consumption
Target 2. Halve, between 1990 and 2015, the proportion of people who suffer from hunger	**4** Prevalence of underweight children under five years of age **5** Proportion of population below minimum level of dietary energy consumption
Goal 2　Achieve universal primary education	
Target 3. Ensure that, by 2015, children everywhere, boys and girls alike, will be able to complete a full course of primary schooling	**6** Net enrolment ratio in primary education (girls, boys, total) **7** Proportion of pupils starting grade 1 who reach grade 5 (girls, boys, total) **8** Literacy rate of 15- to 24-year-olds (women/men/total)
Goal 3　Promote gender equality and empower women	
Target 4. Eliminate gender disparity in primary and secondary education, preferably by 2005, and to all levels of education no later than 2015	**9** Ratio of girls to boys in primary, secondary and tertiary education **10** Ratio of literate women/men of 15- to 24-year-olds **11** Share of women in wage employment in the non-agricultural sector **12** Proportion of seats held by women in national parliament
Goal 4　Reduce child mortality	
Target 5. Reduce by two thirds, between 1990 and 2015, the under-five mortality rate	**13** Under-five mortality rate **14** Infant mortality rate **15** Proportion of one-year-old children immunised against measles
Goal 5　Improve maternal health	
Target 6. Reduce by three quarters, between 1990 and 2015, the maternal mortality ratio	**16** Maternal mortality ratio **17** Proportion of births attended by skilled health personnel
Goal 6　Combat HIV/Aids, malaria and other diseases	
Target 7. Have halted by 2015 and begun to reverse the spread of HIV/Aids	**18** HIV prevalence among 15- to 24-year-old pregnant women **19** Condom use rate of the contraceptive prevalence rate[†] **20** Number of children orphaned by HIV/Aids[‡]
Target 8. Have halted by 2015 and begun to reverse the incidence of malaria and other major diseases	**21** Prevalence and death rates associated with malaria **22** Proportion of population in malaria risk areas using effective malaria prevention and treatment measures[§] **23** Prevalence and death rates associated with tuberculosis **24** Proportion of tuberculosis cases detected and cured under directly observed treatment short course (DOTS)

Goal 7 Ensure environmental sustainability

Target 9. Integrate the principles of sustainable development into country policies and programmes and reverse the loss of environmental resources

25 Proportion of land area covered by forest

26 Ratio of area protected to maintain biological diversity to surface area

27 Energy use (kg oil equivalent) per $1 GDP (PPP)

28 Carbon dioxide emissions (per capita) and consumption of ozone-depleting CFCs (ODP tons)

29 Proportion of population using solid fuels

Target 10. Halve by 2015 proportion of people without sustainable access to safe drinking water

30 Proportion of population with sustainable access to an improved water source, urban and rural

Target 11. By 2020 to have achieved a significant improvement in the lives of at least 100 million slum dwellers

31 Proportion of urban population with access to improved sanitation

32 Proportion of households with access to secure tenure (owned or rented)

Goal 8 Develop a global partnership for development

Target 12. Develop further an open, rule-based, predictable, non-discriminatory trading and financial system (includes a commitment to good governance, development, and poverty reduction – both nationally and internationally)

Some of the indicators listed below are monitored separately for the less developed countries (LDCs), Africa, landlocked countries and small island developing states

Official development assistance

33 Net ODA, total and to LDCs, as percentage of OECD/DAC donors' gross national income

34 Proportion of total bilateral, sector-allocable ODA of OECD/DAC donors to basic social services (basic education, primary healthcare, nutrition, safe water and sanitation)

Target 13. Address the special needs of the less developed countries (includes: tariff and quota-free access for least-developed countries' exports; enhanced programme of debt relief for HIPCs and cancellation of official bilateral debt; and more generous ODA for countries committed to poverty reduction)

35 Proportion of bilateral ODA of OECD/DAC donors that is untied

36 ODA received in landlocked countries as proportion of their GNIs

37 ODA received in small island developing states as proportion of their GNIs

Market access

Target 14. Address the special needs of landlocked countries and small island developing states (through the Programme of Action for the Sustainable Development of Small Island Developing States and the outcome of the 22nd special session of the General Assembly)

38 Proportion of total developed country imports (by value and excluding arms) from developing countries and from LDCs, admitted free of duties

39 Average tariffs imposed by developed countries on agricultural products and textiles and clothing from developing countries

40 Agricultural support estimate for OECD countries as percentage of their GDP

41 Proportion of ODA provided to help build trade capacity[ll]

Target 15. Deal comprehensively with the debt problems of developing countries through national and international measures in order to make debt sustainable in the long term

Debt sustainability

42 Total number of countries that have reached their HIPC decision points and number that have reached their HIPC completion points (cumulative)

43 Debt relief committed under HIPC initiative, US$

44 Debt service as a percentage of exports of goods and services

Target 16. In cooperation with developing countries, develop and implement strategies for decent and productive work for youth

45 Unemployment rate of 15- to 24-year-olds, each sex and total[¶]

Target 17. In cooperation with pharmaceutical companies, provide access to affordable essential drugs in developing countries

46 Proportion of population with access to affordable essential drugs on a sustainable basis

Target 18. In cooperation with the private sector, make available the benefits of new technologies, especially information and communications

47 Telephone lines and cellular subscribers per 100 population

48 Personal computers in use per 100 population and Internet users per 100 population

---

Source: United Nations Statistics Division – Millennium Indicators (http://unstats.un.org/unsd/mi/mi_goals.asp October 2002).

Notes

* For monitoring country poverty trends, indicators based on national poverty lines should be used, where available.

† Amongst contraceptive methods, only condoms are effective in preventing HIV transmission. The contraceptive prevalence rate is also useful in tracking progress in other health, gender and poverty goals. Because the condom use rate is only measured amongst women in union, it will be supplemented by an indicator on condom use in high-risk situations. These indicators will be augmented with an indicator of knowledge and misconceptions regarding HIV/Aids by 15- to 24-year-olds.

‡ To be measured by the ratio of proportion of orphans to non-orphans aged 10–14 who are attending school.

§ Prevention to be measured by the percentage of under five sleeping under insecticide treated bednets; treatment to be measured by percentage of under five who are appropriately treated.

‖ OECD and WTO are collecting data that will be available from 2001 onwards.

¶ An improved measure of the target is underdevelopment by ILO for future years.

- those which evaluate operational results corresponding to the direct products of government action (the construction of facilities, the adoption of a government bill, a budget increase, the recruitment of teachers, the number of cases processed by an administrative department, etc.). For the most part, the source of information is administrative data or registers;
- those which directly measure the effect of the government action on the targeted population group (rate of use of a service, schools or hospitals built or renovated, etc.). In this case, the data must be sufficiently broken down, or must be specific to a given structure (beneficiaries/users).

In monitoring final or outcome indicators, two types of data may be used which in most cases require representative household surveys:

- the more traditional of these evaluate the results according to the final objective being targeted (reduction in poverty, mortality rates, inequality, etc.);
- less widely used surveys measure the level of satisfaction of the population directly (users/beneficiaries), who give their qualitative appreciation of the progress made and of any unexpected negative effects. It should be emphasised that this qualitative information may be

Box 11.1 What can the Millennium Development Goals achieve?

Eight goals and 18 targets for development and poverty eradication and for protecting the environment were set out in the United Nations Millennium Declaration, adopted in September 2000 by 191 countries. Forty-eight indicators were later defined by a group of experts from several international institutions, specialised in different fields, in a view to measuring and monitoring progress in each of the targeted goals (see Table 11.1).

The principles underlying the decision to set out the Millennium Development Goals (MDGs) and the related indicators are an improvement on previous practices. The initiative has at least three major implications that are worthy of note.

- By precisely quantifying the goals to be met, the national and international stakeholders illustrate a greater determination to make firm commitments. It is made quite clear that the international community must be involved, as the last of the goals concerns the resources to be mobilised in terms of support and development partnerships in order to meet the first seven goals. This is a clear recognition that the rich countries have a duty to help the poor countries.
- By clarifying and harmonising priorities the MDGs are a step towards improving coherence between the donors and concentrating resources, that can enhance aid effectiveness.
- A central place is now granted to precise monitoring of progress in the medium and long term. This approach implicitly leads to a better understanding of the situation in the field and an evaluation of the strategies implemented. Considerable efforts are currently being made to collect the data relating to the MDGs, although doubts may be raised as to whether they are sufficient.

Beyond the commendable principles of this initiative, in practice the MDGs raise a large number of questions and provoke debate on issues ranging from their feasibility or pertinence, to the scale of the resources to be mobilised to reach them.

About twelve years before the deadline fixed by the MDGs (2015), a large number of studies are trying to see if progress is on track. The assessments vary significantly from one report to another. Forecasts can be optimistic or pessimistic, depending on the hypotheses retained. Nonetheless, a few solid observations on the realism of the MDGs can be noted:

- at the rate of progress made in the 1990s, only one of the goals, concerning access to water, can be met by 2015 (Vandemoortele 2002);
- although the most optimistic hypotheses may enable us to reach, or at least come close to the MDGs at the world level (World Bank 2002d), for many countries in sub-Saharan Africa, where poverty is the most widespread, such enormous efforts are required that it will be impossible to reach the goals.

In addition, the aim of measuring progress raises questions as to the pertinence of the goals and the indicators chosen in the MDGs.

- The wish to harmonise the goals on a world level is incompatible with the principle of ownership recommended in the PRSPs. Are a country's specific situation and the priorities drawn up on a national level of secondary importance to the international community? In particular, the MDGs ignore social inequalities that are a major problem for many countries.
- The monitoring of the MDGs focuses on average progress made, on a global level. This approach irons out disparities, especially evolutions concerning less-favoured groups. The focus on monitoring the MDGs alone oversimplifies the problem as it is far from effective in evaluating the real successes or failures obtained at the country level.
- Finally, the scale of needs in terms of statistical support for monitoring the MDGs, in particular in the poor countries, where it is the most vital to measure progress, is widely underestimated. There is a vicious circle, given that the availability and quality of data depend on a country's level of wealth. As a result, the lack of data, or its very poor quality in the poorest countries, tends to exclude them from the scope of analyses or to provide a biased picture of evolutions.

The question of the financial resources required to meet the MDGs is also far from being settled. It has been estimated that, for the thirty or so African countries alone that are not in conflict or which have no major problems of governance, an increase in official development assistance of about 20–25 billion dollars is required (African Development Bank 2002). According to declarations made by Koffi Annan at the Monterrey Conference, the total cost worldwide is apparently at least 50 billion dollars per year, which represents the doubling of official development assistance. But there seems to be no programme at the moment for the allocation of a significant volume of aid, with amounts and timings planned sufficiently in advance to enable medium- and long-term strategies to be defined.

Finally, there are still problems in making the commitments materialise, despite increasing concern and calls from the international community. Vandemoortele (2002) refers to the observation made by James Grant in 1993 when he was UNICEF Executive Director, considering that it is still true today: 'The problem is not that we have tried to eradicate global poverty and failed; the problem is that no serious and concerted attempt has ever been made.' Vandemoortele also quotes Nelson Mandela, who asked in 2001: 'Will the legacy of our generation be more than a series of broken promises?'

Table 11.2 Some examples of policies and their monitoring indicators

	Universal primary education	Employment opportunities for the most disenfranchised	Fight against corruption
Objectives			
Policies/measures	Construction and renovation of schools and classrooms Teacher recruitment	Promoting the private sector, and particularly the creation of micro-entreprises (micro-credit, simplification of bureaucracy, etc.) Encouraging highly labour intensive activities (HLI projects)	Raising awareness (information, ethical code, creating a corruption watchdog, a book or letterbox for users' impressions and complaints) Raising public sector salaries Simplifying procedures Adopting checking procedures
Indicators			
Operational result	Number of classrooms built Number of teachers recruited	Creation of a micro-credit institution Simplifying the administrative procedures for setting up a business Implementing HLI projects	Increasing salaries Reorganising the administration Adopting anti-corruption laws (sanctions, setting up a watchdog)
Intermediate result: direct impact	Rate of attendance at new classes Ratio of pupils/teachers	Number of businesses and jobs created Number of HLI projects and direct jobs created	Applying checking and sanctions policies (number of corruption cases tried and punished)
Final result (in relation to the objective)	Proportion of primary age children in education (overall and among the poorest)	Unemployment rate (overall and among the poorest) Percentage of informal jobs (overall and among the poorest)	Improved running of the administration (efficiency, transparency) by analysing its users' impressions (watchdogs) Better tax income
Evolution of appreciation of the population (representative sample)	Rate of parent satisfaction (conditions of access, quality of primary education)	Percentage of the population who are satisfied with their jobs Perception of the difficulty of finding work Perception of employment stability	Reduced incidence of corruption (percentage of victims among the population, companies) Satisfaction index/objective

quantified (through a satisfaction index) if a representative sample of the population (or the target group) is surveyed, and can thus serve as concrete data for decision-makers. This type of indicator is particularly important within the framework of participatory processes, in that the measurement or monitoring/appreciation is carried out by the public concerned. Moreover, it can help to compensate for the difficulties in making measurements in certain areas (such as quantifying progress made), and to identify any negative effects of policies (for example, universal education achieved, but at the cost of a decline in the quality of education).

The distinction between these different levels of monitoring makes clear how the expected results are arrived at. It enables direct links to be made with the policies being enacted, their impact to be evaluated, the extent to which they satisfy needs and objectives to be analysed, and finally any failings to be identified (for example, a targeted population not being affected by a measure). The availability of these indicators provides support for decision-making, and for possible policy redirections. In practice, the link between policies and final objectives is often not made, or is not sufficiently explained. Two scenarios can arise. In the first case, we simply monitor the overall final outcomes, which provide little information in operational terms. These results are often too aggregated, lack direct links with the actions taken, and also depend on external factors (unrelated to the policy being implemented). In the second scenario, we place too much emphasis on intermediate indicators, without measuring the final impact of the policy (for example: a budget rise, a drop in taxation levels, etc.). In both cases, leaders can avoid feeling accountable to the population for the evolution of the situation in relation to the final objectives being targeted.

Finally, it should be underlined that the monitoring and publication of the indicators must be undertaken by a sufficiently independent body in order to avoid any pressure to disguise or massage the information and so that the principle of accountability can be applied effectively.

The main survey types for measuring poverty

Household surveys constitute the best means of appreciating the population's living conditions and measuring the scale of their poverty. Different types of surveys, with different objectives, can be used. Table 11.3 gives a brief summary of the most common survey types, without trying to describe their characteristics in detail.

Clearly, the choice of tool depends on the objective being targeted in terms of measurement or poverty analysis. Given that the human and financial resources of poor countries are generally limited, it is advisable to avoid multiple surveys and to identify the adequate measuring and

Table 11.3 The main types of household surveys in developing countries

Type of survey	Main subjects dealt with	Objectives
LSMS-type survey into living conditions (variations: priority survey or Integral survey)	Multiple subjects: income and spending, health, education, employment, agriculture, access to basic services, etc.	Measurement and understanding of poverty Treating different dimensions of poverty
Demographic and health survey (DHS)	• occurrence of illness • anthropometry (rate of malnutrition) • health and fertility behaviour • housing, education, employment	Detailed analysis of the state of health and access to healthcare
Employment survey	• activities, jobs, unemployment • income • socio-demographic variables • housing	Analysis of employment and conditions of activity Measuring monetary poverty (based on income)
Budget/consumption-type survey	• consumption and income • housing conditions • socio-demographic variables	Measure of living standards Measure of monetary poverty (based on consumption)
Targeted survey	Examples: among users of health or education establishments, violence in certain areas, etc.	Measure of impact on well-identified population groups
CWIQ-type rapid evaluation and monitoring survey	• access to education and healthcare (and degree of population satisfaction) • employment • nutrition • housing	Rapid diagnosis of the impact of policies on the well-being of the population based on a few key indicators Does not aim for a precise measurement of monetary poverty and its evolution
PPA-type qualitative and participatory survey (or participatory evaluation)	• perception of poverty • inequalities within households • problems encountered by the poor and factors involved in poverty • actions given high priority	Detailed knowledge of poverty based on semi-structured interview

Source: This table is primarily based on the presentation by Coudouel and Hentschel (2001).

monitoring systems in order to take into account the various dimensions of poverty (see Box 11.2). In this context, we will continue this chapter by looking specifically at surveys enabling the measurement of monetary poverty (which correlates the best with the different forms of poverty) and its evolution.

Implementation on the ground: diagnosis and proposals

Shortcomings often faced in practice

Surveys into consumption and living conditions, which are the usual tool for measuring poverty in poor countries, often have significant failings which remain neglected or ignored. The quality and the scope of the resulting analyses raise serious problems. Globally, the diagnosis leads us to three major observations:

- the scale of the surveys and the resulting administrative difficulties, particularly in view of the shortage of available skills, prevent the rapid availability of reliable, accurate and up-to-date information likely to be of use in drafting or reshaping policy;
- the absence of regularity, and especially of standard survey methods, makes comparisons over time difficult, obscuring the picture of real economic trends and the evolution of the indicators;
- finally, the proliferation of household surveys since the end of the 1980s has not helped to strengthen the national statistical offices (NSOs). The lack of coordination between different donors, each with different requirements and specific funding procedures over which the NSOs have no influence, has had a disastrous effect on the ability to plan activities (splits between different directions, competition for project funding, etc.).

The low level of involvement of the data's potential users (analysts and decision-makers) in the design and implementation of the surveys, and conversely the limited participation of those responsible for operations on the ground in the use and analysis phase, reduce the effectiveness and the relevance of the system. The former are not fully aware of the underlying limits of statistical surveys and the basic criteria to be respected; while the latter are not sufficiently sensitised to the usefulness and objectives of the operation, and so do not understand the importance of the necessary degree of precision and rigour. To this compartmentalisation of tasks, dissociating data collection from analysis, must be added the further separation between the phases of production and analysis of the data on the one hand and the process of defining the policies that can be drawn from them on the other. In these conditions, it is hardly surprising that the data collected are inadequate and/or of limited reliability.

Box 11.2 Surveys of living standards and conditions in developing countries: the leading role played by the World Bank

Since the middle of the 1980s, the World Bank has played (and continues to play) an indisputable driving role in devising and publishing surveys of living standards in developing countries, and particularly in Africa. The main characteristic of the three survey systems presented below, in relation to previous methods, is the emphasis placed on evaluating policies (policy-oriented surveys) and the economic explanation of behaviour, under the influence of the work on 'new economics of the family' begun by G. Becker.

Living Standard Measurement Studies surveys

The Living Standard Measurement Studies (LSMS) surveys were initially designed to measure and monitor poverty and inequality, but changes in internal priorities at the Bank towards modelling the microeconomic behaviour of households have led to changes in their structure. Based on relatively small sample sizes on a national scale (1,600 households in Côte d'Ivoire), they have become multi-objective studies, covering almost all aspects of the economic and domestic activities of households: consumption, income, agriculture, jobs, transfers, migrations, education, health, anthropometry, etc. The first LSMSs were set up in Peru and Côte d'Ivoire in the middle of the 1980s. Following this, they spread widely to other countries: Bolivia, Ghana, Jamaica, Morocco, Mauritania, Pakistan, etc. In most of these countries, these surveys were the first to take advantage of developments in microcomputers, and their data are therefore available in electronic format. They have been studied extensively, giving rise to many publications on a wide variety of subjects, initiated by the team at the Bank and universities associated with it. The LSMSs have proved difficult to maintain over time, due to their high cost (100 to 200 dollars per household), and especially to the lack of internalisation in the countries where they have been applied. Deaton (2000) shows how, in the case of Côte d'Ivoire, personnel changes within the Bank led to the surveys being abandoned after 1988, with no lasting effect on local survey capacity.

The Integrated, Priority and Community Surveys of the Social Dimensions of Adjustment programme

Launched in 1988 by three development agencies (the World Bank, the African Development Bank and the United Nations Development Programme) in response to criticism of UNICEF's structural adjustment (Cornia *et al.* 1987), the Social Dimensions of Adjustment (SDA) programme developed a system combining three household surveys to measure the social impact of adjustment policies. The first, called the Integrated Survey (IS), took its inspiration directly from the LSMS surveys. The Priority Survey (PS) is a short survey of a large sample group (up to 15,000 households) aiming to capture various indicators for household well-being (basic services, etc.), initially with no detailed measurement of consumption, and to characterise the populations that might be affected by economic policies. Finally, the third, called the Community Survey (CS), provides 'mesoeconomic' information (existence of basic infrastructure, markets, community facilities) captured from privileged sources (managers, politicians, teachers, etc.) at community level (village, neighbourhood, etc.). This data can then be combined with that provided by households. The first result of these surveys was the production and institutionalisation of the 'Poverty Profile', describing the poverty situation of households. This document is now an essential reference for all the Bank's anti-poverty programmes. Several dozen surveys were carried out in Africa (for a total cost of 53 million dollars) before the programme was ended in 1993, following a very critical internal evaluation within the World Bank (Dubois 1996), which revealed initial objectives that were doubtless too ambitious but also an unhealthy degree of competition between two teams within the Bank (LSMS and SDA; in fact, although the promoters of the SDA acknowledged a certain parental influence from the LSMS group, the latter group completely 'disowned' the former). In terms of surveys, the SDA originated a certain number of methodological innovations, which still have a wide influence on new generations of surveys carried out since the middle of the 1980s. However, the SDA surveys and their descendants so far have shown a number of practical weaknesses, and in particular the abandonment of the original system's hierarchical structure, widely varying data quality and especially the fact that the mechanism was not taken up by the African national statistical offices.

The Core Welfare Indicators Questionnaire satisfaction surveys

The Core Welfare Indicators Questionnaire (CWIQ) surveys are the latest in a series of household surveys developed by the World Bank to aid in the formulation and evaluation of social and/or anti-poverty policies. Taking note of the failings of previous surveys, they aim in a way to replace Priority Surveys (PS) as they are carried out on the ground. With time, the PSs have gradually lost their main virtue (shortness). New modules, not initially foreseen, have been incorporated into the basic questionnaire (consumption, expenditures, etc.), without the collection procedures being revised to ensure the reliability of the data. Based on the premise that a short survey cannot give a sufficient measure of monetary poverty and that decision-makers need rapid feedback on the policies that are put into effect, CWIQ surveys focus on measuring *access to, use of and satisfaction with the principal basic socio-economic services*, indicators that are relatively easy to measure. Apart from its common-sense founding principles, aimed at providing results quickly (short questionnaire, single visit to a household, standardised tabulation plan), the main technical innovation of the CWIQ survey is data entry using optical scanning technology. Designed to be repeated annually with large sample sizes, the CWIQ survey is integrated into a complete kit, including all the stages of the operation from the organisation on the ground to the production of the results. Applied in several African countries in recent years, it has proved its viability. The survey's 'turnkey' option leads to obvious advantages (routine procedures for producing data and results), but is also a disadvantage (rigidity, little room to manoeuvre for local teams).

Far from being limited to a particular survey or country, the weaknesses of the poverty measuring and monitoring systems are general in the regions that are most affected by this phenomenon. To illustrate and underline the weaknesses of the statistical surveys that have been carried out, we shall present a few concrete examples. In particular, a study aiming at a comparative approach to urban poverty in three western African countries (DIAL 2000b) has enabled a precise diagnosis to be made of the quality of the 14 household surveys carried out between 1985 and 1998 covering consumption and living conditions (eight in Côte d'Ivoire, three each in Mali and Senegal), as well as of six Demographic and Health Surveys (two per country). In order to use the basic files from the first survey group, significant work was required in terms of cleaning up, harmonising of classifications and imputing erroneous data, to make the estimates more robust. However, despite these efforts, the results obtained remain very fragile due to the poor quality of the surveys. Focusing on one of the most frequent shortcomings, the following observations can be made:

1   The principal problem of the surveys, taken individually, lies in the quality of the data collected. Hardly any of the 14 statistical operations covering the living conditions of the population would have passed the test of validation according to the standard international criteria in this area. Although the measurement of consumption, by its very nature the most complex to estimate, is the most questionable indicator, it is far from being the only such. Thematic fields (activity, employment) and variables (definition of household concept), which should be much simpler to measure, are also affected. In many cases the data have not been cleaned up and the minimal tests for consistency have not been enough;

2   From a comparative point of view, the first source of inconsistency results from the absence of any clear, relevant methodology common to all the surveys (sampling plan, classification, collection method, formulation of the questionnaires, cleaning-up procedures). Given the total absence of standardisation in the survey methods, it is often difficult to be sure whether the meanings behind changes in poverty or country classifications over time should be attributed to real, interpretable economic phenomena or to problems in the statistical data that were collected.

More specifically, as far as the sampling plan is concerned:

- the extreme variation in sample size (for example, ranging from less than 300 to more than 3,000 households for the capitals) reduces the comparability of estimates;
- the definition of the capital's geographical limits is not constant (administrative capital versus entire built-up area including suburbs);
- the 'other urban areas' aggregate (besides the capital) is in reality very heterogeneous and variable from one survey to another. Furthermore, it is poorly measured due to the small size of samples covering different towns from one survey to another. This problem brings into doubt the reliability of the results for all urban areas.

Regarding the measurement of consumption, we can see:

- massive and variable underestimates, particularly in 'Priority Surveys'; they use lists of products under broad headings which are incomplete and pre-coded in advance in the questionnaire;
- no systematic recognition of self-consumption. This problem is inversely proportional to the level of urbanisation;
- the lack of information on regional prices which would enable consumption outside the capital to be deflated; poor estimates of sub-annual seasonal variation and uncertainty about periods of reference in retrospective questions, which afflict the annualisation of consumption, particularly in phases of high inflation (see periods following the CFA franc devaluation in 1994).

All these factors encourage the conclusion that the quality of the information decreases the further one moves from large towns into rural areas.

The examples presented in Box 11.3 are far from being isolated cases. There are many, many more. Madagascar, for instance, has had one of the richest arrays of household surveys in Africa since the beginning of the 1990s: an Integral survey in 1993/4 followed by three Priority surveys (1997, 1999, 2001). In addition, the human resources working at the statistical institute are among the best qualified, and are supported by high-level international economists. But these favourable conditions have not been enough to avoid the pitfalls in terms of data consistency. Household consumption as taken from the surveys represents between one-third and one-half of private consumption according to the national accounts.[1] This ratio is not even a quarter for non-food consumption, and one-eighth for services (Cour 2001). In fact, the generic problem of multi-objective surveys (such as Priority, Integral, LSMS surveys, etc.), the multiplicity of subjects covered, leads to a desire to measure everything – but to do so with an unacceptable level of error. An expert, detailed analysis of the files from the surveys of 1993 and 1997 compared with those of the two Demographic

Box 11.3 Survey quality and the difficulty of measuring monetary poverty

Apart from the methodological questions previously raised (see pp. 283–4), monetary measures of poverty and their monitoring over time require high-quality budget/consumption surveys. Beyond the questions of sampling methods inherent to any survey, budget/consumption surveys require at the very least that the questionnaire be sufficiently precise, from the point of view both of the list of products and of the spending timetable, to corres-pond to spending habits in the country being studied, that the survey be carried out over several visits in order to guide the households properly, that it be accompanied by product price monitoring, and that survey methods be consistent. It has been very damaging that such precautions have not always been taken, either through budgetary constraints, lack of supervision over local teams, or a desire to obtain rapid results.

In this connection, the case of Côte d'Ivoire is significant. This country now has eight budget/consumption surveys, four permanent household surveys (LSMS surveys) conducted in 1985 and 1988, three Priority Surveys conducted in 1992–3, 1995 and 1998, and a West African Economic and Monetary Union (WAEMU) spending survey conducted in 1996. As an example, the table below shows important variations in budget coefficients between the different series of surveys. These are too significant not to suggest problems of survey methods.

Food as a proportion of household spending in Abidjan, 1985–96

	LSMS survey		*Priority survey*		*WAEMU survey*
	1985	*1988*	*1993*	*1995*	*1996*
Food	39	35	48	50	44

Sources: LSMS surveys from 1985, 1988; priority surveys from 1993, 1995; WAEMU spending survey from 1996; Grimm, Guénard and Mèsple-Somps (2000).

Our second example, taken from the World Development Report 2000/1, illustrates the implications of the methodological choices made about monetary poverty. It shows how poverty rates can vary according to whether we take into account a scale of equivalence, economies of scale within households, or the type of data correction in the sample.

Poverty rates according to different hypotheses in Latin America and the Caribbean around 1996 (poverty threshold: 2 dollars PPP per day per person)

The hypotheses	*Average*	*Standard variation*
Scale of equivalence	41.3	4.5
Economies of scale	44.1	2.3
Missing and null values	49.1	1.9
Under-representativity	33.5	11.6
All options	40.1	13.0

Source: World Bank (2001a).

The third example makes clear the fragility of international comparisons of poverty according to the calculation method used for the Purchasing Power Parity (PPP) conversion factor. Analysing poverty in seven African capitals based on an identical survey conducted in 1996 and a common threshold, Backiny-Yetna and Torelli (2000) arrived not only at different levels of poverty but at very different rankings, depending on whether they used the official PPP coefficients estimated by the World Bank or those derived from real Harmonised Consumer Price Indices. Niamey is the poorest city according to the latter, with eight times more poverty than Abidjan, which has the least poverty (24 per cent and 3 per cent respectively). According to the World Bank PPPs, the incidence of poverty would only be 10 per cent. The figure would be less than twice that of Abidjan, and the city would appear in fourth place. The coefficient of the ranks of the two series hardly reaches 0.6. Dominance tests show that the differences in ranking occur whatever threshold is chosen. Therefore, not only are the World Bank PPPs apparently wrong, but they give inconsistent rankings to countries, even though these rankings are used as criteria for allocating international aid.

Incidence of poverty in seven capitals in West Africa (1996) according to the Purchasing Power Parity (PPP) calculation method

P_0 (%) PPP calculation	Poverty threshold: $1 PPP per day per person						
	Niamey	Ouagadougou	Bamako	Dakar	Cotonou	Lomé	Abidjan
Harmonised price index	23.8	22.7	16.6	13.2	12.7	8.8	2.9
World Bank	9.9	13.1	16.9	7.6	11.0	3.0	5.5

Source: Backiny-Yetna and Torelli (2000).

Finally, these inconsistencies do not only affect calculations of monetary poverty, as proved by problems with maternal mortality in Africa:

> rather different numbers can be given for the same series. Maternal mortality, which for Ghana jumped from 400 to 1000 from one issue of the *World Development Report* [by the World Bank] to the next, is often mentioned in this regard. Mauldin (1994) showed that, although they both used the same source, the *WDR* reported for 56 developing countries and the *HDR* [*Human Development Report*, by the UNDP] for 55 of these and a further 48. Counting differences of less than 50 points as the same, *HDR* gave higher values than *WDR* for 26 countries, lower for 12 and about the same for 17. Some differences are substantial e.g. Benin at 800 and 161, Mali at 850 and 2,325 and Malaysia 120 and 26. The correlation coefficient between the two sets of figures is only 0.7, dropping to only 0.4 for high mortality countries.
>
> (Strategic Partnership with Africa 1999)

Source: Taken from DIAL (2000b), with authors' supplements.

and Health Surveys (DHS 1992, 1997) on child anthropometry (Waltis-berger 1999) shows up clearly the lesser reliability of the former. For the year 1997, they observed a rate of emaciation (weight/height) of 18 per cent, against 10 per cent from the DHS. Almost all the subjects pose problems: education (with a highly implausible increase of one million pupils between 1993/4 and 1997), employment (the proportion of managers in employment apparently rose by 234 per cent in three years), agriculture (the production of paddy, estimated at about 2.5 million tonnes in both years, corresponds to a yield of 1.1 t/ha from an area of 2.3 million hectares in 1993 against a yield of 2.2 t/ha from an area of 1.2 million hectares in 1997), health, the informal sector, etc.

From a general viewpoint, *measurement errors are much more serious than sampling errors.* But methodological considerations, when they exist at all, focus on the second point. Surveys are little documented or not at all, leading to a loss of memory of how they were carried out and the problems encountered, and makes the necessary critical evaluation of the data risky.

Furthermore, the lack of rigour in the analyses produced before the statistical operations must be emphasised. This observation can be explained in part by the absence of high-quality data. But the fact that analysts ignore or disguise the shortcomings of surveys, and carry out approximate studies of uncertain validity, does not encourage the production of reliable, relevant information. This brings about a vicious circle. To illustrate this problem, it is not unusual to find, at national and to a lesser extent international level, that the publication of official documents stuffed with gross inconsistencies (level and structure of consumption, incidence of poverty, doubtful extrapolations, etc.) seems to provoke no reaction. As an example, highly surprising results were put forward in studies of poverty in Mali, without giving rise to any questions or comments (DIAL 2000b):

- a level of consumption per head of 440 dollars in 1989, placing Mali ahead of Ghana and Kenya, did not cause the analysts either to revisit their estimation methods or to question the reliability of their data;
- the observation of a sharp drop in total household spending at national level, equivalent to a fall in purchasing power of 50 per cent between 1989 and 1994, is presented without question, despite the improbability of such a development;
- according to the Annual Report of the Sustainable Human Development Observatory on Mali (ODHD 1999), 'poverty rose in Mali between 1994 and 1996, with the numeric poverty index increasing from 68.8 per cent to 71.6 per cent, and that between 1996 and 1998, we could see the beginning of a fall in the incidence of poverty: from a level of 71.6 per cent in 1996, it dropped to 69 per cent in 1998', although no national survey on which such statements could be based

had been conducted since 1994 (see Chapter 8 for the methodology used by ODHD).

The low level, if not absence, of discussion about the relevance of the analyses would seem to reflect the limited interest of decision-makers and experts at all levels in the availability of reliable quantitative diagnoses. Far from being specific to the Mali case, these deficiencies are widely generalised.

Elements of interpretation of a programmed failure

All things considered, it would be reasonable to wonder whether the multiplication of household surveys in the recent period, especially in Africa, has really improved our knowledge of poverty and inequality. The answer to this question is far from trivial. The quantity of accessible information has undoubtedly increased. But at the same time, the quality of the data has just as undoubtedly deteriorated (Deaton 1995).[2] This fault, widely underestimated, generates damaging counter-productive effects.

On the one hand, within countries, the most far-fetched figures circulate, and the ability to look at them critically by going back to the raw data (the initial treatment of the surveys) is almost non-existent. Rather than trying to ensure minimal consistency between these various figures, it is more in the interests of professional statisticians to maximise the number of surveys: even if these are badly conducted they are the only way to complement their derisory salaries.

On the other hand, the second-hand use of surveys by teams from northern universities does not help the situation. Apart from their (frequently) low level of knowledge of the countries, the conditions and the basic processing procedures (maintained by the absence of documentation), the logic of publication which governs the academic world and the criteria for evaluating academic reviews do not encourage them to focus their attention on the quality of the data. Too often, a critical diagnosis which goes too far would lead to refusal to use the surveys in question. But to accept this verdict would be to deprive oneself of the comparative advantage afforded by being able to obtain a database that has not yet been used by potential competitors. Moreover, the excessive value placed on formalisation and (econometric) instrumentation by development economists contributes to a marginal importance being given to the quality of the data used. So in most studies, when the problem is not simply ignored, the most common approach consists of mentioning it briefly in the introduction, and then unfolding the paper's reasoning and conclusions as if the question of quality had no importance for the results obtained. And then when, in the best cases, a real evaluation of the data is completed, this has no impact on the original country, such is the scale of the separation between the two worlds (the academic world of the North, and the technical and political world of the South; see Roubaud 2000c).

Finally, the proliferation of surveys gives the impression that knowledge has advanced, although the images conveyed by the information could well have only a distant connection with the phenomena they are supposed to measure. This is all the more regrettable given that the results of these surveys are then compiled into international databases. As an example, Deininger and Squire (1996) assembled a series of 2,600 observations about inequality measurements from survey reports, covering 112 countries for the period 1947–74. Considerable (although insufficient[3]) critical analysis work led them to conclude that only 700 of them could be classified as being of 'very good quality', of which very few were from poor countries. This judgement still did not prevent armies of economists from starting to mass-produce equations for growth or inequality, without the slightest warning as to their use. Srinivasan (2001), in common with other equally prestigious authors before him (Fields 1994; and for the OECD countries Atkinson and Brandolini 1999), gives an extremely severe judgement on what he terms 'the industry of analysis by growth regression'.

This problem is far from only affecting household surveys. It has an impact on all statistical information systems in poor countries (national accounts, agriculture, investment, balance of payments, population, etc.).[4] In parallel with the domestic responsibilities of failing states and public administrations, we should not minimise those of the international organisations, whose front rank includes the World Bank, and more marginally the UNDP (with regard to poverty). By publishing international databases[5] premised on information that is often deficient or even absurd, these institutions, together with certain well-respected researchers, perform a legitimising function that relieves users of the need for vigilance and encourages all kinds of abuse. This damaging logic was brilliantly demonstrated in an article by J.-D. Naudet (2000d).

Does this mean that it is better, rather than gaily publishing incorrect figures, to publish nothing at all? Such a position is clearly untenable. But it must be recognised that the definition of policy depends on the quality of the analysis provided, which itself already depends on the reliability of the information used to produce it. The stakes are high – the fortunes of entire populations, among the poorest in the world, depend on this. We must stop pretending to know what we do not, and redirect our efforts towards the raw information. The thankless and overlooked work of the statisticians must be given its due. The proposals below aim to make a modest contribution to this long-term goal.

A few basic principles for repairing shortcomings and setting up effective systems

The necessary introduction of reliable methods of poverty monitoring, within the framework of new policies and their evaluation, calls for a radical break with past practice. This break must take place in parallel on two closely connected fronts: technically, in terms of the production and analysis of statistics, and institutionally, in order to reinforce the organisations responsible for the economic and social information systems in the countries of the South. The list of recommendations below may seem nothing more than common sense. Experience nonetheless shows that they are not generally adhered to. This catalogue of good practice constitutes a minimum platform to offset the effects produced by the falling standards of quality over the past 15 years. This is especially true given that the new generation of surveys, launched rapidly to finalise the PRSPs, bodes ill for quick improvement in the situation.

Methodology and frequency for ensuring consistency in sequential monitoring indicators

1   In the context of the human and financial resources available locally, and the complexity of the measurement, it is unreasonable to base the statistical methods for annual monitoring on weighty budget/consumption, LSMS or living conditions surveys. Priority surveys must be vetoed, if the desire is to measure household consumption correctly. The myth of the 'light survey' into consumption has lasted a long time.

2   So precise monitoring of monetary poverty should only be undertaken on the basis of a frequency of more than a year (every five years for example). It can only be derived from surveys which adequately encompass consumption and/or income, both on average *and* from the point of view of dispersion, based on a methodology which remains constant with time. In particular, the use of two different types of survey to measure the same phenomenon (Integral/Priority surveys to measure consumption, for example) is not relevant and causes confusion.

3   For analytical reasons (employment is the main source of household income, especially in poor households) and practical reasons, employment surveys are the best candidate to become the central pillar of household survey methods. To this reference framework, which provides intermediate indicators about the fight against poverty, can be added thematic modules which would change from survey to survey.

4   Furthermore, the introduction of a permanent household survey arrangement should be carried out gradually and continuously. Initially, this might involve limited geographical coverage, enlarging with time as the survey process is mastered.

5   In any case, 'blitz' operations that are not part of the NSOs' fundamental work programmes, corresponding only to the diverging concerns of their various donors, and whose main effect is to undermine local institutions, must be abandoned.

Fieldwork and procedures for ensuring data quality

1   The emphasis must be placed on early checking of the raw data, without waiting for the data entry stage to try to correct the most conspicuous errors.

2   Official nomenclatures must be drawn up and applied uniformly to all surveys referring to the information. They must at least cover the socio-demographic description of households and individuals as well as their economic activities (branch, sector, product, profession, employment status, etc.).

3   All surveys must be accompanied by methodological and financial documents stating objectives, the progress of data collection, the problems encountered, cleaning up and correction procedures used, as well as the main concepts/definitions and layouts of the files. Questions of organisation and costs must also be covered here. This condition is essential to consolidate two basic functions: critical judgement of the information content and capitalising on knowledge processes.

4   All of these principles weigh in favour of the adoption of quality charters or standards (with, why not, certified ISO-type standards for surveys[6]), taking inspiration from international experience in the field. Indeed, once the results are produced, nothing looks so much like a survey as another survey. Nonetheless, they are not all of equal worth. It must be possible to rank two operations, using objective criteria, according to the reliability of the data produced. This direction would enable the institution of a motivation/sanction system encouraging improvements in quality, which is currently totally lacking.

Institutional reinforcement to ensure the permanence of the system

1   The need of capacity building to replace the lost technical capacity within the NSOs is inescapable. Providing external funding will not be enough to ensure the quality of operations. Underestimating the problem of local statistical skills has led to the failure of numerous recent surveys, especially in terms of quality. The solution adopted for the DHS surveys (the whole system at the international level has been taken over by the private consulting firm Macro International Inc.), although it has led to usable high-quality end products, is not satisfactory from the point of view of independence and control for the national teams.

2   In constituting an effective system, there will be an ongoing need for an element of significant and sustained technical assistance,[7] until the necessary skills in quality standards and analysis techniques have been totally internalised.

3   On a wider scale, the stable employment of qualified managers within

the NSOs will mean facing head-on the structural problems from which they suffer: head-hunting of human resources by more prestigious institutions, lack of recruitment of young graduates, salary questions, mobility, career management, continued training, etc.

4   In addition, strong pressure needs to be exerted so that poor countries' governments release extra resources from national budgets for the statistical system.

5   Finally, integrated medium-term planning is needed to coordinate the donors' support to the NSOs.

Making the most of the data to ensure the social and democratic function of access to the information

1   It would be advisable to have the data analysed systematically by independent, professional experts, in order to offset the conflict of interests between producers and users of the statistics.

2   We need to support the creation of centres of analysis by national experts, within and outside the NSOs. In particular, the restriction of the NSOs' activities to statistical production should be combated, in favour of greater integration between data collection and analysis.

3   The unequal division of work between statistical production in the South and economic analysis in the North must be avoided. A balance needs to be found between the accessibility of the data (which should be considered as a public good) to national and international researchers and achieving a return on local investments in information production. It should be required that knowledge be transferred to the NSOs by users of the data outside the institutions.

4   The organisation of debates on the results of surveys within the countries should be systematically promoted. Efforts should be made to inform and communicate through local media in order to increase social demand for surveys and analyses of poverty.

5   On a wider theme, setting up statistical instruments for measurement and monitoring cannot be an end in itself: the figures and analyses provided by these instruments must be used. The communication of the information gathered by the statistical administration to society at large in all developing countries should be encouraged. Recent years have seen growing demand from groups in society for quantitative information, which would give them a better knowledge of the economic and social situation and enable them to measure better the results of their leaders' policies. In emerging democracies the demand for concrete results is all the more urgent and populations are waiting for answers from their governments. It is now widely recognised that poverty in developing countries can only be fought successfully if the societies and governments within the countries – and not only the aid agencies – mobilise their efforts to this end. Wide

dissemination of existing information on the state and evolution of poverty would seem to be an element that could encourage such a mobilisation within society. It also gives reason to hope that, under the pressure of informed public opinion, the governments of these countries will fully acknowledge their responsibilities in this area.

Conclusion

Arrangements for measuring poverty are coming to play a crucial part in drafting, monitoring and evaluating new international development policies. But it is clear that the poverty monitoring tools in poor countries, and indeed the statistical information systems in general, show such deficiencies that they are unlikely to be effective in fulfilling the role they have been assigned. The situation is so catastrophic that an internationally recognised expert has been led to wonder whether 'today, the first priority is not the fight ... against the poverty of existing information systems' (Cour 2001). In this context, it is far from certain that the proliferation of surveys has made (or is leading towards) any progress in our knowledge about the question. Paradoxically, this phenomenon is least known in precisely those countries that are most affected by poverty.

The full scope of this problem has not yet been understood by either national or international institutions. The diagnosis given here is certainly fragmented, and it would be appropriate to proceed to a deeper and more systematic evaluation of the comparative performances of existing systems. But beyond the nuances that would probably be revealed by such an exercise, according to different fields of application and different countries, it is reasonable to think that it would only confirm our conclusions. Rather than just sounding the alarm, we propose a certain number of concrete approaches to how to remedy this state of affairs. However, if the recommended solutions have to be able to meet with relative consensus regarding their form, and not exceed the financial and human resources available, particularly in countries benefiting from the HIPC Initiative, we remain sceptical as to the political will to implement them, on the part of both public authorities and donors, due to the extent to which they represent a break with past and current practice. In any case, they require that the rehabilitation of the public administrations, and in this case the NSOs, be embraced, and that the official line of 'better government' no longer serves as a disguise for the old refrain of 'less government'.

Notes

1 This phenomenon is not limited to Madagascar, as shown by Srinivasan (2001) for India or Naudet (2000d) for 13 African countries. In this connection, it should be emphasised that the reliability of the national accounts is equally uncertain.

2   A simple comparison between the publications taken from the generation of surveys undertaken following independence during the 1960s (for French-speaking Africa among other countries), with a high level of technical assistance, and those available today, is enough to remove any doubt on this question. Among other things, this demonstrates that the current deficiencies are not the result of structural problems linked to insuperable difficulties in grasping the activities, consumption and behaviour of African households, but rather are the direct consequence of several decades of budgetary adjustment and institutional decline in African public administrations.

3   Apart from the fact that household surveys by their nature can only provide very imperfect measures of inequality (problems of distribution queues, individual dispersion, etc.), the absence of documentation on surveys in many developing countries considerably limits any diagnosis we could make about their quality and reliability. Only a return to the raw data would enable us to make a solid judgement as to sampling and measurement errors, but such an undertaking would seem unrealistic.

4   See Deaton (1995) for a summary of quality issues relating to data in developing countries.

5   We have mentioned Deininger and Squire's database on inequalities, but the criticism applies equally to Summers and Heston's on GDP in PPP, or the World Bank's or IMF's on GDP series and the principal aggregates of national accounts.

6   This kind of approach has been successfully undertaken by the National Statistical Office of Colombia (DANE). DANE put in place a quality management system, obtaining its certification by the norm ISO 9001-2000 in July 2002. This guarantees the quality of the whole process (from conception to dissemination of results) for its main periodic statistics: the Consumption Price Index, the Continuous Household Survey, the Census of Dwellings, the Monthly Industrial Survey, the Monthly Retail Sales Survey, the Construction Cost Index, the statistics of Foreign Trade.

7   It should be emphasised that the breed of international statistical specialists with real experience of operations in Africa is in danger of extinction. Where are the successors to Ch. Scott in survey planning, P. François and D. Blaizeau for household surveys and M. Séruzier for national accounts? In French-speaking Africa, the redirection of the French statistical office's (INSEE) co-operation policy towards Eastern Europe has led to a depletion of skills. In this unpromising context, the creation of AFRISTAT in 1996 for the countries in the Franc zone constitutes a notable exception.

12 The different approaches to measuring poverty in Europe
What lessons for the LDCs?

Daniel Verger

Talking about statistics in connection with poverty can often provoke reactions of rejection: investing in constructing a means of observing poverty or exclusion would be a waste of resources, which would be better spent on relieving hardship. However, providing effective help for people in difficulty, and directing aid initially towards those who need it the most, requires that we can identify them and know the specific nature of their behaviour. This is exactly what we would expect from a statistical system. But do existing systems currently provide information that is relevant for this purpose? In a 'rich' country, statistical knowledge of populations in difficulty, although in constant progression, still leaves significant areas in shadow. In a 'poor' country, one of the 'least-developed countries' (LDCs),[1] with a less comprehensive statistical system, is it possible to imagine an affordable system that could give useful information on the populations facing the greatest hardship, the 'poorest of the poor'? It is clearly out of the question to suggest a system along French lines, but it is much more reasonable to review the experience of measuring poverty in European countries to see what lessons might be learned for the development of a system that would be appropriate for the LDCs: which basic concepts should be adopted? What are the pitfalls to be avoided?

We shall therefore attempt to assess the current state of knowledge about disadvantaged populations in a country like France: can we define them, count them or describe them? What problems do we face? Which of them, being ignored in Europe as leading to relatively minor failings, must imperatively be corrected in the case of the LDCs, given the specific characteristics of the societies concerned?

This chapter calls upon the author's experience in this field, as specialist of household surveys at the French Statistical Office (Institut National de la Statistique et des Etudes Economiques, or INSEE). Numerous references are made throughout this chapter to a special issue of the review *Economie et Statistique* devoted to measuring poverty, of which the author was one of the editors (Herpin and Verger 1997a).

The elusive definition of poverty

The first thing that strikes one on looking through the literature on poverty is the absence of a definition: neither sociologists nor economists give a precise definition which would enable quantification; and when an organisation such as the European Council takes the risk of suggesting one, it does not seem workable, and what is more it seems to contradict the methods of European statisticians. According to this definition, dating from 1984, the following should be classified as poor: 'people whose resources (material, cultural or social) are so scarce that they are excluded from the minimum acceptable lifestyles of the member state in which they live'. The link with the European habit of adopting half of the median income per unit of consumption as the poverty threshold seems tenuous at the very least! Nevertheless, this definition offers several principles whose relevance we shall develop, and which will underlie several aspects of our approach.

This lack of definitions reflects the many problems that the analysis of poverty is still confronted with, both in conceptual terms and in terms of measurement: disputes as to the numbers of the poor, or their socio-demographic characteristics, are far from being resolved. These disputes are not just theoretical quibbles between experts: different approaches lead to significant differences in numbers of people living in poverty – the variations can easily amount to several hundred thousand people – and the profile of the populations affected is not the same either. As the variations concern the number of large or single-parent families in particular, we can see that the definition of the corrective policies to be implemented would benefit from approaches that are better defined and better measured, or even more diversified. For example, even for the recent period in France, the INSEE has shown that only slight variations in the values of a few parameters can change the poverty rate among single-parent families from 22 per cent to 26.5 per cent (or from 10.7 per cent to 19.2 per cent for couples with three or more children) and that evaluations of the number of poor people can range from 6.9 to 8.5 million (Hourriez and Olier 1997). The range would be even wider if we considered all the possible definitions of poverty. We are plainly still a long way from being able to publish a 'rubber-stamped' evaluation of the numbers of poor people! Recent speculation seems rather to indicate that the search for a single measure of poverty resembles a fruitless quest for the Holy Grail. Without knowing exactly how many independent dimensions would have to be taken into account to grasp the problem fully, we can be sure that no single concept or evaluation could be enough.

In the special issue of *Economie et Statistique* mentioned above, an effort was made to clarify the concepts. A first, fundamental divergence in approaches to poverty pits the concepts of the absolute and relative nature of poverty against each other. Within each broad family, further varying schools can be distinguished, from those that define poverty based on income to those that prefer a measurement based on consumption, via those for whom it is essentially the inability to ensure a balanced budget.

Absolute versus relative poverty

Absolute approaches reign in the United States, in certain English-speaking countries such as Australia, and in certain Eastern European countries. The details of their concrete implementations may vary, but the general principle is as follows: a norm of consumption establishes the fundamental needs of a given society at a given time[2] – number of calories of food, articles of clothing, rooms in housing – and the poor are considered to be those who cannot achieve this level of consumption even at the lowest market prices. This kind of definition is certainly close to an instinctive representation (the 'poor' do not have enough to feed, clothe and house themselves), but it requires that we accept the risk of ethnocentric bias, since we decide, and not the individuals themselves, what it is important for them to have, and that we suppose the same norms are universally shared.

Western European countries do not accept this approach, and define poverty as being a lower standard of living than that experienced by the majority of the population. In this form, as a simple measure of inequality, relative poverty affects households with a standard of living that is below a certain threshold, a certain percentage of a so-called 'normal' standard. The arbitrariness is still present, although it has changed its form. It now stems from the chosen measure of living standards, the choice of the central value supposed to represent 'normality', and the choice of the thresholds: do we take monetary income per head – or more precisely per unit of consumption – as an indicator, or do we refer to a wider notion of resources? Where do we fix the threshold? At half, 40 per cent or 60 per cent of the central value? For the central value, do we take the mean or the median?

Moreover, the relative nature of the concept makes its interpretation a delicate business. Many misunderstandings remain. How many readers understand that if everybody's income doubled, the rate of poverty would remain unchanged, and that if everybody's income increased, poverty can also increase if incomes increase more slowly at the bottom of the distribution than at the top? Paradoxes such as these, which are in fact the logical consequences of the adopted definition, do not arise with absolute measures. Even if the norm evolves with growth, this evolution is slow, no doubt behind average movements in consumption, and at best concomitant with them: when everybody's income increases, the rate of poverty should not increase. This seems to be a desirable property. Society would have to have an extreme degree of aversion to inequality to believe that the situation has worsened when incomes have risen universally, albeit at the price of a slight increase in inequality or relative poverty.

The relative poverty threshold is usually higher than the absolute poverty threshold, implying that relative poverty is a wider notion than that of absolute poverty. In fact this is how it was developed, at a period when economic growth gave reason to hope that absolute poverty could be quickly and completely eradicated in the developed countries. But actually this is far from inevitable: in certain countries, where the distribution of income is highly concentrated, the relative threshold may be below the absolute threshold.

In current international conferences on these subjects, a trend seems to be emerging towards the combined use of indicators from both of these two families.

Certainly, in the case of the LDCs, the concept of relative poverty is of limited interest. Given the average standard of living of the whole population, the issue is to identify those whose resources enable only imperfect provision of the 'vital' functions: the problem is one of survival, not of inequality. The system to be introduced must aim to measure a concept of absolute poverty appropriate to the current state of the societies concerned. The definition of a minimum 'basket of goods' could not be decreed by statisticians. We will come back to this later when discussing approaches based on living conditions, but we can say now that this is a political decision. The issue is to define for each country what its citizens are collectively prepared to accept as the minimum that should be guaranteed to each inhabitant by a social policy. This phase is obviously very sensitive: it must respect the specific culture of the society, without automatically justifying all the deprivation that occurs; but it must remain realistic as to the degree of development achieved – otherwise the analyses that are carried out will be of no use in guiding possible corrective policies. Each country must define its priorities and list the fundamental goods and values which, when lacking, would indicate a state of poverty. The most revealing indication of the difficulty of such deliberations must be that international organisations, rather than embarking on them for their studies covering several countries, define poverty using a fixed threshold income of one dollar per person per day (or thereabouts), corrected by purchasing power parities (PPP). This solution is obviously full of faults, but it has the merits of simplicity and of cutting short any criticism of the necessarily arbitrary choices involved in an absolute method adapted to the country's situation (Ponty 1998). Nevertheless, we must continue to make progress along a less systematic route, although it is strewn with pitfalls. The general reflections such as Sen's can provide an indispensable guide to a quality approach.

If we had to create such a measure in France (which would be desirable, moreover), we can be sure that discussions would be bitter. Are the French ready to acknowledge that we should help everyone to achieve a certain level of leisure consumption, and, if so, what sort? How many visits to the cinema? How many days' holiday at the seaside or in the mountains? Several experimental studies seem to suggest that the minimum allocation that we define for others is less generous than the one we define for ourselves!

Approaches based on income, consumption or a balanced budget?[3]

A second important choice facing the statistician or sociologist who wishes to describe poverty relates to the choice of the quantity to be used to sort households, which will enable those at the bottom of the scale – the 'poor' – to be distinguished from the others. The choice of monetary income is usual, but not as natural as one might think (Fleurbaey *et al.* 1997). In fact, we could choose to place the observation at several levels along the long river linking causes or opportunities with results: by favouring income we position ourselves upstream, while if we take consumption as a basis we are further downstream, closer to the consequences. The income-based approach may enable a less-distorted view of what is really important, and indicate whether populations in difficulty can feed themselves well enough to conserve their health capital, house themselves and keep warm, all *minima* which are defined in terms of quantities consumed. Before making a detailed assessment of the advantages and limitations of these various types of approach, it should be re-emphasised that the consequences of the socio-demographic choice for the populations identified as poor are significant. Lollivier and Verger (1997) investigated and compared three alternative choices, based on the 'European Community Household Panel': the approaches taken by researchers focusing on monetary income, researchers favouring the observation of living conditions and consumption, and researchers preferring to study difficulties in 'getting by' or 'staying in the black' as declared by the households themselves. They showed how the poor populations revealed by these methods are linked and to what extent they can be unconnected.[4] If we isolate the tenth of the population with the lowest financial resources, the tenth with the worst living conditions, and the tenth that finds it hardest to remain within their budget, we obtain three sub-populations with little in common: only 2 per cent belong to all three sub-groups, while 25 per cent belong to at least one of the three. The three dimensions seem conceptually non-equivalent, each illustrating important aspects of reality but leaving out others, leading to the necessity of observing all of them to determine the extent to which the various symptoms accumulate. (Razafindrakoto and Roubaud arrive at a similar conclusion in the case of Madagascar; see Chapter 4.)

This confirmation of the existence of significant differences between the population of the poor in the monetary sense and the population suffering from a low standard of living is in the end an element that can be contributed to a more general, recurring and sometimes quite bitter debate, opposing the advocates of an approach to poverty based on resources against those who think it preferable to define it as shortages in terms of consumption, proving its concrete effects.

Monetary approaches to poverty: is instantaneous monetary income a good indicator?

In a society such as contemporary Western society, where the market governs almost all trade, a low level of monetary income appears a natural choice as the central indicator to be taken into account if we wish to define poverty as lack of resources. However, the limits of this indicator are apparent, whether they stem from conceptual inadequacies or from problems of observation quality.

From measurement errors . . .

In France, monetary incomes are known both through household surveys and through tax sources, complemented by references to tables for resources that are not declared because they are not taxable. In both types of sources, the extremes of the distribution are less apparent than the centre. From forgetting occasional income, or the resources of certain members of the household – older children or grandparents (for example) living at the same address – to forgetting or hiding certain income seen as embarrassing or coming from more or less illicit activities (black-market work, drug dealing, prostitution, etc.), the sources of imperfection in answers to surveys are many.[5] Finally, it should be emphasised that the instability of the job market, which is often the source of poverty, does not improve the quality of income declaration, regardless of efforts at underestimation. When several casual jobs follow each other, with different earnings from one to another, and different lengths of time spent in the job, it is particularly difficult to produce a precise estimate, and the declared income for the month of reference is likely to be the lowest guaranteed monthly income. The problem of rounding – to multiples of 10 or 100 euros (the nearest or the lower we cannot know, but we can lean towards the latter) – is negligible for high incomes but becomes significant for lower pay – 100 euros is equivalent to one-tenth of the French minimum wage! As for errors between euros and cents (or former national currencies), or conversion errors between monthly and annual estimates, these are rarer but not unheard of. Observing income trends from the 'European Community Household Panel', before cleaning up the data, we can see multiplications (or divisions) by ten or more, although the person declares that his or her income has not changed between the two visits!

Measuring income is particularly difficult in the case of the self-employed, especially for those with lower revenues, who use *forfait fiscal* or lump-sum tax arrangements. For a self-employed worker, the notion of income has little meaning, and the division between money used to maintain or develop the tools of the trade and that withdrawn for private consumption is a particularly arduous distinction to draw. The correct measurement of self-employed income, on a basis which would enable comparison with employees, is a challenge for statisticians worldwide that has not as yet been resolved. In the LDCs there are many small self-employed concerns, especially in the informal sector, for which difficulties of observation accumulate: variable resources, absence of separation between the professional and private spheres (and all the more so, given crude accounting and tax regulations).

Even the exact definition of so-called disposable income is subject to debate. About a dozen possible definitions have been proposed, according to whether or not we include social security contributions (employers' or employees'), whether we take figures before or after tax and rates, and whether or not we include help from other households (from alimony received from an ex-partner to the pocket money a student receives occasionally from his parents). For some, these last elements are resources in the same way as other types of income; for others, the absence of a contractual nature distinguishes them and means they should not be aggregated. It is tempting not to take them into account, because these sums are difficult to observe. But this leads to paradoxes. For example, students whose executive parents provide them with a town-centre flat would be seen as poorer than the young working-class unemployed who cannot leave the parental home for lack of resources. For correct measurements of poverty among the young, it is essential to integrate parental support. Without specific questioning, it is very likely that help received is frequently omitted from surveys; and tax sources only bring to light certain such payments and could not guarantee exhaustive data.

In the years to come, the current definition of 'household' – defined as a group of people sharing the same accommodation – should certainly also be revised, preferring a notion of 'life unit' closer to a behavioural collective – defined as a group of people who share resources and draw on the same budget. This would modify the profile of poor populations, especially among the young.

All these measurement errors have an impact on results. An error-correction procedure reduces by 1.5 points the poverty rate as measured by a cross-section survey (INSEE 1998).

... to conceptual limits

Independently of the problems of income observability, the use of monetary income as the only indicator of poverty raises several points of a more conceptual nature. The first relates to the more or less 'instantaneous' nature of the quantity chosen: the period over which income is measured is the result of a choice; income is currently collected on either a monthly or a yearly basis. But neither of these windows of observation was chosen for theoretical reasons. Social workers, insisting on the difficulties experienced by disadvantaged populations trying to plan their budgets over even a short period and facing late income payments, emphasise the importance of measuring fluctuations in resources over very short periods; this makes them reject the yearly or even monthly framework as too long. On the contrary, economists are anxious to take into account the possibilities of transferring resources from one period to another using the financial market; for this reason, they emphasise that these same periods are too short. The whole life cycle, or a shorter period of a few years, would be more appropriate, and 'permanent income' should be preferred to instantaneous income. The two viewpoints are not necessarily incompatible, and it would seem in fact that a consensus is emerging that poverty is a lack of resources which needs to be examined on average over three or four years. As the saying goes: 'one poor harvest is not enough to make a poor farmer'.

A second problem arises in the case of inconsistency between several types of resources – for example, between income and wealth, as can happen with the self-employed. So how can poverty be defined? An elderly self-employed person, whose turnover is in decline and who is soon to retire, may have a low income but significant wealth in the form of the tools of his trade. Does this mean that he is not poor? Should an elderly widow with a small reversion pension but who either owns her main residence outright or holds it in usufruct therefore lose her right to benefits? Should the right to a pension not be taken into account, whether or not it is considered part of a person's wealth? The question thus arises as to the relevance of enlarging the notion of simple monetary income to cover wider resources, including for example the user value of assets. This question is mainly posed in the following form: should the situation of a person's resources be understood to represent income extended to a certain number of resources such as imputed rent, the value of the use of property by an owner-occupier. An affirmative response would be enough to lift a whole class of propertied elderly people out of the poverty category, but it is far from certain that this position is the correct one. Including an imputed rent does not only affect owner-occupiers: the same type of econometric inclusion would have to be made to quantify the advantage represented by the provision of housing free of charge (the 'benefits in kind' granted by certain employers, parents paying their children's rent during their studies, or, equivalently, lending a flat, etc.). In these cases, although the mechanics of the inclusion present the same difficulties, its indispensability becomes much clearer.

As soon as we realise that monetary income is not enough to describe the real level of resources, we must guard against introducing bias, distorting the comparison between different types of households, by making certain inclusions and not others. Imputed rent is not the only element that needs to be included: while the user value of assets associated with owning – or having the right to use free of charge – consumer durables such as a car would not have much effect on the level of resources, other elements could prove more significant, and primary among these is 'domestic production', or all the goods or services that we produce ourselves in our non-professional daily activities. Although only a minority of households in France now produce their own food, with the decline of the farming population, the value of carpentry, decorating and other domestic work remains, or perhaps is becoming, significant. However, these supplements do not seem to enlarge the resources of the most disadvantaged (Degenne *et al.* 1997). This element is described by certain sociologists as contributing to the 'culture of poverty', but it is no longer central to the approach to poverty in Europe. It remains entirely relevant in dealing with poverty in least-developed countries, or even in France's territories overseas, where it would be a serious mistake to overlook non-monetary supplements to resources (Attias-Donfut and Lapierre 1997). Knowing how to prepare raw foodstuffs from the garden, or obtained by fishing, hunting or gathering, is only one aspect of this culture of poverty.

In the case of the LDCs, taking into account domestic production is of primary importance, especially, but not exclusively, in rural areas. We might even claim that actual monetary income has only a minor role in the domestic economics of these countries. Basing our methodology on income is simply out of the question in this case (although this does not mean that a measure of income should not be included in surveys[6]).

Other elements draw attention to a different kind of resource, which should be given its proper value to obtain a correct evaluation of 'extended resources' – that of social capital. Individuals who remain integrated into a dense and active network of relationships, familial or not, can obtain a level of services to which their lack of purely monetary resources would prohibit access, in terms of loans, insurance, etc. This dimension, still relevant within contemporary developed societies, has not yet been sufficiently observed. With the growth in prevalence of 'reconstituted' families, the nature and volume of this social network tend to change: in observing child poverty, it is essential to take the family network into account. The situation of children brought up in single-parent families is undoubtedly currently presented as being more difficult than it is due to such resources being overlooked. For the LDCs, observing this network is an essential part of measurement methods. Attias-Donfut and Lapierre transposed the questions from the 'Three Generations survey' they had set up in metropolitan France to Guadeloupe. The aim was to observe families with three surviving generations (grandparents, parents and children), each generation being questioned directly. Although this type of survey is costly and relatively difficult to implement, it gives valuable, previously unseen information. It is certainly out of the question to imagine such an operation in an LDC; nevertheless the results obtained by Attias-Donfut and Lapierre for Guadeloupe are partially transposable (with the proviso that anything dealing with the consequences of introducing a European-style welfare state must be adapted to take into account what could happen if such measures were introduced in the country being studied), and show the importance of correctly measuring informal flows, mutual gifts, exchanges of services between neighbours and family members. An ethnographic study of the society in question should be used to describe practices, which statistics will then measure. This would also enable the concept of 'household' to be defined appropriately: the two problems likely to arise differently in different countries relate to polygamy and the degree of cohabitation between generations. The definition of the household will be particularly sensitive when polygamy means the man residing successively in the houses of his different wives, without having a single 'home': surveys of consumption will be even more difficult in this context (underreporting the man's spending, or conversely double accounts, etc.).

On the other hand, another limitation of monetary approaches, the failure to take into account the value of using free public services (education, health, security, etc.), has less impact in the case of LDCs, where these public services have generally a much lesser presence, than in the case of Europe with its well-developed welfare state. We therefore propose not to concern ourselves with this for the moment.[7]

The role of wealth, though, is less easily ignored: the shock of a fall in income can be better dealt with and will be less likely to trigger a vicious circle hurling a household into poverty if the household is well-equipped and able to 'get by'. Attias-Donfut and Lapierre, describing interviews that they have carried out, emphasise cases where the household has declared that owning their house enabled them to survive ill fortune, such as losing a job, better than others. Conversely, problems related to debt are often the origin of the vicious circle leading a household from difficulty to destitution.

Measuring consumption: a tempting alternative?

For advocates of the consumption approach to poverty, the use of income is disqualified by conceptual limitations and by problems concerning the reliability of observations that we have just described. The consumption approach wins out in both areas.

Except for a miser, income is not in itself useful; it is so only indirectly, by what it enables one to acquire, today or tomorrow, and it is the consumption of goods and services that determines the level of well-being. Imagine two households of the same composition, facing different price systems – one can achieve a higher standard of living even though their incomes are identical. In a centralised country such as France, with a dense, efficient communications network, we might think that geographical variations in price are negligible, and that differences in income should directly represent differences in standard of living. But although this argument is true on average, it is weaker at the detailed microeconomic level, and it would seem that differences in price actually applying to neighbouring households are not unusual. Unlike better-off households, disadvantaged populations might not have access to the cheapest varieties of goods on the market: a lower rate of car usage can prevent them from shopping in the most competitive hypermarkets; day-to-day budget management does not always allow them to take advantage of the best bargains, which are often linked to purchases in large quantities or at specific times. Unless we can measure price differentials in detail, population layer by population layer, we would make less errors by focusing on the quantities actually consumed rather than just on capacity to buy. However, this problem remains marginal in a country like France, and should not disqualify an income-based approach. In the LDCs, the phenomenon takes on a totally different scale. Although the causes we have just mentioned become negligible, the frequent variations in price from one region to another, made possible by difficulties in transport and communications between areas or even villages, are essential, and cause differences of such significance that they cannot be overlooked, even in a first approximation, or even with an income-based approach. In a LDC, prices generally need to be deflated by the local pricing level in order to obtain anything interpretable for a study on poverty.

Consumption also tends to be smoother than income, with households trying to avoid jumps in spending with the problems they can cause. Consumption is a directly available indicator of permanent income, so relevant for economists but so difficult to calculate. All these advantages, according to the advocates of this approach, make consumption the best indicator of material well-being.

Sensitive ethical questions remain

In fact, all these arguments can be turned around. In the presence of uncertainty, everyone needs to have savings to fall back on and the usefulness of an altruist depends on what he can give to those around him. Consumption is powerless to take account of these aspects, unlike income. Should someone with pronounced ascetic tendencies, who chooses not to consume but instead to hoard his income or to distribute it through acts of charity, be deemed poor and therefore helped, or not? Taking into account the variety of individual tastes, which gives rise to so much debate when determining absolute thresholds, certainly poses more problems in consumption-based approaches than in income-based approaches. When classifying households, should total consumption be considered, including 'harmful' consumption (drugs, alcohol, tobacco, etc.), or only spending for consumption deemed 'normal', 'basic', or 'fundamental'? In the variant of consumption-based approaches which considers living conditions, mentioned above, it is usual only to consider an absence of consumption or goods as a sign of deprivation contributing to the emergence of poor living conditions in the case of elements that are widespread in the majority of the population (control by frequency) and that are judged to be, if not indispensable, at least important for the majority (control by consensus): not being able to consume tobacco because of lack of money would doubtless not be an indicator in this context in Europe at the beginning of the twenty-first century!

Although sources of information exist about levels of equipment or even the percentage of people who do not have enough money to be able to buy a particular item regularly, there are currently none enabling us to describe a normal state or to define scientifically the so-called basic consumption contour for our times in our societies. This is an echo of the difficulty of determining an absolute poverty threshold, and defining what is seen by society as a set of basic needs is another significant challenge for a statistical system. The Universal Declaration of Human Rights defines the major freedoms that must be guaranteed, but there is nothing of this kind to delimit the level of consumption which should – or could – be considered the minimum to be ensured for all. The literature on economic theories of justice is rich in more or less paradoxical examples of the difficulties faced in trying to base the principles of redistribution on individual utility (Fleurbaey 1995).

The trend is more and more to reject the consideration of utility for all aspects of individual choice. Certain decisions must remain private or even intimate, and the policy of transfer should only ensure a certain equalisation in terms of achievements deemed to be fundamental, such as the right to maintain one's health, or to have access to education and training. On the other hand, it is impossible to draw the line at a single domain, such as food or clothing consumption. The approach must be sufficiently global to be able to avoid equating poverty with absence of aspiration in the chosen sub-domain. So poverty in terms of living conditions cannot be correctly defined without the use of a large number of different indicators covering a wide spectrum of consumption, in order to reduce the effects of certain deliberately chosen lacks (rejection of television in certain intellectual strata, vegetarianism, etc.). Consumption can therefore only be a correct approach to observing poverty if we know how to avoid these two opposite dangers; it must cover a wide area, but still be reduced to certain aspects, whose definition represents the social norm. Once again, the statistician finds himself faced with the recurrent problem that we have already mentioned, which no approach can avoid: the definition of poverty is a political act, which cannot rest solely on scientific considerations.

Difficulties in observing consumption

It is not necessarily simpler to observe consumption than income. It is true that the French consider any question about their income to be indiscreet, to the extent that it has been described as a taboo subject – and that until the 1980s the INSEE studied standards of living by looking at socio-professional categories, made up of professions, levels in the hierarchy, statuses (self-employed or employee) or activity sectors – while no such comment has been made about consumption. But people's supposed willingness to be questioned about consumption is not enough to guarantee the quality of the measurements.

The first point that should be emphasised is that no general consumption survey currently exists in France; the 'Family Budget surveys' are concerned with spending on consumption. The differences are significant. It is possible to consume without spending, as it is symmetrically possible to spend without consuming. Here we find the counterpart of the problem mentioned when discussing the relevance of monetary approaches, which involves domestic production or the consumption of free public services: the 'Family Budget surveys' now include an evaluation of home-grown or self-supplied food products (grown in the garden, or removed from stock by a trader for his own use), but this is a long way from covering all free consumption. Moreover, the survey does not pick up transactions in kind between households. Purchase and consumption are not equivalent: we might make purchases for people outside the household, or even lose what we have bought by keeping it badly, etc. Finally, the surveys do not require that spending be broken down into a price and a quantity. We therefore have little information on the quantity/price ratio that has been achieved. As budget surveys are not true consumption surveys, their data are insufficient for poverty measurement. What is more, even as data on spending the surveys cannot avoid certain problems of quality.

The effects of memory, as to either the nature, value or date of purchases, are such that where consumption is concerned we cannot rely on simple retrospective interviews. All consumption surveys are primarily based on a system of observation using diaries, in which the household records its spending on consumption every day; due to the scale of this task, the length of the study has to be limited. Attempts at surveys that aim to measure consumption over long periods have all ended in failure, and current surveys limit the use of diaries to two weeks. Such a system is completely inappropriate for observing data with meaning at the microeconomic level of the household. If the survey is sufficiently wide-ranging, an average derived from the diaries can provide good estimates for the whole country, but will not allow the consumption of a specific household to be reliably reconstructed. For example, if someone buys a set of false teeth during the diary period he will be assumed to have bought 26 in a full year. Aware of this difficulty, the statisticians of consumption have designed hybrid surveys, combining the mechanism for observing spending using a diary with a system of retrospective interviews for spending which would normally be infrequent (home improvements, clothing, buying consumer durables). This diminishes the effect, but without removing it completely: the retrospective questioning only concerns a limited set of big purchases, with the rest being observed through the diary and thus generating the same difficulties (Herpin and Verger 2000). Other effects arise, which also place a strain on the quality of the survey. The household can manipulate the results by their behaviour. A person who wishes to be truthful but does not want to work too hard in filling in his diary may put off certain purchases, while others, reluctant to reveal the low level of their usual spending, may concentrate all their purchases for the month into the two weeks: it can be seen as demeaning to admit to a low level of consumption, in the same way as a person might hesitate to admit to the interviewer that he receives state unemployment benefit.

Finally, it is no easier to measure consumption than income; it is perhaps even more difficult. It is clear that the individual consumption distribution drawn from the surveys into household budgets has very little value at individual level, and could not be used as the basis of an approach to inequality or poverty. The rating attributed to a household using an income classification is very often inconsistent with its place in a classification by level of consumption spending, and we cannot be sure that the latter case is more accurate. Approaches to poverty using spending on consumption in the strict sense have therefore not been developed in France.

If to these difficulties we add the fact that budget surveys are costly (at least three visits) and complex to organise (if we wish to take proper account of seasonal aspects, data collection must be distributed across the year; for diaries to be kept in the case of an illiterate or semi-literate population, interviewers need to provide active assistance), we might hesitate to recommend basing a mechanism for measuring poverty on such an operation, even though certain recent experiences have shown that consumption surveys can be conducted successfully in African countries (Blaizeau 1999).

Observing living conditions

By contrast, the variant which defines poverty by observing living conditions is now in widespread use in France. It has already been tried in Madagascar (Razafindrakoto and Roubaud 2000a) and should be recommended as the basis of the statistical system for observing poverty in the LDCs. The indicators used in France combine shortages in consumption with absences in consumer durables or home comforts. These last items contribute to a considerable change in the register described by the score for quality of living conditions. The past is reintroduced, where pure consumption approaches are only concerned with the present. Equipment and the current level of comfort is a reflection of past spending, although it may also originate from gifts or inheritances. Finally, it also depends on the quality of care devoted to its upkeep. In this way it incorporates a whole 'domestic production' aspect that is neglected elsewhere, conferring a certain conceptual advantage.

In terms of measurement, the data relating to the equipment installed are of satisfactory quality, although it is not easy to observe whether an absent piece of equipment denotes a lack of resources – and should therefore legitimately count as a deficit – or whether it is deliberate. Similarly, as soon as we try to go beyond the stage of reducing the comfort of accommodation to its surface area and the existence of inside toilets and a bath or shower, we enter an area where judgements tend to be subjective. Is the accommodation dark? Is it damp? Are the neighbours noisy? Is the environment polluted? Do you feel safe here? In an operational setting, all of these indicators appear to be measurements of a person's sensitivity to these various problems as much as of the extent to which they are really exposed to them (Lollivier and Verger 1997). This approach is no more free of measurement errors than the others.

Another criticism that could be made of current statistical sources in this area is that the list of items being researched, and deficits examined, has no theoretical basis. The existence of heating is measured, but not the amount of domestic work it requires: heating a house with wood or coal and having an electric central heating system do not involve the same constraints, and yet the two situations are treated together. We know whether the accommodation is large, but not whether it is in a building with a lift. This brings us once again to the debate we have already mentioned, about how to define a minimum living standard of a person's fundamental needs, and much remains to be done before the list of elements needed to construct a score for quality of living conditions provides an appropriate approach to poverty.

The study by Razafindrakoto and Roubaud mentioned above included an initial stage of consideration given to the indicators to use for Madagascar. In order to extend this to various LDCs, it will have to be systematised through detailed observation of lifestyles, taking care that the list of items be appropriate to both urban and rural living; the question of whether a single score will be enough or whether two will be needed, one for urban and one for rural populations, will have to be analysed.

Recent work on Albania (Hazizaj and Misha 2000) has shown the inadequacy of the available source, which does not provide enough relevant indicators: the research covered the possession of certain items of equipment (which was of little use in areas without electricity), cars or tractors (in mountainous areas without roads), while ignoring the possession of livestock or a donkey cart, the only things likely to give information about the degree of comfort and social status of a traditional rural household.

The comprehensiveness and relevance of this list are crucial elements for the quality of the mechanism to be set up. The list may differ slightly from one country to another in order to take account of cultural details.

'Subjective' poverty: how to interpret difficulties in making ends meet

The third dimension that we have mentioned involves the subjective approach to poverty: a person is poor if he cannot make ends meet at the end of the month on his income, and considers that he needs more resources to live, or even survive.

The distinctive conceptual feature of this approach is to avoid any external normative judgement, and to take the household's own perceptions as the sole basis for defining its needs, ultimately placing a radical level of value on its own individual preferences, with the advantages and disadvantages we have already mentioned (Gardes and Loisy 1997).

Measurement problems are once again significant in this area. The exact wording of questions has a strong impact on responses and, in many countries, certain questions can bring out problems to balance the household budget at the end of the month for a large section of the population (70 per cent or even 80 per cent of the population): there is no doubt about the difficulties, but genuine poverty is less certain. Although such approaches have been used on their own to define poverty thresholds (the so-called Leyden approach), it would seem that they should only be used in combination with other approaches within a multidimensional framework.

What is measured in this way seems to have more to do with the difference between aspiration and reality (in countries in transition, political change has given birth to hopes that may take time to realise), or even a certain specific philosophy of life. Someone who believes that we should be content with what we have will never be 'subjectively' poor, while with those who are culturally conditioned always to see what is wrong the opposite will be observed.

This makes it difficult to use raw indicators. Several solutions have been explored. The Leyden method comes down to only using responses from people in the area under consideration to define the poverty threshold, since asking a billionaire about the minimum needed to live leads to estimates with little relevance. Lollivier and Verger (1997) have instead opted for a scoring method which, as in the living conditions approach, brings together various elements relating to difficulties in getting by at the end of the month, whether this be subjective declarations such as those we have just mentioned, or more objective indicators like the inability to pay electricity bills, rent or service charges. The combined indicator thus obtained is certainly more robust than the individual elementary indicators, since the more items are taken into account, the more each one's individual weaknesses are compensated for. Moreover, the 'subjective' poverty defined by this score should be renamed: defined in this way, the new face of poverty revealed by problems in balancing the budget is just as objective as the others!

For LDCs, questions such as these should play a part in any poverty survey, but great care needs to be taken in testing the wording of the questions, and especially the translations into the languages or dialects used by any sub-populations there may be.

Conclusion

The required statistical methods for measuring poverty could therefore take the form of a survey somewhat similar to the French 'Permanent Living Conditions Survey', which collects the information needed for the construction of social indicators. The survey would be conducted regularly, without the use of a consumption diary, listing a large number of elements of living conditions – equipment, accommodation – with subjective questions on the shortage of consumables and the level of difficulty experienced in balancing the budget at the end of the month. Detailed questioning on exchanges of help and services and on home production should be included.[8] Great care needs to be taken in selecting a representative sample and in the list of elements to be investigated in order to make them as appropriate as possible. The ideas developed in this text underline the difficulty of the questions to be answered and the significance of their impact.

Notes

1   The first version of this text was written for a seminar devoted to Madagascar. However, the ideas it contains have a more general validity, and can be applied to all the less developed countries, either African or Asian. This does not mean that exactly the same survey should be rigorously introduced and the same measures applied to all countries: as we shall see, the approach to poverty must be anchored in the society under consideration. Therefore it is possible that slight differences will need to be introduced to adapt the general framework to the specific culture of each country.

2   We could therefore speak of 'relative absolute poverty', to emphasise that the threshold is adapted to a given society at a given time and is by no means universal.

3   As relative approaches are the only ones currently being developed in France, we shall limit ourselves to this framework from now on. However, most of the ideas we shall develop could easily be transposed to absolute approaches, and thus remain relevant in what we have to say.

4   In this context, we must emphasise a limitation on all the poverty figures currently supplied by surveys from the public statistical system, which stems from the fact that, with a few exceptions, these operations are carried out in the field of 'ordinary housing'. This may certainly include makeshift accommodation (caravans, furnished rooms, etc.), but it excludes by definition the

homeless population. This comment applies to all the measurement types that we shall analyse. The incomes, consumption or budgetary difficulties that we observe are those of populations that have retained a minimal degree of social integration, in that they have accommodation. We still know little about the homeless. The difficulties are enormous: how can we question at random people who are hurrying to a soup kitchen? How can we avoid counting people twice, or, on the other hand, leaving people out? How can we conduct an interview when the abuse of alcohol or drugs fogs the memory and develops aggression? In France, there are probably about 100,000 people with serious problems who are never put on file and are therefore omitted from the analyses. Neither do surveys take account of the population in community housing, children's homes, retirement homes, hospices, asylums or prisons, all of which are places where populations in difficulty are likely to have a strong presence. In a country with a hot climate (the case of most developing countries), where 'bricks and mortar' housing is less essential than in Europe, the problem of whom to observe is certainly more crucial than in France. One of the aspects of the system to be set up is that it must enable high-quality random surveys to be carried out, including those fringes of the population who strictly speaking have no fixed accommodation. The problems posed by individuals who are temporarily housed by members of their extended family will have to be analysed. The solutions to be implemented will certainly be different in the rural and urban environments.

5   Taxation sources are not perfect either; we shall not go into detail about the problems here, since it seems unlikely that such sources could be used in most LDCs.

6   This measurement is made all the more difficult by the fact that in LDCs there are often significant amounts of emigration/immigration: in many families, a member goes to live in a richer country, bordering their own or further away, and sends or brings back to the rest of the family an income which constitutes an essential part of their resources. These incomes must obviously be measured, as equally, in consumption surveys, must the consumption of individuals who are part of the household but spend a part of their time abroad. Indeed, immigrants also pose problems for poverty statistics (makeshift housing, language problems, consumption and income straddling the original country and the adopted country, etc.). The Albanian survey mentioned on p. 309, for example, had to confront such observational difficulties.

7   Obviously, this does not mean that installing free and effective health and education systems would not be an extremely valuable means of reducing the damaging effects of poverty, particularly for the long-term future of children.

8   A pioneering survey was conducted in France in 1988 by the INSEE working together with the Centre National de la Recherche Scientifique (CNRS). This *Modes de vie – Production Domestique* (Modes of life – domestic production) survey could serve as a basis for developing the questioning and certain parts of the survey in the LDCs.

13 Two original poverty monitoring tools

The 1-2-3 surveys and the Rural Observatories

Mireille Razafindrakoto and François Roubaud

Despite their primary importance, methods of measuring and monitoring poverty remain one of the weak points of the current PRSP processes. In Chapter 11 we revealed the main failings of household surveys as they are currently being implemented in poor countries, particularly in Africa. We suggested a certain number of directions for consideration by which these shortcomings could be resolved. Going beyond these corrective principles, we shall now present two original instruments that have been successfully applied on the ground in various developing countries: the 1-2-3 survey and Rural Observatories.[1] These two survey systems illustrate the possibility of combining a certain number of basic criteria to put together an appropriate mechanism. After a general introduction to these two statistical operations, illustrated principally by the example of Madagascar, where for the moment experiments have progressed the furthest, we shall put into perspective their respective advantages and limitations, in particular by comparing them with the properties of other types of surveys covering the same subjects. Finally, we shall look at the common elements in the implementation of the two tools in order to determine the main strengths leading to their success. We shall pay particular attention to the characteristics distinguishing them from traditional methods, which enable them partially to overcome the shortcomings of such methods. As an example, we shall set out a few analytical results based on the data obtained by applying the two tools in Madagascar. By emphasising the figures and conclusions which are usually inadequate for drafting and evaluating policy, we shall uncover concrete means of improving the state of our knowledge of poverty and answering decision-makers' questions, while at the same time demonstrating the possibility of achieving this at lower cost.

Presentation of the two survey systems

The 1-2-3 survey: A simple, flexible method for monitoring poverty and urban governance

Initially designed at the beginning of the 1990s to study the informal sector (Roubaud 1992), the 1-2-3 survey was gradually extended to measure and monitor poverty and urban governance, adapting itself to the increasing importance of these subjects which now constitute the heart of development policy. After an initial partial experiment in Mexico (1986, 1989), the 1-2-3 survey was applied for the first time in its entirety in Cameroon in 1993 (Roubaud 1994b). The methodology was then consolidated in Madagascar, where the mechanism was introduced in 1995 and is still in operation today. Initially limited to the capital, it was extended in 2000 after five years of successful operation to the country's seven principal urban centres. Strengthened by this success, the 1-2-3 survey has spread widely over the last few years. It has been conducted, is in the process of being conducted or is in preparation on three continents: in Africa (Morocco, seven capitals in West Africa), Latin America (El Salvador, Bolivia, Colombia, Equator, Peru, Venezuela) and Asia (China, Bangladesh). The 1-2-3 survey was designed to act as a generic framework with a flexible structure, which respects a certain number of common characteristics but whose configurations in practice vary according to the needs and specific architecture of the existing information systems in the different countries.

Based on the principle of grafting surveys together, the 1-2-3 survey is made up of an arrangement of three interlocking surveys, aimed at different statistical populations: individuals, production units, households.

The first phase of the method is a survey of employment, unemployment and the conditions of activity of households (phase 1: labour force survey). It is designed to be conducted annually (or even continuously), as in Madagascar since 1995. Apart from the central theme of this phase, focusing on the labour market, it plays a pivotal role in drawing up a much wider framework for household surveys. Two techniques are used to extend the subject of the questions covered: grafting on extra surveys[2] and adding modules on varying subjects to the core questionnaire. In the first category, we could mention phase 2 on the informal sector and phase 3 on consumption, sources of purchases and poverty, which are an integral part of the method's basic architecture. These structural surveys, more complex to implement, are not designed to be conducted every year, but with a lesser frequency. For example, in Mexico, phase 2 is carried out every two years, while in Madagascar phases two and three are repeated every three years (1995, 1998 and 2001).

The second phase consists of carrying out a specific survey among heads of informal production units on their working conditions,

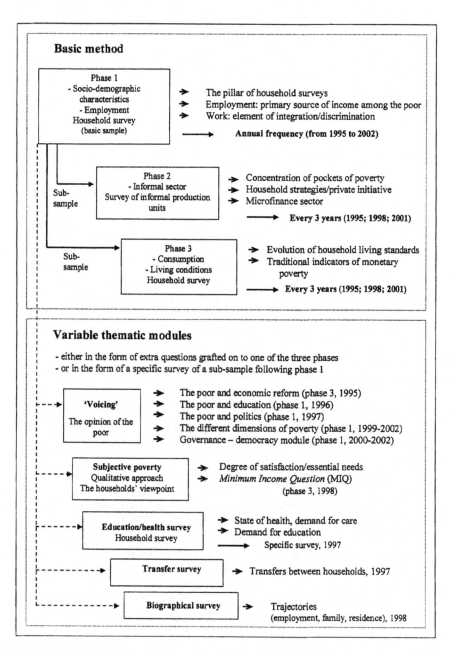

Figure 13.1 The 1-2-3 survey scheme: the example of Madagascar.

economic performance, the way in which they are integrated into the fabric of production and their perspectives. Finally, the third phase is a survey on household consumption. It aims to estimate the living standards of households, to measure the relative weights of the formal and informal sectors in their consumption, and to analyse the factors of poverty.

Specific statistical operations are added to this basic architecture, corresponding to varying thematic modules. These modules may take two forms. According to a first configuration, they are presented as entirely separate surveys applied to a sub-sample of households and/or individuals taken from phase 1 (as is phase 3), following the principle of survey grafting. In Madagascar, the SET97 survey on health, education and household transfers, and the BIOMAD98 survey on biographical trajectories (family, migration, employment) were carried out in this way. According to a second configuration, different themed modules can be added to the basic questionnaire of the three phases according to requirements. Examples from Madagascar include, among others, the supplementary modules on perceptions of economic reforms and the role of the state (1995), demand for education and educational policies (1996), ethnic identity, religious observance, electoral participation and the role of political parties and the political class (1997), reform of the civil service and privatisation (1998), new dimensions of poverty (vulnerability, subjective approaches, 'participation', violence, etc.: 1999–2002), or the 'governance' and 'democracy' modules applied in seven capitals in West Africa. In fact, these modules are similar to opinion polls. By responding to a desire for representativity in the opinions gathered, they contribute to applying the participatory process, promoted by the PRSP approach. We will not develop the aims and advantages of this type of approach any further here, as they are covered in Chapter 5.

The labour force survey: pillar of household statistical framework

In most countries in the world, primarily the developed countries but also the developing countries of Latin America, Asia, North Africa, etc. – in fact everywhere except for sub-Saharan Africa – the labour force survey is at the heart of statistical methods based on households. We are taking labour force survey in this context to mean a generic type of household survey using regular, internationally standardised concepts and methods covering the labour market in general and the population's working conditions (employment, unemployment, income, etc.). Not only is this the most widespread form of household survey, it is also the one around which there has been the most work on harmonising concepts and methodologies of measurement in order to enable international comparison, particularly at the instigation of the International Labour Organisation (Hussmanns, Mehran and Verma 1990).

Two types of arguments weigh in favour of using labour force surveys for monitoring poverty in developing countries. First we could mention analytical reasons. The question of employment is central in poor countries, with the vast majority of the population, and especially the most disadvantaged, obtaining its income through work, and with institutional transfers of funds (welfare benefits) and income from capital playing only a marginal role. Even more than in other countries, improving the operation of the labour market and access to employment is central to economic policy.

Beyond these economic and social considerations, the introduction of labour force surveys is justified on technical grounds, involving both the statistical management of surveys and strengthening the institutional capacities of the national statistical offices (NSOs). Labour force surveys are in fact particularly simple to implement. The questionnaire is short and can be applied on the ground in a limited time. This level of performance compares favourably with more complex surveys, where it is not unusual for questionnaires to exceed 100 pages, requiring several hours if not days of interviews. This is the case, for example, with multi-objective surveys ('LSMS surveys' type, see Chapter 11), or even income/expenditure surveys, in that reliable estimators can only be obtained using complex, tiresome procedures. Indeed this complexity has contributed to the failure of numerous operations of this kind. As a result, the cost of labour force surveys is limited, for the reasons mentioned above. Finally, they provide an ideal basis for producing operational stratifications of households, which are relevant for various lines of questioning, and enable further surveys or modules on the most varied subjects to be added, as shown by the experience of the MADIO[3] project in Madagascar.

The operationality of labour force surveys in a context of scarce resources (financial as well as human) combines two significant advantages that should be taken into account:

1   They enable us to imagine the implementation of chronological series, which goes right to the foundations of economic analysis. The continuity of viable surveys, where both concepts and results are standardised (levels of activity, levels of unemployment, etc.), facilitates the use of (particularly econometric) methods for analysing both microeconomic and macroeconomic behaviour.
2   They are a useful instrument for motivating teams of statisticians, particularly in poor countries, where household survey systems are still at an embryonic stage. Confronted with immense difficulties, these statisticians need motivating projects with a low risk of failure. As a result, it is advisable to favour surveys that can be controlled by limited teams, for which the results to be communicated are known in advance and which are not vulnerable to the risks caused by too great a requirement for funding, which by definition are unpredictable and which cannot be charged to meagre national budgets.

As an example, the Malagasy labour force survey has been in existence since 1995, and is carried out every year. It supplies rapid annual information on the state and the development of the labour market, and analyses how it operates. It is the only source of information available to Madagascar, which provides a real-time diagnosis of the effects of economic policy on the population (employment, unemployment, income, etc.). The labour force survey now covers a representative sample of 6,000 households in the large urban centres, including 3,000 in and around the capital (or about 26,000 individuals, with 13,000 in Antananarivo). One-third of the sample changes from year to year. It is possible to follow individual careers through time due to this 'panel' dimension.

Figure 13.2 and Table 13.1 illustrate concrete examples of the appeal of the labour force survey, in its twin dimensions of annual monitoring (cross-section of the population) and panel. In poor countries, this type of result cannot be obtained with the existing systems. Here, the correlation between increased salaries and the reduction in child labour is made clear (for a more detailed analysis, see Razafindrakoto and Roubaud 1999a).

In addition, monitoring the panel enables transitory poverty to be distinguished from chronic poverty. In the Malagasy capital during the period studied, about one person out of six found themselves in a

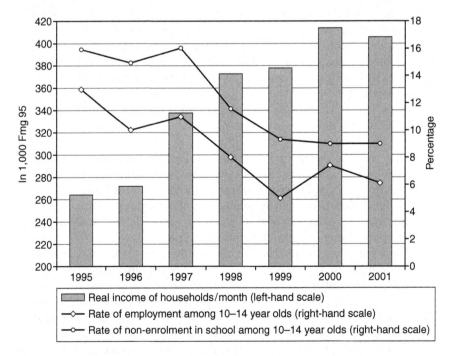

Figure 13.2 Increase in salaries and change in rate of employment among children.

Sources: 1-2-3 surveys, 1995 to 2001, phase 1, MADIO/INSTAT, authors' calculations.

Table 13.1 Chronic and transitory poverty from panel data 1997–9

Years	Never poor	Sometimes poor	Always poor	Total
1997–8	35%	27%	38%	100%
1998–9	36%	25%	39%	100%

Sources: 1-2-3 surveys, 1997 to 1999, phase 1, MADIO/INSTAT, authors' calculations.

situation of chronic poverty, and one in four lived temporarily in poverty. Identifying these two forms of poverty has considerable implications in terms of targeting and means of combating poverty (Herrera and Roubaud 2001).

The informal sector survey, a light cast on a concentration of pockets of poverty

The second phase of the system is carried out among heads of informal production units identified during the first phase (the labour force survey). Its appeal in the context of monitoring poverty lies in the fact that pockets of poverty are concentrated in the informal sector, especially in urban areas. Paying particular attention to this sector enables a large proportion of the poor to be targeted. Analysing the conditions under which these activities are carried out, economic performance and how informal units are integrated into the productive system, following the input/output table approach, gives a clear picture of the impact of policy on the sector and the strategies of households for which it is a main source of employment or income.

The survey aims to answer precise questions on the role of the sector in the economy, as well as its actual and potential contribution to improving the population's living conditions. As an example, setting up micro-finance systems aims to help the most disadvantaged by encouraging the development of micro and small enterprises. But we have to ask: who benefits from these systems, and what is their impact? On another level, given the limited employment opportunities in the formal sector, does the encouragement of informal activities constitute a viable alternative enabling the creation of a growth dynamic? To answer these questions, we have to understand clearly the economic circuit around the centre of which the informal sector gravitates, by analysing the evolution of its structure and production, the origin of its intermediate consumption, capital, investment, financing and the demand to which it responds.

As an example of results from phase 2, Table 13.2 shows the evolution of the principal economic aggregate values for the informal sector between 1995 and 1998 in the Malagasy capital Antananarivo (MADIO 1998a). This process requires not only the availability of two comparable informal sector surveys but also the capacity to make volume/price

Table 13.2 Evolution of the principal aggregates for the informal sector, 1995–8

| | Level aggregates | | | | Evolution 95/8 | |
	1995 (Fmg 1995)	1995 (Fmg 1998)	1998 (Fmg 1998)		Nominal	Real
Number of						
IPUs	123,000	–	164,000		–	+33.7%
Employment	191,900	–	241,200		–	+25.7%
Capital	199 Bn Fmg	356 Bn Fmg	596 Bn Fmg		+199.5%	+67.4%
Turnover	1,309 Bn Fmg	2,352 Bn Fmg	3,004 Bn Fmg		+129.5%	+27.7%
Production	721 Bn Fmg	1,291 Bn Fmg	1,769 Bn Fmg		+145.4%	+37.0%
Added value	405 Bn Fmg	706 Bn Fmg	1,139 Bn Fmg		+181.2%	+61.3%

Sources: 1-2-3 surveys 1995, 1998, phase 2, MADIO/INSTAT.

Note
To deflate the values of the aggregates, specific indices for sale price, production price and added value price for the informal sector were produced. Between 1995 and 1998, they grew by +85.8 per cent, 79.1 per cent and 74.3 per cent respectively. During the same period, the CPI (consumer price index) rose by +64.8 per cent. The price of production was assigned to the capital value, in the absence of specific information.

breakdown, based on a specific price index for the informal sector. To our knowledge, there is no equivalent data source in other developing countries.

The survey on consumption, the degree of satisfaction of household needs and monetary poverty

Phase 3 of the 1-2-3 survey is an income/expenditure survey. It aims to determine the level and structure of household consumption. Following the example of other surveys of the same kind, it enables poverty lines to be calculated and the traditional indicators of monetary poverty to be estimated (incidence, intensity, etc.).

From a methodological viewpoint, it is confronted to the usual trade-off between reliable estimators and rapid communication of results. The option chosen was to position phase 3 halfway between the traditional income/expenditure survey and the LSMS survey. The use of accounts diaries covering two weeks provides a better measure of consumption and thus of poverty than is given by LSMS surveys, which are based solely on retrospective questioning. The fact that the survey takes less account of seasonality than traditional income/expenditure surveys, where data are collected throughout a full year, is partially compensated for by shorter timescales for delivering information, making a simpler survey that is more useful for decision-makers.

From an analytical viewpoint, its originality lies in its estimates of amounts spent in different categories of households by product, keeping track of where products were purchased, and in particular their origins in the formal or informal sector. Among other things, it describes the behaviours of different categories of households (according to their wealth, sources of income, etc.) in their decisions to buy a product in the formal or informal sector, and the countries of origin of all products consumed.

Figure 13.3 shows that in a phase of rapid income growth, the informal sector's share of household consumption diminishes differently according to the type of budget item and the type of household, the poorest remaining much more dependent on the informal sector than the richest (MADIO 1998b).

Modules on governance and democracy

The failure of structural adjustment policies, combined with the extension of the concept of poverty to cover non-economic dimensions, has made governments and donors aware of the importance of previously underestimated conditions for the success of development policies. Consequently, governance, accountability, empowerment and participation of the population have been placed at the heart of their strategies. It is more and more apparent that development questions cannot be approached solely

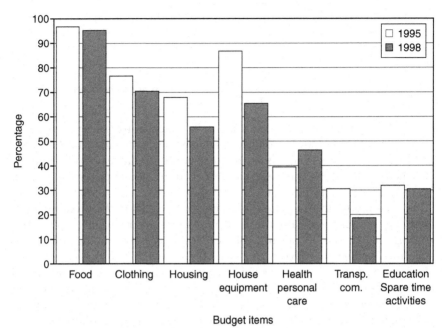

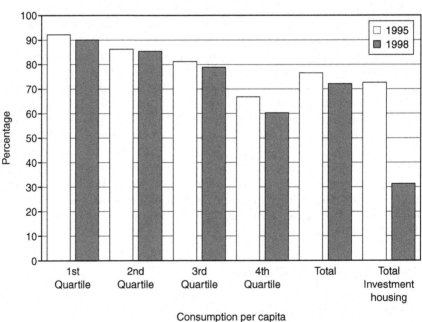

Figure 13.3 Evolution of the informal sector's share of household consumption 1995–1998.

Sources: 1-2-3 surveys, 1995, 1998, phase 3, MADIO/INSTAT.

Note
Self-consumption and imputed rents are excluded.

through the perspective of economic growth. In fact, drafting effective anti-poverty policies must take account, and aim for better understanding, of the interactions between at least four dimensions: growth of course, but also distribution (of income or assets), the quality of institutions (particularly public institutions) and the type of political regime. For this reason, notions of good governance and democracy are now emphasised as fundamental determiners of the success of economic policies and, more generally, the path of development of a country. They do not play a solely instrumental role (with democracy contributing to good governance which itself favours growth and limits inequality), but represent elements of a population's well-being in themselves. For example, respect for individual liberties (political liberty, freedom of expression, etc.) can be seen as an intrinsic component of development; in the same way, an administration with integrity will increase the perception of justice by reducing discriminatory practices (by fighting corruption, among other things).

This is why the 1-2-3 survey was extended to cover questions of governance and democracy. On the one hand, this is a question of understanding the administration's operation, the quality of public services and the opinion of different sections of society on the role of the state (what it is or should be doing). On the other hand, the survey provides a means of researching the population's point of view on the functioning (or dysfunction) of democracy, the appropriateness of the political regime in the context of the country, and more widely on the values that the society considers essential (see Figure 13.4). Ultimately, the aim is to explore the links between democracy (or, more globally, the political regime), public institutions, their effective mode of operation, the society's values system and the population's living conditions.[4]

Finally, the 1-2-3 survey enables the chronological evolution of three types of information to be combined and monitored: *subjective questions*, associated with opinion polls (perception of the operation of democracy and the state, level of support for policies that have been implemented, party-political preferences, concepts of ethnicity, subjective experience of exclusion or discrimination, systems of values and representation, etc.), *objective data on behaviour and social practices* (political and social participation, religious practice, access to public services, violence or corruption, etc.) and *individual socio-economic characteristics* traditionally collected in household surveys (sex, age, education, migration, work, unemployment, income, etc.).

As an example, Figure 13.5 illustrates the link between improving public sector salaries and a sharp drop in the incidence of corruption[5] between 1995 and 2001. The measurement of this type of indicator is quite exceptional in developing countries.

Table 13.3 presents the principal characteristics of the 1-2-3 survey system introduced in Madagascar from 1995. The average costs of the surveys are very affordable. Clearly, they cannot be applied in exactly this

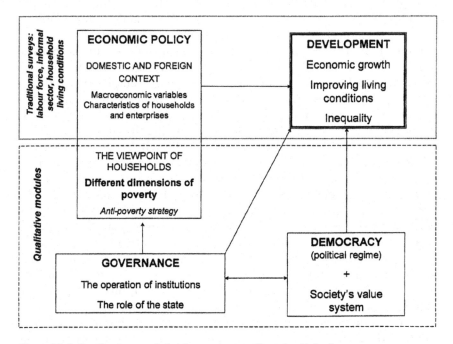

Figure 13.4 Qualitative modules for understanding the links between governance, democracy, economic policy and populations' living conditions.

form in other national contexts, where prices are generally higher. But even in the framework of Madagascar, they compare favourably with the costs of other types of household surveys carried out in the country: Integral or Priority Surveys, Demographic and Health Surveys, etc. (see definitions in Chapter 11).

Rural Observatories: an original methodology for analysing and monitoring the rural world

Although pockets of poverty are mainly concentrated in rural areas, traditional methods are not only complex to implement but also inappropriate to handle this phenomenon. First, agricultural surveys, by focusing on farms, do not give an overall picture of the activities and income of rural households. Second, national surveys such as LSMS surveys, either priority or integral, have the disadvantage of failing to capture enough of the characteristics and diversity of the rural world. However, it is essential to take these characteristics into account when defining appropriate policies. To counteract these shortcomings, the principle of socio-economic 'observatories', inspired by 'village monographs', has proved its relevance. It is advisable, however, to strengthen the economic – and more specifically

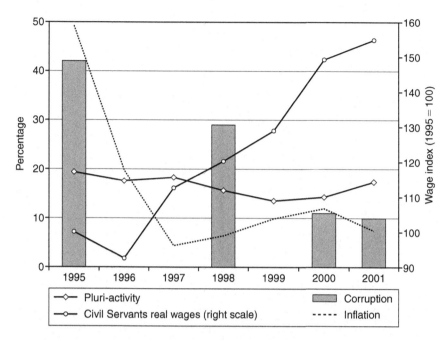

Figure 13.5 Public wages and corruption in Madagascar, 1995–2001.

Source: Razafindrakoto and Roubaud (2001a) based on employment surveys 1995–2001, MADIO/INSTAT.

macroeconomic – purpose of questioning, as well as the statistical and quantitative component, both of which are usually limited in this type of approach. The Rural Observatories set up by the MADIO project in Madagascar constitute an original experiment in this perspective.

A Rural Observatory is a restricted space, limited to a few villages chosen to illustrate a key problem in the rural environment, within which repeated surveys are carried out on production and households' living conditions. The sites of the Rural Observatories were selected by a method of reasoned choice, in the absence of a basis of recent and reliable surveys. The criteria used were as follows: the agroclimatic zone and the dominant system of production (cash crops, food crops, fishing or livestock); demographic density, the ethnic composition of the population, migratory movements; accessibility or isolation; the availability of community services (health, education) and basic infrastructure (water, electricity, post, telephone), as well as access to state or private sector economic support services (supervisory services, financial establishments, marketing companies, etc.), the existence of development projects funded by donors or non-governmental organisations.

Table 13.3 Principal characteristics of the 1-2-3 survey system as used in Madagascar (1995–2001)

	Phase 1: labour force survey	Phase 2: informal sector survey	Phase 3: consumption, poverty survey
Subject	Labour market	Informal sector	Consumption, poverty
Coverage	Antananarivo*	Antananarivo	Antananarivo
Frequency	Annual	Every 3 years	Every 3 years
Number of times conducted	7, 1/3 of panel rotating	3, cross-sections	3, cross-sections
Sample size	3,000 households, 15,000 individuals	1,000 IPUs	600 households
Unit cost (euros)	5 euros/household	9 euros/IPU	9 euros/household

	SET 97: health, education and transfers survey	BIOMAD 98: biographical survey	
Subject	Health, education, transfers	Career biographies	
Coverage	Antananarivo	Antananarivo	
Frequency	Every 5 years	Occasional	
Number of times conducted	1	1	
Sample size	1,000 households	2,400 individuals	
Unit cost (euros)	9 euros/household	4 euros/individual	

Note
The costs include all the operations on the ground, data entry and auditing, including publishing the initial results.
* Surveys extended to major urban centres from 2000.

Table 13.4 Population surveyed in the four Rural Observatories (1998)

	Antalaha	Antsirabe	Marovoay	Tuléar	Total
Number of households	553	598	553	504	2,208
Corresponding population	2,850	3,581	3,192	2,934	12,557
Average size of households	5.2	6.0	5.8	5.8	5.7
Panel of households 1995–8	297	288	303	227	1,115

Sources: Rural Observatories, 1995 to 1998; MADIO.

In this way, four Rural Observatories were set up in 1995, and each illustrates one key issue concerning Malagasy agriculture. The choice was initially limited to four due to limited human and financial resources and the experimental nature of the method (see Table 13.4). These observatories are:

- in the south-west region, the Mahafaly coastal plains observatory (Tuléar): for the populations of fishermen and livestock farmers in an arid and isolated region;
- in the north-east, the vanilla observatory (Antalaha): for producers of vanilla (and secondarily coffee, cloves and pepper) faced with the liberalisation of trade for cash crops;
- in the highlands, the Vakinankaratra observatory (Antsirabe): a zone of mixed family-based farming, mostly of rice, but with an overall rice deficit;
- in the west, the observatory of the Lower Betsiboka plains (Marovoay), a large irrigated rice-growing area currently being restructured, following a management crisis during the 1980s and the disengagement of the state at the end of this period. Producer households, deeply integrated into the market economy, have had to use adaptive strategies.

Following this, a Network of Rural Observatories (NRO) was set up in Madagascar. With the methodology gradually being consolidated, the number of observatories rose from four between 1995 and 1998 to 13 in 1999 and 17 in 2000. Each one has an operator (a non-governmental organisation, research consultancy, etc.) in charge of implementation and donors providing the funding. Putting together the network fulfils three objectives:

- extending the coverage of the arrangement put in place by the MADIO project to other areas;
- providing instruments for measuring the local impact of development action in the rural environment;

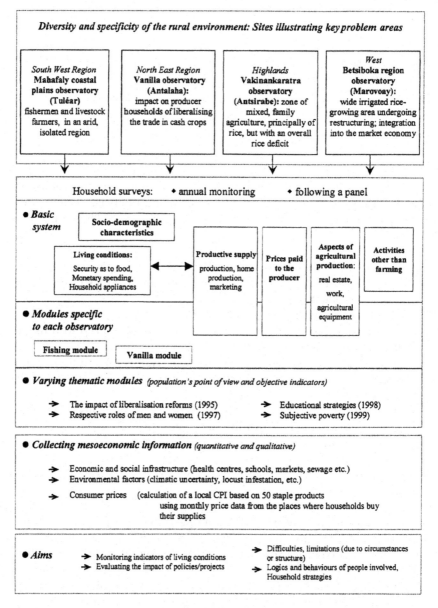

Figure 13.6 The Rural Observatories for studying the rural environment.

- creating a forum for information exchange between different operators working in rural areas in order to capitalise on experience (assessing failures and successes).

Although these surveys are not statistically representative, they have many advantages:

- The annual follow-up, and particularly the 'panel' dimension (monitoring the same households through time), gives an understanding of adaptation strategies and individual behaviour in the macroeconomic environment.
- The geographical concentration of the areas under observation makes the surveys easier to manage – a pitfall that has tripped up many a statistical operation in the rural environment. The affordable costs (4,000 euros per year per observatory), reliable data (better control over operations on the ground) and reduced timescales for producing results (less than three months after data collection has ended) are all advantages stemming from this geographical concentration.
- The focus on localised areas offers the possibility of collecting mesoeconomic information at lower cost. This type of information covers economic and social infrastructure (presence of schools, health centres, roads, markets, credit institutions, etc.), but also prices for consumption in local markets (essential for evaluating the real evolution of purchasing power in rural households). These data provide the means of enriching the diagnosis through multi-level analyses, taking account of demand as well as supply.
- The arrangement enables specific subjects to be researched which are beyond the scope of traditional national surveys in poor countries, given the small sample sizes and the concentration of areas of production (for example, producers of vanilla).
- The observatories are particularly well-suited to a real monitoring/ evaluation of the impact of rural development projects, which are by their very nature localised in space (setting up a control sample).
- Finally, in a context of crumbling agricultural statistics mechanisms, the Rural Observatories enable indicators and rough estimates to be uncovered for analysing the rural world in the absence of data at the national level (for example, the evolution of rice yields).

As an illustration, Figures 13.7 and 13.8 – produced from the panel data – give a basis for analysing the link between the evolution of rice production, yield and producer prices, compared to the consumption price of staple products.

The stagnation of the yields appears to be a major hindrance to growth in production. This means that producer households are unable to react favourably to the rise in price for the producer. Additionally, in order for the price rise to have a real motivational effect, it has to be lasting, translating into improved purchasing power for the income drawn from paddy sales. However, the evolution of the relative price of paddy compared with

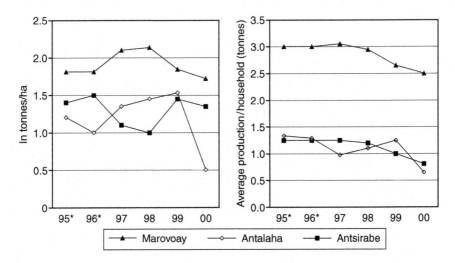

Figure 13.7 Evolution of rice yield and production, 1995–2000.

Source: Rural Observatories, 1995 to 2000, MADIO.

Note
The calculation covers a panel of households for the period from 1997–2000.
* For 1995 and 1996, the average trend has been reproduced.

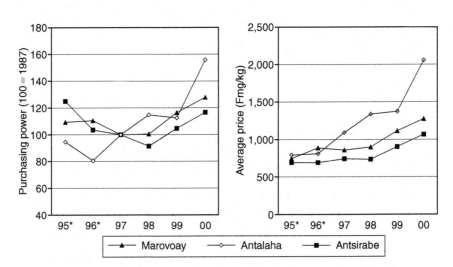

Figure 13.8 Evolution of the producer and consumer price, 1995–2000.

Source: Rural Observatories, 1995 to 2000, MADIO.

Note
The calculation covers a panel of households for the period from 1997–2000.
* For 1995 and 1996, the average trend has been reproduced.

the staple products shows no clear trend, even though it appears favourable over the later years.

Characteristics and benefits of the two survey systems

The foundations of these two methods, initially experimental, are now solidly established. Their main strengths are reliable information, regular monitoring, the ability to make comparisons over time, low costs, the ease with which they can be taken over by technicians from the country in question. Apart from the richness of the information gathered, these properties explain the success of these operations in Madagascar, but also in other developing countries. To understand fully the benefit they provide, we can try to identify their specific characteristics in terms of analytical content, particularly by comparing them with the most widespread survey systems, and we can also outline several intrinsic properties that have contributed to their success.

Putting the two systems in perspective: a comparison with traditional instruments

As an element of comparison we have chosen the 'World Bank' surveys (LSMS type, Integral or Priority), both because they are by far the most widespread, and because they have in common with the 1-2-3 surveys and the Rural Observatories the capacity to provide measures of monetary poverty, which is not the case for other survey systems such as CWIQ or DHS (see Chapter 11).

Table 13.5 summarises the practical characteristics of each survey, as they have been implemented in Africa, rather than their theoretical characteristics. The major advantages of the two methods presented here are, first, the quality of the data, and, second, the costs, the richness of the information and the ability to monitor over time. By contrast, their limited geographical coverage in comparison with the 'World Bank' surveys, which cover the whole national territory, constitutes their main disadvantage.

It should however be noted that in the case of 1-2-3 survey this limit is not inherent in the survey. In most cases, the limitation arises both from financial constraints and especially from a deliberate strategy of capacity building and ownership by the country concerned. In fact, certain recent experiences have extended the sample to the national level (El Salvador, Morocco, Peru, Venezuela). Nonetheless, these are occasional surveys, whose performance remains to be evaluated from the perspective of making the arrangement permanent.

We can also examine the different types of survey according to the types of poverty indicators they enable us to calculate. It is clear (see Table 13.6) that 1-2-3 surveys and Rural Observatories are more appropriate for

Table 13.5 Main characteristics of the 1-2-3 survey and Rural Observatories: comparison with the standard LSMS-type system as applied in Africa

	1-2-3 survey	Rural Observatories	LSMS-type survey
Scope of the survey	More appropriate for the urban environment (in its current design)	More specific to the rural environment	Can cover a whole country
Sample	Representative of the town, the urban area or the urban centre being surveyed	Representative at local level of the villages surveyed (chosen to illustrate specific key problem areas)	Representative at national and urban/rural level (but not at local level)
	One-third of the household panel rotates	Integral household panel	Household survey of a cross-section
Frequency	Annual (phase 1) Every 3 years (phases 2 and 3) (same methodology)	Annual (conducted each time with the same methodology)	Often every 3 or 5 years (irregular)
Characteristics of the questionnaire	Simple and adaptable with variable themed modules (particularly opinion surveys)	More or less simple, with a specific module adapted to the local reality (activity type)	Complex questionnaire
Cost	Low	Low	High
Main aims	– Precise measurement and monitoring of working conditions and living standards – Analysis of individual and household behaviour – Measuring the significance of the informal sector; monitoring its trends – 'Participatory' monitoring: gathers the hopes/perceptions of individuals who are representative of the population	– Precise monitoring of the living conditions of rural producers – Evaluating the impact of projects/programmes (witness sample) – Detailed analysis of the choices and behaviour of people involved in a specific context – Availability of indicators (if lack of national data)	– Global measurement of living standards indicators – Monitoring possible (if the survey is repeated regularly with the same methodology) – Analysis of individual and household behaviour

Table 13.5 continued

Type of information gathered (in standard versions)	– Socio-demographic – Work, unemployment and working conditions (careers and perspectives) – Characteristics and trends of informal production units (IPUs) – Consumption and living conditions – Social capital/exclusion; vulnerability/insecurity – Governance: opinion/degree of satisfaction with policies/reforms, the role and functioning of institutions (level of corruption)	– Socio-demographic – Productive supply (production, home production, marketing) – Production factors (real estate, work, agricultural equipment, etc.) – Price for the producers – Living standards (spending on equipment/accommodation) – Security as to food – Mesoeconomic information (local consumption prices, infrastructure, etc.)	– Socio-demographic – Employment/activity – Productive supply (production, home production) – Living standards (consumption, housing conditions) – Access to education and health services – Anthropometric – Community-level data (infrastructure, etc.)
Quality control procedures	– Test for internal and chronological consistency (at household and overall level) – Checking at each stage (on the ground/data entry/auditing) – High level of supervision by highly qualified personnel	– Test for internal and chronological consistency (at household and overall level) – Checking at each stage (on the ground/data entry/auditing) – High level of supervision by highly qualified personnel	Most often: – no opportunity for chronological testing – need for significant auditing work (correction/elimination of questionnaires)
Main limitations	Application in rural areas would require development to adapt the questionnaire	Cannot be extrapolated to national or regional level	– Difficult to manage from data collection to analysis, and high cost prevents the country ownership – Could not be considered for an annual survey – Timescale for data collection and analysis
Main strengths	– Simplicity and reliability of the system – Regular monitoring – Results available quickly – Handling different kinds of information in different years: households, individuals, employment, IPUs, opinions	– Management made easier by geographical concentration – Monitoring a panel (trends at individual level) – Specific handling of a key problem area	National coverage Wide thematic coverage (possibility of intersecting treatment of data but over a single year)

an approach to the new dimensions of poverty underlined by the most recent research (subjective approaches, vulnerability, participation, voicing, etc.). In theory, nothing prevents 'World Bank' surveys from doing the same thing.[6]

Joint characteristics of the two surveys systems: factors in their success

Several reasons have contributed to the success of these surveys: a simple, flexible mechanism, repetition of a single methodology leading to economies of scale, quality control at all stages, training competent supervisors and strengthening institutional capacities, integration into the national statistical information system, rapid publication of results and, finally, their wide dissemination through the media. These are in fact the same reasons which led to the initial choice of limited geographical coverage (the capital for 1-2-3 and the four focal points for the Rural Observatories), and only to conceive of extending the system once the methods had been consolidated and the survey process perfectly mastered.

An important investment to ensure the quality of data

Several means have been used to maximise the quality of the responses for the two surveys. Managing data collection and data entry is a central element: clear, precise concepts; the survey staff controlling the order of questions and the internal logic of the forms; a reasonable workload for the staff and the people being surveyed; training for supervisors and survey staff; appropriate level of supervision; systematic double data entry, etc.

We would emphasise two points, which distinguish the surveys conducted in Madagascar within the framework of the MADIO project from the others. First, the level of formal and professional qualifications held by the teams is well above average. High-level supervisors (statistical engineers and economists) participate to a great extent in the training and in operations on the ground. Second, a whole battery of consistency tests has been developed. Only when all the quality criteria have been fulfilled, after returning to stage one where necessary, are the questionnaires definitively validated.

Comparisons over time feature among the tests. Independent of the monitoring of a panel of households, conducting successive surveys enables measurement errors to be checked for that which would be impossible to detect in an occasional survey. As the latter are most common in poor countries, the statisticians of these countries are rarely confronted with this problem. The quality of the estimates can be judged in the light of the consistency of the progress obtained from one year to the next.

If a number of consistency tests (internal consistency, consistency over

Table 13.6 Types of indicators available for measuring and monitoring poverty

	Indicator type	Variables/methods	Surveys
The traditional dimensions of poverty	Monetary poverty	Consumption or income per head	1-2-3; RO LSMS
	Poverty in terms of living conditions	Characteristics of housing, assets	1-2-3; RO LSMS
	Poverty in terms of human capital	Level of education	1-2-3; RO LSMS
Subjective approach	Subjective poverty	Degree of satisfaction of households/needs Subjective perception of living standards	1-2-3
New approaches (favouring indicators of means rather than of results)	Opportunities	Access and means of integration into the labour market Educational strategies	1-2-3; RO (partially LSMS)
	Discrimination	Consumption strategies (products, supplies) Access to physical assets/local environment Domestic constraints Impact of public service inefficiency (example: corruption)	
	Poverty in terms of exclusions	– Social capital: participation in associations, transfer . networks, etc. – Means of continuing access to information – Political participation (elections)	1-2-3; RO
	Vulnerability/insecurity	Job stability; income stability; forms of social protection (social security, contracts, etc.); access to credit, property elements Physical safety (victims of acts of violence)	1-2-3; RO
Approach to trends	Transitory or chronic poverty	– Monitoring over time of a panel of households/individuals, – Transition matrix (into/out of poverty, transitory/chronic poverty) Analysis of explanatory factors	1-2-3; RO

Table 13.5 continued

Indicator type	Variables/methods	Surveys
Social mobility (poverty trap)	Social origin of parents (education, occupation, ethnicity, castes, etc.)	1-2-3
Opinion (representative poll)	Needs/difficulties Opinions on priorities	1-2-3; RO
Participatory process – Consultation – Participatory monitoring	Monitoring the impact of policies/reforms	– Population's perception of measures or policies applied and their effects (positive/negative); users/beneficiaries satisfaction to public good – Monitoring of objective indicators (direct incidence of corruption, discrimination or difficulties experienced by the poor in their contact with public services)	1-2-3; RO

time) are programmed in to the data entry procedures, the problem is also handled upstream. Certainly, statisticians have too great a tendency to count on the virtues of information technology, as miraculous as they are misunderstood, only considering these issues when auditing is carried out. At this stage it is often too late to correct the data, and cleaning up then consists more of reinventing the information to provide the appearance of internal consistency than trying to obtain reliable responses. To minimise this problem, a large number of consistency tests are carried out 'by hand' by the supervisors themselves, before the data are even sent for capture.

Disseminating the results – confronting the verdict of the demand

The automatic publication of the main results as part of the survey is another strength of these two methods. The cycle is completed with the public presentation, publication and dissemination of a document containing the initial results, about three months after the data have been collected. For the purpose of comparison, this timescale is extended to over a year on average for a survey of the LSMS type. In contrast with traditional survey publications, voluminous and often limited to an accumulation of unrefined or briefly commented statistical tables, the series of initial results from the MADIO surveys are presented as a brochure of fifty or so pages, in a smart, high-quality format, where the text is more important than the tables. All of the survey's principal results, with a strong analytical component, are thus put forward for review. This summary overview, using various tools from the field of descriptive statistics, emphasises the most important points of the survey, which can then be subject to more detailed thematic analyses. This feature responds to the objective of making the information drawn from the survey available to the wider public, with the aim of encouraging democratic debate (Razafindrakoto and Roubaud 2000c).

Reliable data available in real time

As the purpose of the system of statistical monitoring of households is to assist in defining and shaping economic policy, it is imperative that reliable information be made available as quickly as possible. The inevitable conclusion is that survey systems of the LSMS type do not satisfy this demand, at least in the form in which they exist in poor countries. On the one hand, as we have already emphasised, the second-rate quality of the data and the changes in methodology do not enable robust diagnosis of current trends (DIAL 2000b), which produces damaging effects. For example, in many countries in West Africa the second half of the 1990s corresponded to a phase of relatively rapid growth (of about 5 per cent per year), in contrast with the period preceding the devaluation of the CFA franc in January 1994. Yet the few surveys available speak of an increase in poverty (except for Côte d'Ivoire until 1998). It is perfectly probable that these counterintuitive results do not correspond to the reality, and can be explained by the poor quality of data in the surveys and/or the methodological changes from one survey to the next. However, these results have a negative impact on the public in these countries: they contribute to strengthening the widely-held belief that growth is not favourable to the reduction of poverty, an idea that has been considerably undermined by international experience and the absence of any clear trend towards increased inequality in the region.

On the other hand, the irregularity and excessive delay in publishing the results of surveys place tight limits on the use that can be made of them for adjusting economic policy. For example, in 1997 the GDP per head began to rise in Madagascar, after long years of decline. Growth has continued to accelerate ever since, until the political crisis at the very end of 2001. Madagascar is also one of the African countries where the statistical programme financed by the World Bank is the most intensive, with four LSMS-type surveys in recent years (1993, 1997, 1999 and 2001). The results of the 1997 survey, released to the public during 1999, showed that poverty had risen since 1993. Not until the end of 2000 will the surveys identify a turnaround in the situation that happened nearly four years previously. There is clearly good reason to wonder about the relevance of such a system. In contrast, the 1-2-3 survey enabled the change in circumstances to be announced in 1997, and confirmed year after year since then (certainly, only in the capital). In addition, the survey shows that there is no comparison between the slight improvement in the income and consumption of urban households and that resulting from the evolution of private consumption in the national accounts, which places a question mark over the degree of validity of these accounts.

Conclusion

In this chapter we have presented two original tools for monitoring poverty, and the living conditions of households more generally. They were developed in part to address the shortcomings of existing survey systems used in developing countries. Furthermore, they have been tested operationally in fairly varied contexts, confirming by example the validity of our hypothesis about the reasons for the weaknesses shown by certain types of surveys. It is obviously not our intention to promote these two methods as the only possible alternative to their competitors, but rather to diversify the set of tools available for monitoring poverty. Certainly, the World Bank's effective monopoly[7] in this area has necessarily had a softening effect, which has proved counter-productive. In addition, it would seem essential to carry out a more systematic evaluation of the mass of surveys that have accumulated over the last decade in poor countries, in order to arrive at a sounder diagnosis of the advantages and disadvantages of each and thus to draw conclusions with an eye to the future. Only thus can we hope that methods of monitoring and evaluating policies will respond effectively to the ambitious objectives assigned to them by the PRSPs.

Notes

1 This chapter is based on various documents which present the surveys in greater detail. A few references for 1-2-3 surveys are Rakotomanana, Ramilison and Roubaud (2000); Rakotomanana, Ravelosoa and Roubaud (2000); DIAL (2000c). For Rural Observatories, the reference is Droy, Ratovoarinony and Roubaud (2000).

2 The employment survey is used to provide a sub-sample, to which a second questionnaire on a specific subject is then applied.

3 The MADIO project (Madagascar-Dial-Instat-Orstom) aims to support economic analysis and the rehabilitation of the national statistical system; see Roubaud (2000c).

4 On this issue, three regional household survey projects have been launched recently in Africa. The Afrobarometer surveys project, initiated by the Michigan State University (Department of Political Science) in collaboration with various African partners, aims to build comparative series of national public attitudes surveys on democracy, markets and civil society in Africa (see http://www.afrobarometer.org). The United Nations Economic Commission for Africa (UNECA) project for Monitoring and Measuring Good Governance in Africa, to provide information for the Peer Review process of the NEPAD (http://www.uneca.org). Fourteen national surveys have been launched in 2001 and 19 more countries are supposed to be covered in a second phase. Finally, the PARSTAT project, conducted by AFRISTAT and DIAL with local NSOs, realised the 1-2-3 survey module on subjective poverty, governance and democracy in seven WAEMU capitals in 2001 and 2002. This methodology will be extended to the five Andean countries in Latin America, within the framework of the European Project on Measuring Democracy, Human Rights and Good Governance (see http://dial.prd.fr).

5 The incidence of corruption is defined as the proportion of inhabitants of the capital who have fallen victim to corruption during the past year. By definition therefore, the issue is one of small-scale corruption rather than large-scale corruption (public contracts, etc.).

6 A first intent has been experimented in Madagascar by introducing in the Enquête permanente auprès des ménages (EPM 2001) some questions directly based on the MADIO 'subjective poverty module'; see note 7.

7 It should be noted, in fact, that in certain countries the 'World Bank' surveys have started to follow the lead set by some of the useful properties of the 1-2-3 survey system. This is the case, for example, with the measurement of consumption by the Enquête Camerounaise sur les ménages (ECAM II) survey in Cameroon in 2001, and the measurement of employment and subjective poverty approaches in the EPM 2001 survey in Madagascar. In another field, also in Madagascar, the whole policy on publishing and disseminating results has been adopted.

14 Evaluating poverty reduction policies

The contribution of micro-simulation techniques

Denis Cogneau, Michael Grimm and Anne-Sophie Robilliard

As part of the PRSP process, the World Bank is responsible for offering guidance on Poverty and Social Impact Analysis (PSIA), designed to assess the impact of economic policies on poverty. The Bank proposes a detailed review of the 'toolkits' used by economists and social scientists, which it puts in correspondance with the reform policies recommended by the PRSPs (World Bank 2002e). This sort of exercise is perfectly understandable and legitimate in a national or multilateral bureaucratic context, as all modern economic administrations have their 'methods' departments. Nonetheless, it has the disadvantage of producing a 'shopping list' that fails to take into account either the concrete conditions for applying the proposed methods, or the hypothetical and experimental nature of many of the evaluation methods. Indeed, these two aspects are connected, as good practice in evaluation methods requires that a certain number of conditions should be met among the users. These conditions include not only technical skills but also, and perhaps above all, an institutional infrastructure such that the 'evaluation messages' can, first, be demanded, second, understood, and third, integrated in a wider decision-making process. However, in a large number of countries concerned by the PRSPs, the world's poorest countries, the conditions for implementing participatory evaluation and debate on the policies are often far from being met. In particular, it is clear that politicians and administrative staff take little note of work carried out by their Statistics, Forecasting and Planning departments. It is also clear that the democratic requirement to justify political decisions is weak. Hence, the problem with PSIAs is not so much the result of technical difficulties with the evaluation methods or data availability, but rather of the conditions under which the results of the evaluations are received. An initial evaluation of the PRSP process by the World Bank and the IMF observed that: 'Poverty and Social Impact Analysis (PSIA) of major policies and programs has not been undertaken as part of PRSPs' (IDA and IMF 2002). It explains the situation by underlining the lack of qualified staff within the administrations, technical difficulties and the lack of data, as it goes on to say: 'for reasons to do with national capacity constraints and its inherent technical difficulties. The data and capacity needs are formidable and serious methodological issues remain unresolved, despite some analytical advances in this area.' We believe that the focus on technical difficulties, or what we could call the 'technocratic' explanation, is exaggerated. On the other hand, it is fair to point out that the methods have not been perfected yet, but surely the same can be said for all scientific activities. In the end, the problem in adopting the methods comes back to the more general problem of democratic ownership of the reforms, a subject that is referred to in detail in other chapters of this book.

This chapter focuses on the methods, insisting on the inevitable risks to be run in any attempt at evaluation. It in no way aims to cover all the methods available,[1] but presents and illustrates the contributions made by the different micro-simulation techniques used to analyse poverty reduction policies in developing countries.[2] In line with what we have just said, the techniques are presented like a research programme and not as off-the-shelf, finished tools. The first section discusses the relationship between evaluating and designing policies, explains the difference between *ex ante* and *ex post* evaluation, and reviews the new questions that the poverty reduction strategies pose for econometricians, whether it be for evaluating old-style policies seen from a poverty perspective or new-style policies directly designed to attack poverty. The second section describes the different micro-simulation techniques that seek to meet these new demands, and the third section presents a few concrete examples. Finally, the conclusion looks at future challenges concerning technical progress and how the evaluation criteria can be fine-tuned and the issue broadened.

The new challenges for policy evaluation

Policy design and **ex ante** *and* **ex post** *evaluation*

Designing and evaluating economic policies are two closely related processes. From an optimistic standpoint, the history of development policies can be seen as a learning process, with each new policy drawing lessons from the failures or disadvantages of former policies, in a more or less radical manner. For instance, following the financial crisis that hit the Latin American countries at the beginning of the 1980s, structural adjustment policies were drawn up as a remedy for the supposed shortcomings of the previous policies, based on the substitution of national production for imports. The need to restore fiscal balance and balance of payments figures not only led to the introduction of corrective macroeconomic stabilisation policies, but also to a concern to find more structural policies designed to reduce state intervention and promote exports. Worries about unequal growth patterns that had already been voiced at the beginning of the 1970s, when growth was high, resurfaced at the end of the 1980s and led to the reorientation of structural adjustment towards poverty reduction. The Russian and Asian crises also called into question the role of state and non-state institutions in the workings of free market economies. They inspired greater prudence in reform policies, and the idea of more detailed evaluations of the policies was keenly promoted. As a result of this, the 'new policies' were based in part on a more or less precise *a posteriori* or *ex post* evaluation of the previous policies.[3] This critical assessment meant that new normative criteria could be put forward (private sector efficiency, poverty reduction, etc.), and new policies designed to improve these criteria could be proposed. This brought up the difficult issue of a priori or *ex ante* evaluation.

From an epistemological standpoint, the terms *ex post* and *ex ante* are not clear-cut or sufficient in themselves,[4] because there is also a border between experimental evaluation and prospective evaluation, or between experiment and simulation. In fact, econometric theory is now relatively good at delimiting the gradation between direct experiment methods by random sample and those that provide a structural representation of the agents' behaviour and enable prospective simulations.[5] Strictly speaking, *ex post* evaluation seeks to check retrospectively whether the (in principle clearly identified) objectives of a policy (already put into practice) have been met, with a positive approach. It comes close to a pharmacological type of question, such as: 'is the drug effective?' which suggests an experimental approach. However, experimental or pseudo-experimental evaluations cannot be applied to a great number of policies because it is practically impossible to form a control group. This is the case for all non-targeted or non-graduated policies and, even more so, for any policies that, although targeted, may have external or macroeconomic effects on the population as a whole.

Let's take the case of a policy fixing a minimum wage level and address the question of its impact on employment and poverty. This is typically a non-targeted policy, so the evaluation cannot be made by an econometrically controlled comparison of certain agents a priori concerned by the minimum wage and others who are not. From the moment that there is a single minimum wage, it is not possible either to establish a scale between agents to whom a certain level is applied and others to whom another level is applied, which would enable a similar comparison. We can observe, this time over a period of time, how increases in the minimum wage affected employment in different labour categories, particularly for individuals whose wages were initially close to the minimum wage (then considered as a targeted group). We can also model the numbers of individuals leaving poverty and try to identify the impact of earned income received in $t - 1$ on the state of poverty in t. In this case, the economic situation applicable to the different periods must be carefully controlled, in order to avoid attributing economic factors that have no relation whatsoever to the level of the minimum wage to the variations in employment and income observed. Furthermore, if the increase in minimum wage has a strong macroeconomic impact, whatever its characteristics, purely microeconomic evaluations can prove to be completely misleading.

Now let's take the case of a public works policy, offering low-paid jobs, for instance at half of the current minimum wage, and again look at the question of its impact on poverty. This time certain agents can be selected (or select themselves) and others not, and it is possible to control differences between the two groups, either a priori by selecting beneficiary agents amongst a population of candidates at random, or *a posteriori*, by jointly modelling participation in the programme and its impact on the participants' income.[6] However, if the programme is sufficiently wide in scale, the choices made by the programme's beneficiaries and the resulting redistribution of income have consequences for the rest of the labour market and on overall demand for goods and services. The two above examples demonstrate that, in economics, an evaluation process can be far removed from the pharmacological model of applying a treatment to a group of sick people. In many cases, both *ex post* and *ex ante* evaluations require representations of the workings of the economy as a whole.

Obviously, another problem with *ex ante* evaluation is that it involves making prospective rather than retrospective simulations. When a policy results in a significant, long-term change in the structure of a population, as, for instance, in the case of education or health policies (fighting Aids, for example), the prospective dimension is of fundamental importance. In practice, *ex ante* evaluation is also required to compare several alternative policies. Whereas *ex post* evaluation is part of a positive process: 'such and such a policy more or less achieved its objectives', *ex ante* evaluation is closer to a normative approach: 'this policy is better than that one'.[7] In that case, the greater the political stakes, the more it is vital to ensure an independent evaluation. There are numerous examples where the theoretical structure of the models used postulates more or less explicitly that a recommended policy will have a positive impact, with their empirical application serving merely to quantify its scale. For instance, the structure of many computable general equilibrium (CGE) models built to assess structural adjustment or free trade policies tended to put the emphasis on static gains in efficiency obtained by reducing domestic or external taxes. However, they minimised the potentially considerable short-term Keynesian impact of a reduction in public spending, the contractionary consequences of a rapid fall in the protection of the economy, or a certain number of dynamic longer-term gains in efficiency depending on the supply of public goods or the protection of local innovations. Conversely, policies in the 1970s were evaluated using fixed-price planning models which ignored the problems arising from a heavily distorted relative prices structure. The success or failure of policy experiments therefore provides lessons not only for the new policies but also for the corresponding methods of evaluation. The first of these lessons is clearly modesty.

Different chapters in this book have already presented in detail the theoretical and practical content of the new poverty reduction strategies, particularly pointing out how a transition is currently underway between the structural adjustment policies applied for the last 20 years or so and new policies designed to fight more effectively against the phenomenon of poverty. The 'participatory' approach to drafting these policies results in more freedom of manoeuvre, which should hopefully encourage policies that are better suited to democratic demands, but will also lead to greater heterogeneity. The new methods of negotiating international aid, using medium and long-term schedules of objectives, should also provide enough time for a full evaluation of the results, stage by stage.

The new political demands

Putting the accent on poverty reduction fixes obvious targets for the evaluation methods. They must be capable of providing satisfactory estimates of the policies' distributive impact, in terms of income distribution but also distribution of all the other primary factors of well-being such as access to public goods, health and education. This is highly ambitious and implies that the heterogeneity of the different populations must be taken into account far more than in the past, both in terms of differences in resources (income, capital, education, health), and in terms of the economic agents' characteristic behaviour and the environments in which they are immersed.

Certain elements of stabilisation and structural adjustment policies that are still applied must be examined, no longer just in macroeconomic and financial terms or in terms of efficiency, but also in distributive terms. For instance, international institutions now tend to accept that public finance or monetary policies that could possibly lead to a significant increase in poverty are no longer tenable and that, in cases where they are nonetheless considered inevitable, they must be backed up by palliative policies such as safety nets, tariffs or subsidies to protect certain vulnerable groups.

Suitable evaluation methods must therefore be capable of simulating the distributive impact of macroeconomic policies at the same time as the impact of targeted palliative policies. However innovative they may be, labour market policies generally raise the same type of difficulties. Hence, labour-intensive public works programmes or workfare policies must be evaluated taking into account the heterogeneity of the agents' behaviour regarding labour supply and their job opportunities, but also the potential macroeconomic effects of these interventions. The same is true in this respect for more traditional policies for farm prices or wage policies. In addition, policies dealing with domestic and external indirect taxes must take into account heterogeneous consumption habits and the existence of an informal sector with little taxation (Gautier 2002).

Policies for education, health and, more generally, the provision of public goods (e.g. water supplies) call on slightly different methods. First of all, it is not possible to start from an income and prices generation model as certain fairly specific elements of behaviour must be taken into account.

Tariff policies for public services or on demand subsidies can be assessed using a microeconomic model of demand for these services. The evaluation presents two types of difficulties: first, estimating the price elasticity of the various agents' demand for these services; second, estimating the impact of the quantity and quality of available supply of the services. Price variance for such services is often by definition limited in cross-sectional microeconomic data, which is often also relatively crude concerning consumption of these services (school or health centre attendance over the long term, water consumption in volume, etc.). In addition, the efficiency of tariff policies rests on the existence and quality of local supply, which is often difficult to measure precisely. Furthermore, such evaluation implies that it is possible to address the question of arbitration between the quantity and the quality of the services offered and be able to put a figure, on the supply side, on the cost of an improvement in quality and, on the demand side, on the impact of the same improvement in terms of take-up (Cogneau *et al.* 2002).

However, as part of a poverty reduction strategy, policies for the provision of public goods also have longer-term objectives, particularly when it comes to education and health. Education policies aim to equal out opportunities and increase income for the next generation; their effectiveness in these areas is part of a dynamic process, depending on demographic change and the labour market. In this way, policies targeting occupational qualifications are highly dependent on other policies aimed at developing labour demand and trade specialisation. Health policies aim to lower mortality rates over the long term, to offer equal chances in the face of illness and in terms of survival, and to increase income opportunities. There is wide recognition of the dynamic complementarity of education and health policies and, in the very long term, their combined impact on fertility policies. For an epidemic such as Aids, with its very long incubation period, the dynamic consequences of current policies must be viewed in a timescale of at least 15 years (Cogneau and Grimm 2002).

Finally, the question of the distribution of access to public services should be seen in a geographical perspective: first, there are considerable spatial disparities in most developing countries; second, supply and tariff policies are more and more often designed in a context of administrative decentralisation. These concerns led to the recent development of poverty mapping.[8]

Structural heterogeneity, variety of behaviour and demo-economic change

In all these areas, progress in distribution analysis and micro-simulation methods (see following section) has made it possible to produce data that takes into account the heterogeneity of populations whilst preserving a statistically representative diagnosis. Progress in the microeconomic analysis of households also shows greater respect for the impact that differences in resources and contexts have on economic agents' behaviour. On the macroeconomic side, it is now possible to break away from the models based on a small number of representative agents, and, on the microeconomic side, from the simplistic application of the standard consumer model. These two possibilities are in fact necessities. Nonetheless, if they are to be put into practice it is necessary to give up the intellectual comfort provided by the formal competitive general equilibrium model.

First of all, descriptive analysis of the distribution of income, education or health variables reveals that the observation of a few typical cases or average representative agents is not enough to account for inequalities between the real agents or the evolution of such inequalities. Historically, applied CGE models were the first tools used to address this type of question. CGE models were gradually improved by building Social Accounting Matrices (SAM) where household accounts were increasingly detailed and disaggregated,[9] meaning that analyses could be carried out on the basis of a 'typology' of households with different characteristics and levels of income.

The first two general equilibrium models applied to developing economies and the issue of the distributive impact of different macroeconomic policies were Adelman and Robinson's model for Korea (1978) and Lysy and Taylor's model for Brazil (1980). The two models produced different results concerning the impact of macroeconomic policies on income distribution. At the time, the differences were thought to stem from the structural characteristics of the two economies and the choice of specifications for the models. Later on, Adelman and Robinson (1988) went back to the two models and defended the idea that the differences were mainly due to a different definition of income distribution, and not to different choices for macroeconomic closure.[10] The neoclassical approach is centred on the personal, essentially individualistic distribution of income, whereas the Latino-American structuralist school is built on a Marxist vision of society, comprised of classes characterised by their endowments in factors of production with diverging interests. In other words, whereas the structuralists defend a 'functional' approach to income distribution, which characterises households by the factors of production at their disposal, the neoclassics have more often adopted a 'personal' approach, which classifies households according to their level of income. At the end of this debate, the approach most commonly used

---

Box 14.1 The theoretical problems posed by the hypothesis of the representative agent in the general equilibrium model

Disaggregating Social Accounting Matrices did not allow the applied general equilibrium models to do away with the hypothesis of representative agents, but merely multiplied their number. From a theoretical standpoint, the existence and unicity of the equilibrium in the Arrow–Debreu model is only guaranteed when an economy's net demand has certain properties (Hildenbrand 1998). The hypothesis of a representative agent with a quasi-concave utility function ensures that these properties are respected on the individual level, hence giving the model a microeconomic basis whilst not having to solve distributive problems. According to Kirman (1992), this hypothesis poses a number of problems. First, there is no plausible justification for the assumption that the aggregate of several individuals, even if they are all maximisers, acts in the same way as an individual maximiser. Individual maximisation of utility does not necessarily lead to collective rationality, neither does the fact that a community shows a certain degree of rationality mean that the individuals in the community act rationally. Also, even if we accept that the choices of the aggregate can be considered to be those of an individual maximiser, the reaction of the representative agent to a change in the parameters of the initial model may not be the same as the aggregate reaction of the individuals that the agent represents. There may be cases where, faced with two situations, the representative agent prefers the second to the first, whereas each individual prefers the first to the second. Finally, it is restrictive to try to explain group behaviour by that of an individual. The sum of simple, plausible economic behaviour observed in a multitude of individuals can generate complex dynamics, whereas constructing a model of an individual whose behaviour corresponds to these complex dynamics can result in imagining an agent with very peculiar characteristics. In other words, the dynamic complexity of the behaviour of an aggregate can emerge from the aggregation of heterogeneous individuals with simple behaviour patterns.

---

today is an extended functional classification, combining the two types of criterion (Bourguignon, Branson and de Melo 1989).

To go from income distribution in a few groups of households to a global inequality index, or to calculate poverty measurements, it is important to specify the income distribution within the groups in question. The simplest solution consists in assuming that the distribution of income in each group is parametric, and depends on the average income and other parameters that characterise the dispersion of income around this average.[11] In this case, the average can be adjusted to tie in with results from the CGE model. On the other hand, it is impossible to do away with the hypothesis of fixed intra-group income dispersion. And yet, however fine-tuned the household typology may be, descriptive analysis of empirical

Table 14.1 Decomposition of total inequality of household income in Madagascar and Indonesia

	Madagascar (14 groups)		Indonesia (10 groups)	
	Theil index	*Breakdown (%)*	*Theil index*	*Breakdown (%)*
Between groups	0.127	24.3	0.126	25.6
Within groups	0.395	75.7	0.367	74.4
Total	0.522	100.0	0.493	100.0

Sources: EPM 93 and SUSENAS 96 surveys, and authors' computations using 1995 SAMs classification of households for each country.

income distributions shows that intra-group inequality still represents the majority of the total inequality observed (see Table 14.1). Even if part of intra-group inequality can be attributed to measurement errors and idiosyncratic,[12] transitory elements of income, part of it is also due to structural heterogeneity.

The structural heterogeneity of different households first of all covers the wide variety of endowments of factors of production, whether it be assets such as land or physical capital, or the structure of labour supply by age and level of qualification. It also covers observable elements (e.g. spatial location) and non-observable (i.e. entirely idiosyncratic) elements affecting the productivity of assets or the individuals' work. Finally, for analyses of the distribution of purchasing power, the heterogeneity of cost-of-living indexes stemming from differences in needs and preferences is also taken into account.

Tools that pay no attention to the structural heterogeneity of households and individuals run the risk of making significant errors in their conclusions regarding income or poverty distribution, education or health. In addition, study by simulation of targeted policies (safety nets, workfare, education or health subsidies) on the basis of the observable characteristics of households or individuals, such as the number of children or housing characteristics, is precisely only possible if the variables which served for the targeting are retained in the final model.

In the short term, this structural heterogeneity is liable to be affected by recompositions of labour supply through, on the one hand, behaviour relating to people's choice of occupation or of migration and, on the other, to their leaving the school system or the workplace at the end of their lives (including mortality), and finally by recompositions of household consumption baskets resulting from demand-for-products behaviour. It is therefore vital to model such recompositions correctly, respecting the market contexts in which the agents are immersed. For instance, it has been clearly shown that when the failure or imperfections of labour markets, products or credit facilities are taken into account, this significantly modifies the agents' behaviour. For farming households, the absence of a local labour market leads to non-recursive intertwinned production and consumption behaviour which strongly modifies their response to prices incentives. For urban households, the rationing of formal salaried jobs leads to a segmentation of the labour market, restricting the choices of activity and occupation; non-random selection of individuals for hirings or lay-offs in the formal sector is also a significant source of intra-categorial heterogeneity. Finally, the degree of imperfection in credit markets has a significant impact on behaviour concerning schooling or job-leaving.

In the long term, structural heterogeneity is mainly determined by demographic change and by the accumulation of assets. Demographic change may be the consequence of the political and economic change itself (endogenous), or of long-term trends in demographic behaviour (fertility transition for instance), independently of the economic and political change (exogenous). In the context of structural adjustment, a worsening of living conditions, through a decline of real incomes for example, may lead to worse nutrition (or even starving) and thus increase morbidity and mortality, in particular for the children of the poor. Like-wise, a worsening of health conditions through reduced supply of care centres may increase morbidity and mortality. A slowdown in economic activity may also delay marriage and fertility and extend the breast-feeding period and thus post-partum infecundity. In contrast, a reduction of family planning programmes or an increase in the price of contraception, mostly imported goods, may increase fertility. The development of an export sector may attract immigrants. In contrast, a boom in agriculture may slow down or even invert the urbanisation process.[13]

Demographic shocks, such as the fertility transition in relation to edu-cational expansion or the recent increase in mortality in sub-Saharan Africa through the Aids epidemic, may also modify income distribution. These demographic changes may be considered largely independent of short-term economic fluctuations. The distributional impact will, on the one hand, be the consequence of changes in the composition of the population – age structure, distribution of household size, matching behaviour on the marriage market – and, on the other, of changes in labour supply behaviour and earnings induced by the demographic change (on this issue, see Lam 1997). To sum up, it should be noted that there may be strong interactions between economic and demographic change even in the short term. These interactions should be taken into account when analysing the distributional shocks of macroeconomic or demographic shocks or policy reforms. However, until now, little effort has been made to develop analytical tools able to evaluate and quantify such interactions.[14]

A number of different approaches based on the use of a representative sample of microeconomic units have recently been developed to capture these elements of structural heterogeneity for households and individuals with a view to providing a satisfactory means of analysing, *ex ante*, the distributive impact of poverty reduction strategies.

Micro-simulation techniques applied to the evaluation of poverty reduction policies

The term 'micro-simulation' spans a number of different approaches used in social sciences. Their common denominator is to focus primarily on the economic behaviour of agents and investigate the impact of public policy and shocks at the micro level. These models typically take representative samples of micro agents (households or firms) and measure the effect of government policy on these samples. The field originated from a paper by Orcutt (1957) who was concerned that macroeconomic models had little to say about the impact of government policy on the income distribution of agents in the economy. In developed countries, micro-simulation techniques are now extensively used to evaluate the impact of such policies as pension systems, social security and fiscal reforms. The application of micro-simulation techniques to developing countries, however, raises a number of specific problems.

The micro-units examined in the micro-simulation models used to evaluate poverty reduction policies, of particular interest to us here, are individuals and households. In most cases, these models focus on monetary poverty and income distribution As a result, all mechanisms related to income generation – such as wage formation, occupational choice, labour supply – are central. But micro-simulation models also permit examining other types of behaviour, such as schooling decision or health demand. Instead of aggregating the observations taken from a household survey and defining a few representative groups according to standard practice using CGE models (see p. 346), these models work directly with all the observations gathered in the survey. This is made possible thanks to continual improvements in data processing capacities and the growing number of income and consumption surveys available on representative household samples.

Another key characteristic of micro-simulation models is their ability to produce meaningful aggregates (either at the regional or national level), calculated by adding-up the results obtained at the individual level. This quality relates to the use of representative household samples, the aim being to ensure consistency between macroeconomic reasoning and poverty evaluation.

The basic principle underlying micro-simulation models is to take the household sample as a reference population to which economic shocks and, in the case of dynamic models, demographical processes such as births, deaths, migration, etc. are applied. In the case of static models, the 'final' population is the same as the reference population, but household income and consumption (or any other relevant characteristic at the

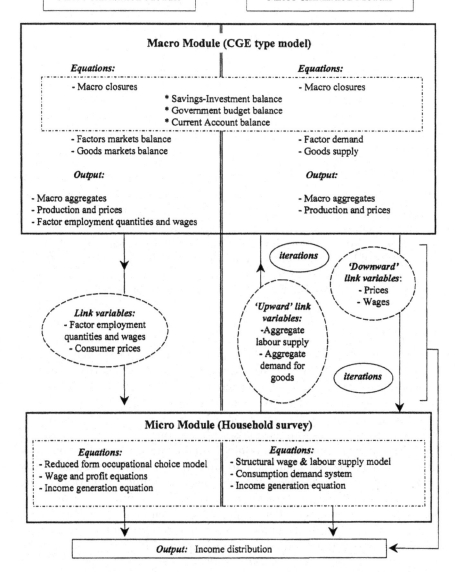

Figure 14.1 Generic structures of micro–macro models.

household level that has been incorporated in the model) have changed. In dynamic models, the simulated population is different because demographical processes change its structure. In both cases, the aim is to compare the distribution of income or consumption (or any other welfare measure) before and after the simulated shock, using standard measures and methods for poverty analysis.

In order to evaluate poverty reduction policies, micro-simulation models are typically linked to a macroeconomic framework, which can be more or less comprehensive. The term 'micro-macro model' will be used to refer to the combination of a micro-simulation model with a macroeconomic framework.

Three levels of analysis should be taken into account to ensure satisfactory analysis of the impact of economic policies on poverty and income distribution:

- at the macroeconomic level it is the economy's structural characteristics that are important, together with the macroeconomic constraints liable to limit its margin to adjust to changes in price systems and incentives;
- at the microeconomic level it is important to capture the different aspects of household heterogeneity;
- between these two levels at the 'meso' level, the structure and workings of the factors markets play a central role in determining factor returns.

Some key characteristics seem relevant to describe and classify macro-micro models used to evaluate poverty reduction policies. These characteristics relate either to the features of the micro simulation 'module', or to those of the macroeconomic framework, or to the characteristics of the linkage between these two levels.

Concerning the micro-simulation module, a fundamental feature is whether agents' behaviours are taken into account. When this is not the case, the micro-simulation module contains at least an 'accounting' income equation. We shall refer to this type of model using the term 'micro-accounting' model. When microeconomic behaviours are represented, their types constitute another discriminating feature of micro-simulation models. For instance, some models focus on labour supply and occupational choices, while others represent decisions concerning schooling, migration or consumption. The representation of microeconomic behaviour can be based on a reduced or a structural formalisation. Structural models are systems of equations that link exogenous and endogenous variables and parameters. Solving a system of equations so that the endogenous variables are expressed according to exogenous variables gives one or several equations referred to as the reduced form of the system. By definition, these reduced specifications are therefore derived from structural neoclassical models of constrained optimisation and have these models' standard properties. However, given their reduced form, they cannot explicitly account for the endogenous phenomena of decision-making, segmentation and/or rationing at work on the micro-economic level.

A second characteristic that distinguishes macro-micro models concerns the modelling of phenomena at the aggregate level; that is, establishing whether there is macroeconomic closure and, if so, defining its characteristics. First, a distinction can be made between models with no closure, which address first-round effects or measures with low feedback, and 'closed' models that take into account the general equilibrium effects through price variations or macroeconomic quantities. Prices determination mechanism can then either be 'integrated' into the micro-simulation model, or formalised in an 'independent' aggregate model that feeds the micro-simulation, in what is then referred to as a sequential model.

The two characteristics mentioned above (reduced versus structural, sequential versus integrated) are in fact not entirely independent. Integrating macroeconomic closure into a micro-simulation model imposes a structural specification of microeconomic behaviour.

A final criterion that can be used to classify micro-simulation models is the time dimension. Demo-economic models are generally developed to study the impact of a change in demo-economic behaviour and therefore focus on the dynamic aspects and on modelling demographic processes. In contrast, static models designed to examine the short or medium-term impacts of changes in the economic environment are based on a more comprehensive modelling of short or medium-term behaviour, in particular with respect to the workings of markets for goods and factors.

Using relevant combinations of the classification criteria presented above, different approaches can be distinguished which we will now describe, outlining their advantages and their limits. Several examples of models implemented to date are presented in Table 14.2, three of which are developed in the last section.

Micro-accounting and disaggregated CGE models

This first approach basically corresponds to a more extensive disaggregation of a standard multi-sector and multi-market model. It corresponds to examples [1], [2] and [3] in Table 14.2.

The construction of any micro-simulation model applied to poverty analysis starts by computing the reference income distribution for the sample of households using the information contained in the household survey. This can be a delicate exercise, particularly when it comes to collecting data on income from independent activities. Once the distribution of income has been established, household income can be disaggregated into different sources (wage income, agricultural income, income from

Table 14.2 Micro-simulation and micro-accounting models for development and poverty analysis

No.	Reference	Country or region	Microeconomic part	Population structure	Macroeconomic part	Macro–micro link
Micro-accounting and disaggregated CGE models						
1	World Bank (2001e) (RMSM-X+LP for PRSPs)	Several developing countries	Expansion of household incomes by socio-economic groups according to factor returns given by the macro-part	Static	Static, financing gap model	Sequential
2	Devarajan and Go (2001) (123-PRSP)	Zambia, but easily transferable to any other country	Expansion of household incomes by decile observed in a survey according to factor returns given by the macro-part	Static	Static, multi-sector CGE model	Sequential
3	Agénor, Izquierdo and Foffack (2002) (IMMPA)	Hypothetical database, but transferable to any country	Expansion of household incomes by socio-economic groups observed in a survey according to factor returns given by the macro-part	Static	Dynamic, multi-sector CGE model	Sequential
Sequential approach and reduced models						
4	Bourguignon, Fournier and Gurgand (1999, 2001), Bourguignon, Ferreira and Lustig (2001), Bourguignon, Ferreira and Leite (2001), Grimm (2001)	Several Asian and Latin-American middle-income countries, Côte d'Ivoire	Reduced form household income generating model	Use of two or more empirically obs. pop. structures	Empirically based hypotheses on the evolution of returns on the labour market and labour supply behaviour	No

Table 14.2 continued

			Static, but with varying education and household size distributions	Hypotheses on the evolution of the return to education	No
5	Ferreira and Leite (2002)	Ceará (Brazil)	Same as in [4] plus reduced form schooling and household-size models		
6	Robilliard, Bourguignon and Robinson (2001), Bourguignon, Robilliard and Robinson (2001)	Indonesia	Same as in [4]	Static	Static, multi-sector CGE model	Sequential
	Integrated approach and structural models					
7	Cogneau (1999, 2001)	Antananarivo (Madagascar)	Structural household income generating model	Static	Static, three-sector CGE model	Integrated
8	Cogneau and Robilliard (2001)	Madagascar	Structural household income generating model	Static	Static, three-sector CGE model	Integrated
	Dynamic models					
9	Cogneau and Grimm (2002), Grimm (2002a)	Côte d'Ivoire	Structural household income generating model plus dynamic demographic model	Dynamic	Hypotheses on the evolution of the return to education and labour demand	No

Source: Authors' representation.

informal independent activities, transfers, etc.). If the structure of household consumption is available, specific price indexes for each household can also be constructed. This allows taking into account differences in budget shares, and in particular capturing the fact that poor households tend to have bigger food shares than rich ones.

At the macro level, the evolution of prices corresponding to the different types of income can be extracted from a CGE-type macro model (see pp. 346–7). For example, the evolution of factor prices following a change in the economic environment can be used as the basis for a micro-simulation exercise, as long as it is possible to match the sources of income of households in the sample with the factors contained in the Social Accounting Matrix, and thereby in the CGE model. This matching can sometimes pose problems because Social Accounting Matrices are mainly built using national accounts and are likely to use nomenclatures different from those used in the household surveys.[15] Furthermore, dividing value added between remuneration from labour and remuneration from capital, which may seem easy when dealing with formal sectors, is more delicate when it comes to agricultural or informal activities. In these cases, households hold the capital and use family labour, so the disaggregation of income for each household must be based on a certain number of assumptions concerning the returns to these factors.

Once the structure of income and consumption of the sample households has been determined in accordance with the structure of the macroeconomic model, it is relatively simple to proceed with the micro-simulation accounting exercise. For instance, if one assumes that agricultural income went up by 10 per cent, it is relatively straightforward to recompute household incomes using that information and compare the new income distribution with the initial one. The first step is to simulate a new price vector using a standard CGE model; the second is to compute new households' incomes given the aggregate evolution of the corresponding price system. The limits of this type of model are inherent to the assumption that households do not respond to changes in the price system. Indeed, it implicitly assumes that households hold fixed shares of factors for which only returns are liable to change. This hypothesis is particularly debatable in the case of labour supply and is likely to limit the scope of this type of model to cases where adjustments on the labour market are marginal.

Sequential approach and reduced models

Introducing households' behaviours constitutes a more advanced stage of micro-simulation. As we pointed out above, the formalisation of microeconomic behaviour can be reduced or structural. One possible approach is based on a 'reduced-form' micro-simulation module that describes the income generation process for a sample of households, taking into account occupational choices. It corresponds to examples [4] to [6] in Table 14.2. But whereas the models [4] and [5] use aggregate hypotheses built up from observed data, only example [6] develops, strictly speaking, a micro-macro simulation model with a CGE model as the macro framework.

This approach is inspired by a model developed by Bourguignon, Fournier and Gurgand (2001) and applied to analysing the evolution of income distribution in Taiwan from 1979 to 1994. The micro-simulation model is based on the representation of income generation by a model of individual occupational choice and wage and profit equations. This framework has been extended and linked to a standard CGE model to analyse the social impact of the financial crisis in Indonesia (Robilliard, Bourguignon and Robinson 2001; see example on pp. 360–2). The two models are used sequentially: the CGE model generates vectors of price, wages and employment which are then transferred to the micro-simulation model, which in turn generates a new distribution of incomes, consistent with the earnings and employment aggregates given by the CGE model.

The advantage of this type of approach is that it is based on a micro-econometric model of household behaviour that takes into account decisions concerning production and labour supply. Nevertheless, one of the problems posed by this approach is the consistency between the aggregate and microeconomic representations of behaviour and the functioning of the factor markets. At the macro level, the functioning of the factor market is based on aggregate supply and demand functions and on assumptions concerning intersectoral mobility. At the micro level, occupational choices and labour earnings are generated independently in the absence of structural modelling of microeconomic behaviour. Due to the sequential structure, there is not always a consistent relationship between the behaviour specification in the macro model and that implied by the equations in the micro-simulation module. In addition, this type of specification limits the ability to represent complex interactions between production and consumption decisions linked to the failure, or absence, of certain markets.

Integrated approach and structural models

The introduction of a structural specification of household decisions permits capturing more complex behaviours and allows implementing an integrated framework. Compared to the sequential approach where microeconomic behaviour needs to be specified twice (in an aggregated form in the macro module and in a disaggregated form in the micro-simulation module), the integrated approach has the advantage of being completely consistent in terms of the specification of microeconomic behaviour: all the flows that are related to household behaviour (like labour supply, consumption, etc.) are computed by adding-up results obtained at the household level, not by using an aggregate labour supply or consumption function.

One key characteristic of this type of approach – which corresponds to examples [7] and [8] in Table 14.2 – is to focus more on the microeconomic side of the model, on the basis of a comprehensive structural modelling of occupational choices, income generation and consumption decisions. To our knowledge, Cogneau (1999, 2001) was the first to develop a micro-simulation model of household income within a general equilibrium framework. This model was used to study the labour market in Antananarivo. In line with it, a general equilibrium micro-simulation model was developed and applied to the Malagasy economy as a whole in order to analyse the impact of different development strategies on poverty and income distribution (Cogneau and Robilliard 2001; see example on pp. 362–4).[16]

In terms of consistency, this type of approach appears more satisfactory than the sequential approach described above, but the complexity of the structural specifications makes an exhaustive disaggregation of goods and sectors more difficult, due to the intrinsic econometric difficulties posed by estimating systems of equations. Hence, contrary to the previous approaches, this type of model must be content with a less sophisticated representation of the macroeconomic and multi-market framework. This aspect limits the scope of the approach to cases where intersectoral reallocation does not play a central role. For example, the economic impact of certain macroeconomic or liberalisation policies generally depends on the position of the goods produced by the economy *vis-à-vis* foreign trade. One of the contributions of applied general equilibrium models stems from their ability to take into account structural effects by disaggregating activities and goods. From that perspective, the integrated structural approach is relatively better adapted to exploring demo-economic issues or general growth strategies for instance, or targeted policies such as labour market interventions or price policies. Another limit has to do with the fact that, although it may be possible in theory, it is hard in practice to devise a full structural econometrical model of household behaviour, including production, labour supply, consumption, schooling and migration decisions. The model either has to focus on the features of behaviour most relevant to the policy question under review, or use a 'piecemeal modelling' approach in the spirit of Orcutt's micro-simulation analysis. This means that it is practically impossible to build a multi-purpose model with this approach.

Dynamic models

One way of explicitly taking into account the temporal dimension of economic policies as well as the heterogeneity of individual behaviour and resources is to integrate a household income micro-simulation model (as presented above) into a dynamic micro-simulation model able to project the population structure and the accumulation of human and possibly physical capital through time. This corresponds to example [9] in Table 14.2. The demographic model has to be similar to those used in developed countries for the study of pension reforms, of the distribution of life-cycle incomes, or the accumulation of wealth.[17]

Two of us have made a first attempt to produce such a model for the case of Côte d'Ivoire (see example on pp. 364–6). This model integrates a structural household income generating model into a dynamic demographic micro-simulation model. This model is based on various data sources such as household income surveys, demographic surveys, census data and United Nations' demographic projections. It simulates fertility, marriage, household formation, mortality, migration, school enrolment of children, labour supply, and earnings in each period, on the individual level. The model was tested over a validation period of five years (1993–8). Not only does it produce a sequence of cross-sections, but even individual demographic and economic trajectories through time in a 15- to 25-year timescale. To date, it has been used to study the economic, especially distributional, impact (a) of Aids (Cogneau and Grimm 2002), and (b) of educational policies (Grimm 2002a) in Côte d'Ivoire.

Both issues typically need a dynamic approach. The Aids epidemic, although it strongly modifies the age mortality rates, only has a significant impact on the age structure in the long or very long term. During this period the mortality change interacts with other demographic and economic behaviours such as fertility, marriage and labour supply. The expansion of education begins by increasing the dependency ratio. The surplus only arises when the children enter the labour market. During this period as well, the change in the distribution of education interacts with demographic behaviour.[18] In addition, the dynamic framework allows us to compare the distributional effects of today – in particular the negative effect of financing this policy on current income – with those in 15 or 25 years.

In contrast with the other approaches described above, a drawback of the dynamic micro-simulation model remains the lack of hypotheses concerning macroeconomic closures and the long-term evolution of the economy and the structure of economic growth. Future work will address this issue, but much effort will be needed to resolve this problem in a satisfactory manner. Furthermore, the model parameters are mainly estimated using cross-section data, which hampers the modelling of behavioural changes or phenomena such as consumption smoothing. A significant improvement of our model in this respect would call for panel data.

Micro-simulation to evaluate policies: a few applications

In this section we will present three examples where micro-simulation models have been applied in practice. These examples correspond to three of the approaches described in the previous section. We do not present any applied model corresponding to the micro-accounting framework because, to our knowledge, existing models are merely stylised exercises that have not yet been applied to meaningful policy questions. A wide range of shocks and policies are explored through the examples presented. In the first example, the micro-macro model was used to decompose the social impact of the Indonesian financial crisis. In the next example, alternative development strategies for the Malagasy economy are examined with respect to their impact on poverty and income distribution. Finally, the effect of an expansion of education on income distribution is examined using a dynamic model for Côte d'Ivoire. The three countries for which models are presented are currently developing poverty reduction strategies under the PRSP initiative and the policies examined can be related to poverty reduction.

Decomposing the social impact of the Indonesian financial crisis

This reduced form sequential macro-micro model was developed by Robilliard, Bourguignon and Robinson (2001) to quantify the effects on poverty and inequality of the financial crisis that hit Indonesia in 1997. The macro framework is a CGE model based on a Social Accounting Matrix with 38 sectors and 14 factors of production. It captures structural features of the economy, binding macro constraints, and incorporates general equilibrium effects. The micro-simulation model is based on a detailed representation of the real income generation mechanism at the household level. It is based on a sub-sample of 9,800 households, a module of the 1996 SUSENAS survey that contains information on occupational choices, income and consumption. It captures household heterogeneity in terms of income sources, area of residence, demographic composition, endowment in human capital, and consumption preferences.

The CGE scenarios seek to reproduce and decompose the evolution of the Indonesian economy between 1997 and 1998 in terms of changes in employment, wages, and macroeconomic aggregates. The most important external shocks during that period were the financial crisis and the extended El Niño drought. The drought is simulated through a negative shock on the total productivity factor in agricultural sectors. It is also assumed that there was a 25 per cent increase in the marketing cost of food. This reflects the fact that traders, more than producers, are expected to benefit from the food price increase. The financial crisis is simulated through a combination of different shocks. First, it is assumed that the need to adjust the current account led to a real devaluation, which is simulated through a 30 per cent decrease in foreign saving flows to the economy (SIMDEV scenario). As a result of the devaluation, all sectors experienced a 'credit crunch', simulated through a cut in the supply of working capital. Two types of working capital are considered in the CGE model. In a first stage the impact of a 25 per cent cut in the availability of foreign working capital is examined in combination with the real devaluation described above (the DEVCCF scenario). In a second stage, the impact of a 20 per cent cut in the availability of domestic credit crunch (FINCRI scenario) is considered. The domestic credit crunch shock is viewed as stemming from the foreign credit crunch. As a result, it is simulated in combination with the two previous components of the financial crisis. The resulting simulation can then be analysed as mimicking a 'pure' financial crisis shock, without any other historical shock. The effect of El Niño drought is simulated through a 5 per cent decrease in the total factor productivity of the agricultural sector. The drought is first simulated alone (SIMELN scenario) and then in combination with the financial crisis, thus yielding something that is close to what actually happened in Indonesia between 1997 and 1998 (the SIMALL scenario).

When all components of the crisis are taken into account (SIMALL), the modelling exercise yields a 140.9 per cent increase in the poverty head-count ratio (see Table 14.3). This surge in poverty appears to be fuelled both by the drop in the average income per capita and by an important increase in inequality indicators. All shocks contribute to the negative income impact and the increase in inequality. In terms of the rural–urban

Table 14.3 Decomposing the social impact of the Indonesian financial crisis

	BASE	SIMELN	SIMDEV	DEVCCF	FINCRI	SIMALL
Per capita income (Rp. thousands)						
Urban	170.9	−12.7	−7.6	−21.3	−22.9	−30.1
Rural	90.6	−10.0	−2.0	−7.1	−12.6	−21.2
All	121.1	−11.5	−5.0	−14.7	−18.1	−26.0
Theil index ($\times$ 100)						
Urban	53.9	8.5	6.2	5.6	7.7	15.8
Rural	33.1	5.1	3.9	6.6	10.8	15.9
All	49.3	5.2	2.4	−1.1	2.9	9.3
Poverty head-count index (P_0)						
Urban	4.0	78.6	47.1	129.3	165.0	279.4
Rural	12.4	43.0	13.0	36.7	63.2	113.5
All	9.2	48.9	18.6	51.9	80.0	140.9

Source: Robilliard, Bourguignon and Robinson (2001).

Notes
Base values for BASE column and percentage change for other simulations.
SIMELN   El Niño drought
SIMDEV   Real devaluation
DEVCCF   Real devaluation + foreign credit crunch
FINCRI   Real devaluation + foreign credit crunch + domestic credit crunch
SIMALL   Real devaluation + foreign credit crunch + domestic credit crunch + El Niño drought.

divide, the simulations are able to capture the fact that the poverty increase was much higher in the urban sector. Two reasons can explain this result: first, wage earnings, which represent a higher income share in urban areas, decreased more than self-employment incomes; second, food prices increased relatively to non-food prices, a shock that typically benefits rural households on average. Nevertheless, results show that poverty increased within the rural sector as well. Again, this increase appears to stem from a strong decrease in per capita income and a significant worsening in income distribution. A comparison of these results with results obtained using representative household groups shows that the latter approach would have led to underestimate poverty increase at the aggregate level by 20 per cent and inequality increase by 150 per cent.

Impact on poverty and income distribution of alternative development strategies in Madagascar

This integrated structural model was developed by Cogneau and Robilliard (2001) to study the impact on poverty and income distribution of alternative development strategies in Madagascar. The model represents the behaviour of a sample of 4,500 households, representative of the Malagasy population, in an economy with three sectors (agricultural, formal and informal) and four goods (food products, agricultural exports, informal and formal). The structural microeconomic model represents the decisions of households in terms of occupational choice and labour supply, taking into account their heterogeneity in terms of qualifications, preferences and opportunities of work allocation. Consumption preferences are also treated explicitly at the microeconomic level.

In terms of development strategy, one can consider that there are at present two options for the Malagasy economy: either continuation of the formal sector 'push', through, in particular, development of the Export Processing Zone, or the massive investment in the development of the agricultural sector, which suffered from under-investment during the last decades and whose performance is poor. The first two simulations concern value added in the formal sector. In the first simulation (EMBFOR), growth in the formal sector corresponds to the creation of new firms, leading to an increase in 10 per cent in stock of capital and in employment. It is simulated through an increase in income provided by the capital dividends from formal enterprises for shareholder households, and in the demand for formal labour. The increase is simulated by selecting individuals in the population of non-formal active workers and non-active persons of 15 years and over. The hiring pattern is partially random. Its structure is defined in terms of sex, age, education and milieu (rural/urban) and corresponds to the structure of formal hiring in the last five years. In the second simulation (SALFOR), the value added in return for formal labour increases by a rise of 10 per cent in formal wages but with no impact on employment. The value added in return for formal capital increases in the same way as in the previous simulation. The direct effect of this shock is an increase in income for households receiving formal wages. The following two simulations concern the agricultural sector. The first (PGFAGRI) simulates an increase of 10 per cent in overall productivity of factors affecting agricultural households. This leads to an increase in agricultural incomes and in agricultural production. In the fourth simulation (PGFALIM), the increase in productivity concerns the production of agricultural foodstuffs only.

The results are presented in partial equilibrium (fixed prices) and general equilibrium (prices determined endogenously). Results show that general equilibrium mechanisms have important redistributive effects. For instance, when considering the impact of the PGFAGRI simulation, the partial equilibrium simulation yields an average decrease of poverty of −2.0 per cent, with an increase in the urban sector, while the general equilibrium simulation yields an average decrease of poverty of −3.7 per cent, with a decrease in the urban sector. This difference can be explained by the fact that the strategy of agricultural growth also benefits urban households via a drop in the corresponding food product prices, a typical general equilibrium effect that the partial equilibrium framework

Table 14.4 Impact on poverty and income distribution of alternative development strategies in Madagascar

	BASE	EMBFOR		SALFOR		PGFAGRI		PGFALIM	
Equilibrium		*Partial*	*General*	*Partial*	*General*	*Partial*	*General*	*Partial*	*General*
Per capita income (francs Malagasy thousands)									
Urban	1,628	5.4	4.2	6.7	5.9	−0.2	1.9	−0.2	1.6
Rural	605	4.0	5.8	1.9	3.5	1.1	5.0	0.9	4.2
All	863	4.7	5.0	4.2	4.7	0.5	3.5	0.4	3.0
Theil index (×100)									
Urban	90.9	1.6	−1.0	3.0	2.0	0.2	−0.8	0.3	−0.0
Rural	51.0	4.7	5.9	3.3	3.1	−2.3	0.3	0.2	9.4
All	81.6	3.0	0.8	4.6	3.1	−1.2	−1.5	−0.2	2.0
Poverty head-count index (P_0)									
Urban	43.4	−3.9	−3.3	−2.5	−2.1	2.9	−2.6	2.9	−1.8
Rural	74.9	−1.2	−2.4	−0.3	−1.5	−2.9	−3.9	−1.9	−2.0
All	67.0	−1.7	−2.6	−0.7	−1.6	−2.0	−3.7	−1.2	−2.0

Source: Cogneau and Robilliard (2001).

Notes
Base values for BASE column and percentage change for other simulations.
EMBFOR   Formal hiring (10 per cent)
SALFOR   Increase in formal wages (10 per cent)
PGFAGRI   Increase in total factor productivity in agricultural sector (10 per cent)
PGFALIM   Increase in total factor productivity in agricultural foodstuffs sector (10 per cent).

does not capture. From the point of view of development strategy, the results also show that one point of growth 'pulled' by the agricultural sector leads to a 1.5–2 times greater reduction in the poverty rate than a 'formal' point of growth. As mentioned above, this result depends on the evolution of food prices, whose decrease benefits the urban households. In case the drop in food price is too strong, the agricultural growth strategy could nevertheless hurt agricultural households. From that perspective, rural growth cannot be considered independently of urban growth (see Chapter 4) since the price impact of an increase in agricultural production depends on the position of food products *vis-à-vis* foreign trade, on the tradability of these products and on the linkages between the urban and the rural sectors.

The dynamic effects of an expansion of education on the income distribution in Côte d'Ivoire

The micro-simulation model used by Grimm (2002a) is designed to simulate at the individual level the most important demographic and economic events through time. The base unit is the individual, but each individual belongs in each period to a specific household. The model is a discrete time model. Each period corresponds to one year. A fixed order concerning the different events is assumed: marriage, household formation, school enrolment, fertility, mortality, migration, reallocation of land, occupational choices, generation of individual earnings and household income. The labour income module draws from the spirit of Roy's model (1951) as formalised by Heckman and Sedlacek (1985). It is competitive in the sense that no segmentation or job rationing prevails, but only weakly because labour mobility across sectors does not equalise returns to observed and unobserved individual characteristics. Household members compare their potential earnings in different activities, including employment, within the household by taking into account past labour supply decisions of the other household members. Finally they choose the activity which provides the highest potential income. The population of departure is constructed using the *Enquête Prioritaire* (EP 1993), which covers 9,600 households and 58,000 individuals. The modelling of the different events is based on various other data sources (for details see Grimm 2002b and Cogneau and Grimm 2002).

The study uses 1992 to 2015 as the simulation period. The reforms are assumed to start in 1998. REFSIM is the reference simulation, which assumes a roughly constant enrolment age pattern from 1998 on. PRIMED simulates the case of almost universal primary schooling for the generations enrolled in 1998 and after. HIGHED simulates in addition increased progression rates into higher education. Finally, ALPH adds literacy programmes for adults, in particular for women and the rural population. This last scenario is simulated under four different hypotheses:

constant (CR), increasing (IR), and decreasing returns to education (DR), and a segmentation of the labour market through a rationed labour demand in the (formal) wage sector (SM).

First of all, only reforms which include a huge adult literacy programme with a particular attention to women and rural population will reduce the illiteracy rate below 20 per cent in the considered timescale. Table 14.5 shows that the economic effects of an expansion of education depend very crucially on the hypothesis made for the evolution of the return to education and the labour demand. It should be noted that even in the reference simulation income, inequality and poverty change due to changes in the population structure. All the scenarios draw a rather optimistic picture of the evolution of the Ivorian economy, but given the difficulty in predicting the long run evolution of the economy and the structure of economic growth, the results should principally be interpreted in relation to the reference scenario and not in absolute terms. Over the period 1992 to 2015, the growth gain per capita of the most optimistic policy (ALPH) relative to the persistence of the status quo (REFSIM) is about 0.3 of a point per year if the return to education remains constant (ALPHCR), about −0.9 of a point per year if the return to education decreases (ALPHDR) and about 1.8 points per year if the return increases (ALPHIR). The literature is very controversial on the evolution of the relation between education and its return (see, for instance, Bils and Klenow 2000; Katz and Murphy 1992); in consequence the uncertainty is very high. Therefore, we assumed three alternative return scenarios, where returns either remain constant or decrease (increase) with the share of the workforce having more than five years of schooling with an elasticity of decrease/increase of $-1/3$, $1/3$. The share of the workforce having more than five years of schooling increases in the simulation ALPH by approximately 3 per cent per year, this implies that the return to education between 1998 and 2015 in the wage-earner sector, for instance, increases from 17.1 per cent to 20.5 per cent under the hypothesis of increasing returns and decreases from 17.1 per cent to 14.3 per cent under the hypothesis of decreasing returns. If the share of the workforce employed in the (formal) wage sector remains rationed to that of 1997 (ALPHSM), which, in our opinion, seems a quite likely scenario, no growth gain will be generated at all. Likewise, the evolution of income distribution and poverty depends in a decisive way on these hypotheses. A decreasing return relatively quickly produces a Kuznets curve, whereas an increasing return results in a rise of the Gini coefficient of 0.4 points per year relative to REFSIM. Poverty is predicted to decrease due to changes in the population and education structure even in the reference scenario. However, a much more rapid decrease only seems possible with an increasing return to education and without a rationed labour demand in the (formal) wage sector. Otherwise, the expansion of education has, at least in the considered time period, only a modest effect on the poverty

Table 14.5 Some results on education strategies in Côte d'Ivoire

	1998	2005	2010	2015	Growth p.a. 1997–2015
Per capita income (CFA francs thousands)					
REFSIM	351	457	498	546	2.61
PRIMED	−0.3	−0.7	−0.6	−2.6	−0.15
HIGHED	2.0	−2.2	−0.6	−0.5	−0.02
ALPHCR	−0.3	−2.0	1.4	5.3	0.30
ALPHDR	−2.6	−10.5	−11.4	−15.0	−0.92
ALPHIR	−1.1	5.3	17.9	36.8	1.80
ALPHSM	0.0	−4.2	0.6	0.9	0.06
Gini index over the distribution of household income per capita					
REFSIM	0.598	0.609	0.609	0.609	0.18
PRIMED	−0.2	−0.8	−0.7	−1.0	−0.06
HIGHED	−0.8	0.2	1.0	1.3	0.07
ALPHCR	0.0	0.0	0.2	0.2	0.00
ALPHDR	−0.7	−3.1	−2.6	−4.8	−0.28
ALPHIR	−0.3	2.5	3.9	6.9	0.37
ALPHSM	−0.3	−0.8	0.2	0.0	0.00
Poverty head-count index (P_0) (household income per capita under 1 USD PPP)					
REFSIM	0.348	0.300	0.271	0.254	−1.75
PRIMED	0.0	−2.0	−2.2	0.0	−0.01
HIGHED	−0.3	−0.7	4.8	4.3	0.22
ALPHCR	1.7	−1.0	−0.7	−0.8	−0.05
ALPHDR	0.6	3.3	7.0	5.1	0.27
ALPHIR	0.0	−3.0	−5.5	−10.6	−0.62
ALPHSM	0.6	0.7	2.2	2.4	0.12

Source: Grimm (2002a).

Notes
Simulation from 1992 to 2015, income in 1000 CFA francs 1998-Abidjan
REFSIM in levels, other for levels in percentage deviations from REFSIM, and for growth rate in absolute deviations
REFSIM   Reference simulation, constant enrolment age pattern from 1998 on
PRIMED   Universal primary school for the generations enrolled in 1998 and after
HIGHED   PRIMED + higher progression rates into higher education
ALPH–   HIGHED + literacy programmes for adults
–CR   ALPH with constant returns to education
–DR   ALPH with decreasing returns to education
–IR   ALPH with increasing returns to education
–SM   ALPH with rationed labour demand in the (formal) wage sector.

head-count index, because, among other things, the higher progression rates in higher education are only marginally beneficial to the poor. The simulations also show that a policy, which is limited to universal primary education (PRIMED), does not contribute to a further poverty reduction relative to the reference case. One explanation is that, in the early stages, the rise in schooling reduces the workforce. The average household income per capita only starts rising faster after 2005, when the first better-educated cohorts enter the labour market. Furthermore, the return to education for up to six years of schooling is not sufficient to achieve significantly higher income. In any case, purely universal primary education can only foster growth in the very long run, when a large part of the population benefits from it.

Conclusion: future challenges

In this chapter, we have described the current *ex ante* evaluation techniques for poverty reduction policies, placing them in the historical context of econometric evaluation and in relation to the new policies proposed by the international institutions. There is currently a strong focus on adapting policies to each national situation and to democratic demands, leading to demands for more, and better, evaluation. When such evaluation is carried out *ex post*, once the policies have been implemented, several econometric methods are possible, particularly in the case of targeted policies. When the evaluation is carried out *ex ante*, in order to choose between several alternative policies, we hope to have demonstrated that micro-simulation techniques are the best suited. We have also argued that *ex post* evaluation can also require structural modelling of microeconomic behaviour patterns, or modelling of external or macroeconomic effects, so that in fact, in a large number of cases, the difference between *ex ante* and *ex post* evaluation is mainly a question of the statistical information available rather than the method itself.

A distinction can be made within the policy packages recommended by the PRSPs, between relatively traditional stabilisation or adjustment policies concerned with the level and/or structure of prices or demand, and sectoral and/or targeted policies concerned with access to the labour market or access to social services. Before carrying out an evaluation of the distributive impact of the first type of policy, the first step is to ensure the consistency of the macroeconomic framework and the microeconomic database. This can be done to a greater or a lesser extent, and can focus more on one or other of the two scales of analysis (macro or micro). As for the second type of policy, some of the effects can be evaluated by micro-simulation with partial equilibrium of the relative behaviour in terms of labour supply or demand for services, involving more or less complex micro-econometric estimates. The evaluation of their macroeconomic effects or their long-term effects (intergenerational in particular) requires the analytical framework to be opened further, either on the side of general equilibrium or of demo-economic dynamics. Finally, we proposed a typology of the micro-simulation techniques used to date to evaluate the poverty reduction strategies, and presented different evaluation experiments in which we have taken part. The methods and experiences presented are all quite recent and are still research programmes rather than proven, routine techniques. This is why we would like to conclude with our ideas on the future challenges facing this research, which we believe can be found on three levels: methods, already widely developed in this chapter (and, for databases, Chapter 11); criteria, particularly covered in Chapter 2; and the processes involved in choosing and implementing the policies, which are studied in detail in the chapters in the second part of this book.

In our view, three areas are really crucial today as far as the methods of analysis are concerned. First, the consistency between macro and micro-economic variables still raises a number of unresolved questions, regarding the simulation techniques as such (see pp. 350–9), but also, upstream, regarding the statistical data.[19] Second, we believe that it is vital to further our knowledge, not only of the behaviour of the agents, but also of the real workings of the markets. For instance, spatial or sectoral segmentation, the prevalence of high transaction costs or the existence of community-based redistribution mechanisms are all likely to impose great constraints on the agents' behaviour and thereby to change the impact of the policies significantly. Third, in a number of cases there appears to be a need to develop simulation tools that are better able to take into account the time dimension of demo-economic phenomena, particularly in order to promote long-term, intergenerational redistribution strategies instead of short-term interventions that may be more profitable from a political standpoint, but are often socially inefficient.

As for the evaluation criteria, progress must be made in applying the theory of justice to the problems of poor countries and fragmented societies, in a view to improving the definition of the policies' objectives (reduction of income poverty or multidimensional poverty, equal opportunities, etc.), their measurement and evaluation. Clarifying the objectives is doubtless one of the conditions required if better connections are to be established between the emergence of a democratic debate and the work of national and international 'experts'. Before deciding how poverty can be reduced, it is obviously important to agree on what sort of poverty we are talking about. It is not right that the experts should be the only people present, at all the stages of the policies' design and evaluation.

Finally, the increasing concern expressed on the subject of institutions underlines that two other types of evaluation must go hand in hand with the formal policy evaluation, namely the evaluation of the policies' selection and design processes and the evaluation of the policies' implementation processes. What is the point of a formal evaluation of policies that will never be decided on, or that will be very poorly implemented? The evaluation processes must give just as much weight to the logical design of 'good policies' as to the social and institutional conditions required to implement them in practice.[20] The participatory and administrative processes conditioning any action count just as much as a sound definition of the action itself. Lastly, there is an *evaluation of the evaluation*, the methodology of which is still to be designed, which we have only begun to outline here.

Notes

1 A parallel paper on the analytical challenges raised by the PSIA specifically reviews this question. Cf. Bourguignon, Pereira da Silva and Stern (2002).

2 This choice obviously stems from the fact that the authors of these lines use these techniques widely. In fact they are also taking part in a World Bank research programme on this subject.

3 It is nonetheless obvious that policies are also conditioned by the international balance of power, and by political changes in developed countries.

4 We must point out that our use of the terms *ex ante* and *ex post* only remotely ties in with the meaning they are given in the modern theory of justice where *ex ante* (resp. *ex post*) refers to an assessment of a state of the world before (resp. after) the occurrence of idiosyncratic shocks, particularly contrasting the approach in terms of equality of opportunities to that in terms of equality of conditions (see Chapter 2). There is also a purely macroeconomic sense of the *ex ante/ex post* comparison which distinguishes partial equilibrium (in jargon, 'first round' results) from general equilibrium.

5 Including those aimed at simulating such experimentation *a posteriori* ('matching estimators') and those designed to determine the causal impact of a given variable by a strategy of so-called 'natural' instrumentation; see Heckman (1999).

6 As in the case of the evaluation of the Argentinian workfare programme 'Trabajar' proposed by Jalan and Ravallion (2002), applying the matching estimators technique.

7 Two stages can be distinguished. The first consists in examining and clarifying the logical coherency of the criteria put forward and the policies proposed, and is more or less related to theories of justice. The second consists in imagining the impact of the policies (i.e. in simulating their application in a prospective manner), and is related once more to econometrics.

8 See Elbers, Lanjouw and Lanjouw (2001). See also Chapter 2 on the risks of a static approach to poverty.

9 CGE models are based on a database called the Social Accounting Matrix, which records the different economic flows between agents and/or accounts each year. In this type of model, household incomes are modelled as the sum of all income from the different factors held by the households.

10 A macroeconomic closure is the way by which market equilibrium is achieved between supply and demands for goods, factors and monetary assets, through either price or quantities adjustments. It also makes precise the consequences of fiscal balance and external balance constraints, and how investments meet with savings.

11 For example, De Janvry, Sadoulet and Fargeix (1991) assume a log-normal distribution of income; Decaluwé *et al.* (1999) a beta distribution.

12 Idiosyncratic, that is, individually specific.

13 Tapinos, Mason and Bravo (1997) analysed such phenomena for Latin America in the 1980s, a period of economic crisis and structural adjustment. They showed that, for an average Latin American country, a GDP decrease of 10 to 15 per cent, a usual value for this region and period, implied a loss of almost one year in life expectancy at birth, mainly attributable to a rise in infant mortality. This change affected primarily the poor population. The study also suggested that the crises delayed marriages. In some countries the

total fertility rate decreased three times faster during the crisis than before. The effects on income distribution are not directly analysed by the authors, but one may speculate that they are complex, because the transmission channels have, among other things, ambiguous effects on the dependency ratio.

14 Several explanations may be given. First, during the period of structural adjustment, economic analysis was more concerned with the evaluation of the impact of monetary and exchange rate policies, budget policies, and international trade policies. Second, even if macroeconomic stability was at the centre of structural adjustment policies, the considered timescale rarely exceeded the short and medium term. Third, for a long time, microeconomic data necessary for the quantification of such interactions was not available, although this is no longer the case today.

15 On problems posed by reconciling data from microeconomic surveys and data from national accounts, see, among others, Robilliard and Robinson (1999).

16 Hence, contrary to the view expressed by Bourguignon, Pereira da Silva and Stern (2002), an integrated approach does not conflict with taking into account imperfect market situations.

17 See for example the literature reviews in Merz (1991) (general presentation), Harding (1993, 1996, 2000) (dynamic models), Genier (1996) (models for the health sector), Gokhale *et al.* (2001) (models for the transmission of wealth), and Kotlikoff, Smetters and Walliser (2001) (models for the study of pension reforms).

18 Ferreira and Leite (2002) also try to address the distributional effects of an expansion of education, in their case for the region of Ceará (Brazil). They use a static household income micro-simulation model of the type usually used for the decomposition of distributional changes over time. Besides labour supply and earnings, they actualise only the distribution of education and the household size, but keep constant all other dimensions of the population structure, including the age structure. Doing so gives this exercise a very hypothetical character. Furthermore, their analysis is carried out in a static comparative way, and therefore does not enable the reproduction of the trajectory between the point of departure and the point of arrival.

19 In particular, the different structural aggregrates and coefficients obtained from microeconomic surveys are generally difficult to match with National Accounting data when this exists; for example, for consumption by product (see Chapter 11, and also Robilliard and Robinson 1999). The upper end of income distribution is poorly represented in the statistical surveys, which can require significant adjustments in terms of capital income or income from transfers, whereas national accounts frequently underestimate the importance of informal income and the lower end of income distribution, which are accounted for better in certain surveys (Chapter 13).

20 See the example of 'Quantitative Service Delivery Surveys' quoted by Bourguignon, Pereira da Silva and Stern (2002).

References

Adelman, I. and Robinson, S. (1978) *Income Distribution Policy: A Computable General Equilibrium Model of South Korea*, Stanford: Stanford University Press.

—— (1988) 'Macroeconomic adjustment and income distribution: alternative models applied to two economies', *Journal of Development Economics*, 29(1): 23–44.

Aerts, J.-J., Cogneau, D., de Monchy, G., Herrera, J. and Roubaud, F. (2000) *L'économie camerounaise: un espoir évanoui*, Les Afriques, Paris: Karthala.

AFD (2001) *L'AFD et la réduction de la pauvreté et des inégalités. Note de doctrine* (mimeo), Paris: Agence Française de Développement.

African Development Bank (2002) *Achieving the Millennium Development Goals in Africa. Progress, Prospects, and Policy Implications*, Global Poverty Report 2002, in collaboration with the World Bank, Abidjan: African Development Bank.

AFRISTAT (1998) 'Etat du système statistique dans les Etats membres d'Afristat. Rapport de synthèse de l'enquête réalisée en 1996', Study series No. 1, Bamako: Afristat.

Agénor, P.-R., Izquierdo, A. and Foffack, H. (2002) IMMPA: *A macroeconomic quantitative framework for the analysis of poverty reduction strategies*, (mimeo), Washington, DC: World Bank.

Aghion, P. and Bolton, P. (1997) 'A theory of trickle-down growth and development', *Review of Economic Studies*, 64: 151–72.

Ames, B., Brown, W., Devarajan, S. and Izquierdo, A. (2001) 'Macroeconomic policy and poverty reduction', in World Bank, *A Sourcebook for Poverty Reduction Strategies*, Available online: http://www.worldbank.org/poverty/strategies/chapters (accessed on 1 September 2002).

Andrews, D., Boote, A., Rizavi, S. and Singh, S. (1999) *Debt Relief for Low-Income Countries: The Enhanced HIPC Initiative*, IMF Pamphlet Series No. 51, Washington, DC: International Monetary Fund.

Antoine, Ph. (2002) *L'approche biographique et ses possibilités pour l'analyse des systèmes de genre*, Working Paper DT2002-04, April, Paris: DIAL.

Antoine, Ph., Razafindrakoto, M. and Roubaud, F. (2001) 'Contraints de rester jeunes! Evolution de l'insertion dans trois capitales africaines: Dakar, Yaoundé, Antananarivo', *Autrepart*, 18: 17–36.

Atkinson, A.B. and Brandolini, A. (1999) *Promise and Pitfalls in the Use of 'Secondary' Data Sets: Income Inequality in OECD Countries* (mimeo), Oxford: Nuffield College.

Atkinson, A.B. and Stiglitz, J.E. (1980) *Lectures in Public Economics*, New York: McGraw-Hill International Editions.

Attias-Donfut, C. and Lapierre, N. (1997) *La famille providence: trois générations en Guadeloupe*, Paris: La Documentation française.

Backiny-Yetna, P. and Torelli, C. (2000) 'Comparaison de la pauvreté dans sept capitales d'Afrique de l'Ouest: annexe méthodologique', in DIAL, *Etude de la pauvreté urbaine en Afrique de l'Ouest. Côte d'Ivoire, Mali, Senegal*, Paris: DIAL.

—— (2001) 'Pauvreté en Afrique de l'Ouest et à Madagascar: Perspectives comparatives', Paper presented at the Conference entitled 'La pauvreté à Madagascar: Etat des lieux, réflexions sur les politiques de réduction et leur mise en œuvre', DIAL/IRD/INSTAT/RESAL, Antananarivo, February 2001.

Bako-Arifari, N. and Le Meur, P.-Y. (2001) 'Les dynamiques locales face aux interventions de développement', in G. Winter (ed.) *Inégalités et politiques publiques en Afrique; pluralité des normes et jeux d'acteurs*, Paris: Karthala-IRD.

Banegas, R. and Meyer, P. (2002) *Etude sur la gouvernance: stratégies comparées et choix opérationnels*, Rapport pour le Ministère des Affaires étrangères.

Banerjee, A.V. and Newman, A.F. (1993) 'Occupational choice and the process of development', *Journal of Political Economy*, 101: 274–99.

Barclay, P. (chairman) (1995) *Joseph Rowntree Foundation Inquiry into Income and Wealth*, York: Joseph Rowntree Foundation.

Becker, G.S. and Tomes, N. (1986) 'Human capital and the rise and fall of families', *Journal of Labor Economics*, 4, S1–S39.

Behrman, J.R. and Wolfe, B.L. (1987) 'Investments in schooling in two generations in pre-revolutionary Nicaragua', *Journal of Development Economics*, 27: 395–419.

Behrman, J.R., Gaviria, A. and Székely, M. (2001) 'Intergenerational mobility in Latin America', *Economía*, 2(1): 1–43.

Berthélemy, J.C. (2001) 'HIPC Debt Relief and Policy Reform Incentives', Paper presented to the WIDER Conference on Debt Relief, 17–18 August, Helsinki.

Berthélémy, J.C. and Söderling, L. (2001) *L'Afrique Emergente*, Paris: OECD.

Besley, T. and Burgess, R. (2001) *The Political Economy of Government Responsiveness* (mimeo), London: London School of Economics.

Bils, M. and Klenow, P.J. (2000) 'Does schooling cause growth?', *American Economic Review*, 90(5): 1160–83.

Birdsall, N., Claessens, S. and Diwan, I. (2001) 'Will HIPC Matter? The Debt Game and Donor Behavior', Paper presented to the WIDER Conference on Debt Relief, 17–18 August, Helsinki.

Blaizeau, D. (1999) 'Sept enquêtes sur les dépenses des ménages dans les pays de l'UEMOA', *Stateco*, 92/93(1/2): 39–81, Paris: INSEE.

Blondiaux, L. (1998) *La fabrique de l'opinion. Une histoire sociale des sondages*, Paris: Seuil.

Bloom, D. and Sachs, J. (1998) *Geography, Demography and Economic Growth in Africa*, Brookings Papers on Economic Activity 2, Washington, DC: The Brookings Institution.

Boote, A. and Thugge, K. (1997) *Debt Relief for Low-Income Countries and the HIPC Initiative*, IMF Working Paper, WP/97/24, Washington, DC: International Monetary Fund.

Booth, D. (eds) (2002) *Fighting Poverty in Africa: Are PRSPs Making a Difference?*, London: Overseas Development Institute for the Strategic Partnership with Africa.

Booth, D. and Lucas, H. (2002) *Good Practice in the Development of PRSP Indicators and Monitoring Systems*, Working Paper 172, London: Overseas Development Institute.

Bourdet, Y. (2001) *Mali, Coping with Adversity* (mimeo), Department of Economics, Sweden: University of Lund.

Bourdieu, P. (1980a) *Le Sens Pratique*, Paris: Editions de Minuit.

—— (1980b) 'L'opinion publique n'existe pas', in P. Bourdieu *Questions de sociologie*, Paris: Editions de Minuit.

Bourguignon, F. (1990) 'Growth and inequality in the dual model of development: the role of demand factors', *Review of Economic Studies*, 57: 215–28.

—— (1998) 'Equité et croissance économique: une nouvelle analyse?', *Revue Française d'Economie*, 3: 25–84.

—— (2002) *The Growth Elasticity of Poverty Reduction: Explaining Heterogeneity Across Countries and Time Periods*, Working Paper 2002-03, Paris: DELTA.

Bourguignon, F. and Fields, G. (1997) 'Discontinuous losses from poverty, generalized measures and optimal transfers to the poor', *Journal of Public Economics*, 62: 155–75.

Bourguignon, F. and Morisson, C. (1998) 'Inequality and development: the role of dualism', *Journal of Development Economics*, 57(2): 233–58.

—— (1999) *The Size Distribution of Income Among World Citizens*, Delta and Université de Paris, Paris: DELTA.

Bourguignon, F. and Verdier, T. (2000) 'Oligarchy, democracy, inequality and growth', *Journal of Development Economics*, 62(2): 285–314.

Bourguignon, F., Branson, W.H. and de Melo, J. (1989) *Adjustment and Income Distribution: A Counterfactual Analysis*, NBER WP 2943, Cambridge: National Bureau of Economic Research.

Bourguignon, F., Ferreira, F.H.G. and Leite, P.G. (2001) *Prices, Preferences or Endowments? Accounting for Excess Inequality in Brazil* (mimeo), Paris: DELTA and Rio de Janeiro: Pontificia Universidade Católica.

Bourguignon, F., Ferreira, F.H.G. and Lustig, N. (2001) *The Microeconomics of Income Distribution Dynamics: A Comparative Analysis of Selected Countries* (mimeo), Washington, DC: World Bank.

Bourguignon, F., Fournier, M. and Gurgand, M. (1999) 'Distribution des salaires, éducation et développement: Taiwan (1979–1994)', *Revue d'Economie du Développement*, 3: 3–33.

—— (2001) 'Fast development with a stable income distribution: Taiwan, 1979–1994', *Review of Income and Wealth*, 47(2): 139–63.

Bourguignon, F., Robilliard, A.-S. and Robinson, S. (2001) *Representative Versus Real Households in the Macro-economic Modelling of Inequality* (mimeo), Washington, DC: World Bank.

Bourguignon, F., Pereira da Silva, L. and Stern, N. (2002) *Evaluating the Poverty Impact of Economic Policies: Some Analytical Challenges* (mimeo), Washington, DC: World Bank.

Bratton, M. and van de Walle, N. (1997) *Democratic Experiments in Africa. Regime Transitions in Comparative Perspective*, London: Cambridge University Press.

Bréchon, P. (ed.) (2000) *Les valeurs des français. Evolutions de 1980 à 2000*, Paris: Armand Colin.

Bréchon, P., Laurent, A. and Perrineau, P. (eds) (2000) *Les cultures politiques des français*, Paris: Presses de Sciences Po.

Burnside, C. and Dollar, D. (1997) *Aid, Policies, and Growth*, Policy Research

Working Paper No. 1777, Development Research Group, Washington, DC: World Bank.

Capdevielle, J. (forthcoming) *La légitimité démocratique à l'épreuve de la mondialisation néolibérale*, Cahiers du CEVIPOF.

Cayrol, R. (2000) *Sondages: Mode d'emploi*, Paris: Presses de Sciences Po.

Cellule Croissance Accélérée et Développement (1998) *Le Mali, propositions pour une stratégie de croissance et développement à l'horizon 2010*, Bamako (March).

Chambas, G. and Kerhuel, F. (2001) 'La réforme de l'État: Implications des Cadres stratégiques de réduction de la pauvreté', *Afrique Contemporaine*, numéro spécial (3): 78–85.

Champagne, P. (1990) *Faire l'opinion. Le nouveau jeu politique*, Paris: Editions de Minuit.

Chaudhuri, S. and Ravallion, M. (1994) 'How well do static indicators identify the chronically poor?', *Journal of Public Economics*, 53: 367–94.

Chavagneux, C. (1998) 'Les copains d'abord', *Alternatives économiques*, 94 (November).

—— (2001) 'Lutte contre la pauvreté: les enjeux politiques d'un slogan', *Politique africaine*, 82: 161–8.

Chavagneux, C. and Tubiana, L. (2000) 'Quel avenir pour les institutions de Bretton Woods? Les transformations de la conditionnalité', in F. Bourguignon, C. Chavagneux, L. Tubiana, P. Salama and J. Valier, *Développement*, Report of the Conseil d'Analyse Economique, Paris: La Documentation française.

Cling, J.-P. (2001) 'Réforme agraire et démagogie électorale au Zimbabwe', *Afrique Contemporaine*, 197: 64–75 (January–March).

Cogneau, D. (1998) 'Perspectives et contraintes de la croissance à Madagascar', *Economie de Madagascar*, 3: 49–64.

—— (1999) 'La formation du revenu des ménages à Antananarivo: une micro-simulation pour la fin du siècle', *Economie de Madagascar*, 4: 131–56.

—— (2001) *Formation du revenu, segmentation et discrimination sur le marché du travail d'une ville en développement: Antananarivo fin de siècle*, Working Paper DT2001-18, November, Paris: DIAL.

Cogneau, D. and Grimm, M. (2002) *The Distribution of AIDS over the Population in Africa: Hypothesis Building from Individual Answers to a Demographic and Health Survey with an Application to Côte d'Ivoire*, Working Paper DT2002-02, March, Paris: DIAL.

Cogneau, D. and Guénard, C. (2002) *Les inégalités et la croissance: une relation introuvable?*, Working Paper DT2002-03, January, Paris: DIAL.

Cogneau, D. and Maurin, E. (2001) *L'effet du revenu parental sur la décision de scolariser les enfants dans un pays pauvre: une analyse semiparamétrique*, Working Paper DT2001-16, November, Paris: DIAL.

Cogneau, D. and Robilliard, A.-S. (2001) *Growth, Distribution and Poverty in Madagascar: Learning from a Microsimulation Model in a General Equilibrium Framework*, DIAL Working Paper DT2001-19, November, and IFPRI TMD Discussion paper No. 61.

Cogneau, D., Maurin, E. and Pasquier, L. (2001) *Social Mobility in Africa, a Comparative Analysis of Five sub-Saharan Societies* (mimeo), Presented at the meeting of the RC28 group of ISA in Mannheim, May.

Cogneau, D., Dumont, J.C., Glick, P., Razafindrakoto, M., Razafindravonona, J., Randretsa, I. and Roubaud, F. (2002) 'Madagascar', in C. Morrisson (ed.) *Educa-*

tion and Health Expenditure, and Poverty Reduction: The Cases of Madagascar and Tanzania, Paris: OECD Development Centre.

Cohen, D. (2000) *The HIPC Initiative: True and False Promises*, Discussion Paper, CEPR 2632, December, London: Centre for Economic Policy Research.

Collier, P. (1997) 'The failure of conditionality', in C. Gwin and J. Nelson (eds) *Perspectives on Aid and Development*, Policy Essay 22, Washington, DC: Overseas Development Council.

Collier, P. and Dollar, D. (1998) *Aid Allocation and Poverty Reduction*, Development Research Group, Washington, DC: World Bank.

Collier, P. and Gunning, J.W. (1997) *Explaining African Economic Performance*, Working Paper No. 21, Oxford University, Centre for the Study of African Economies.

Cornia, G.A., Jolly, R. and Stewart, F. (eds) (1987) *Adjustment with a Human Face: Protecting the Vulnerable and Promoting Growth*, Paris: Oxford University Press/UNICEF.

Coudouel, A. and Hentschel, J. (2001) 'Données et mesure de la pauvreté', in World Bank, *A Sourcebook for Poverty Reduction Strategies*. Available online: http://www.worldbank.org/poverty/strategies (accessed 1 September 2002).

Coulibaly, M., Diarra, A. and Traore, A. (1999) *Macro-économie, emploi et changements structurels au Mali* (mimeo), November, Bamako: GREAT.

Cour, J.-M. (2001) *Compte-rendu de la mission pour le PAGDI, Madagascar 29 novembre–3 décembre 2000* (mimeo), Report for the PAGDI.

Dante, I., Gautier, J.-F., Marouani, M.A. and Raffinot, M. (2001) *Mali Final Country Report*, London: Overseas Development Institute.

De Janvry, A., Sadoulet, E. and Fargeix, A. (1991) 'Politically feasible and equitable adjustment: some alternatives for Ecuador', *World Development*, 19(11): 1577–94.

Deaton, A. (1995) 'Data and econometric tools for development analysis', in J. Behrman and T.N. Srinivasan (eds) *Handbook of Development Economics*, Vol. 3A, Amsterdam: North-Holland.

—— (2000) *The Analysis of Household Surveys. A Microeconometric Approach to Development Policy*, Baltimore: Johns Hopkins University Press.

Decaluwé, B., Patry, A., Savard, L. and Thorbecke, E. (1999) *Poverty Analysis within a General Equilibrium Framework*, CREFA WP 9909, Québec: Université Laval.

Degenne, A., Grimler, G., Lebeaux, M.O. and Lemel, Y. (1997) 'La production domestique atténue-t-elle la pauvreté?', *Economie et Statistique*, 308/309/310(8/9/10): 159–86.

Deininger, K. and Squire, L. (1996) 'A new data set measuring income inequality', *The World Bank Economic Review*, 10(3): 565–91.

Demery, L. (1999) *Poverty Dynamics in Africa: An Update*, Poverty Reduction and Social Development Unit, Washington, DC: World Bank.

Devarajan, S. and Go, D.S. (2001) *A Macroeconomic Framework for Poverty Reduction Strategy Papers (with an application to Zambia)* (mimeo), Washington, DC: World Bank.

Devarajan, S., Dollar, D. and Holmgren, T. (2001) *Aid and Reform in Africa; Lessons from Ten Case Studies*, Washington, DC: World Bank.

DGCID (2001) *Lutte contre la pauvreté, les inégalités et l'exclusion: une contribution au débat*, Paris: Ministère des Affaires étrangères.

DIAL (1998) 'Selectivity: where are the guidelines?', *Dialogue*, DIAL Newsletter No. 10, December.

—— (1999) 'From multilateral debt reduction to debt write-offs for the poorest countries', *Dialogue*, DIAL Newsletter No. 11, June.

—— (2000a) 'Sous le marché, les pauvres; commentaires critiques sur la première version du rapport Attacking Poverty', *Dialogue*, DIAL Newsletter No. 13, June.

—— (2000b) *Etude de la pauvreté urbaine en Afrique de l'Ouest: Côte d'Ivoire, Mali, Senegal*, Report produced for the World Bank, Paris: DIAL.

—— (2000c) *The 1-2-3 Survey: A Poverty Monitoring Tool*, May, Paris: DIAL.

—— (2001) 'Dynamique de la pauvreté en Afrique de l'Ouest', *Dialogue*, DIAL Newsletter No. 15, June.

Diallo, C.S. and Raffinot, M. (1999) *Evaluation du programme National de Lutte contre la pauvreté au Mali*, Bamako: UNDP.

Dollar, D. and Kraay, A. (2001) *Growth is Good for the Poor*, Working Paper No. 2587, April, Washington, DC: World Bank.

Droy, I., Ratovoarinony, R. and Roubaud, F. (2000) 'Les observatoires ruraux à Madagascar 1995–1998: une méthodologie originale pour le suivi des campagnes', *Stateco*, 95/96/97(1/2/3): 123–40, Paris: INSEE.

Dubois, J.-L. (1996) 'L'expérience du programme Dimensions sociales de l'ajustement. Apports méthodologiques et réflexions d'ensemble', *Cahiers de Sciences Humaines*, 32(2): 379–402.

Easterly, W. and Levine, R. (1997). 'Africa's growth tragedy: policies and ethnic divisions', *Quarterly Journal of Economics*, 112(4): 1203–50.

Elbers, C., Lanjouw, J.O. and Lanjouw, P. (2001) *Welfare in Villages and Towns: Micro-Level Estimation of Poverty and Inequality* (mimeo), Washington, DC: World Bank.

Elias, N. (1987) *La société des individus* (trans. J. Etoré 1991), Paris: Fayard.

Englebert, P. (2000) 'Solving the mystery of the Africa dummy', *World Development*, 28(10): 1821–35.

Erikson, R. and Goldthorpe, J.H. (1993) *The Constant Flux: A Study of Class Mobility in Industrial Societies*, New York: Oxford University Press.

Esping-Andersen, G. (1990) *The Three Worlds of Welfare Capitalism*, Cambridge: Polity Press.

Eurodad (2001a) *Many Dollars, Any Changes? Executive Summary.* Available online: http://www.eurodad.org (accessed on 1 September 2002).

—— (2001b) *Debt Reduction for Poverty Eradication in the Least Developed Countries, Analysis and recommendations on LDC debt*, May, Brussels.

European Commission (2001) *PRSP Review: Key Issues*, October, Brussels.

Evans, M., Paugam, S. and Prélis, J.A. (1995) *Chunnel Vision: Poverty, Social Exclusion and the Debate on Social Welfare in France and Britain*, London School of Economics, STICERD, Welfare State Programme/115.

Ferguson, J. (1990) *The Anti-politics Machine: Development, Depolitization and Bureaucratic Power in Lesotho*, London: Cambridge University Press.

Ferreira, F.H.G. and Leite, P.G. (2002) *Educational Expansion and Income Distribution. A Micro-simulation for Ceará*, PUC-RIO WP 456, Departamento de Economica, Rio de Janeiro: Pontificia Universidade Católica.

Fields, G. (1994) 'Data for measuring poverty and inequality changes in the developing countries', *Journal of Development Economics*, 44(1): 87–102.

Fleurbaey, M. (1995) 'Equal opportunity or equal social outcome?', *Economics and Philosophy*, 11(1): 25–55.

—— (1998) *Les théories économiques de la justice*, Paris: Economica.

Fleurbaey, M., Herpin, N., Martinez, M. and Verger, D. (1997) 'Mesurer la pauvreté', *Economie et Statistique*, 308/309/310(8/9/10): 43–64.

Forbes, K.J. (2000) 'A reassessment of the relationship between inequality and growth', *American Economic Review*, 90(4): 869–87.

Foster, J.E., Greer, J. and Thorbecke, E. (1984) 'A class of decomposable poverty measures', *Econometrica*, 52(3): 761–6.

Foster, M., Fozzard, A., Naschold, F. and Conway, T. (2002) *How, When and Why does Poverty get Budget Priority; Poverty Reduction Strategy and Public Expenditure in Five African Countries, Synthesis Paper*, Working Paper 168, London: Overseas Development Institute.

Galor, O. and Zeira, J. (1993) 'Income distribution and macroeconomics', *Review of Economic Studies*, 60: 35–52.

Gardes, F. and Loisy, C. (1997) 'La pauvreté selon les ménages: une évaluation subjective et indexée sur leur revenu', *Economie et Statistique*, 308/309/310(8/9/10): 95–112.

Garenne, M., Waltisperger, D., Cantrelle, P. and Ralijaona, O. (1999) 'Impact démographique d'une famine ignorée: Antananarivo, 1985–1987', *Economie de Madagascar*, 4: 247–64, Antananarivo: Banque centrale and INSTAT.

Gautier, J.-F. (2002) 'Taxation optimale de la consommation et biens informels', *Revue Economique*, 53(3): 599–610.

Genier, P. (1996) 'Les micro-simulations dans le domaine de la santé: revue de quelques études', Paper presented at 'Applications des méthodes de microsimulation', November, Paris, INSEE.

Ghura, D., Leite, C.A. and Tsangarides, C. (2002) *Is Growth Enough? Macroeconomic Policy and Poverty Reduction*, IMF WP 02/118, July, Washington, DC: International Monetary Fund.

Gokhale, J., Kotlikoff, L.J., Sefton, J. and Weale, M. (2001) 'Simulating the transmission of wealth inequality via bequests', *Journal of Public Economics*, 79: 93–128.

Goody, J. (1976) *Production and Reproduction, A Comparative Study of the Domestic Domain*, London: Cambridge University Press.

Grimm, M. (2001) *A Decomposition of Inequality and Poverty Changes in the Context of Macroeconomic Adjustment. A Microsimulation Study for Côte d'Ivoire*, United Nations University/WIDER Discussion Paper No. 2001/91, UNU/WIDER, Helsinki (and forthcoming in A.F. Shorrocks and R. Van der Hoeven (eds) *Growth and Poverty*, Oxford: Oxford University Press).

—— (2002a) *Les effets d'une expansion d'éducation en Côte d'Ivoire. Une étude par microsimulation dynamique* (mimeo), Paris: DIAL.

—— (2002b) *Modéliser les trajectoires démo-économiques des individus et des ménages dans un pays en développement à l'aide d'un modèle de micro-simulation dynamique*, Working Paper DT2002-01, Paris: DIAL.

Grimm, M., Guénard, C. and Mesplé-Somps, S. (2000) 'Analyse de la pauvreté urbaine en Côte d'Ivoire (1985 à 1998)', in DIAL, *Etude de la pauvreté urbaine en Afrique de l'Ouest. Côte d'Ivoire, Mali, Senegal*, Report produced for the World Bank, Paris: DIAL.

—— (2002). 'What has happened to the urban population in Côte d'Ivoire since the Eighties? An analysis of monetary poverty and deprivation over 15 years of household data', *World Development*, 30(6): 1073–95.

Gubert, F. and Robilliard, A.-S. (2002) 'Summary of Requirements for Statistics and Information about the Rural Sector for PRSPs', Paper presented at the Paris

21 Seminar on New Partnership to Strengthen Agricultural and Rural Statistics in Africa for Poverty Reduction and Food Security, 16–17 September, Paris.

Gunter, B.G. (2002) 'What's wrong with the HIPC Initiative and what's next?', *Development Policy Review*, 20(1): 5–24.

Gupta, S., Clements, B., Guin, S. and Leruth, L. (2001) 'Debt relief and public health spending in heavily indebted poor countries', *Finance and Development*, September.

Haan, A., Lipton, M., Darbellay, E., O'Brien, D. and Samman, E. (1997) *The Role of Government and Public Policy in Poverty Alleviation in SSA*, Collaborative Research Project, Poverty, Income Distribution and Labour Market Issues in Sub-Saharan Africa, AERC, December, Nairobi: African Economic Research Consortium.

Habbard, P. (2001) 'Les enseignements des processus d'élaboration de stratégie de réduction de la pauvreté dans les pays du Resal en 2000', Solagral, Paper presented to the Conference entitled 'La pauvreté à Madagascar: Etat des lieux, réflexions sur les politiques de réduction et leur mise en œuvre', DIAL/IRD/INSTAT/RESAL, Antananarivo, 5–7 February.

—— (2002) 'Les processus d'élaboration des documents stratégiques de lutte contre la pauvreté', in J.-P. Cling, M. Razafindrakoto and F. Roubaud (eds) *Les nouvelles stratégies internationales de lutte contre la pauvreté*, Paris: Economica.

Habermas, J. and Rawls, J. (1997) *Débat sur la justice politique* (trans. by R. Rochlitz), Paris: Cerf.

Hanmer, L. and Naschold, F. (1999) *Are the International Development Targets Attainable?*, Report for the Department for International Development, London: Overseas Development Institute.

Harding, A. (1993) *Lifetime Income Distribution and Redistribution. Applications of a Microsimulation Model*, Amsterdam: North-Holland.

—— (1996) *Microsimulation and Public Policy*, Amsterdam: North-Holland.

—— (2000) 'Dynamic microsimulation: recent trends and future prospects', in A. Gupta and V. Kapur (eds) *Microsimulation in Government Policy and Forecasting*, Amsterdam: North-Holland.

Haubert, M. (2001) 'Le risque idéologique', *Courrier de la Planète*, No. 63, Vol. 63, June.

Hazizaj, T. and Misha, A. (2000) 'Poverty in Albania; Albania, a very poor country trying to find its way in the market economy', Conference proceedings from *International Comparisons of Poverty*, Bratislava: SUSR-INSEE-EUROSTAT.

Heckman, J. (1999) *Causal Parameters and Policy Analysis in Economics: A Twentieth Century Retrospective*, NBER Working Paper No. 7333, Cambridge: National Bureau of Economic Research.

Heckman, J. and Sedlacek, G. (1985) 'Heterogeneity, aggregation, and market wages functions: an empirical model of self-selection in the labor market', *Journal of Political Economy*, 93: 1077–125.

Héran, F. and Rouault, D. (1995) 'La présidentielle à contre-jour: abstentionnistes et non-inscrits', INSEE *Première* No. 397.

Herpin, N. and Verger, D. (1997a) 'Mesurer la pauvreté aujourd'hui', *Economie et Statistique*, 308–309–310(8/9/10).

—— (1997b) 'Les étudiants, les autres jeunes, leur famille et la pauvreté', *Economie et Statistique*, 308/309/310(8/9/10): 211–27.

—— (2000) *La consommation des français*, Paris: La Découverte.

Herr, H. and Priewe, J. (2001) *The Macroeconomic Framework of Poverty Reduction – An Assessment of the IMF/World Bank Strategy*, Berlin: University of Applied Science.

Herrera, J. and Roubaud, F. (2001) *Dynamique de la pauvreté urbaine au Pérou et à Madagascar 1997–1999: une analyse sur données de panel*, Working Paper DT2001-13, December, Paris: DIAL.

Hicks, J.F. (1998). 'Enhancing the Productivity of Urban Africa', World Bank conference paper, International Conference of the Research Community for the Habitat Agenda, Forum of Researchers on Human Settlements, Geneva, 6–8 July.

Hildenbrand, W. (1998) 'How relevant are specifications of behavioral relations on the micro-level for modelling the time path of population aggregates?', *European Economic Review*, 42: 437–58.

Hirschman, A. (1991) *Deux siècles de rhétorique réactionnaire*, Collection L'espace Politique, Paris: Fayard.

Hoddinott, J. (2002) 'Participation and poverty reduction: an analytical framework and overview of the issues', *Journal of African Economies*, 11(1): 146–68.

Hoekman, B., Michalpoulos, C., Schiff, M. and Tarr, D. (2002) 'Trade policy reform and poverty alleviation', in World Bank, *A Sourcebook for Poverty Reduction Strategies*. Available online: http://www.worldbank.org/poverty/strategies/chapters (accessed on 1 September 2002).

Hourriez, J.-M. and Legris, B. (1997) 'L'approche monétaire de la pauvreté: méthodologie et résultats', *Economie et Statistique*, 308/309/310(8/9/10): 35–63.

Hourriez, J.-M. and Olier, L. (1997) 'Niveau de vie et taille du ménage: estimation d'une échelle d'équivalence', *Economie et Statistique*, 308/309/310(8/9/10): 65–94.

Hubbard, M. (2001) 'Attacking poverty, a strategic dilemma for the World Bank', *Journal of International Development*, 13: 293–8.

Hussmanns, R., Mehran, F. and Verma, V. (1990) *Surveys of Economically Active Population, Employment, Unemployment and Underemployment: An ILO Manual on Concepts and Methods*, Geneva: International Labour Organisation.

Huw, E. (1999) 'Debt relief for the poorest countries: why did it take so long?', *Development Policy Review*, 17: 267–79.

IDA and IMF (1999) *Strategic Frameworks for Poverty Reduction – Operational Questions*, 10 December, Document SM/99/290 (F), Washington, DC: International Development Agency and International Monetary Fund.

—— (2002) *Review of the Poverty Reduction Strategy Paper (PRSP) Approach: Early Experience with Interim PRSPs and Full PRSPs*, 26 March. Available online: www.worldbank.org/poverty/strategies/review (accessed 1 September 2002).

IMF (2000) *Key Features of PRGF-Supported Programs*, 16 August, Washington, DC: International Monetary Fund.

—— (2001) *The IMF's Poverty Reduction and Growth Facility (PRGF): A Factsheet*. Available online: http://www.imf.org/external/np/exr/facts/prgf (March), Washington, DC: International Monetary Fund.

IMF and World Bank (2001a), *Poverty Reduction Strategy Papers (PRSPs): Progress in Implementation*, Development Committee, DC2001-0026, 26 September, Washington, DC: International Monetary Fund and World Bank.

—— (2001b) *Heavily Indebted Poor Countries Initiative: Status of Implementation*, Development Committee, DC2001-0027, 28 September, Washington, DC: International Monetary Fund and World Bank.

—— (2002) *Heavily Indebted Poor Countries Initiative: Status of Implementation*, Development Committee, DC2002-0009, 14 April, Washington, DC: International Monetary Fund and World Bank.

Inglehart, R. (1993) *La transition culturelle dans les sociétés industrielles avancées*, Paris: Economica.

—— (1997) *Modernization and Postmodernization. Cultural, Economic and Political Change in 43 Societies*, Princeton: Princeton University Press.

INSEE (1998) *Synthèses Revenus et Patrimoine des ménages*, Edition No. 28, Paris.

—— (1999) *France Portrait Social 1999*, INSEE/Statistiques Publiques, Paris.

ISTED (1998) *Dynamique de l'urbanisation de l'Afrique au Sud du Sahara* (edited by Michel Arnaud), Paris: ISTED.

Jacoby, H. (1994) 'Borrowing constraints and progress through school: evidence from Peru', *Review of Economics and Statistics*, LXXVI(1): 151–61.

Jalan, J. and Ravallion, M. (2002) *Income Gains to the Poor from Workfare: Estimates for Argentina's Trabajar Programme* (mimeo), Indian Statistical Institute and World Bank, Washington DC: World Bank.

Jolliffe, D. (1998) *The Impact of Education in Rural Ghana: Examining Productivity and Labor Allocation Effects* (mimeo), Prague: Charles University.

Joseph, A. (2000) *Resolving the Debt Problem: From the HIPC Initiative to Cologne*, Technical Document 163, August, Paris: OECD Development Centre.

Juarez, M. (ed.) (1994) *Informe sociológico sobre la situación social en España*, Madrid: Fundación Foessa.

Kaase, M., Newton, K. and Scarbrough, E. (eds) (1995) *Beliefs in Government*, 5 vols., New York: Oxford University Press.

Kanbur, R. (2000) 'Aid, conditionality and debt in Africa', in F. Tarp (ed.) *Foreign Aid and Development: Lessons Learnt and Directions for the Future*, London and New York: Routledge.

Kanbur, R. and Squire, L. (1999) *The Evolution of Thinking About Poverty: Exploring the Interactions*, Washington, DC: World Bank.

Kankwenda, M., Grégoire, L.J., Legros, H. and Ouédraogo, H. (1999) *La lutte contre la pauvreté en Afrique subsaharienne*, Paris: UNDP/Economica.

Katz, L. and Murphy, K. (1992) 'Changes in the wage structure 1963–87: supply and demand factors', *Quarterly Journal of Economics*, 107: 35–78.

Khan, M.S. and Sharma, S. (2001) *IMF Conditionality and Country Ownership of Programs*, IMF Working Paper, WP/01/42, September, Washington, DC: International Monetary Fund.

Killick, T. (1998) *Adjustment, Income Distribution and Poverty in Africa: A Research Guide*, Collaborative Research Project, Poverty, Income distribution and Labour Market Issues in Sub-Saharan Africa, June, Nairobi: African Economic Research Consortium.

—— (2000) *HIPC II and Conditionality: Business as Before or a New Beginning?*, Paper commissioned by The Commonwealth Secretariat Policy Workshop on Debt, HIPC and Poverty Reduction, London: ODI.

—— (2002) *The Streamlining of IMF Conditionality: Aspirations, Reality and Repercussions*, A Report for the Department for International Development, March, London ODI.

Kirman, A. (1992) 'Whom or what does the representative individual represent?', *Journal of Economic Perspectives*, 6(2):117–36.

Klasen, S. (2001) 'In search of the Holy Grail: how to achieve pro-poor growth?',

Background Paper to SPA Task Team 'Growth and Equity', Eschborn: GTZ. Presented to SPA Task Team Meetings, 6–9 November, Addis-Ababa, Ethiopia.

Klugman, J. (2001) 'Poverty Reduction Strategy Sourcebook: Overview', in World Bank, *A Sourcebook for Poverty Reduction Strategies.* Available online: http://www.worldbank.org/poverty/strategies/chapters (accessed on 1 September 2002).

Kotlikoff, L.J., Smetters, K. and Walliser, J. (2001) *Finding a Way Out of America's Demographic Dilemma*, NBER WP 8258, Cambridge: National Bureau of Economic Research.

Krugman, P. (1988) 'Financing versus forgiving a debt overhang', NBER Working Paper No. 2486, Cambridge: National Bureau of Economic Research.

Kuznets, S. (1955) 'Economic growth and income inequality', *American Economic Review*, 45(1): 1–28.

Lafore, R. and Borgetto, M. (1996) *Droit de l'aide et de l'action sociale*, Paris: Montchrétien.

Lalmant, C. (2001) *Les Cadres Stratégiques de Lutte contre la Pauvreté*, Haut Conseil de la Coopération Internationale, September.

Lam, D. (1997) 'Demographic variables and income inequality', in M.R. Rosenzweig and O. Stark (eds) *Handbook of Population and Family Economics*, Amsterdam: North-Holland.

Lampedusa, G. T. di (1958) *Il Gattopardo* (trans. Alexander Colquhoun, as *The Leopard*, New York: Pantheon Books, 1960).

Lancelot, A. (1984) 'Sondage et démocratie', in SOFRES, *Opinion publique*, Paris: Gallimard.

Lautier, B. (2001) 'Sous la morale, la politique. La Banque mondiale et la lutte contre la pauvreté', *Politique africaine*, 82(2): 169–76.

—— (2002) 'Pourquoi faut-il aider les pauvres? Une étude critique du discours de la Banque mondiale sur la pauvreté', *Revue Tiers Monde*, Tome XLIII, 169(1): 137–75.

Leandro, J., Schafer, H. and Frontini, G. (1999) 'Towards a more effective conditionality: an operational framework', *World Development* 27(2): 285–99.

Lillard, L.A. and Willis, R.J. (1992) 'Intergenerational educational mobility, effects of family and State in Malaysia', *Journal of Human Resources*, XXIX (4): 1126–66.

Lipton, M. (1997) 'Poverty – are there holes in the consensus?' (Editorial), *World Development*, 25(7): 1003–7.

Lok Dessallien, R., Sanoussi Gouné, A., Diarra, B., Larivière, S. and Martin F. (eds) (2001) *Poverty Reduction Strategy, the Malian Experience*, UNDP, Université Laval, Québec: IDEA International.

Lollivier, S. (1999) *Inégalités de niveaux de vie et générations*, Données sociales, Paris: INSEE.

Lollivier, S. and Verger, D. (1997) 'Pauvreté d'existence, monétaire ou subjective sont distinctes', *Economie et Statistique*, 308/309/310(8/9/10): 113–42.

Loury, G. (1981) 'Intergenerational transfers and the distribution of earnings', *Econometrica*, 49: 843–67.

Lysy, F. and Taylor, L. (1980) 'The general equilibrium model of income distribution', in L. Taylor, E. Bacha, E. Cardoso and F. Lysy (eds) *Models of Growth and Distribution for Brazil*, Oxford: Oxford University Press.

McGee, R., Hughes, A. and Levene, J. (2001) *Assessing Participation in Poverty*

Reduction Strategy Papers: A Desk-Based Synthesis of Experience in Sub-Saharan Africa, Participation Group Draft Report, October, Brighton: Institute of Development Studies.

MADIO (1997a) *L'Etat de santé de la population et la demande de soins dans l'agglomération d'Antananarivo en 1997. Premiers résultats de l'enquête SET 1997*, December, Antananarivo: INSTAT/MADIO.

—— (1997b) *Transferts entre les ménages et réseaux de solidarité dans l'agglomération d'Antananarivo. Premiers résultats de l'enquête SET 1997*, December, Antananarivo: INSTAT/MADIO.

—— (1998a) *Le secteur informel dans l'agglomération d'Antananarivo: performances, insertion, perspectives. Enquête 1-2-3, premiers résultats de la phase 2*, Antananarivo: INSTAT/MADIO.

—— (1998b) *La consommation et le rôle du secteur informel dans la satisfaction des besoins des ménages dans l'agglomération d'Antananarivo. Enquête 1-2-3, premiers résultats de la phase 3*, Antananarivo: INSTAT/MADIO.

Mahieu, F.R. (1990) *Les fondements de la crise économique en Afrique*, Paris: L'Harmattan.

Malgoubri, E., Mesplé-Somps, S., Muguet, J. and Zongo, B. (2002) *Results-oriented Expenditure Management, Burkina Faso Case Study*, Report produced for the ODI-CADE, Paris: DIAL.

Maoz, Y.D. and Moav, O. (1999) 'Intergenerational mobility and the process of development', *Economic Journal*, 109: 677–97.

Maxwell, S. (2001) 'Innovative and important, yes, but also instrumental and incomplete: the treatment of redistribution in the new New Poverty Agenda', *Journal of International Development*, 13: 331–41.

Meade, J.E. (1976) *The Just Economy*, London: George Allen & Unwin.

Meltzer, A. (2000) *Report*. Available online: http://www.ids.ac.uk/eldis/ifiac.htm or http://www.gsia.cmu.edu/afs/andrew/gsia/meltzer/ (accessed on 1 September 2002).

Merrien, F.-X. (1994) 'Divergences franco-britanniques', in F.-X. Merrien (ed.) *Face à la pauvreté. L'Occident et les pauvres hier et aujourd'hui*, Paris: Les Editions de l'Atelier.

Merz, J. (1991) 'Microsimulation – a survey of principles, developments and applications', *International Journal of Forecasting*, 7: 77–104.

Meynaud, H. and Duclos, D. (1996) *Les sondages d'opinion*, Repères 38, Paris: La Découverte.

Milano, S. (1989) *Le revenu minimum dans la CEE*, (2nd édition, revised, published in 1995), coll. 'Que sais-je', Paris: Presses Universitaires de France.

Ministère des Affaires Etrangères (1999) *L'allégement de la dette et le développement, les vraies questions les fausses évidences*, Notes de travail DGCID/DCT No. 4/99, Paris.

Ministère des Affaires Etrangères and Ministère de l'Economie, des Finances et de l'Industrie (2001) *Principes, modalités de préparation et de mise en œuvre des contrats de désendettement et de développement*, Paris.

Moisseron, J.-Y. and Raffinot, M. (1999) *Dette et pauvreté, Solvabilité et allégement de la dette des pays à faible revenu*, Paris: Economica.

Mosley, P. (2001) 'Attacking poverty and the post-Washington consensus', *Journal of International Development*, 13: 307–13.

Myrdal, G. (1968) *Asian Drama: An Enquiry into the Poverty of Nations*, New York: The 20th Century Fund and Pantheon Books.

Narayan, D., Chambers, R., Shah, M.K. and Petesch, P. (2000) *Crying out for Change* (*Voices of the Poor*, Vol. 2), New York: Oxford University Press (for the World Bank).

Narayan, D., Patel, R., Schafft, K., Rademacher, A. and Koch-Schulte, S. (2000) *Can Anyone Hear Us? Voices from 47 Countries* (*Voices of the Poor*, Vol. 1), New York: Oxford University Press (for the World Bank).

Naudet, J.-D. (2000a) *Finding Problems to fit the Solutions: Twenty Years of Aid to the Sahel*, Paris: Sahel and West Africa Club/OECD.

—— (2000b) 'L'aide extérieure est-elle un instrument de justice? Une analyse des évolutions des fondements éthiques de l'aide au développement', *L'économie Politique*, 7(3): 71–87.

—— (2000c) *Accounting for Aid Flows to Mali: Summary*, SAH/REFA (2002)2, Paris: Club du Sahel/OECD (original in French).

—— (2000d) 'Les "guignols de l'info": Réflexions sur la fragilité de l'information statistique', in J.-P. Jacob (ed.) *Sciences sociales en Afrique: les rendez-vous manqués*, Collection Enjeux, Nouveaux Cahiers de l'IUED, 10, Paris and Geneva: Presses Universitaires de France.

ODHD (1999) *Croissance, équité et pauvreté, Rapport national sur le développement humain durable*, Bamako: Ministère de l'Economie, du Plan et de l'Intégration, UNDP and World Bank.

—— (2001) *Aide, Endettement, Pauvreté*, Rapport national sur le Développement Humain Durable 2000, Bamako: Ministère de l'Economie, du Plan et de l'Intégration, UNDP and World Bank.

OECD (1997) *Evaluation of Programs Promoting Participatory Development and Good Governance, Synthesis Report*, Development Assistance Committee Expert Group on Aid Evaluation, Paris: OECD.

—— (2001) *The DAC Guidelines on Poverty Reduction*, Paris: OECD.

OECD and UNDP (1998) *Mali Aid Review: Synthesis and Analysis*, Provisional Report, Paris.

—— (1999) *Improving the Effectiveness of Aid Systems, the Case of Mali*, SAH/D(99)502, Paris: Sahel and West Africa Club/OECD.

Orcutt, G. (1957) 'A new type of socio-economic system', *Review of Economics and Statistics*, 58: 773–97.

Overseas Development Institute (2001) *PRSP Institutionalisation Study: Final Report*, submitted to the Strategic Partnership for Africa, October.

Oxfam (2002) *Rigged Rules and Double Standards: Trade, Globalisation and the Fight against Poverty*, Oxford: Oxfam.

Panos (2002) *Reducing Poverty: Is the World Bank's Strategy Working?* Panos Report No. 45, August, London.

Paugam, S. (1993) *La société française et ses pauvres. L'expérience du revenu minimim d'insertion*, (2nd edition, revised, published in 1995), Paris: Presses Universitaires de France.

—— (1996) 'Pauvreté et exclusion: la force des contrastes nationaux', in Serge Paugam (ed.) *L'exclusion, l'état des savoirs*, Paris: La Découverte.

—— (1999) *L'Europe face à la pauvreté. Les expériences nationales de revenu minimum*, Paris: La Documentation française.

Piketty, T. (1994) *Introduction à la théorie de la redistribution des richesses*, Paris: Economica.

—— (1997) 'The dynamics of wealth distribution and the interest rate with credit rationing', *Review of Economics Studies*, 64: 173–89.

—— (2001) *Les hauts revenus en France au XXe siècle. Inégalités et redistribution: 1901–1998*, Paris: Grasset.

Polanyi, K. (1944) *The Great Transformation*, Boston: Beacon Hill.

Ponty, N. (1998) 'Mesurer la pauvreté dans un pays en développement', *Stateco*, 90–9: 53–67.

Raffinot, M. (1999) 'L'initiative FMI-Banque Mondiale de réduction de la dette: un grand pas pour les organisations internationales, un petit pas pour les pays à faible revenu', *L'économie politique*, (3): 73–86.

—— (2000) 'Réductions de dette et pauvreté: Faut-il annuler la dette des pays les plus pauvres?', *Techniques financières et développement*, 57–58(4/1): 74–84.

Raffinot, M. and Roubaud, F. (2001) 'Recherche fonctionnaires désespérément', in *Les fonctionnaires du Sud entre deux eaux: sacrifiés ou protégés?*, *Autrepart*, 20: 5–10, Paris: Editions de l'Aube-IRD.

Raison-Jourde, F. (1991) *Bible et pouvoir à Madagascar au XIXe siècle. Invention d'une identité chrétienne et construction de l'État (1780–1880)*, Paris: Karthala.

Rakotomanana, F., Ramilison, E. and Roubaud, F. (2000) 'La mise en place d'une enquête annuelle sur l'emploi à Madagascar: un exemple pour l'Afrique Sub-saharienne', *Stateco*, 95/96/97(1/2/3): 25–40, Paris: INSEE.

Rakotomanana, F., Ravelosoa, R. and Roubaud, F. (2000) 'L'enquête 1-2-3 sur le secteur informel et la satisfaction des besoins des ménages dans l'agglomération d'Antananarivo 1995, 1998: la consolidation d'une méthode', *Stateco*, 95/96/97(1/2/3): 41–62, Paris: INSEE.

Ranis, G. and Stewart, F. (2001) 'HIPC: Good news for the poor?', Paper presented to the WIDER Conference on Debt Relief, 17–18 August, Helsinki.

Ravallion, M. (2001) 'Growth, inequality and poverty: looking beyond averages', *World Development*, 29(11), November, 1803–15.

Ravelosoa, R. and Roubaud, F. (1998) 'La dynamique de la consommation des ménages dans l'agglomération d'Antananarivo, 1965–1995', *Autrepart*, 7: 63–87, Paris: Editions de l'Aube-IRD.

Rawls, J. (1971) *A Theory of Justice*, Cambridge, Mass.: Harvard University Press (quoted from the New York: Oxford University Press edition, 1999).

—— (1999) *The Law of Peoples*, Cambridge: Harvard University Press.

Razafindrakoto, M. and Roubaud, F. (1999a) 'La dynamique du marché du travail dans l'agglomération d'Antananarivo entre 1995 et 1999: la croissance macro-économique profite-t-elle aux ménages?', *Economie de Madagascar*, 4: 103–29, December, Antananarivo: BCM/INSTAT.

—— (1999b) *La politique d'immigration favorise-t-elle la venue des investisseurs étrangers à Madagascar? Analyse des résultats de l'enquête EPTVS99*, Antananarivo: Secrétariat Technique à l'Ajustement.

—— (2000a) 'The multiples facets of poverty in a developing country: the case of Madagascar's capital city', Conference proceedings from *International Comparisons of Poverty*, Bratislava: SUSR-INSEE-EUROSTAT.

—— (2000b) 'Pauvreté et récession dans les métropoles africaines: éléments de diagnostic', Paper presented to the HEXAPOLIS conference 'Six mégapoles face au défi des nouvelles inégalités: mondialisation, santé, exclusion et rupture sociale', organised by the Institut de l'humanitaire and INED at the UNESCO headquarters, 2–3 November.

—— (2000c) 'La statistique au service du débat démocratique en Afrique: l'exemple du projet MADIO à Madagascar', Paper presented to the International

Conference on Statistics and Human Rights, IAOS, Montreux, 4–8 September.

—— (2001a) 'Vingt ans de réforme de la fonction publique à Madagascar', in M. Raffinot and F. Roubaud (eds) *Les fonctionnaires du Sud entre deux eaux: sacrifiés ou protégés?, Autrepart*, 20: 43–60, Paris: Editions de l'Aube-IRD.

—— (2001b) *La voix des pauvres à travers les enquêtes statistiques*, Working Paper DT2001-13, June, Paris: DIAL.

—— (2002) 'Madagascar à la croisée des chemins: la croissance durable est-elle possible?', in F. Roubaud (ed.) *Madagascar après la tourmente: regards sur dix ans de transitions politique et économique, Afrique Contemporaine*, 202–203(1/2): 75–92, Paris: La Documentation française.

Renard, D. (1995) 'Assistance et Assurance dans la constitution du système de protection sociale française', *Genèses*, 18: 30–46.

Richard, J.-L. (2000) 'Les valeurs économiques: entre libéralisme et interventionnisme', in P. Bréchon, A. Laurent and P. Perrineau (eds) *Les cultures politiques des Français*, Paris: Presses de Sciences Po.

Robilliard, A.-S. and Robinson, S. (1999) *Reconciling Household Surveys and National Accounts Data Using Cross-entropy Estimation*, IFPRI/TMD Division WP 50, Washington, DC: International Food Policy Research Institute.

Robilliard, A.-S., Bourguignon, F. and Robinson, S. (2001) *Crisis and Income Distribution: a Micro-macro Model for Indonesia* (mimeo), Paris: DIAL and Washington DC: IFPRI.

Rodrik, D. (2001) 'Trading in illusions', *Foreign Policy*, March–April.

Roemer, J. (1998) *Equality of Opportunity*, Cambridge: Harvard University Press.

Roubaud, F. (1992) *Enquête 1-2-3: propositions pour un système d'enquêtes intégrées auprès des ménages*, Working Paper DT1992-18, Paris: DIAL.

—— (1994a) 'Dynamique du marché de travail à Yaoundé 1983–1993: la décennie perdue', *Revue Tiers-Monde*, Tome XXXV, 140(4): 751–78.

—— (ed.) (1994b) 'L'enquête 1-2-3 sur l'emploi et le secteur informel à Yaoundé', *Stateco*, 7: 81–135, Paris: INSEE.

—— (1999) 'Education et ajustement structurel à Madagascar', *Autrepart*, 11: 81–100, Paris: Editions de l'Aube-IRD.

—— (2000a) *Identités et transition démocratique: l'exception malgache?*, Paris: Tsipika-L'Harmattan.

—— (2000b) 'Enquêtes auprès des ménages et élections politiques dans les pays en développement: l'exemple de Madagascar', Paper presented to the International Conference on 'Statistics and Human Rights, AISO, Montreux, 4–8 September.

—— (2000c) 'Le projet MADIO à Madagascar: objectifs, démarches, résultats', *Stateco*, 95/96/97(1/2/3): 5–24, Paris: INSEE.

—— (2001) Démocratie électorale et inertie institutionnelle à Madagascar, in *l'Afrique politique, réformes des Etats africains*, CEAN, Paris: Karthala.

Rowntree, B.S. (1902) *Poverty: A Study of Town Life*, London: Thomas Nelson and Sons.

—— (1941) *Poverty and Progress: A Second Social Survey of York*, London: Longman Green.

Rowntree, B.S. and Lavers, G.R. (1951) *Poverty and the Welfare State. A Third Social Survey of York Dealing only Economic Questions*, London: Longman Green.

Roy, A. (1951) 'Some thoughts on the distribution of earnings', *Oxford Economic Papers*, 3: 135–46.

Rubio, G., Prennushi, G. and Subbarao, K. (2001) 'Monitoring and evaluation', in World Bank, *A Sourcebook for Poverty Reduction Strategies*. Available online: http://www.worldbank.org/poverty/strategies/chapters (accessed on 1 September 2002).

Sachs, J. (1988) 'The debt overhang or developing countries', in L. Calvo *et al.* (eds) *Debt, Growth and Stabilization: Essays in memory of Carlos Díaz Alejandro*, Oxford: Blackwell.

Sachs, J. and Warner, A. (1996) *Sources of Slow Growth in African Economies*, Development Discussion Paper 545, Cambridge: Harvard Institute for International Development.

Sahel and West Africa Club (2001) *Managing the Economy Locally in Africa, ECOLOC Manual Volume 1, Synthesis Report*, February, Paris: Sahel and West Africa Club/OECD.

Sahn, D. and Stifel, D. (2000) 'Poverty comparisons over time and across countries in Africa', *World Development*, 28(12): 2123–55.

Salamon, L.S. and Anheier, H.K. (eds) (1997) *Defining the Nonprofit Sector. A Cross-national Analysis*, Manchester and New York: Manchester University Press.

SAPRIN-Mali and IREPAS (1999) *Revue des Programmes d'Ajustement Structurel au Mali, 1988–1995*, June, Bamako.

Scholte, J.A. (2002) 'Société civile et gouvernance mondiale', in P. Jacquet, J. Pisani-Ferry and L. Tubiana, *Gouvernance mondiale*, Report of the Conseil d'Analyse Economique, Paris: La Documentation française.

Schultheis, F. (1996) 'L'etat et la société civile face à la pauvreté en Allemagne', in S. Paugam (ed.) *L'exclusion, l'état des savoirs*, Paris: La Découverte.

Schultheis, F. and Bubeck, B. (1996) 'Theorical and methodological problems in intercultural comparison of the phenomenon of extreme poverties', in P. Guidicini, G. Pieretti and M. Bergamaschi (eds) *Extreme Urban Poverties in Europe. Contradictions and Perverse Effects in Welfare Policies*, Milan: Franco Angeli.

Schultz, T.B. (1998) *Inequality in the Distribution of Personal Income: How it is Changing and Why*, Yale University, Economic Growth Center, Discussion Paper 784, January.

Sen, A. (1981) *Poverty and Famines*, New York: Oxford University Press.

—— (1983) 'Poor relatively speaking', *Oxford Economic Papers*, 35: 153–69.

—— (1992) *Inequality Reexamined*, Cambridge: Harvard University Press.

—— (1997) 'Editorial: human capital and human capability', *World Development*, 25(12): 1959–61.

—— (1999) 'Global justice: beyond international equity', in I. Kaul, I. Grunberg and M.A. Stern (eds) *Global Public Goods: International Cooperation in the 21st Century*, New York: UNDP/Oxford University Press.

—— (2000) *Un nouveau modèle économique: développement, justice, liberté*, Paris: Odile Jacob.

Serra, R. (1999) *Mali Country Study, Creating a Framework for Reducing Poverty: Institutional and Process Issues in National Poverty Policy in Selected African Countries*, SPA Working Group on Poverty and Social Policy, 10 December, Washington, DC.

—— (2001) 'Poverty and governance reforms in Mali', Wolfson College, University of Cambridge. Communication to the symposium of capitalising growth and poverty research on Mali (CSLP) Bamako, 12–15 June.

Severino, J.-M. (2001a) 'Les fondements stratégiques de l'aide au développement au XXIe siècle', *Critique Internationale*, 10(1): 75–99.

——— (2001b) 'On n'échappe pas au politique quand on fait de l'aide au développement', *L'économie politique*, 10(2): 8–17.

Simmel, G. ([1908] 1997) *Les Pauvres*, coll. 'Quadrige' (first edition in Germany, 1908). Preceded by 'Naissance d'une sociologie de la pauvreté' by S. Paugam and F. Schultheis, Paris: Presses Universitaires de France.

Snerch, S. (1994). *Pour préparer l'avenir de l'Afrique de l'Ouest: une vision à l'horizon 2020*, Synthesis of the study on long-term prospects in West Africa, Paris: OECD/ADB/CILLS.

Société Civile du Mali (2001) *Point de vue de la société civile sur le cadre stratégique de lutte contre la pauvreté au Mali, atelier national de validation de la synthèse des ateliers régionaux* (6–7 June) CCA-ONG, Bamako.

Srinivasan, T.N. (2001) 'Croissance et allégement de la pauvreté: les leçons tirées de l'expérience du développement', *Revue d'économie du développement*, 1–2: 115–68.

Stiglitz, J. (1974) 'Alternative theories of wage determination and unemployment in LDCs: the labor turnover model', *Quarterly Journal of Economics*, 88(2): 194–227.

——— (2002) *Globalisation and its Discontents*, London: Penguin.

Stöckli, B. (2000) 'Fonds de contrepartie, un mécanisme de réduction de la dette: le programme suisse de désendettement', in Centre Universitaire Luxembourg, Actes du colloque Endettement, marginalité, pauvreté, quels financement et refinancement du Tiers-Monde?, Luxembourg, 20–22 January.

Strategic Partnership with Africa (1999) *Africa Poverty Status Report 1999*, Report prepared for the SPA Working Group on poverty and Social Policy, September, Washington, DC.

Summers, L. (2001) 'Remarks by Larry Summers at the World Bank Country Directors' Retreat', May, Speech to World Bank country directors. Available online: http://www.eurodad.org/articles (accessed on 1 September 2002).

Tapinos, G.P., Mason, A. and Bravo, J. (1997) *Demographic Responses to Economic Adjustment in Latin America*, Oxford: Clarendon Press.

Tarp, F. (ed.) (2000) *Foreign Aid and Development; Lessons Learnt and Directions for the Future*, London and New York: Routledge.

Thin, N., Underwood, M. and Gilling, M. (2001) *Sub-Saharan Africa's Poverty Reduction Strategy Papers from Social Policy and Sustainable Livelihoods Perspectives*, A report for the Department for International Development, Oxford: Oxford Policy Management.

Tikare, S., Youssef, D., Donnelly-Roark, P. and Shah, P. (2001) 'Organizing Participatory Processes in the PRSP', in World Bank, *A Sourcebook for Poverty Reduction Strategies*. Available online: http://www.worldbank.org/poverty/strategies/chapters (accessed on 1 September 2002).

Toka, G. (1995) 'Political support in East Central Europe', in M. Kaase, K. Newton and E. Scarbrough, *Beliefs in Government*, Vol. 1, New York: Oxford University Press.

Transparency International (2000) *Annual Report 2000*, Berlin: Transparency International.

Traoré, A.D. (1999) *L'Etau. L'Afrique dans un monde sans frontières*, Arles: Actes Sud.

UNAIDS (2000) *AIDS Epidemic Update*, Joint United Nations Programme on HIV/AIDS, Geneva: World Health Organisation, December.

UNCTAD (2002) *The Least Developed Countries Report 2002; Escaping the Poverty Trap*, New York and Geneva: United Nations.

UNDP (1999) *Coopération pour le Développement, Mali, Rapport 1997/98*, Bamako: United Nations Development Programme.

—— (2002) *Deepening Democracy in a Fragmented World*, Human Development Report 2002, New York: Oxford University Press.

United Nations (2001) *World Population Prospects*, UN Population Division, New York: United Nations.

United States General Accounting Office (GAO) (2000) *Developing Countries: Debt Relief Initiative for Poor Countries Facing Challenges*, Washington, DC: United States General Accounting Office.

Urfer, S. (1993) 'Quand les Eglises entrent en politique', *Politique Africaine*, spécial 'Madagascar', 52: 31–9, Paris: Ambozontany/Karthala.

Vandemoortele, J. (2002) 'Are the MDGs feasible?', UNDP, Bureau for Development Policy, New York, Paper presented to the ABCDE-Europe conference organised by the World Bank in Oslo, 24–26 June.

Wade, R.H. (2001) 'Making the World Development Report 2000: Attacking Poverty', *World Development*, Vol. 29 (8): 1435–42.

Waltisberger, D. (1999) *Compte-rendu de mission à Tananarive, pour le compte de Macro International Inc.* (mimeo), November, Paris.

Walzer, M. (1983) *Sphères de justice, une défense du pluralisme et de l'égalité* (trans. by P. Engel), Paris: Seuil.

Whaites, A. (2000) *PRSP: Good News for the Poor? Social Conditionality, Participation, Poverty Reduction*, Monrovia: World Vision International.

—— (ed.) (2002) *Masters of their Own Development? PRSPs and the Prospects for the Poor*, Monrovia: World Vision International.

Winter, G. (ed.) (2001) *Inégalités et politiques publiques en Afrique; pluralité des normes et jeux d'acteurs*, Paris: Karthala-IRD.

Wolfensohn, J. (1997) *The Challenge of Inclusion*, Hong Kong: IMF–World Bank Annual Meetings Address.

Wood, A. and Mayer, J. (1998) 'Africa's export structure in a comparative perspective', Study No. 4, *African Development in a Comparative Perspective*, Geneva: United Nations Conference for Trade and Development.

World Bank (1980) *World Development Report 1980*, Washington, DC: World Bank.

—— (1981) *Accelerated Development in Sub-Saharan Africa: An Agenda for Action*, Washington, DC: World Bank.

—— (1990) *World Development Report 1990: Poverty*, Washington, DC: World Bank.

—— (1994) *Adjustment in Africa: Reforms, Results and the Road Ahead*, World Bank Report on Development Policy, Washington, DC: World Bank.

—— (1995) *A Continent in Transition: Sub-Saharan Africa in the Mid-1990s*, Africa Region, Washington, DC: World Bank.

—— (1997) *World Development Report 1997: The State in a Changing World*, Washington, DC: World Bank.

—— (1998a) *Assessing Aid: What Works, What Doesn't and Why*, World Bank Policy Research Report, New York: Oxford University Press.

—— (1998b) *Urban in the Regions. Snapshot of Sub-Saharan Africa: Regional Urban Statistics and Projections* (mimeo). Available online: http://www.worldbank.org/external/urban/urbanDev (accessed on 1 September 2002).

—— (1999) *Core Welfare Indicators Questionnaire: Handbook and CD ROM*, Washington, DC: World Bank.

—— (2000a) *World Development Report 2000/2001: Attacking Poverty*, New York: Oxford University Press.

—— (2000b) *Global Economic Prospects and the Developing Countries*, Washington, DC: World Bank.

—— (2000c) *Can Africa Claim the 21st Century?* Washington, DC: World Bank.

—— (2000d) *The Quality of Growth*, New York: Oxford University Press.

—— (2001a) *Poverty Reduction Strategy Sourcebook: Chapters and Related Materials*, April. Available online: http://www.worldbank.org/poverty/strategies/chapters (accessed on 1 September 2002).

—— (2001b) *Global Economic Prospects and the Developing Countries*, Washington, DC: World Bank.

—— (2001c) African Forum on Poverty Reduction Strategies, Quotations from Day 1. Available online: http://www.worldbank.org/wbi/attackingpoverty (accessed on 1 September 2002).

—— (2001d) *World Development Report 2002: Building Institutions for Markets*, New York: Oxford University Press.

—— (2001e) *RMSM-X for PRSPs. A New Module to Measure the Impact of Macroeconomic Policies and Programs on Poverty and Income Distribution. A Research Proposal* (mimeo), Washington DC: World Bank.

—— (2002a) *The Role and Effectiveness of Development Assistance: Lessons from World Bank Experience*, Research Paper from the Development Economics Vice-Presidency of the World Bank, Washington, DC: World Bank.

—— (2002b) *Overview of Poverty Reduction Strategies*, Washington, DC: World Bank. Available online: http://www.worldbank.org/poverty/strategies/overview.htm (accessed on 1 September 2002).

—— (2002c) *World Development Report 2003: Sustainable Development in a Dynamic World: Transforming Institutions, Growth and Quality of Life*, New York: Oxford University Press.

—— (2002d) *World Development Indicators 2002*, Washington, DC: World Bank.

—— (2002e) *A User's Guide to Poverty and Social Impact Analysis* (mimeo), Washington DC: World Bank.

The PRSPs referred to in this book are all available on the World Bank website: http://poverty.worldbank.org/prsp

Index

Printed in the United States
by Baker & Taylor Publisher Services